# MASTERPLOTS
## FIFTEEN-VOLUME
## COMBINED EDITION

*Volume Twelve*
*Purp-Scho*

# MASTERPLOTS

*15-Volume Combined Edition*
FIFTEEN HUNDRED AND TEN
*Plot-Stories and Essay-Reviews*
*from the*
WORLD'S FINE LITERATURE

*Edited by*
FRANK N. MAGILL

*Story Editor*
DAYTON KOHLER

VOLUME TWELVE — PURP-SCHO

SALEM PRESS
INCORPORATED
NEW YORK

This work also appears under the title of
MASTERPIECES OF WORLD LITERATURE IN DIGEST FORM

5-82 gift

# THE PURPLE LAND

*Type of work:* Novel
*Author:* W. H. Hudson (1841-1922)
*Type of plot:* Adventure romance
*Time of plot:* Nineteenth century
*Locale:* Uruguay and Argentina
*First published:* 1885

> Principal characters:
> RICHARD LAMB, an English adventurer
> PAQUITA, his wife
> DOÑA ISIDORA, her aunt
> LUCERO, a horse tamer
> MARCOS MARCO, General Coloma
> MARGARITA, his daughter
> DON PERALTA, a mad landowner
> DEMETRIA PERALTA, his daughter

## Critique:

The Purple Land is a story of romantic adventure, perhaps not quite so entertaining as *Green Mansions,* but with merits of its own. The reader gets an insight into the lives and environment of the people of an unhappy far-off purple land in revolutionary South America. Hudson is one of the great masters of sensuous prose. Perhaps the reason for this stylistic skill is the fact that he was a botanist and the keenness of observation required in scientific writing is reflected in his choice of adjectives and verbs.

## The Story:

Richard Lamb married Paquita without her father's consent and eloped with her to Montevideo. There they went to see Doña Isidora, a relative of Paquita, and stayed with her for some time. Doña Isidora gave Lamb a letter to the overseer of the *Estancia de la Virgen de los Desamparados,* a ranch called in English Vagabond's Rest.

Lamb departed with the letter, and in the Florida department he began to learn the history of the unhappy land of Uruguay. The Argentines and Brazilians interfered in the country's politics, and, as if the foreign influences were not enough to cause trouble, there was constant friction between the country and the town districts. At a pulpería, or tavern, he met Lucero, a horse tamer, and went to stay at his house; but he soon left Lucero and continued his journey to the estancia.

Lamb took advantage of rustic hospitality throughout his journey. One night he stayed at a house in which lived a family with many children. The children were all named after particular Christian concepts, such as Conception and Ascension. However, there were far too many insects infesting the house for his comfort, and he departed early the next day. Lamb continued his journey through Lucuarembó department and then entered the county of his destination. There he discovered that Doña Isidora's letter meant nothing; there was no employment for him.

During his stay at the estancia he had a fight with a man called Barbudo and gained a reputation for being a great fighter. When he discovered that his reputation as a fighter would only lead to more and bloodier fights, he decided to return to Montevideo.

At Toloso, Lamb met a group of English expatriates in a pulpería, and he remained with his fellow countrymen for a time. Finally he found them to be quite worthless and quarreled with them. Then he headed once more for Montevideo. In the Florida department he met a lovely girl named Margarita and helped her get her doves from a branch in a tree.

THE PURPLE LAND by W. H. Hudson.   Published by E. P. Dutton & Co., Inc.

Margarita was so different from the rest of her family that Lamb could not help wondering how she came to be born into such a rough, coarse family. There he met Anselmo, who was an indefatigable talker and teller of pointless tales. There, too, he met Marcos Marco.

Lamb and Marcos started out to go to Montevideo together, but on the way they were captured by an army detail and taken prisoners because Lamb had neglected to get a passport. They were taken before a justice of the peace at Las Cuevas. Through the machinations of the justice's fat wife, Lamb was free to move about until his trial. Marcos, however, was imprisoned. Lamb talked the fat wife into giving him the key to the fetters which bound his friend Marcos. Lamb freed his friend so that Marcos would be able to sleep comfortably in his captivity, but Marcos took advantage of his opportunity and escaped during the night. Lamb, being a lover of nature, captured a small snake and used it as a means to ward off the attentions of the justice's wife. He was finally released.

Later, at the estate of Alday, he first heard of General Santa Coloma, who in reality was Marcos Marco. He told Anita, an orphan living with the Aldays, the story of Alma, who wanted a playmate, and Little Niebla. Anita wanted a playmate too and the next morning she ran off to find one. Monica, the daughter of the household, searched for and found Anita. Monica then asked Lamb to tell her a story out of the great store of anecdotes he knew.

Lamb was taken to see General Coloma, whom he recognized as his friend Marcos. He joined the general and fought in the battle of San Paulo. The general explained to Lamb the mystery of Margarita; she was Coloma's daughter.

When the battle of San Paulo ended badly for the general's army, Lamb escaped. At a pulpería he met Gandara, who wanted to take him prisoner because he had been a member of General Coloma's army. Lamb shot Gandara and escaped. He stayed for a time at the home of an expatriate Scotsman named John Carrickfergus, but soon he continued his journey to Montevideo.

His next important stop was at the home of Don Peralta, who was demented. Don Peralta had lost a son, Calixto, who had been killed in battle several years before. Demetria Peralta, the daughter, was the heir to the estate, but she and everyone else were under the thumb of Don Hilario, the supervisor of the estate. When Lamb rode away, he left with Santos, a servant, who told him the history of the Peralta family. Demetria wished to marry Lamb and thus be able to take over and administer the property which was really hers. Lamb could not marry her, but he arranged to abduct her and take her to Montevideo, where she would be safe from Hilario. When they arrived safely in Montevideo, Paquita looked after Demetria as if she were her own sister. From Montevideo they went to Buenos Aires, where the unsanctioned marriage of Lamb and Paquita promised to give still more trouble for the young couple.

# PYGMALION

*Type of work:* Drama
*Author:* Bernard Shaw (1856-1950)
*Time:* c. 1900
*Locale:* London
*First presented:* 1913

Principal characters:
HENRY HIGGINS, a phonetician
ELIZA DOOLITTLE, a flower girl
ALFRED DOOLITTLE, her father, a dustman
COLONEL PICKERING, another phonetician
FREDDY EYNSFORD HILL, a poor young gentleman

Throughout his career Shaw agitated for the reform of the vagaries of English spelling and pronunciation; nevertheless his assertion is immaterial that *Pygmalion* was written to impress upon the public the importance of phoneticians in modern society. *Pygmalion,* like all of Shaw's best plays, transcends its author's didactic intent. The play will continue to be performed and read, not for indoctrination into one of Shaw's pet theories, but for the laughter its characters provoke.

The play is a modern adaptation of the Pygmalion myth (though some have claimed that it is a plagiarism of Tobias Smollett's *Peregrine Pickle),* in which the sculptor-king Pygmalion falls in love with a creature of his making, a statue which Aphrodite, pitying him, brings to life. The Pygmalion of Shaw's play turns up as Henry Higgins, a teacher of English speech; his Galatea, Eliza Doolittle, a cockney flower girl whom Higgins transforms into a seeming English lady, mainly by teaching her to speak cultivated English. In the process of transforming a poor girl into a lady, Higgins irrevocably changes a human life. By lifting Eliza above her own class and providing her with only the appurtenances of another, Higgins makes her unfit for both. On this change and Higgins' stubborn refusal to accept its reality and its consequences, Shaw builds his play.

From the beginning, when Higgins first observes her dialectal monstrosities, Eliza is characterized as a proud, stubborn girl, even though educated only by the cru-

dities of poverty and the gutter. Brassy enough to ask Higgins to make good his boast that he can pass her off as a duchess within three months, she calls on him and offers to pay him for elocution lessons which will take her off the streets and into a position as saleswoman in a flower shop. Like all the proud, she is also sensitive, and she tries to break off the interview when Higgins persists in treating her as his social inferior. Little wonder, then, that months later, when Higgins has indeed proved his boast, she resents his indifference toward her and her future, and, after telling him what a cad he is, runs away to his mother, who has befriended her.

Higgins can best be understood in contrast to Colonel Pickering, his foil, who finances the transformation. As a fellow phonetician, Pickering approves of the project as a scientific experiment, but as a gentleman he sympathizes with Eliza as a sensitive human being. It is Higgins' uproariously tragic flaw that he, like all of Shaw's heroes, is not a gentleman. He is brilliant and cultured, but he lacks manners and refuses to learn or even affect any, believing himself to be superior to the conventions and civilities of polite society and preferring to treat everyone with bluntness and candor. He is, or so he thinks until Eliza leaves him, a self-sufficient man. When he discovers that she has made herself an indispensable part of his life, he goes to her and in one of the most remarkable courtship scenes in the history of the theater pleads with her to live with Pickering and himself as three dedicated bachelors. At the end of the play he is confident that she will accept his unorthodox proposition, even when she bids him goodbye forever.

As a matter of fact, Shaw himself was never able to convince anyone that Eliza and Higgins did not marry and live happily ever after. The first producer of the play, Sir Herbert Beerbohm Tree, insisted on leaving the impression that the two were reconciled in the end as lovers, and this tradition has persisted. Enraged as always by any liberties taken with his work, Shaw wrote an essay which he attached to the play as a sequel denouncing any sentimental interpretation of *Pygmalion*.

He concedes that *Pygmalion* is a romance in that its heroine undergoes an almost miraculous change, but he argues that the logic of the characterization does not permit a conventional happy ending. Higgins is, after all, a god and Eliza only his creation, so that an abyss separates them. Furthermore, Shaw contends, their personalities, backgrounds, and philosophies are irreconcilable. Higgins is an inveterate bachelor and likely to remain one because he will never find a woman who can meet the standards he has set for ideal womanhood—those set by his mother. Eliza, on the other hand, being young and pretty, can always find a husband whose demands on a woman would not be impossible to meet. Therefore, Shaw insists, Eliza marries Freddy Eynsford Hill, a penniless but devoted young man who played only an insignificant role in the play itself. Stubbornly, Shaw would not even permit them the luxury of living happily ever after: they have financial problems which are gradually solved by opening a flower shop subsidized by Colonel Pickering. Shaw's Pygmalion is too awe-inspiring for his Galatea ever to presume to love him.

Even with the addition of such an unconventional ending to the play, *Pygmalion* would be highly atypical of Shavian drama were it not for the presence of Alfred Doolittle, Eliza's father. Through Doolittle, Shaw is able to indulge in economic and social moralizing, an ingredient Shaw could not dispense with. Like Eliza, Doolittle undergoes a transformation as a result of Higgins' meddling, a transformation that is unpremeditated, however, in his case. Early in the play Doolittle fascinates Higgins and Pickering by his successful attempt to capitalize on Eliza's good fortune. He literally charms Higgins out of five pounds by declaring himself an implacable foe of middle-class morality and insisting that he will use the money for a drunken spree. Delighted with the old scoundrel, Higgins mentions him in jest to a crackpot American millionaire who subsequently bequeathes Doolittle a yearly allowance of three thousand pounds if he will lecture on morality. Thus he becomes a dustman transformed into a lion of London society, a reprobate changed into a victim of bourgeois morality. Although he appears only twice in the play, Doolittle is so vigorous and funny that he is almost as memorable a comic character as Higgins.

The truth of the matter is that the play itself is memorable because of its vigor and fun, notwithstanding Shaw's protestations about its didacticism. The reason why Shaw did protest so much in his insistence on the serious intent of the play may lie in his realization that *Pygmalion* was his least serious, least didactic, play.

# QUALITY STREET

*Type of work:* Drama
*Author:* James M. Barrie (1860-1937)
*Type of plot:* Comedy of manners
*Time of plot:* Napoleonic wars
*Locale:* English provincial village
*First presented:* 1902

Principal characters:
    MISS PHOEBE THROSSEL, a spinster
    MISS SUSAN THROSSEL, her sister
    VALENTINE BROWN, loved by Phoebe

*Critique:*

This play contains acute if not very penetrating observations on the problem of a wartime love affair in which the lovers are apart for ten years, during which time both change superficially. Most of the action is based on the heroine's successful attempt to bring her lover to his senses. Barrie employs dramatic irony quite effectively throughout and the minimum of privacy in the lives of people in a small village is brought out with good comic effect.

*The Story:*

In the days of the Napoleonic wars, two sisters, Phoebe and Susan Throssel, lived in a little house in Quality Street, the main thoroughfare of a provincial English village. Both were single, both were pretty. One day they entertained a needlework party in their charming blue and white parlor. One of the ladies present repeated a rumor that a gentleman of the village had enlisted to go to the wars. All wondered who the gentleman could be.

Phoebe told her sister that Valentine Brown, a dashing doctor who had come to the village two years before, had walked with her in the street, and had said that he wanted to tell her something important. The retiring Phoebe had asked Brown to come to the house to tell her. Both sisters assumed that Brown was coming to propose marriage to Phoebe, a likely conclusion since a venture in which Brown had invested their savings had

failed and he would naturally feel responsible for their welfare. In anticipation of his proposal, Susan gave Phoebe a wedding dress which she had made for her own marriage, a wedding which had never materialized.

But to Phoebe's disappointment and humiliation, Brown said nothing of marriage. Instead, he told them that he was the man who had enlisted. He declared his friendship for both sisters and his liking for the little blue and white parlor, but he gave no indication of love for Phoebe, who had given her heart to him. Ironically, Phoebe revealed her disappointment by telling Brown that she had thought he was going to announce his marriage and that they were curious to know the name of the fortunate young lady. The sisters, out of pride, did not mention that the loss of their investment left them all but destitute. They planned to set up a school in their house.

Ten years later Susan and Phoebe were still conducting their school, which had prospered in spite of their many shortcomings as teachers. They were loved, but hardly respected by the older children. Dancing and the more gentle acquirements they taught with pleasure, but they detested Latin, and would teach algebra only at the request of their pupils' parents. They could not bring themselves to whip the older boys, most of whom they feared.

The wars were over at last, and everywhere people were celebrating the victory at Waterloo. On Quality Street all but Susan and Phoebe were preparing for a village ball that night. While Phoebe was out of the house, Captain Valentine Brown, who had lost his left hand during a battle on the continent, came to call on his dear old friends. Disappointed at the disappearance of the delightful blue and white parlor, he paid his respects to Miss Susan and asked to see Phoebe of the ringlets and the dancing eyes. When Phoebe returned, Captain Brown could not hide his dismay at the way she had changed into a drab, mouselike spinster. Phoebe was hurt by his unconcealed feelings. She was further hurt later in the day when a former pupil, now Ensign Blades and a veteran, asked her, under duress, to attend the ball with him. Miserable, Phoebe declined. But Phoebe was only thirty and tired of teaching. Inspired by Susan and by Patty, the maid, she transformed herself into the Phoebe of ten years before. When Brown came again, he failed to recognize Phoebe, and he was told that she was the sisters' niece. Completely taken in and charmed by "Miss Livvy," he asked her to accompany him to the ball. "Livvy" teased him, to his discomfort, about his gray hairs.

At later balls and parties of the victory celebration, "Livvy" continued to capture the fancy of all the young men of the village. Difficulties posed by the dual existence of Phoebe-"Livvy" were met by the explanation that Phoebe or "Livvy" was either out or indisposed.

At one ball the swains hovered about "Livvy" constantly, but Captain Brown stoutly held his place as her escort. The sisters' gossipy spinster neighbors, who lived across the street and observed their comings and goings, began to suspect that something was not quite right. They were almost in a position to expose Phoebe at the ball, but Susan saved the day by lending another young lady "Livvy's" coat. Captain Brown, alone with "Livvy," told her of his love for Phoebe, explaining that he had fallen in love with Phoebe during the balls because of "Livvy's" resemblance to the Phoebe of days gone by. "Livvy," the flirt, had made Captain Brown realize that he was no longer twenty-five and that he preferred, after all, the retiring, modest, quiet Phoebe.

School over, the parlor was redecorated with its blue and white frills for the summer holiday. Phoebe, tiring of her dual role, announced that "Livvy" had been taken sick again, and became the tired schoolteacher again. The gossips who came to call were more suspicious than ever because no doctor had visited "Livvy." They almost discovered that there was no one in the sick room, but they prudently did not go beyond the partly opened door.

That day Captain Brown came to propose to Phoebe. When the sisters left the parlor for a moment, he entered the sick room and found it empty. Then he heard the entire story from Patty, the maid. Captain Brown was amused, but carried on the masquerade when "Livvy" came out of the sick room and announced her recovery. The sisters were stupefied when he offered to take "Livvy" to her home twenty miles away. They stepped out of the parlor to have a hurried consultation, but they knew that Captain Brown had found them out when they heard him talking to a "Livvy" he devised with pillows and a shawl and which he carried out to a waiting coach, to the satisfaction of the gossips who were watching from their windows.

Miss Susan Throssel announced the forthcoming marriage of her sister Phoebe to Captain Valentine Brown. The reopening of school was quite forgotten.

# THE QUEEN'S NECKLACE

*Type of work:* Novel
*Author:* Alexandre Dumas, father (1802-1870)
*Type of plot:* Historical romance
*Time of plot:* Eighteenth century
*Locale:* France
*First published:* 1848

*Principal characters:*
MARIE ANTOINETTE, Queen of France
JEANNE DE LA MOTTE VALOIS, an impoverished noblewoman
CARDINAL DE ROHAN
PHILIPPE DE TAVERNEY, a courtier
ANDRÉE DE TAVERNEY, his sister
COUNT DE CHARNY, a naval officer
OLIVA, a girl resembling the queen
COUNT CAGLIOSTRO, an Italian adventurer and supposed magician

## Critique:

Always a defender of the integrity of the monarchy, Dumas here presents a lively picture of court intrigue and royal passion. As a mystery story this novel presents not one loose thread or irrelevant detail. As historical fiction it attempts to describe the person of Marie Antoinette as a woman of extreme charm, intelligence, and honor. Count Cagliostro, a character in several romances by Dumas, is again in this book a sinister and mysterious figure motivating the action.

## The Story:

The Countess Jeanne de La Motte Valois, a descendant of the fallen royal house of Valois, aspired to return to favor in the court of Louis XVI. Suffering extreme poverty, she was honored by a visit from the queen, who gave her money and promised her assistance.

The queen was always a victim of intrigues by her enemies. Even on the night when she had, with the assistance of Andrée de Taverney, made a charitable visit to the Countess de La Motte, one of her enemies had whispered into the king's ear that her majesty had gone on a nocturnal mission of doubtful purpose. Her honesty and proud demeanor put the king to shame, however, and as a conciliatory gesture he offered her a fabulously expensive necklace, which she refused on the grounds that France needed a new battleship more than the queen needed jewels.

Andrée's brother, Philippe de Taverney, was favored by Marie Antoinette for his courtesy and grace. He promptly fell in love with her. At a court reception Philippe was thwarted in his love by perceiving that Count de Charny had won the queen's favor. It was Andrée's fate to have fallen in love with de Charny also, and she watched with jealousy the queen's innocent flirtation.

While Jeanne de La Motte was plotting to gain entrance to the royal court, Cardinal de Rohan, disliked by the queen because of his former disapproval of her marriage to King Louis, was also hoping to win a place at court. These two hopefuls, combining talents, agreed to aid one another in their ambitious projects.

Count Cagliostro, a mystic and a malicious conspirator against the nobility of France, plotted to create a public scandal about the queen. To aid him he produced an unknown girl, Oliva, whose amazing resemblance to Marie Antoinette deceived even the queen's closest friends. First Count Cagliostro sent Oliva to the salon of M. Mesmer, where she exploited her emotions publicly, drawing attention to herself. Her witnesses mistook her for the queen. Next Count Cagliostro brought the girl to a masquerade ball attended by many of the nobility in disguise, but an affair beneath the dignity of the queen. Again it was said that Marie Antoinette

3099

had appeared in public in a most ungracious manner. At the salon and at the ball Jeanne de La Motte had seen the woman who was not really the queen at all. Cardinal de Rohan had been with Jeanne at the ball. Jeanne had perceived that he loved Marie Antoinette, whose disdain for him was well-known.

Widespread gossip about her conduct reached the queen, who, anxious to belie her accusers, brought Jeanne to the king and asked her to assure the monarch that the queen had not degraded herself in the salon of M. Mesmer. The king loyally asserted that he needed no assurance from an outsider that his queen did not lie. But the gossip about Marie Antoinette's presence at the masquerade ball was not so easily explained away. The queen denied having been there; Jeanne claimed that she had seen her. Others were called as witnesses. Both Philippe and de Charny said that they had recognized her when her mask dropped off. King Louis came to the queen's rescue by vowing that he had been with her in her apartment on the night of the ball.

Jeanne, guided by her intuition, knew that the queen coveted the beautiful necklace that the king had wanted to purchase for her from the jewelers, Boehmer and Bossange. When Jeanne assured de Rohan that the queen would be pleased to own the necklace, he, hoping to buy her royal favor, arranged to purchase it by delivering a down payment of five hundred thousand francs. Jeanne, at Versailles, promptly told Marie Antoinette of de Rohan's generous intention. Her reaction was to assume responsibility for the payment of the necklace herself; as queen, she could not accept so generous a favor from a subject. When de Rohan brought the necklace to her, she graciously dismissed the old enmity between them. Unfortunately, King Louis chose that time to be frugal and refused to grant the queen the sum of money she desired. With timely malice Count Cagliostro collected from de Rohan an old debt of five hundred thousand francs. Hearing of the transaction from Jeanne, the queen ordered her to take the necklace back to Boehmer and Bossange.

But Jeanne had her own plans. She forged a note from the jewelers to the queen acknowledging receipt of the necklace. Next she forged a note from the queen to the jewelers promising to pay the balance due them within three months. Meanwhile Jeanne kept the jewels. To safeguard her theft, she had to prevent de Rohan, who assumed that the queen had kept the necklace, from meeting Marie Antoinette. He had been told by the deceived jewelers that the queen would pay for the necklace.

Count Cagliostro assisted Jeanne in her plan by taking Oliva to live in a house close to that of Jeanne. When the two women met, Jeanne knew at once she was facing the woman who had compromised the queen by her conduct at M. Mesmer's salon and at the ball. She escorted Oliva to the park on three successive nights, and there de Rohan courted the woman he mistook for Marie Antoinette. De Charny, witnessing the amorous meeting, thought that he saw the queen. Angry and grieved, he reproached Marie Antoinette for her conduct. Again she realized that someone had been impersonating her.

When the day of payment for the necklace arrived, the jewelers petitioned the queen for their money. After an exchange of angry words, Marie Antoinette and the jewelers realized that they had been duped and that their respective notes were forgeries.

The scandal broke. De Rohan, believing that the queen was his mistress but wishing to conceal the fact for his own protection, still assumed that the queen would pay for the jewels. The jewelers thought that he would pay for them. The public thought that the queen retained the necklace so that de Rohan, for love of her, would be forced to pay, or that the king, to avert scandal, would satisfy the jewelers.

When de Charny came to offer the queen his money, she declared her intention to prove her innocence, and she placed de Charny in hiding while she conducted an interview with de Rohan.

When the deceived cardinal discreetly hinted at their secret love affair, the queen, outraged, sent for the king. De Rohan had no proof of his accusation. Still believing that he had possessed the queen and that she had kept the necklace, he was sentenced to the Bastille.

De Charny emerged from hiding to throw himself at the queen's feet just as the king returned. To explain de Charny's supplicating position, Marie Antoinette had to invent a lie. She said that he was begging for permission to marry Andrée de Taverney, who had entered a convent.

Brought before the queen, Jeanne de La Motte refused to divulge any enlightening evidence and followed de Rohan to the Bastille. Jeanne knew, however, that she controlled the situation. If pressed too hard, she could intimate that the queen and de Rohan had a reason for charging her with the theft of the necklace. Then the police discovered Oliva. Seeing her, the queen understood the intrigue that had been worked against her, but Jeanne was still able to connive and to lie about her association with Oliva so that, in the end, no one was convinced of the queen's innocence. The public, believing Marie Antoinette guilty of adultery and theft, assumed that the person known as Oliva had been invented to conceal the queen's guilt.

After the trial, Cardinal de Rohan and Count Cagliostro, also arrested, were freed. Jeanne de La Motte was publicly branded. The queen was still suspected of being involved in a scandal. No one in the palace realized all involved in the affair were themselves on the threshold of the Bastille and that the Revolution was impending.

# QUENTIN DURWARD

*Type of work:* Novel
*Author:* Sir Walter Scott (1771-1832)
*Type of plot:* Historical romance
*Time of plot:* 1468
*Locale:* France and Flanders
*First published:* 1823

Principal characters:

QUENTIN DURWARD, a Scottish cadet
LUDOVIC LESLEY (LE BALAFRÉ), his maternal uncle
ISABELLE, Countess of Croye, disguised as Jacqueline, a servant
LADY HAMELINE, her aunt
KING LOUIS XI
COUNT PHILIP DE CREVECOEUR, of Burgundy
CHARLES, Duke of Burgundy
WILLIAM DE LA MARCK, a Flemish outlaw
HAYRADDIN MAUGRABIN, a Bohemian

## Critique:

Quentin Durward was one of the many Scotsmen who sought their fortunes abroad in the service of foreign kings, and the story of his adventures is the first of Scott's novels with a foreign setting. There is no doubt in the mind of the reader that Scott liked this Scotsman very much because the character of the hero is the idealized younger son who goes out to seek fortune with nothing but his own wit and bravery. *Quentin Durward* is among the best of Scott's novels, its authenticity little marred by some slight reorganization of actual events to implement the plot.

## The Story:

When Quentin Durward, a young Scottish gentleman, approached the ford of a small river near the castle of Plessis-les-Tours, in France, he found the river in flood. Two people watched him from the opposite bank. They were King Louis XI in his common disguise of Maitre Pierre, a merchant, and Tristan l'Hermite, marshal of France. Quentin entered the flood and nearly drowned. Arriving on the other side and mistaking the king and his companion for a respectable burgher and a butcher, he threatened the two with a drubbing because they had not warned him of the deep ford. Amused by the lad's spirit and daring, Maitre Pierre took him to breakfast at a nearby inn to make amends. At the inn Quentin

met a beautiful young peasant girl, Jacqueline. Actually, Jacqueline was Isabelle, Countess of Crove. Quentin tried to learn why the merchant, Maitre Pierre, acted so much like a noble. He saw many other things which aroused his curiosity but for which he found no explanation.

Shortly afterward Quentin met Ludovic Lesley, known as Le Balafré, his maternal uncle, who was a member of King Louis' Scottish Archers. Le Balafré was exceedingly surprised to learn that Quentin could read and write, something which neither a Durward nor a Lesley had heretofore been able to do.

Quentin discovered the body of a man hanging from a tree. When he cut the man down, he was seized by two officers of Tristan l'Hermite. They were about to hang Quentin for his deed when he asked if there were a good Christian in the crowd who would inform Le Balafré of what was taking place. A Scottish archer heard him and cut his bonds. While the two were defending themselves from the mob, Le Balafré rode up with some of his men and took command of the situation, haughtily insisting that Quentin was a member of the Scottish Archers and beyond the reach of the marshal's men. Quentin had not joined the guards as yet, but the lie saved his life. Le Balafré took Quentin to see Lord Crawford, the commander of the guards, to enroll him. When the Scottish Archers

3102

were summoned to the royal presence, Quentin was amazed to see that Maitre Pierre was King Louis.

Count Philip de Crèvecoeur arrived at the castle and asked audience with the king in the name of his master, the Duke of Burgundy. When the king admitted de Crèvecoeur, the messenger presented a list of wrongs and oppressions, committed on the frontier, for which the Duke of Burgundy demanded redress. The duke also requested that Louis cease his secret and underhand dealings in the towns of Ghent, Liège and Malines, and, further, that the king send back to Burgundy, under safeguard, the person of Isabelle, Countess of Croye, the duke's ward, whom he accused the king of harboring in secret. Dissatisfied with the king's replies to these demands, de Crèvecoeur threw his gauntlet to the floor of the hall. Several of the king's attendants rushed to pick it up and to accept the challenge, but the king ordered the Bishop of Auxerre to lift the gauntlet and to remonstrate with de Crèvecoeur for thus declaring war between Burgundy and France. The king and his courtiers then left to hunt wild boars.

During the chase Quentin Durward saved the king's life by spearing a wild boar when Louis slipped and fell before the infuriated beast. The king decided to reward Quentin with a special mission. He was ordered to stand guard in the room where the king entertained de Crèvecoeur and others, and at a sign from the king Quentin was to shoot the Burgundian. But the king changed his mind; the signal was not given. Then the king made Quentin the personal bodyguard of Isabelle and her aunt, Lady Hameline, on their way to seek the protection of the Bishop of Liège.

Quentin set out with the ladies to conduct them to Liège. In the party was Hayraddin Maugrabin, a Bohemian, whose brother it was whom Quentin had cut down earlier. On the road they were assaulted by the Count de Dunois and the Duke of Orleans. Quentin defended himself with great courage and received timely help from his uncle, who arrived with a body of Scottish Archers. Le Balafré took de Dunois prisoner. Nothing untoward occurred until the small party reached Flanders. There Quentin discovered, by following Hayraddin, that a plot had been hatched to attack his party and carry off the women to William de la Marck, the Wild Boar of Ardennes. Quentin frustrated these plans by going up the left bank of the Maes instead of the right. He proceeded safely to Liège, where he gave over the women into the protection of the bishop at his castle of Schonwaldt. Four days later William de la Marck attacked the castle and captured it during the night. Lady Hameline escaped. In the bishop's throne room in the castle William de la Marck murdered the churchman in front of his own episcopal throne. Quentin, aroused by the brutality of William, stepped to the side of Carl Eberson, William's son, and placed his dirk at the boy's throat, threatening to kill the lad if William did not cease his butchery. In the confusion Quentin found Isabelle and took her safely from the castle in the disguise of the daughter of the syndic of Liège. They were pursued by William's men, but were rescued by a party under Count de Crèvecoeur, who conducted them safely to the court of the Duke of Burgundy at Peroune.

The king came to the castle of the Duke of Burgundy, asserting the royal prerogative of visiting any of his vassals. Disregarding the laws of hospitality, the duke imprisoned Louis and then held a council to debate the difficulties between France and Burgundy. Hayraddin appeared as a herald from William de la Marck, who had married the Lady Hameline. But Toison d'Or, the duke's herald, unmasked Hayraddin because he knew nothing of the science of heraldry. The duke released Hayraddin and set his fierce boar hounds upon him, but ordered the dogs called off before they tore Hayraddin to shreds. Then he ordered that Hayraddin be hanged with the proper ceremony.

The king and the duke also debated

the disposal of Isabelle's hand and fortune. But Isabelle had fallen in love with Quentin and announced that she preferred the cloister to any other alliance. The duke solved the problem, at least to his satisfaction, by declaring that Isabelle's hand would be given to the man who brought him the head of William de la Marck.

The king and the duke joined forces to assault Liège. Their combined forces gallantly besieged the city but were forced to go into bivouac at nightfall. That night William made a foray but was driven back into the city. Next day the forces of the king and the duke attacked once more, made breaches in the wall, and poured into the city. Quentin came face to face with William de la Marck, who rushed at him with all the fury of the wild boar for which he was named. Le Balafré stood by and roared out for fair play, indicating that this should be a duel of champions. At that moment Quentin saw a woman being forcibly dragged along by a French soldier. When he turned to rescue her, Le Balafré attacked de la Marck and killed him.

Le Balafré was announced as the man who had killed de la Marck, but he gave most of the credit to Quentin's valiant behavior and deferred to his nephew. While it was agreed that Quentin was responsible for de la Marck's death, there was still the question of his lineage, which the duke questioned. Indignant, Le Balafré recited the pedigree of Quentin and thereby proved his gentility. Without more ado, Quentin and the Countess Isabelle were betrothed.

# QUO VADIS

Type of work: Novel
Author: Henryk Sienkiewicz (1846-1916)
Type of plot: Historical novel
Time of plot: c. A. D. 64
Locale: Rome
First published: 1895

Principal characters:
VINICIUS, a young Roman patrician
LYGIA, a foreign princess whom Vinicius loves
PETRONIUS, Vinicius' uncle, intimate friend of Nero
NERO, the Roman emperor
CHILO, a Greek sycophant
PETER, leader of the Christians
TIGELLINUS, Petronius' enemy, Nero's friend

Critique:

Quo Vadis is a tremendous achievement, both as a historical re-creation and as a vivid and dramatic work of fiction. Those who enjoy learning history by reading novels will find it extremely satisfactory. Others who are willing to settle for a good story will be moved by its sharply depicted characters, its tremendous tensions and energy. No one has succeeded better than Sienkiewicz in portraying the broad panorama of Roman civilization in the last, degenerate days of the Empire, and no one else has so credibly presented the early Christians as real, live people.

The Story:

When Vinicius returned to Rome, after duty in the colonies, he called on his uncle, Petronius, who was one of the most influential men in Rome. A friend of the Emperor Nero, Petronius owned a beautiful home, choice slaves, and numerous objects of art. Petronius had no delusions about the emperor. He knew quite well that Nero was coarse, conceited, brutal, thoroughly evil.

Petronius was happy to see his handsome young nephew. Vinicius had fallen in love with Lygia, daughter of a foreign king, now living with Aulus Plautius and Pomponia. He asked his uncle to help him get Lygia as his concubine. Petronius spoke to Nero, and Lygia was ordered brought to the palace. The giant Ursus was sent as Lygia's devoted servant by her foster parents.

At a wild orgy in the palace, Vinicius attempted to make love to Lygia. Through the watchfulness of Acte, who was a Christian and a former concubine of Nero, he did not succeed. Lygia herself was a Christian and she feared both the lust of Vinicius and that of the emperor himself. Then Acte received information that Lygia would be handed over to Vinicius. At the same time, the daughter of the Empress Augusta died. The empress and her circle believed that Lygia had bewitched the child. Alarmed at the dangers threatening the girl, Acte and Ursus planned Lygia's escape.

That night the servants of Vinicius came and led Lygia away from the palace. Meanwhile Vinicius waited at his house, where a great feast was to take place in honor of his success in securing Lygia. But Lygia never arrived, for on the way to his house a group of Christians had suddenly attacked the servants of Vinicius and rescued the girl. Her rescuers took Lygia outside the city walls to live in a Christian colony.

Vinicius was furious. Petronius sent some of his own men to watch the gates of the city. Day after day Vinicius grew more and more upset. Finally, Chilo, a Greek who passed as a philosopher, offered for a sufficient reward to find Lygia. By pretending to be a convert, he learned where the Christians met in secret. He and Vinicius, together with a giant named Croton, went there, and then followed Lygia to the house where she was staying. When they attempted to seize the girl, Ursus killed Croton. Vinicius was injured in the scuffle. For a few days he stayed with the Christians who took care of him. Lygia herself nursed him until she became aware of her love for the pagan patrician. Afterward, rather than succumb to temptation, she left him to the attentions of others.

Vinicius had heard the Christians speaking at their meeting. While recuperating, he was amazed at their goodness, at their forgiveness, at their whole religious philosophy. He heard their leader, Peter, talk of Christ and of Christ's miracles, and his mind became filled with odd and disturbing thoughts. He realized that he must either hate the God who kept Lygia from him, or love Him. Strangely enough, he became convinced that he no longer had the desire to take Lygia by force. He maintained his contacts with the Christians. At last, after he had accepted their faith, Lygia agreed to marry him.

In the meantime Nero had gone to Antium. There the noble Tigellinus planted in his mind the idea that he should burn Rome in order to write and sing a poem about the tremendous catastrophe. Accordingly, Nero fired Rome, and almost all of the city was destroyed. Vinicius rushed from Antium to save Lygia. Luckily, she had left the city before the fire gained headway. The populace was angry and violent about the fire. Rebellion was in the air. The empress and the Jews at court persuaded Nero to blame the Christians for the fire. Chilo, who had been befriended by the Christians and whose abominable crimes had been wiped away by Christian forgiveness, turned traitor. He gave the emperor all the information he had about the Christians and led the guards to the hiding places of the sect. Cruel persecutions began.

Petronius tried desperately to stop Nero and save Vinicius. Failing in his attempt, he knew that his own days were numbered. The Christians were crammed first into prisons and then brought into the arena for the entertainment of the populace. Virgins were raped by the gladiators and then fed to starving lions. Christians were crucified, burned alive. After Lygia had been seized and imprisoned, Vinicius failed in an attempt to rescue her.

At last her turn came to be led into the arena to amuse the brutal populace. Stripped, she was tied to the back of a raging bull. When the bull was sent running into the arena, Ursus rushed forward and locked his strong arms around the animal. To the astonishment of all, the bull yielded and died. Then the people demanded that Lygia and Ursus be set free, and the emperor had to obey the public clamor. Petronius advised Vinicius that they should all leave the city, for Nero had subtle ways of removing people who had offended him.

The persecutions continued, the spectacles in the arena growing more and more ghastly. At last the people sickened of the bestial tortures. One of the dying Christians looked straight at Nero and accused him of all his infamous crimes. While Glaucus, a martyr, was being burned alive, he looked at Chilo, the Greek who had betrayed them. Glaucus, who had been left for dead by Chilo, forgave the Greek who had caused the Christian's wife and children to be sold into slavery. Moved by the dying man's mercy, Chilo cried out in a loud voice that the Christians were innocent of the burning of Rome, that the guilty man was Nero. Despairing of his own fate, Chilo was on the point of complete collapse. But Paul of Tarsus took him aside and assured him that Christ was merciful to even the worst of sinners. Then he baptized the Greek. When Chilo went back home, he was seized by the emperor's guards and led away to his death in the arena.

Vinicius and Lygia escaped to Sicily. When Petronius heard that the emperor had ordered his own death, he invited some of the patricians to his house at Cumae, where he had gone with Nero and the court. There at a great feast he read an attack against Nero and astounded everyone by his foolhardiness. Then he and Eunice, a slave who loved him, stretched out their arms to a physician.

While the party continued and the astonished guests looked on, Petronius and Eunice bled to death in each other's arms.

Nero returned to Rome. His subjects hated him more than ever. A rebellion broke out at last, and he was informed that his death had been decreed. He fled. With some of his slaves around him, he attempted to plunge a knife into his throat. But he was too timid to complete the deed. As some soldiers approached to arrest him, a slave thrust the fatal knife into his emperor's throat.

# THE RAINBOW

*Type of work:* Novel
*Author:* D. H. Lawrence (1885-1930)
*Type of plot:* Psychological realism
*Time of plot:* Nineteenth and early twentieth centuries
*Locale:* England
*First published:* 1915

*Principal characters:*
TOM BRANGWEN, a farmer
LYDIA LENSKY, his wife
ANNA LENSKY, Lydia's child by her first husband
WILL BRANGWEN, Anna's husband
URSULA BRANGWEN, Anna's and Will's daughter
ANTON SKREBENSKY, Ursula's lover

*Critique:*

The Rainbow has been the center of much controversy. The author used it as a lever to bring intelligent consideration of basic human relations into the open, where those relationships could be reviewed in a clear-eyed, objective manner, and in doing so he made use of the sexual aspects of marriage and love. The book is essentially a comparison of the matings of three successive generations. The book was not well received when it appeared. The author was ostracized and the novel was suppressed for a time by the police. That such a tempest was occasioned by The Rainbow is hard for the reader to understand today, for by present standards the book can be read and appreciated for what it is, an excellent psychological study.

*The Story:*

Tom Brangwen was descended from a long line of small landholders who had owned Marsh Farm in Nottinghamshire for many generations. Tom was a man of the soil, living alone on his farm with only an old woman for his company and housekeeper. Then a Polish widow, Lydia Lensky, became the housekeeper of the vicar of the local church. She brought her small daughter, Anna, with her. Within a few months Tom Brangwen found enough courage to present the widow with a bouquet of daffodils one evening in the vicar's kitchen and to ask the woman to be his wife.

Their marriage was a satisfactory one, judged by the standards of the world. Tom was kind to his stepdaughter. Later he had two sons by his wife. But knowing his stepdaughter was easier for him than knowing Lydia. The fact that they were of different nationalities, cultures, and even languages kept the couple from ever becoming intellectually intimate with one another. There were times when either one or both felt that the marriage was not what it should be for them, that they were not fulfilling the obligations which their mating had pressed upon them. On one occasion Lydia even suggested to her husband that he needed another woman.

Little Anna was a haughty young girl who spent many hours imagining herself a great lady or even a queen. In her eighteenth year a nephew of Tom Brangwen came to work in the lace factory in the nearby village of Ilkeston. He was only twenty years old; the Brangwens at Marsh Farm looked after him and made him welcome in their home.

Anna Lensky and young Will Brangwen fell in love, with a naïve, touching affection for each other. They soon announced to Tom and Lydia that they wished to be married. Tom leased a home in the village for the young couple and gave them a present of twenty-five hundred pounds so they would not want because of Will's small salary.

The wedding was celebrated with rural pomp and hilarity. After the ceremony the newly-married couple spent two weeks alone in their cottage, ignoring the world and existing only for themselves. Anna was the first to come back to the world of reality. Her decision to give a tea party both bewildered and angered her husband, who had not yet realized that they could not continue to live only for and by themselves. It took him almost a lifetime to come to that realization.

Shortly after the marriage Anna became pregnant, and the arrival of the child brought to Will the added shock that his wife was more a mother than she was a married lover. Each year a new baby came between Will and Anna. The oldest was Ursula, who was always her father's favorite. The love which Will wished to give his wife was given to Ursula, for Anna refused to have anything to do with him when she was expecting another child, and she was not satisfied unless she was pregnant.

In the second year of his marriage Will Brangwen tried to rebel. He met a girl at the theater and afterward took her out for supper and a walk. After that incident the intimate life of Will and Anna began to gain in passion, intense enough to carry Will through the daytime when he was not necessary to the house until the nighttime when he could rule his wife. Gradually he became free in his own mind from Anna's domination.

Since Ursula was her father's favorite child, she was sent to high school. That privilege was a rare thing for a girl of her circumstances in the last decade of the nineteenth century. She drank up knowledge in her study of Latin, French, and algebra. But before she had finished, her interest in her studies was shared by her interest in a young man. The son of a Polish friend of her grand-

mother's was introduced into the house, young, blond Anton Skrebensky, a lieutenant in the British Army. During a month's leave he fell in love with Ursula, who was already in love with him. On his next leave, however, she drove him away with the love she offered to him. He became afraid of her because of that love; it was too possessive.

After finishing high school, Ursula took an examination to enter the university. Having passed the examination, she decided to teach school for a time, for she wanted to accumulate money to carry her through her education without being a burden to her parents. Anna and Will were furious when she broached the subject of leaving home. They compromised with her, however, by securing for her a position in a school in Ilkeston. Ursula spent two friendless, ill-paid, and thankless years teaching at the village elementary school. At the end of that time she was more than ready to continue her education. She decided to become a botanist, for in botany she felt she was doing and learning for herself things which had an absolute truth.

Then one day, after the Boer War ended, Ursula received a letter which upset her completely. Anton Skrebensky had written that he wished to see her again while he was in England on leave. Within a week he arrived in Nottingham to visit her at school. Their love returned for each of them with greater intensity than they had known six years before. During the Easter holidays they went away for a weekend at a hotel, where they passed as husband and wife. They went to the continent as soon as Ursula had finished classes for the summer. Even then, however, Ursula did not want to marry Skrebensky; she wanted to return to college to take her degree. But Skrebensky continued to press increasingly for marriage. He wanted Ursula to leave England with him when he returned to service in India.

Meanwhile Ursula had so neglected her studies that she failed her final examinations for her degree and had to study to take them over again before the summer was finished. When Ursula failed her examinations a second time, Skrebensky urged her to marry him immediately. In India, he insisted, her degree would mean nothing anyway. In the meantime they went to a house party, where they realized that there was something wrong in their mating, that they could not agree enough to make a successful marriage. They left the party separately and a few weeks later Skrebensky was on his way to India as the husband of his regimental commander's daughter.

After he had gone, Ursula learned that she was pregnant. Not knowing that he was already married, she wrote to Skrebensky and promised to be a good wife if he still wished to marry her. Before his answer came from India, Ursula contracted pneumonia and lost the child. One day, as she was convalescing, she observed a rainbow in the sky. She hoped that it was the promise of better times to come.

# RAINTREE COUNTY

*Type of work:* Novel
*Author:* Ross Lockridge, Jr. (1914-1948)
*Type of plot:* Regional chronicle
*Time of plot:* Nineteenth century
*Locale:* Raintree County, Indiana
*First published:* 1948

*Principal characters:*
JOHN WICKLIFF SHAWNESSY, a teacher
SUSANNA DRAKE, his first wife
ESTHER ROOT, his second wife
NELL GAITHER, his sweetheart
PROFESSOR JERUSALEM WEBSTER STILES, his friend
SENATOR GARWOOD B. JONES, a politician

*Critique:*

Raintree County is a long novel, panoramic in scope. The story deals with the events of a single day, but by a series of flashbacks it encompasses almost half a century of American history and life. Through the story pass statesmen, soldiers, prostitutes, gamblers, shoddy politicians, simple people of the soil, all fused into the picture that is America. Here are the men and women of the new Republic, struggling through greed, lust, and war to produce the freedom that had been promised one hundred years before.

*The Story:*

July 4, 1892: That was the day Raintree County, Indiana, had been waiting for. Her most illustrious son, Senator Garwood B. Jones, would make the main address of the day, introduced by his old friend, John Wickliff Shawnessy, teacher. And as John Shawnessy awoke on the morning of that fateful day, his life began to pass before his eyes. It was a fitful picture—events and people crossed each other without regard to time. Some of the pictures were symbolic, some real. But through them all John Shawnessy searched for the meaning of his life. Somewhere was the key to the secret of his existence. During the day he visited the graveyard, studied an old atlas of the county, talked with old friends. Pieced together, the events of that day told the

story of John Wickliff Shawnessy, teacher.

Johnny's father was a preacher, a doctor, a teetotaler. His mother was a gentle woman whom he loved more than he was aware of. Johnny's childhood and adolescence were spent like those of most youths in Raintree County, in playing, working, and dreaming of greatness to come. Two people stood out above all others in those days. One was Garwood B. Jones, the other, Nell Gaither. Garwood, showing signs of becoming a politician, was a smooth talker, a shrewd judge of character, a man without principles. Nell was the girl Johnny had loved since he was old enough to know such feelings. She was a combination of lady and hoyden.

Life in Raintree County was brightened by the appearance of Professor Jerusalem Webster Stiles, who established an academy of higher learning. The "Perfessor," as he was affectionately called, was a cynic and a fraud. His training of the young men was devoted slightly to Greek and Latin and heavily to methods of seducing desirable women. His caustic tongue and vivid history drew young men like a magnet.

On the day he had his graduation picture taken, Johnny met Susanna Drake, a southern girl of wealth and sensuous beauty, but questionable reputation. She was an orphan, lately moved to the village from New Orleans to occupy a house she had inherited. She spoke boldly to Johnny and filled him with desire. Although he desired Susanna's beauty, his heart remained true to Nell.

A picnic was held on graduation night. Nell went with Garwood, who escorted her most of the time, but she and Johnny slipped off together and confessed that they loved each other. In Paradise Lake the two went swimming, nude. Johnny never knew what might have happened next, for they were forced back to decency by the yells of their comrades. It seems that the "Perfessor" and the minister's wife had run off together, and a posse with a rope was hunting the scoundrel. They found the woman at home—the elopers had missed their train—and Johnny later helped the "Perfessor" to escape. Many years were to pass before the man and the boy met again.

On July Fourth of that same year, Johnny found himself again at Paradise Lake, this time with Susanna. As he yielded to his desire and possessed the girl, he knew that it was Nell he really loved.

Susanna returned to New Orleans. In October, Johnny received a letter saying she was coming back to him, pregnant. By the time Susanna arrived, Johnny had made his peace with himself and decided to marry her, although he still loved Nell. Even when Susanna confessed on the night before the wedding that she was not pregnant but only loved him so much that she must marry him, Johnny forgave her.

After the wedding Johnny and Susanna spent a long honeymoon in the South. The year was 1859 and war was fast approaching. Johnny was anti-slavery and Susanna violently pro-South. She seemed to be driven by some mad obsession about Negroes. In New Orleans, Johnny learned a little of her history. Her father had loved a slave and had installed the woman in his house, giving her equality with his insane wife. All three had died in a fire, but it was rumored that the husband and slave had been shot first, locked in an embrace.

Home again, Susanna gave birth to a baby who soon became the greatest joy of his father. Susanna grew more and more withdrawn, alternately spitting out hate and melting in passion. She was driven by desperation, for what Johnny could only suspect. In one last frenzy, she set fire to their house and burned the baby to death. She was rescued, her mind completely gone, and Johnny sent her back to her people to be cared for. He knew at last what he had long suspected. Susanna was the daughter of the slave woman, reared as his own by her father because he loved the Negro woman above all else. Susanna had also known, but she had fought against the knowledge. Unable to escape it, she had tried to expiate the sin through fire, as her father's wife had done.

Johnny enlisted in the war and lived through many bloody campaigns. He ceased to be John Shawnessy, a human being, and became only John Shawnessy, a soldier. He was wounded, reported dead, present at the theater when Lincoln was shot. None of these events really touched Johnny. His soul was back in Raintree County, rooted in the soil of his homeland.

After the war he spent two years in New York with the "Perfessor," now a newspaperman. Johnny had planned through the war years to get his marriage annulled and return home to marry Nell. But he found that Nell had married Garwood after Johnny's reported death and had died in childbirth. There was nothing now to keep him in Raintree County. But New York provided nothing substantial to his life, and when he was called home by his mother's death, he put his roots down for good. He taught school and became the local philosopher. Susanna, he learned, had escaped her relatives; she was believed dead. On the strength of that information, Johnny married a former pupil, Esther Root. Esther's father, considering Johnny an atheist and a bigamist, would not give

3112

his consent. The couple eloped, and Mr. Root would never again receive his daughter. The years were good to Johnny and Esther. They had a fine family and a respected place in the community. There were people, however, who considered John Shawnessy evil and plotted to expose him to the world.

On the night of July 4, 1892, after the departure of Senator Garwood B. Jones, a delegation from the revival meeting accused Johnny and a local widow of immorality. But the "Perfessor," back to cover the celebration, showed the crowd instead that it was the minister, leader of the posse, who had seduced one of his flock. The "Perfessor" thought it a huge joke that he who had once been run out of town by a preacher could now turn the tables after so many years.

The day having ended, John Shawnessy walked the deserted streets of this village in Raintree County. He was thinking of the yesterdays and tomorrows that are America.

# RALPH ROISTER DOISTER

*Type of work:* Drama
*Author:* Nicholas Udall (1505-1556)
*Type of plot:* Farce
*Time of plot:* Sixteenth century
*Locale:* England
*First presented:* c. 1553

Principal characters:
RALPH ROISTER DOISTER, a well-to-do, cowardly braggart
MATHEW MERYGREEKE, Roister Doister's hanger-on
DAME CHRISTIAN CUSTANCE, a well-to-do widow
GAWIN GOODLUCK, Dame Custance's fiancé
SYM SURESBY, Gawin Goodluck's friend

*Critique:*

This drama is one of the early English plays acted by schoolboys and patterned after the Roman drama popular in the schools at the time. Neither the plot nor the characters demanded much subtlety from the youthful actors who originally played it. The humor is broad and the language at times very earthy. Some scenes are truly slapstick, as the scene in which grown men armed with swords are routed by a widow and her servants armed only with household utensils. Some of the characters in the play are modeled on the stock figures of Roman drama, and some are not. Merygreeke is quickly recognizable as the parasite of Roman drama, and Roister Doister himself is found to be the braggart so typical of classical comedy. Dame Christian, on the other hand, is an English addition to the drama, in her way a sixteenth-century version of Chaucer's Wife of Bath. Her humor can, in fact, be traced to the broad comedy of early mystery plays, as presented in the Towneley Cycle.

*The Story:*

Mathew Merygreeke, a gay young rascal who likened himself to the grasshopper of the fable, had often had fun and money at the expense of Ralph Roister Doister, a well-to-do, doltish young man who bragged long and loud of his bravery but failed to act anything but the coward when called to action.

In addition, Ralph Roister Doister imagined himself in love with every woman he met, and he swore each time he fell in love that he could not live without the woman who had most lately caught his eye. One day, meeting Merygreeke on the street, he asserted that he was now madly in love with Dame Christian Custance, a widow reported to be wealthy. She had captivated Roister Doister when he saw her at supper.

Merygreeke, anxious to please the man he constantly gulled, agreed to help Roister Doister pursue his suit. He assured the foolish braggart that the widow was certain to accept him and that Roister Doister ought really to try to marry someone of higher station and greater fortune.

Merygreeke went for musicians to serenade Dame Custance, while Roister Doister waited in front of the widow's home. As he waited, three of the widow's servant women came from the house and talked and sang. When they noticed Roister Doister, he came up, talked to them, and tried to kiss them. After talking with them for a time, Roister Doister gave them a love letter to deliver to their mistress. He boasted that he had written it himself.

Given the letter by her serving-woman, Dame Custance was furious. She reminded her servants that she was an honorable woman, affianced to Gawin Goodluck, who had been for some months on a sea voyage. Dame Custance refused to break the seal of the letter, much less read it.

Meanwhile, to further his suit, Roister Doister sent his servant to the widow's house with some love gifts, a ring and a token in a cloth. The young servant, after some trouble, convinced the widow's serving-women to take the gifts to their mistress, even though she had been angry at receiving the letter.

Handed the gifts, the widow became even angrier, lectured her servants on their conduct, and finally sent a boy to find the man who had delivered the gifts to her house.

Merygreeke, after many a laugh over what happened during Roister Doister's suit, finally went to Dame Custance and revealed his scheme for gulling Roister Doister. The widow said she would never marry such a doltish man, but agreed to join in the fun at the braggart's expense. She went so far as to read the letter he had written to her and said she would make a reply.

Rejoining Roister Doister, Merygreeke listened to the suitor's woeful tale and then told him in outrageous terms that the widow had refused his suit, called him vile names, and accused him of cowardice. Roister Doister immediately vowed that he would assault the widow's house with intent to kill her in combat, along with all her servants. Over Merygreeke's protests, Roister Doister set out to get his men together. Merygreeke laughed and waited, knowing that the cowardly braggart would never carry out his vow.

When they arrived at the widow's house, Merygreeke offered Roister Doister an excuse for not leading the assault. Instead, the braggart began once more to woo the widow with music and song. He sent Merygreeke to call the widow from her house.

Dame Custance went out to Roister Doister and repeated her refusal of his foolish proposal. Then she read his letter aloud, and by rephrasing it and repunctuating it she made the letter as insulting as Roister Doister had meant it to be loving. The result thoroughly confused the suitor, who vowed it was not the letter he had sent to her. After she left, Roister Doister sent for the scrivener who had actually written the letter for him. The scrivener took the letter, read it aright, and convinced Roister Doister that someone had tricked him.

In the meantime Sym Suresby, friend of the widow's fiancé, arrived to tell Dame Custance that her affianced suitor, Gawin Goodluck, had returned from his voyage and would be with her shortly. Suresby saw and heard enough of the conversation between the widow and Roister Doister to think that the widow was unfaithful to Goodluck. He went off, leaving the widow furious at the tomfoolery of Roister Doister. When she chased Roister Doister off, he again vowed to have revenge on the widow and her servants. Gathering his men, he approached her house a second time.

The widow, meanwhile, had gone to a trusted friend to enlist his support in getting rid of the troublesome Roister Doister, who threatened to ruin her approaching marriage to Goodluck. The friend consented to aid her. They also enlisted Merygreeke, who agreed to help them and at the same time pull more tricks at the expense of Roister Doister.

The foolish suitor and his men were routed by the widow with household utensils used as weapons. Having proved himself a coward as well as a fool, Roister Doister renounced his suit for the widow's hand. When Goodluck appeared soon afterward, Dame Custance was able to assure him that the reports he had had from Sym Suresby were muddled and that she had never broken her vows to him. She did, however, berate Suresby for not making certain of the truth before repeating what he had heard.

Merygreeke returned on behalf of Roister Doister and asked forgiveness of the widow and Goodluck. When he promised them that they should have much fun at Roister Doister's expense if they would but agree, they assented heartily and invited Merygreeke and Roister Doister to have dinner with them that very day.

# THE RAMAYANA

*Type of work:* Poem
*Author:* Valmiki (fl. fourth century B.C.)
*Type of plot:* Religious epic
*Time of plot:* Remote antiquity
*Locale:* India
*First transcribed:* c. 350 B.C.

*Principal characters:*
RAMA, a prince and incarnation of Vishnu
SITA, his wife
LAKSHMAN, his brother and loyal follower
DASA-RATHA, his father, King of the Kosalas
RAVAN, Demon-king of Lanka (Ceylon)
KAIKEYI, one of King Dasa-ratha's wives and enemy of Rama

## Critique:

Although relatively unknown to Western readers, the story of Rama is one of the most popular tales among the people of India, where the story holds great religious significance. In India, where the tale has been recounted for untold generations, there are several versions of the story, but the main outlines remain the same, with Rama and Sita the idealized versions of Man and Woman. To the Western reader the characters may appear to be human beings with supernatural powers, roughly equivalent to certain figures in Greek legend and myth, but to Hindus the characters of the *Ramayana* (*The Fortunes of Rama*) are more than this; they are gods, to be reverenced today as they have been in ages past. Scholars disagree on the various versions of the *Ramayana,* and the problem of the original story and additions by later generations of storytellers will perhaps never be solved. The best approach for a general reader is probably to accept the story and enjoy it.

## The Story:

King Dasa-ratha of the Kosalas, who kept his court at Ayodhya, had four sons, though not all by the same mother. According to legend, the god Vishnu, in answer to King Dasa-ratha's supplications, had given a divine liquor to each of the king's wives, so that they might bring forth sons, each of whom was partly an incarnation of Vishnu. Of the sons born, Rama was the handsomest and strongest of all, his mother having drunk more of the magic beverage than Dasa-ratha's other wives.

When Rama grew to manhood he heard of Sita, beautiful, talented, and virtuous daughter of King Janak and the Earth-mother. King Janak was the possessor of a wondrous bow, a mighty weapon that had belonged to the gods, and King Janak resolved that whoever could bend the bow should have Sita for his wife. The king knew, of course, that no ordinary mortal could possibly accomplish the feat.

Rama and his brothers traveled to the court of King Janak and were granted permission to try drawing the mighty bow. With ease Rama bent the bow, with such strength that the weapon snapped in two. King Janak promised that Sita should be Rama's bride and that each of his half-brothers, too, should have a noble bride from the people of Videha.

So Sita became the wife of Rama; her sister Urmila became the bride of Lakshman, Rama's favorite brother; Mandavi and Sruta-kriti, cousins of Sita, became the wives of Bharat and Satrughna, the other half-brothers of Rama. When all returned to Ayodhya, Dasa-ratha, fearing that rivalry between his children might create unhappiness and tragedy in his house, sent Bharat and Satrughna to live with their mothers' people.

Years passed, and King Dasa-ratha grew old. Wishing to have the time and opportunity to prepare himself for the next life, he proposed that Rama his favorite son, should become regent. The king's council and the populace rejoiced in the proposal, and plans were made to invest Rama with the regency and place him on the Kosala throne. Before the preparations had been completed, however, Manthara, a maid to Queen Kaikeyi, one of King Dasa-ratha's wives, advised the queen that Rama's succession to the throne should be prevented and that Bharat, Queen Kaikeyi's son, should become regent. The ill advice was heard, and Queen Kaikeyi remembered that she had been promised two boons by her husband. So when King Dasa-ratha came to her she asked that Bharat should be made regent and that Rama should go into exile for fourteen years. King Dasa-ratha was sad, but he had given his word and he must fulfill his promises. Like a dutiful son, Rama heard his father's decision and prepared to go into exile. He expected to go alone, but his wife Sita and his brother Lakshman prepared to go with him to share his lonely and uncomfortable exile in the dismal Dandak forest. The Kosala people mourned his departure and accompanied him on the first day of his journey away from Ayodhya.

Leaving his native country, Rama journeyed south. He and his companions crossed the Ganges River and came to the hermitage of Bharad-vaja, a holy man. After visiting with him they went on to the hill of Chitrakuta, where stood the hermitage of Valmiki, a learned and holy man. There they learned that King Dasa-ratha had died the day after Rama's departure from Ayodhya, remembering in his hour of death a curse laid on him by a hermit whose son he had accidentally killed. Rama stayed with Valmiki for a time. Bharat returned to Ayodhya to become regent, as his mother had planned. However, he recognized Rama's claim and set out on a journey to find Rama and to ask him to become King of the Kosalas. But Rama, having given his word, remained in exile as he had vowed to do. Bharat returned to Avodhya to place Rama's sandals on the throne as a symbol of Rama's right to the kingship.

In order that his kinsmen might not find him again, Rama left Valmiki's hermitage and after a long journey he established his own hermitage near the dwelling of Agastya, a holy and learned man. There Rama, Sita, and Lakshman lived in peace until they were disturbed by a demon-maiden, enamored of Rama, who had been repulsed in her addresses by both Rama and Lakshman. Spurned and seeking revenge, she went to her brother, Ravan, demon-king of Lanka (Ceylon) and asked his help. Ravan was a powerful being who through asceticism had achieved power even over the gods. His domination, according to legend, could be broken only by an alliance of men and the monkey people. Ravan sent a demon in the disguise of a deer to lead Rama astray while on the hunt. When Rama failed to return, Sita insisted that Lakshman go look for him. In the absence of the brothers, Ravan came and abducted Sita.

Rama, having learned what had happened, allied himself with the monkey people in order to make war upon the demons and win back his beloved wife. Hanuman, one of the monkey people's leaders, found Sita at Ravan's palace and led Rama and the forces of the monkey people to Ceylon. There Ravan's city was besieged and many battles were fought, with combat between the great leaders of both sides and pitched battles between the forces of good and evil. Finally Ravan and his demon forces were defeated, Ravan was killed, and Sita was rescued and restored to her husband. Sita, who had remained faithful to Rama throughout her captivity, proved in an ordeal by fire that she was still virtuous and worthy to be Rama's wife.

Rama, Sita, and Lakshman returned in triumph to Ayodhya, where Rama was welcomed and became king of the Kosala people. Rumors were spread. however, that Sita had not been faithful to her husband, until at last Rama sent his wife away, and she went to live at the hermitage of Valmiki. Shortly after her arrival at the hermitage she gave birth to Rama's sons.

More years passed and the two sons grew up, tutored in their youth by the wise Valmiki, who took his charges eventually to Ayodhya. There Rama, recognizing them as his sons, sent for Sita and had her conducted to his court. Since her virtue had been in doubt she was asked for a token that she had been true to her marriage vows. The earth opened to a great chasm, and the Earth-mother herself rose up on her throne to speak on behalf of Sita and to take her to the land of the gods. Thus Sita was taken away from the husband and the people who had doubted her.

# RAMEAU'S NEPHEW

Type of work: Novel in the form of a dialogue
Author: Denis Diderot (1713-1784)
Time: 1761
Locale: Paris
First published: In German, translated by Goethe, 1805; in French, 1823

Principal characters:
    RAMEAU, nephew of Jean Philippe Rameau, a French composer
    DIDEROT, the author, French encyclopedist and writer

Rameau's Nephew could hardly have been other than the work of a French author. It submits to no simple classification: although fictional, the characters were actual persons and their ideas, in all probability, were their own. But there is the problem—for those who concern themselves about such matters—of deciding how much of Diderot can be found in the character Rameau, and how much of Rameau was in Diderot. On the one hand, the character Diderot is a mild champion of traditional values, and Rameau is a vivacious apologist for roguery. But the brilliant turns of this satirical dialogue suddenly force upon the reader the suspicion that Diderot the author is delighted with the convention-defying attitudes of his friend Rameau; perhaps Diderot believes Rameau more than Rameau believes himself.

The dialogue is a satirical critique of manners and morals. It makes particular reference to prominent writers, musicians, politicians, critics, and other leading figures of eighteenth-century France. Many of the comments are unkind, and some are painfully so—or would have been had the work been published at the time of its composition. But Diderot kept his lively satire under wraps, not only because of its references to living persons, but also because of a reluctance to stir up the censor and all others to whom Rameau's carefree morality might prove intolerable.

The character Rameau is marvelously wrought to suit Diderot's intention. Although Rameau is clearly an individual and is convincing, as witty rogues in literature usually are, he is not simply one thing or another. On the contrary, Dide-

rot states that Rameau is his own opposite. Sometimes Rameau is thin, sometimes fat; sometimes he is filthy, sometimes powdered and curled. His physical vacillation is matched by a vacillation of mood. Sometimes he is gay, sometimes depressed; sometimes he is courageous, sometimes timid to the point of fear. Rameau is a sensualist, a lover of wine and wenches. But his passionate defense of an egoistic hedonism is a sign of his need to apologize for his manner; his morality is a device to prop up his manner. Underneath Rameau's abandon the reader perceives a poignant longing for depth and respectability.

Having created a character whose contrary traits reveal the human being at odds with himself—thus providing the motive for a discussion of morality—Diderot provides Rameau with a gentlemanly antagonist, the man of ideas, Diderot himself. Diderot's mild responses, ostensibly intended to counter Rameau's philosophy, actually prompt Rameau with the acuity of a Socrates, stimulating Rameau to a lively defense of the sense-gratifying life of a social parasite.

Rameau, who contradicts himself within himself, and Diderot, who contradicts Rameau, together bring out the difficulty of all moral problems and of morality itself. Man is neither merely intellectual nor merely sensual; his desire to understand is often in conflict with his desires, and his desires are in conflict with each other. Consequently, no one moral rule or set of principles will do. To be a good man, a person must have a kind of moral genius. For such a person, rules are instruments to be used only with ingenuity and sometimes to be discarded altogether. If a person is at war with himself, or with another, as Rameau is with himself, or with Diderot, a just victory is not always possible. Sometimes there is no such thing as the proper answer. For a good man, life is a creative struggle that must be judged as works of art are judged, without dogmatism and with respect for the impossible goals the human spirit sets for itself. Perhaps the theme of the dialogue is best understood dialectically: without the restraint of reason and human consideration, the human being becomes something worse than a fool, but without attention to the fact of human appetites the moralist becomes something less than a human being.

For Rameau is the fool and Diderot is the moralist. But Rameau fancies himself as something of the classic fool, the darling of the courts, the discerning jester who makes the bitter truth palatable. The fact is that he comes close to being a compromising sponger, a guest in great houses only because he is sometimes an amusing conversationalist. Although he comes close to being merely parasitical, he is saved by his own need for apology. A man who must speak to Diderot is already more than a professional guest.

The dialogue is presented against a background of chess. The narrator takes shelter in the Regency Café where the finest chess players of Paris compete with each other. When Rameau enters and engages Diderot in conversation, he begins a kind of verbal chess game that shows him to be the brilliant and erratic player while Diderot is slower but more canny. Rameau's attitude is revealed at once. In response to Diderot's expression of interest in the games, Rameau speaks scornfully of the players—although they are the best in Paris—and when Diderot remarks that Rameau forgives nothing but supreme genius, Rameau retorts that he has no use for mediocrity.

One must read carefully for, to continue the chess metaphor, the moves are deceptive. Rameau argues that evil comes from men of genius, that the genius—and he cites his uncle as an example—is so

absorbed in his own work that he neglects family and state, and he concludes that a child showing the mark of genius should be smothered or thrown to the dogs. Diderot asks whether it would have been better if Voltaire had been a "good soul" attending to his business and family and doing nothing more, or whether it was better that, though deceitful, ambitious, and mean, he wrote great plays. The implication is that Diderot prefers the latter. But when Rameau says it would have been better for Voltaire himself if he had been the former, Diderot acknowledges that this is true.

As the conversation continues, each man forces upon the other an appreciation of a perspective quite different from his own. Diderot is fascinated by the antics of Rameau, for Rameau is not only a rascal and a wit but also a great mime whose conversation is enlivened by spontaneous performances in which he shows, by the economy of caricature, the manners of those with whom he must associate.

Because Diderot responds to Rameau's zest for life, he is saved from unrealistic moralizing. Nevertheless, Rameau can go too far. When he applauds the behavior of an informer whose act resulted in the execution of the informer's friend, Diderot is quick to say that he finds such an attitude repulsive. He considers it almost unbearable to be in the presence of a man who regarded a great crime as something worthy of the same critical admiration one might give to a work of art. But although nothing more is said on the subject, the fact that Diderot admits to being pursued by "dark fancies" suggests that the moralist has caught something of Rameau's aesthetic attitude toward great acts, whether heroic or foul, and feels himself at grips with the problem of evil within himself.

Diderot and Rameau fall into a long critical discourse on music. Rameau is all for music which honestly expresses the passions. The true, the good, and the beautiful are his Father, Son, and Holy Ghost—but his truth and beauty are close to the earth, allied to the passions of men. Diderot admits that there is a great deal of sense in what Rameau says, but he regrets that Rameau talks of nothing but gold, wine, good food, and women.

The moralist must reconcile himself and his morality to the facts of human passion. Somehow Diderot must come to acknowledge Rameau's importance as the creative beast, but as a man of ideas he finds it almost intolerable that not everything about human action can be reduced to a categorical formula. For Diderot the problem was what it remains for contemporary man, the problem of reconciling Freud's view of man with Christ's conception. In fact, Diderot anticipates Freud twice, within two pages: once, by having Rameau envious of Diderot's literary talent, for in so doing, Rameau accords with Freud's theory of the artist's motive; again, when Rameau asserts that were his son to develop without interference, he would want good food and dress, fame, and the love of women, Diderot replies that if the child were left in his natural state, he would grow to manhood knowing no better than to murder his father as a rival and then seduce his own mother.

Like Dostoevski, Diderot appreciated the exceptional man who stepped beyond the bounds of conventional morality; unlike Nietzsche, he did not deify the immoralist. *Rameau's Nephew* is a skillful and satirical attempt to do justice to man the moralist and also to man the animal.

# THE RAPE OF LUCRECE

*Type of work:* Poem
*Author:* William Shakespeare (1564-1616)
*Type of plot:* Tragedy
*Time of plot:* 500 B.C.
*Locale:* Ancient Rome
*First published:* 1594

Principal characters:
COLLATINE, a Roman general
LUCRECE, his wife
TARQUIN, Collatine's friend and son of the Roman king

## Critique:

The story of Tarquin's violation of Lucrece is an ancient Roman legend which has been presented in many versions other than in this poem by Shakespeare. Because the Elizabethans were especially fond of this legend, Shakespeare had numerous sources upon which to draw. Compared with his other writings, this poem is far more conventionally Elizabethan, yet its passages of great emotion and its consistently beautiful poetry rank it above other interpretations of the story known in his day.

## The Story:

At Ardea, where the Romans were fighting, two Roman leaders, Tarquin and Collatine, spoke together one evening. Collatine, in the course of the conversation, described his beautiful young wife Lucrece in such glowing terms that Tarquin's passions were aroused. The next morning Tarquin left the Roman host and journeyed to Collatium, where he was welcomed by the unsuspecting Lucrece as one of her husband's friends. As he told her many tales of Collatine's prowess on the battlefield, Tarquin looked admiringly at Lucrece and decided that she was indeed the most beautiful woman in Rome.

In the night, while the others of the household were asleep, Tarquin lay restless. Caught between desire for Lucrece and dread of being discovered, to the consequent loss of his honor, he wandered aimlessly about his chamber. On the one hand there was his position as a military man who should not be the slave of his emotions; on the other hand was his overwhelming desire.

But what dreadful consequences might be the result of his lustful deed! His disgrace would never be forgotten. Perhaps his own face would show the mark of his crimes and the advertisement linger on even after death.

He thought for a moment that he might try to woo Lucrece but decided that such a course would be to no avail. Since she was already married, she was not mistress of her own desires. Again he considered the possible consequences of his deed.

At last emotion conquered reason. As Tarquin made his way to Lucrece's chamber all sorts of petty annoyances deterred him. The locks on the doors had to be forced; the threshold beneath the door grated under his footstep; the wind threatened to blow out his torch; he pricked his finger on a needle. Tarquin ignored these omens of disaster. In fact, he misconstrued them as forms of trial which only made his prize more worth winning.

When he reached the chamber door, Tarquin began to pray for success. Realizing, however, that heaven would not countenance his sin, he declared that Love and Fortune would henceforth be his gods. Entering the room, he gazed at Lucrece in sleep. When he reached forward to touch her breast, she awoke with a cry of fear. He told her that her beauty had captured his heart and that she must submit to his will.

3122

First he threatened Lucrece with force, telling her that if she refused to submit to him he would not only kill her but also dishonor her name. His intention was to murder one of her slaves, place him in her arms, and then swear that he killed them because he had seen Lucrece embracing the man. But, if she yielded, he promised to keep the whole affair secret. Lucrece began to weep and plead with Tarquin. For the sake of her hospitality, her husband's friendship, Tarquin's position as a warrior, he must pity her and refrain from this deed. Her tears serving only to increase his lust, Tarquin smothered her cries with the bed linen while he raped her.

Shame-ridden, he stole away, leaving Lucrece desolate. She, horrified and revolted, tore her nails and hoped the dawn would never come. In a desperate fury, she railed against the night; its darkness and secrecy that had ruined her. She was afraid of the day, for surely her sin would be revealed. Still worse, through her fall, Collatine would be forever shamed. It was Opportunity that was at fault, she claimed, working for the wicked and against the innocent. Time, the handmaiden of ugly Night, was hand-in-hand with Opportunity. But Time could work for Lucrece now. She implored Time to bring misery and pain to Tarquin. Exhausted from her emotional tirade, Lucrece fell back on her pillow. She longed for a suicide weapon; death alone could save her soul.

As the dawn broke she began to consider her death. Not until she had told Collatine the complete details of her fall would she take the step, however, for Collatine must revenge her on Tarquin.

Lucrece called her maid and asked for pen and paper. Writing to Collatine, she asked him to return immediately. When she gave the messenger the letter, she imagined that he knew of her sin, for he gave her a sly, side glance. Surely everyone must know by now, she thought. Her grief took new channels. Studying a picture of the fall of Troy, she tried to find the face showing greatest grief. Hecuba, who gazed mournfully at Priam in his dying moments, seemed the saddest. Lucrece grieved for those who died in the Trojan War, all because one man could not control his lust. Enraged, she tore the painting with her nails.

Collatine, returning home, found Lucrece robed in black. With weeping and lamentations she told him of her shame, but without naming her violator. After she had finished, Collatine, driven half-mad by rage and grief, demanded the name of the traitor. Before revealing it, Lucrece drew promises from the assembled soldiers that the loss of her honor would be avenged. Then, naming Tarquin, she drew a knife from her bosom and stabbed herself.

Heartbroken, Collatine cried that he would kill himself as well, but Brutus, his friend, stepped forward and argued that woe was no cure for woe; it was better to revenge Lucrece. The soldiers left the palace to carry the bleeding body of Lucrece through Rome. The indignant citizens banished Tarquin and all his family.

# THE RAPE OF THE LOCK

*Type of work:* Poem
*Author:* Alexander Pope (1688-1744)
*Type of plot:* Mock-heroic epic
*Time of plot:* Early eighteenth century
*Locale:* London
*First published:* 1712

Principal characters:
BELINDA, Miss Arabella Fermor
LORD PETRE, Belinda's suitor
THALESTRIS, Belinda's friend
ARIEL, a sprite
UMBRIEL, a gnome

## Critique:

The Rape of the Lock, generally considered the most popular of Pope's writings as well as the finest satirical poem in the English language, was written at the suggestion of John Caryll, Pope's friend, ostensibly to heal a family row which resulted when an acquaintance of Pope, Lord Petre, playfully clipped a lock of hair from the head of Miss Arabella Fermor. Pope's larger purpose in writing the poem, however, was to ridicule the social vanity of his day and the importance that was attached to affected manners.

## The Story:

At noon, when the sun was accustomed to awaken both lap dogs and lovers, Belinda was still asleep. She dreamed that Ariel appeared to whisper praises of her beauty in her ear. He said that he had been sent to protect her because something dreadful — what, he did not know — was about to befall her. He also warned her to beware of jealousy, pride, and, above all, men.

After Ariel had vanished, Shock, Belinda's lap dog, thought that his mistress had slept long enough, and he awakened her by lappings of his tongue. Rousing herself, Belinda spied a letter on her bed. After she had read it, she promptly forgot everything that Ariel had told her, including the warning to beware of men.

Belinda, aided by her maid, Betty, began to make her toilet. Preening before her mirror, she was guilty of the pride against which Ariel had cautioned her.

The sun, journeying across the sky, witnessed its brilliant rival, Belinda, boating on the Thames with her friends and suitors. All eyes were upon her, and like the true coquette she smiled at her swains but favored no one more than another.

Lord Petre, one of Belinda's suitors, admired a lock of her hair and vowed that he would have it by fair means or foul. So set was he on getting the lock that before the sun rose that morning he had built an altar to Love and had thrown on it all the trophies received from former sweethearts, meanwhile asking Love to give him soon the prize he wanted and to let him keep it for a long time. But Love granted him only half his prayer.

Everyone except Ariel seemed happy during the cruise on the Thames. That sprite summoned his aides, and reminded them that their duty was to watch over the fair Belinda, one sylph to guard her fan, another her watch, a third her favorite lock. Ariel himself was to guard Belinda's lap dog, Shock. Fifty sylphs were dispatched to watch over the maiden's petticoat, in order to protect her chastity. Any negligent sylphs, warned Ariel, would be punished severely.

After her cruise on the Thames, Belinda, accompanied by Lord Petre and the rest of the party, visited one of the palaces near London. There Belinda decided to play ombre, a Spanish card game, with two of her suitors, including Lord Petre. As she played, invisible sylphs sat on her important cards to protect them.

Coffee was served after the game. Sylphs guarded Belinda's dress to keep it from being spotted. The fumes from the coffee sharpened Lord Petre's wits to the point where he thought of new stratagems for stealing Belinda's lock. One of his cronies handed him a pair of scissors. The sylphs, aware of Belinda's danger, attempted to warn her before Lord Petre could act, but as the maid bent her head over her coffee cup he clipped the lock. Even Ariel was unable to warn Belinda in time.

At the rape of her lock, Belinda shrieked in horror. Lord Petre cried out in triumph. He praised the steel used in the scissors, comparing it with the metal of Greek swords that overcame the Trojans. Belinda's fury was as tempestuous as the rage of scornful virgins who have lost their charms. Ariel wept bitterly and flew away.

Umbriel, a melancholy gnome, took advantage of the human confusion and despair to fly down to the center of the earth to find the gloomy cave of Spleen, the queen of all bad tempers and the source of every detestable quality in human beings, including ill-nature and affectation. Umbriel asked the queen to touch Belinda with chagrin, for he knew that, if she were gloomy, melancholy and bad temper would spread to half the world. Spleen granted Umbriel's request and collected in a bag horrible noises such as those uttered by female lungs and tongues. In a vial she put tears, sorrows, and griefs. She gave both containers to Umbriel.

When the gnome returned to Belinda's world, he found the girl disheveled and dejected. Pouring the contents of the magic bag over her, Umbriel caused Belinda's wrath to be magnified many times. One of her friends, Thalestris, fanned the flames of the maiden's anger by telling her that her honor was at stake and that behind her back her friends were talking about the rape of her lock. Thalestris then went to her brother, Sir Plume, and demanded that he confront Lord Petre and secure the return of the precious lock. Sir Plume considered the whole episode much magnified from little, but he went to demand Belinda's lock. Lord Petre refused to give up his prize.

Next Umbriel broke the vial containing human sorrows, and Belinda was almost drowned in tears. She regretted the day that she ever entered society and also the day she learned to play ombre. She longed for simple country life. Suddenly she remembered, too late, that Ariel had warned her of impending evil.

In spite of Thalestris' pleas, Lord Petre was still adamant. Clarissa, another of Belinda's circle, wondered at the vanity of women and at the foolishness of men who fawn before them. Clarissa felt that both men and women need good sense, but in making her feelings known she exposed the tricks and deceits of women and caused Belinda to frown. Calling Clarissa a prude, Thalestris gathered her forces to battle with Belinda's enemies, including Clarissa and Lord Petre. Umbriel was delighted by this Homeric struggle of the teacups. Belinda pounced upon Lord Petre, who was subdued when a pinch of snuff caused him to sneeze violently. She demanded the lock, but it could not be found. Some thought that it had gone to the moon, where also go love letters and other tokens of tender passions. But the muse of poetry saw it ascend to heaven and become a star.

# RASSELAS

*Type of work:* Novel
*Author:* Samuel Johnson (1709-1794)
*Type of plot:* Philosophical romance
*Time of plot:* Eighteenth century
*Locale:* Abyssinia and Cairo
*First published:* 1759

Principal characters:
RASSELAS, Prince of Abyssinia
NEKAYAH, his sister
PEKUAH, her maid
IMLAC, a poet

## Critique:

The History of Rasselas, Prince of Abyssinia, one of the most popular works of Samuel Johnson during his own lifetime, is still widely read. However, it is a weighty novel, ponderous in style and slow moving. There is almost no narrative, for the plot deals with the efforts of four people to find a working philosophy by which they can guide their lives. The age in which Johnson lived was characterized by superficial optimism, and this novel is an attack on that optimism. There is a popular theory that Johnson wrote *Rasselas* in one week, in order to pay his mother's funeral expenses, but many scholars refute this theory. The novel shows that Johnson hated pretense of any kind, and he used his pen to fight it at every opportunity.

## The Story:

It was the custom in Abyssinia for the sons and daughters of the emperor to be confined in a remote place until the order of succession to the throne was established. The spot in which Rasselas and his brothers and sisters were confined was a beautiful and fertile valley situated between high mountains. In the valley was everything needed for a luxurious life. Entertainers were brought in from the outside world to help the royal children pass the time pleasantly. These entertainers were never allowed to leave, for the outside world was not to know how the royal children lived before they were called on to rule.

It was this perfection which caused Rasselas in the twenty-sixth year of his life to become melancholy and discontented. He was unhappy because he had everything to make him happy; he wanted more than anything else to desire something which could not be made available to him. When he talked of his longing with an old philosopher, he was told that he was foolish. The old man told him of the misery and suffering of the people outside the valley and cautioned him to be glad of his present station. But Rasselas knew that he could not be content until he had seen the suffering of the world.

For many months Rasselas pondered on his desire to escape from the valley. He took no action, however, for the valley was carefully guarded and there was no chance for anyone to leave. Once he met an inventor who promised to make some wings for him so that he could fly over the mountains, but the experiment was a failure. In his search for a way to escape, his labor was more mental than physical.

In the palace there was a poet, Imlac, whose lines pleased Rasselas by their intelligence. Imlac was also tired of the perfect life in the valley, for in the past he had traveled over much of the world. He had observed the evil ways of mankind and had learned that most wickedness stemmed from envy and jealousy. He had noticed that people envy others with more worldly goods and oppress those who are weak. As he talked, Rasselas longed more than ever to see the world and its misery. Imlac tried to discourage him, for he believed that

3126

Rasselas would long for his present state should he ever see the violence and treachery which abounded in the lands beyond the mountains.

But when Imlac realized he could not deter the prince, he agreed to join him in his attempt to leave the perfect state. Together the two men contrived to hew a path through the side of a mountain. When they were almost ready to leave, Rasselas saw his sister Nekayah watching them. She begged to accompany the travelers for she too was bored with the valley and longed to see the rest of the world. Because she was the favorite sister of Rasselas, he gladly allowed her and her maid, Pekuah, to join them. The four made their way safely through the path in the mountainside. They took with them enough jewels to supply them with money when they reached a city of trade. They were simply dressed and no one recognized them as royalty.

In Cairo they sold some of their jewels and rented a magnificent dwelling. They entertained great men and began to learn the customs of people different from themselves. It was their object to observe all possible manners and customs so that they could make their own choices about the kind of life each wanted to pursue. But they found many drawbacks to every form of living.

Rasselas and Nekayah believed that it was only necessary to find the right pursuit to know perfect happiness and contentment. Imlac knew that few men lived by choice but rather by chance and the whims of fortune. But Rasselas and Nekayah believed that their chance birth had at least given them the advantage of being able to study all forms of living and thus to choose the one most suitable for them to pursue. So it was that the royal pair visited with men of every station. They went into the courts and into the fields. They visited sages of great fame and hermits who had isolated themselves to meditate. Nowhere did they find a man completely happy and satisfied, for each desired what the other had and thought his neighbor more fortunate than he.

Only once did Rasselas find a happy man. This man was a philosopher who preached the doctrine of reason. He stated that by reason man can conquer his passions and disappointments and thus find true happiness. But when Rasselas called on the sage the following day, he found the old man in a fit of despair. His daughter had died in the night, and the reason which he had urged others to use failed completely in his own life.

Imlac and Nekayah spent long hours discussing the advantages of one kind of life over another. They questioned the state of marriage as compared with celibacy and life at court as compared with pastoral pleasures, but at no time could they find satisfactory solutions for their questions. Nowhere could they find people living in happiness. Imlac suggested a visit to the pyramids so that they might learn of people of the past. While they were in a tomb, Pekuah was stolen by Arabs, and it was many months before she was returned to Nekayah. Pekuah told her mistress that she had spent some time in a monastery while she waited for her ransom, and she believed that the nuns had found the one truly happy way of life.

Their search continued for a long period. Often they thought they had found a happy man, but always they would find much sorrow in the life they thought so serene. Nekayah at one time decided that she would cease looking for happiness on earth and live so that she might find happiness in eternity. A visit to the catacombs and a discourse on the soul prompted her decision.

When the Nile flooded the valley, confining them to their home for a time, the four friends discussed the ways of life which promised each the greatest happiness. Pekuah wished to retire to a convent. Nekayah more than anything desired knowledge and wanted to found a woman's college, where she could both teach and learn. Rasselas thought he wanted a small kingdom where he could rule justly and wisely. Imlac said he would be content to drift through life, with no particular goal. Because all knew their desires would never be fulfilled, they began to look forward to their return to the Abyssinian valley where everyone seemed happy and there was nothing to desire.

# RAVENSHOE

*Type of work:* Novel
*Author:* Henry Kingsley (1830-1876)
*Type of plot:* Domestic romance
*Time of plot:* Early nineteenth century
*Locale:* England
*First published:* 1862

Principal characters:
CHARLES RAVENSHOE, of the old House of Ravenshoe
FATHER MACKWORTH, a resident priest
WILLIAM HORTON, a groom, friend of Charles
ADELAIDE SUMMERS, a vain girl
MARY CORBY, ward of the Ravenshoes
CUTHBERT, older brother of Charles
LORD SALTIRE, an atheist and dandy

*Critique:*

This very long novel is slow in pace, and to some modern tastes Kingsley may seem arch with his interminable asides and his painful foreshadowing. In summary form the novel attempts to cover several centuries in the story of an English family, but the bulk of the book is concerned with the affairs of one generation; rather than a panorama of a family, Kingsley gives the adventures of one son. Divested of its paraphernalia, the tale is a lively one in the Regency tradition. The malevolent priest is perhaps the outstanding character.

*The Story:*

The House of Ravenshoe had long been a bastion of Catholicism in England, and the Church of Rome had for generations assigned a resident priest to the household. Densil Ravenshoe, when he reached manhood, showed a rebellious spirit by going off to London and consorting with Lord Saltire, a notorious atheist. After he had been imprisoned for his debts, his father sent the resident priest to bail him out.

For a while Densil was reconciled to priestly rule, but the new Father Mackworth had his difficulties with him. Densil at last married a Protestant woman, to the consternation of the Church. Five years went by and Densil had no children. Father Mackworth was thinking of asking for another assignment, but he was eavesdropping one evening and what

he heard caused him to stay on at Ravenshoe. Cuthbert, Densil's first son, was born, and the priest had the satisfaction of baptizing him in the true faith.

Five years later a second son, Charles, was born. Densil's wife died in childbirth, and shortly the terrible truth came out: Densil had promised to bring up his second son as a Protestant. Charles was given to a nurse, Norah, wife of James Horton, the gamekeeper. She had a boy, William, just a week older than Charles, and she gladly accepted her new charge. Father Mackworth, resolved that a Protestant should never own Ravenshoe, made his plans early.

Charles was a cheerful lad, well liked by all. When he was ten, he went to visit at Ranford, the estate of the Ascots, who were related to the Ravenshoes. Charles was immediately accepted by his Protestant relations; Cuthbert had never been able to win their love. At Ranford Charles met beautiful, imperious Adelaide Summers, a ward of Lady Ascot, and promptly fell in love with her. Another new friend was the famous Lord Saltire, who became fond of the boy.

There was a great storm at Ravenshoe. In the bay a ship went down, split on a rock. Only a few were saved, among them Mary Corby, the daughter of the captain. She was a lovely girl who was accepted as one of the family. She soon fell in love with Charles.

At Oxford, Charles had two intimate

friends, Lord Welter, his cousin from Ranford, and John Marston, a scholar. Marston was a good influence over Charles but Welter was a brutal, arrogant bully. Unfortunately Charles followed Welter's habits of drinking, brawling, and gaming. After a wild night of carousing, both Charles and Welter were sent down from the university. To delay his homecoming, Charles stopped off for a visit at Ranford. Lord Saltire helped him make his peace with his father. During his visit he became engaged to Adelaide.

Charles spent several months of enforced vacation at Ravenshoe. During that time Welter and Marston both came to see him. Marston proposed to Mary but she refused him. This period was marred by Father Mackworth, who seemed to Charles an evil genius. Ellen Horton, William's younger sister, ran away because of some trouble which seemed to be connected with Father Mackworth. At the beginning of the next term Charles went back to Oxford.

His stay was brief, for he was recalled by the death of his father. Father Mackworth was in possession of a ruinous secret which Cuthbert offered to buy for ten thousand pounds. Father Mackworth refused money, but to keep Charles from inheriting Ravenshoe he revealed that Norah had switched babies long ago; Charles was really her own son, and William Horton, the groom, was a Ravenshoe. William, a Catholic, became second in line to own Ravenshoe. Distraught, Charles rushed to Ranford to see Adelaide, only to learn that she had run away with Welter.

Calling himself Charles Horton, he took service with Lieutenant Hornby. As a servant he learned that Ellen, his own sister, had been Welter's mistress; now she was a maid in the same household with Adelaide, Welter's new mistress. Welter and Adelaide lived by gambling. Charles had an interview with Welter, who excused his villainy by saying that he had not known that Ellen was Charles' sister. In reality, Charles was well rid of the scheming Adelaide. After seeing Mary, who had become a governess, from a distance, Charles enlisted in the army to fight against the Russians.

The Ascot family, heavily in debt, had put all their hopes on a horse they had entered in the Derby. In a desperate attempt to recoup his fortunes, Lord Ascot substituted a less famous jockey and bet against his own horse. The Ascot entry won and the family was ruined. At his father's death, Welter became Lord Ascot. Although he had married Adelaide by that time, society ignored her.

In the Crimea, Charles took part in the famous charge of the Six Hundred at Balaklava. Hornby was killed and Charles was wounded. Invalided home, he took service again as a groom under an officer with whom he had served. He hoped to remain and eventually to find his sister Ellen. His health remained poor.

When William made a trip to Sevastopol to look for Charles, a lying soldier had convinced him that Charles was dead. When he heard the news, Lord Saltire made a new will, bequeathing a large sum to Mary but leaving the bulk of his fortune to Welter and Adelaide.

Thinking themselves at last secure, Welter and his wife began to move freely in society. One night, to his horror, Welter recognized Charles in a tavern. Adelaide wanted Welter to keep still, but her husband, conscience-stricken, informed Lord Saltire, who prepared to make a new will immediately. But the great lord died before morning.

Charles was nursed back to health at Ranford after an operation to heal his war wound. When he returned to Ravenshoe, he was a guest of William, now in control of the estate since Cuthbert's death by drowning. But Lady Ascot had started a chain of inquiries which threatened Father Mackworth's design. Finally paralyzed after a stroke, he summoned Ellen, now a nun, and through a wedding certificate in her keeping the truth came out. James Horton, father of Charles and Ellen, had always been looked upon as the illegitimate son of

Densil's father, Petre Ravenshoe. But Petre had really married James' mother, and so Charles was the true heir of Ravenshoe after all. Father Mackworth had at one time possessed the marriage certificate, but Ellen had stolen it when she ran away. Her return with the certificate provided proof of Father Mackworth's duplicity.

Ellen returned to her nursing duties; Father Mackworth died after begging forgiveness of the heir he had dispossessed. Charles, the Protestant owner of Ravenshoe, made ample provision for his good friend William and the two were married in a double ceremony, Charles to the faithful Mary and William to his childhood sweetheart. At the celebration Welter acknowledged that Lord Saltire's estate really belonged to Charles. Adelaide had become a permanent invalid after a riding accident; hence they would never have children. In reparation, Welter had willed his entire fortune to Charles.

# REBECCA

*Type of work:* Novel
*Author:* Daphne du Maurier (1907-    )
*Type of plot:* Mystery romance
*Time of plot:* 1930's
*Locale:* England
*First published:* 1938

*Principal characters:*
MAXIM DE WINTER, owner of Manderley
MRS. DE WINTER, Maxim's wife and the narrator
MRS. DANVERS, the housekeeper at Manderley
FRANK CRAWLEY, estate manager of Manderley
JACK FAVELL, Rebecca's cousin
COLONEL JULYAN, a magistrate

## Critique:

*Rebecca* is an excellent example of the suspense novel. From the time the drab little companion marries Maxim de Winter, the reader is aware that there is something wrong with the situation at Manderley, the fine house where Rebecca was formerly the mistress. All through the novel there are hints that some startling disclosure about Rebecca is to come, a revelation which will explain many strange events. In development of situation and in character portrayal there is ample evidence of the author's technical skill.

## The Story:

Manderley was gone. Since the fire which had destroyed their home, Mr. and Mrs. de Winter had lived in a secluded hotel away from England. Occasionally Mrs. de Winter recalled the circumstances which had brought Manderley and Maxim de Winter into her life.

A shy, sensitive orphan, she had been traveling about the continent as companion to an overbearing American social climber, Mrs. Van Hopper. At Monte Carlo Mrs. Van Hopper forced herself upon Maxim de Winter, owner of Manderley, one of the most famous estates in England. Before approaching him, Mrs. Van Hopper had informed her companion that Mr. de Winter was recovering from the shock of the tragic death of his wife, Rebecca, a few months pre-. viously.

During the following days the young girl and Mr. de Winter became well acquainted; when Mrs. Van Hopper decided to return to America, Maxim de Winter unexpectedly proposed to her companion. Already deeply in love with him, the girl accepted and they were married shortly afterward.

After a long honeymoon in Italy and southern France, Mr. and Mrs. de Winter returned to Manderley. Mrs. de Winter was extremely nervous, fearing that she would not fit into the life of a great estate like Manderley. The entire staff had gathered to meet the new mistress. Mrs. Danvers, the housekeeper, had been devoted to her former mistress and immediately began to show her resentment toward the new Mrs. de Winter.

Gradually Mrs. de Winter pieced together the picture of Rebecca. She learned that Rebecca had been a beautiful, vivacious woman, a charming hostess. As she became acquainted with the relatives and friends of her husband, she became convinced that they found her lacking in those qualities which had made Rebecca so attractive and gracious. One day she went secretly to the closed rooms Rebecca had occupied. Everything was as Rebecca had left it before her fatal sail in her boat. Mrs. Danvers suddenly appeared and forced her to view Rebecca's lovely clothes and other personal possessions.

When the bishop's wife suggested that the traditional Manderley fancy dress ball be revived, Mr. de Winter gave his consent. Mrs. de Winter announced her intention of surprising them all with her costume. At Mrs. Danvers' suggestion, she planned to dress as an ancestress whose portrait hung in the hall at Manderley. But as Mrs. de Winter descended the stairs that night a silence fell over the guests, and her husband turned angrily away without speaking. Realizing that something was wrong, Mrs. de Winter returned to her room. Beatrice, Mr. de Winter's sister, went to her immediately and explained that Rebecca had worn the identical costume to her last fancy dress ball. Again Mrs. Danvers had humiliated her new mistress. Although Mrs. de Winter reappeared at the ball in a simple dress, her husband did not speak to her all evening; and her belief that he had never ceased to love Rebecca became firmly established in her mind.

The next day a steamer ran aground in the bay near Manderley. A diver sent down to inspect the damaged steamer discovered Rebecca's boat and in its cabin the remains of a human body. Mr. de Winter had previously identified the body of a woman found in the river as that of Rebecca.

Unable to keep silent any longer, Mr. de Winter told his wife the whole story of Rebecca and her death. The world had believed their marriage a happy one, but Rebecca had been an immoral woman, incapable of love. To avoid the scandal of a divorce, they made a bargain; Rebecca was to be outwardly the fitting mistress of Manderley, but she would be allowed to go to London periodically to visit her dissolute friends. All went well until she began to be careless, inviting her friends to Manderley and receiving them in the boathouse. Then she began to plague Frank Crawley, the estate manager of Manderley, and Giles, Mr. de Winter's brother-in-law. There had been gossip after Frank

and others had seen Rebecca's cousin, Jack Favell, at the boathouse with her. One evening Mr. de Winter had followed her to the boathouse to tell her that their marriage was at an end. Rebecca taunted him, suggesting how difficult it would be to prove his case against her, asserting that should she have a child it would bear his name and inherit Manderley. She assured him with a smile that she would be the perfect mother as she had been the perfect wife.

She was still smiling when he shot her Then he put her in the boat and sailed out on the river. There he opened the seacocks, drilled holes with a pike, and leaving the boat to sink, rowed back in the dinghy.

Mrs. de Winter was horrified, but at the same time she felt a happiness she had not known before. Her husband loved her; he had never loved Rebecca. With that discovery, her personality changed. She assured her husband that she would guard his secret.

A coroner's inquest was held, for the body in the boat was that of Rebecca. At the inquest it was established that a storm could not have sunk the boat; evidence of a bolted door, the holes, and the open seacocks pointed to the verdict of suicide which the coroner's jury returned.

That night Jack Favell, drunk, appeared at Manderley. Wildly expressing his love for Rebecca and revealing their intimate life, he tried to blackmail Mr. de Winter by threatening to prove that de Winter had killed his wife. Mr. de Winter called the magistrate, Colonel Julyan, to hear his case. Favell's theory was that Rebecca had asked her husband to free her so that she could marry Jack, and that de Winter, infuriated, had killed her.

From Rebecca's engagement book it was learned that she had visited a Doctor Baker in London on the last day of her life. Colonel Julyan and Mr. and Mrs. de Winter, with Jack Favell following in his car, drove to London to see Doctor Baker. On checking his records,

3133

the doctor found that he had examined a Mrs. Danvers on the day in question. They realized that Rebecca had assumed the housekeeper's name. Doctor Baker explained that he had diagnosed Rebecca's ailment as cancer in an advanced stage. The motive for suicide established, Colonel Julyan suggested that the matter be closed.

Driving back to Manderley after leaving Colonel Julyan at his sister's home, Mr. de Winter told his wife that he believed that Colonel Julyan had guessed the truth. He also realized that Rebecca had intimated that she was pregnant because she had been sure that her husband would kill her; her last evil deed would be to ruin him and Manderley. Mr. de Winter telephoned Frank from the inn where they stopped for dinner, and the estate manager reported that Mrs. Danvers had disappeared. His news seemed to upset Mr. de Winter. At two o'clock in the morning they approached Manderley. Mrs. de Winter had been sleeping. Awaking, she thought by the blaze of light that it was dawn. A moment later she realized that she was looking at Manderley, going up in flames.

# THE REBEL GENERATION

*Type of work:* Novel
*Author:* Johanna van Ammers-Küller (1884-    )
*Type of plot:* Social chronicle
*Time of plot:* 1840-1923
*Locale:* Leyden, Holland
*First published:* 1925

*Principal characters:*
LOUIS CORNVELT, an upper middle-class Hollander
NICHOLAS, and
DAVID CORNVELT, his sons
SARAH, and
KATIE CORNVELT, his daughters
MARIE ELIZABETH SYLVAIN (LYSBETH, "SYLVIA"), his niece
DR. WILLIAM WISEMAN, Katie Cornvelt's husband
(DR.) ELIZA WISEMAN, daughter of William and Katie
LOUIS CORNVELT, David's son
CLARA CORNVELT, David's daughter
MILLICENT CORNVELT, great-granddaughter of Louis Cornvelt, Sr.
STEPHEN CORNVELT, Millicent's cousin, in love with her
DOROTHY CORNVELT, Stephen's wife
PUCK, and
KITTY CORNVELT, daughters of Stephen and Dorothy

## Critique:

*The Rebel Generation* is a sociological novel presenting the changes in middle-class Dutch culture through several generations of a single family. It demonstrates how the ethical standards and the mores of the people changed, especially the relationships between parents and children. The novel also presents the struggle by women for equality with men. The presentation of the attempts by women to achieve equality with men shows how seriously nineteenth-century women faced the problem and how the solution appeared to women of a later generation to be a mixed blessing. *The Rebel Generation* is usually considered Johanna van Ammers-Küller's greatest success. It has been translated into several languages and has had a successful production on the stage.

## The Story:

In 1840, Louis Cornvelt was a prosperous owner of a weaving mill in Leyden. Strongly orthodox and conservative in every way, he was a stanch Calvinist whose beliefs colored his treatment of his family and his employees. His wife, his sons, and his daughters were expected to be completely submissive to his will and the way of life he represented.

Outwardly, at least, they were, until the arrival in the Cornvelt home of an orphaned niece, Marie Elizabeth Sylvain. Reared in a much more permissive atmosphere in the home of her French father, she brought new ideas and an air of rebellion into the Cornvelt home. Three of the sons fell in love with her, but she refused their overtures of love and marriage, for she could not stand the idea of placing herself under the domination of a man. Her rebellion extended so far as to cause her to run away to France when her uncle refused to allow her to earn a living for herself; he felt that such a course might demean him and his family in the eyes of their friends and neighbors.

Marie Elizabeth Sylvain's cousins, fired by her arguments and example, tried to rebel, too, but in the end each

THE REBEL GENERATION by Johanna van Ammers-Küller. Translated by M. W. Hoper. By permission of the agent, Curtis Brown, Ltd. Copyright, 1928, by E. P. Dutton & Co., Inc. Renewed. All rights reserved.

submissively accepted their father's domination. Katie Cornvelt married a young medical doctor, William Wiseman, as her father wished, although she found the man's profession and person repugnant to her. Nicholas Cornvelt ran his father's woolen mill in the old way, as his father dictated, even though the younger man realized that more progressive methods were needed if the mill were to compete with more progressive business houses. Sarah Cornvelt gave up the young man she loved when their fathers refused to countenance their marriage. David Cornvelt, in love with his French cousin, gave her up too when his father demanded that he do so. The young people had been so used to domination that they could not break from the habit of obedience, even after they were grown.

By 1872 the children of Louis Cornvelt were themselves middle-aged and had children of their own who were approaching maturity. Having been reared in a home completely dominated by their father, the children attempted to rule their families in much the same way and to require of the new generation absolute obedience to parents and loyalty to a harshly conservative code. In their time, however, the new generation was supported and encouraged to rebellion by changes in the life of the time. In Holland, as in other European countries, new liberality in politics, new theories in sociology, a breakdown of orthodox religion, and other changes contributed to an outlook that fostered rebellion against paternal domination of children and masculine domination of women.

Dr. William Wiseman and his wife were horrified when their daughter Eliza announced she wished to become a doctor, for such a career had previously been unheard of for a woman. Although her father wanted a son to be a doctor, he could not imagine his daughter becoming one, and he fought to check her interest in medical studies.

Eliza Wiseman found help and encouragement when her mother's cousin, Marie Elizabeth Sylvain, returned to Holland from France to work for the emancipation of women. Marie Elizabeth had received a considerable fortune which she devoted to the cause of equality of the sexes, using the money to assist capable young women to gain an education and to publish periodicals in support of feminine equality. Eliza Wiseman was not the only one in the Cornvelt clan to receive help from their cousin, who called herself Sylvia.

Sarah Cornvelt had married a retired army officer. When her husband died, leaving her with almost no income and several daughters almost grown, Sarah's brothers attempted to take over her affairs, offering her a small allowance from their pockets in return for their domination. Encouraged by her French cousin, Sarah refused to accept the men's proposals and established herself and her daughters as professional dressmakers. Sarah, like her sisters, had had too much domination under the rule of father and husband to accept the domination of her brothers.

David Cornvelt, a distinguished professor, found rebellion in other quarters than his sister Sarah's household. In his own home the younger generation refused to follow his dictates, even though rebellion hurt them and other members of the family. David's son Louis became a political radical and wrote pamphlets that kept his father from appointment to a post in the national cabinet. David's daughter Clara persisted in being a social worker among the lowest classes, even though she gave in to her father in matters of love.

In 1923 the senior members of the Cornvelt family found themselves in their turn faced with a generation of young people who were in rebellion against their parents. By this time even the older generation was dissatisfied. The changes in family relationships were unsatisfactory. So far as women were concerned, emancipation and equality with men had been achieved. Dorothy Cornvelt, married to Dr. Eliza Wiseman's nephew, was a lawyer and a member of Parliament. But her home life was empty, for both her husband and children were indifferent to her professional and political life. Her husband, Stephen Cornvelt, became infatuated with Millicent Cornvelt, a distant cousin from a branch of the family which had migrated to England. His infatuation with the girl was so great that he asked for a divorce, and neither he nor the young girl could see why his wife should deny the request.

The children of Stephen and Dorothy Cornvelt also felt that life was too loose for them. Although they were well educated and free from most parental restraints, they were unhappy. They felt a need for a return to the safety of a stable home and the guidance of older people, even though they disliked interference by their elders. When Stephen tried to dissuade his daughter Kitty from a career as a dancer, she rebelled as violently as any earlier Cornvelt had done. Her sister Puck, however, a successful businesswoman, indicated by her behavior the course that later generations might take. She gave up her career to marry the man she loved, expecting to find happiness in family life and the influence of her husband. She also rebelled, but her rebellion was against too much freedom, rather than too little.

# THE RECRUITING OFFICER

*Type of work:* Drama
*Author:* George Farquhar (1678-1707)
*Type of plot:* Comedy of intrigue
*Time of plot:* Early eighteenth century
*Locale:* Shrewsbury, England
*First presented:* 1706

### Principal characters:

CAPTAIN PLUME, the recruiting officer, a gay blade
SYLVIA BALANCE, Captain Plume's fiancée
MR. WORTHY, Captain Plume's friend
MELINDA, Mr. Worthy's fiancée and cousin of Sylvia Balance
JUSTICE BALANCE, Sylvia's father
ROSE, the pretty young daughter of a farmer
SERGEANT KITE, Captain Plume's aide

## Critique:

This is not Farquhar's best-known play —that honor goes to *The Beaux' Stratagem*—but it is superior to many of the other Restoration comedies. Perhaps the most richly comic soldier in English drama is to be found here in Sergeant Kite, who doubles as a fortune-teller and a pander for his master. It is a long step from the *Miles Gloriosus* of the Plautine comedy, through Captain Bobadil of Ben Jonson's comedy, to this grandly comic figure. In this play the reader is taken from London to Shrewsbury, a welcome change in comedies of this period, most of which were laid in London. In moving his scene from London, Farquhar followed the example of Thomas Shadwell, the poet and playwright who succeeded John Dryden as Poet Laureate. Indeed, the reader is constantly reminded of similarities of incident and tone between the plays of Shadwell and Farquhar. There is less of the elegant tone in this play, however, for it rather leans to the sentiment of later eighteenth-century drama.

## The Story:

Captain Plume, commander of a company of grenadiers, and his aide, Sergeant Kite, went to Shrewsbury to enlist a number of recruits for Captain Plume's command. They went to Shrewsbury because of success in gaining recruits in that city some months before, and because of Captain Plume's amorous successes at the same time. Upon the arrival of the pair they were greeted with the news that a young woman who had just given birth to a child had named Captain Plume as the father. At the captain's request, Sergeant Kite married the woman and went on record as the father of the child. This was not the first time he had done as much for the captain; he had accumulated a list of six wives in the same manner.

Captain Plume also found his good friend, Mr. Worthy, at Shrewsbury. Mr. Worthy had been a happy-go-lucky chap, much like Captain Plume, until his fiancée had inherited a fortune. The girl, Melinda, had taken on airs after becoming a rich woman, and she proceeded to make life miserable for Worthy. His latest grievance was that another officer on recruiting duty, one Captain Brazen, had apparently become a successful rival for Melinda's hand and fortune. Captain Plume asked Worthy about Sylvia Balance, whom the captain loved but could not marry because his life was too uncertain and he had too little money. Worthy told Captain Plume that Sylvia Balance still thought very well of him.

While Worthy and Captain Plume talked, Melinda and Sylvia were having a conversation of their own, in which Sylvia told her cousin that she was determined that the captain should not

3138

leave Shrewsbury alone. The two women quarreled, and after Sylvia's departure Melinda wrote a letter to Sylvia's father telling him that Captain Plume intended to dishonor Sylvia.

That evening Captain Plume had dinner with Sylvia and her father, Justice Balance, who considered the captain a fine match for his daughter. During the evening news came from Germany by mail that Justice Balance's son and heir had died. Immediately the attitude of Justice Balance toward Captain Plume changed, for he did not like to think of the captain as the husband of his daughter if she were to have all his fortune. Calling Sylvia into private conference, he told her of the change in his attitude. Although the girl was very much in love with the captain, she promised that she would not marry without her father's consent. Captain Plume left the house without learning what had happened. A short time after his departure Melinda's spiteful letter to Sylvia's father arrived. In order to get her away from the captain, Justice Balance immediately sent Sylvia by coach to one of his country estates.

Both Worthy and Captain Plume interpreted Sylvia's departure erroneously. They thought that she believed herself too good for the captain after she had inherited a fortune of two thousand pounds a year. The captain, claiming that he would get along as well without her, proceeded to go about his business of recruiting. While doing so he met a farmer's pretty young daughter, named Rose. Rose and he immediately fancied one another, and the captain went so far as to give his half-promise that he would make the girl his wife. In return, she helped him to add almost a dozen more recruits to his company. These included her own brother and her former sweetheart.

One day Sylvia, disguised in some of her brother's clothes, returned to Shrewsbury, where she met the two recruiting officers, Captain Plume and Captain Brazen, in the company of Melinda. When she told them that she was Mr. Willful, a young man of good family who wished to enlist, they both bid for the new recruit, who finally agreed to join Captain Plume's company. The captain was so pleased with young Mr. Willful that he proffered his friendship, even though the recruit was to be an enlisted man in the company.

Saying that he would be censured for entering the army voluntarily, the recruit asked Captain Plume to have him impressed into service by the provisions of the acts of Parliament. The captain agreed to do so. To help her deception, and also to test the direction of Captain Plume's affections, Sylvia in her disguise pretended to be in love with Rose.

The fiancée of Worthy, meanwhile, had been to see a fortune-teller who was really Sergeant Kite in disguise. The fortune-teller told Melinda that she would die unmarried if she let a man who was to call on her at ten o'clock the following morning leave the country. He had also managed to secure a copy of her handwriting, which he showed her in an attempt to make her think the devil was his helper. Melinda was so impressed that she promised herself to follow the fortune-teller's advice.

Justice Balance decided that the best way to keep his daughter's honor and fortune from falling into the hands of Captain Plume was to provide the officer with the soldiers he needed and to draft them according to the provision made by Parliament. In order to do so, the justice opened his court and had the bailiff bring in a number of men who were eligible for the draft. Among the men was Sylvia in her disguise as Mr. Willful. She had been accused, as a man, of having taken Rose as a common-law wife. In the courtroom Mr. Willful behaved impudently, and the justice decided to punish the brash young man by sending him off as a private in Captain Plume's company of gendarmes. Thus Sylvia tricked her father into sending her away with the captain. In fact, the justice ordered Captain Plume not to discharge Mr. Willful for any reason.

After the hearing Justice Balance went to his home, where he learned that his daughter, dressed in her deceased brother's clothes, had disappeared from his country estate. The justice immediately realized that he had been tricked, that the Mr. Willful whom he had sent off with Captain Plume was really Sylvia. He also thought that Captain Plume had been a party to the deception. When the captain called at the justice's home a short time later, it was soon apparent that he knew nothing of the scheme, for he agreed to discharge the new soldier at Justice Balance's request.

Mr. Willful was called in and unmasked as Sylvia. Then the father, realizing how much his daughter loved the captain, gave them permission to marry. Immediately thereafter Worthy and Melinda arrived to say that they had also reached an agreement and were to be married shortly. Melinda also apologized for the spiteful letter she had sent to Justice Balance. Captain Plume, pleased over the prospect of a handsome fortune coming to him with his wife, announced that he was retiring from the army. He turned over all the recruits he had enlisted to Captain Brazen, who had been unsuccessful in finding any men for his company.

# THE RED AND THE BLACK

*Type of work:* Novel
*Author:* Stendhal (Marie-Henri Beyle, 1783-1842)
*Type of plot:* Psychological realism
*Time of plot:* Early nineteenth century
*Locale:* France
*First published:* 1830

> Principal characters:
> JULIEN SOREL, an opportunist
> M. DE RÊNAL, mayor of Verrières
> MADAME DE RÊNAL, his wife
> MATHILDE DE LA MOLE, Julien's mistress
> FOUQUÉ, Julien's friend

## Critique:

This novel is unusual in that its chief character is a villain. He is an interesting villain, however, for Stendhal analyzes the psychological undercurrents of his nature in an attempt to show clearly how struggle and temptation shaped his energetic but morbidly introspective character. The author analyzes the actions of Julien's loves in the same way. This method of writing slows down the action of the plot considerably, but on the other hand it makes the characters real and understandable and shows much of the sordid conditions of French society at the end of the Napoleonic wars.

## The Story:

Julien Sorel was the son of a carpenter in the little town of Verrières, France. Napoleon had fallen, but he still had many admirers, and Julien was one of these. Julien pretended to be deeply religious. Now that Napoleon had been defeated, he believed that the church rather than the army was the way to power. Because of his assumed piety and his intelligence, Julien was appointed as tutor to the children of M. de Rênal, the mayor of the village.

Madame de Rênal had done her duty all her life; she was a good wife and a good mother. But she had never been in love with her husband, a coarse man who would hardly inspire love in any woman. Madame de Rênal was attracted to the pale young tutor and fell completely in love with him. Julien, thinking it his duty to himself, made love to her in order to gain power over her. He discovered after a time that he had really fallen in love with Madame de Rênal.

When Julien went on a holiday to visit Fouqué, a poor friend, Fouqué tried to persuade Julien to go into the lumber business with him. Julien declined; he enjoyed too much the power he held over his mistress.

The love affair was revealed to M. de Rênal by an anonymous letter written by M. Valenod, the local official in charge of the poorhouse. He had become rich on graft and he was jealous because M. de Rênal had hired Julien as a tutor. He had also made unsuccessful advances to Madame de Rênal at one time.

The lovers were able to smooth over the situation to some extent. M. de Rênal agreed to send Julien to the seminary at Besançon, principally to keep him from becoming tutor at M. Valenod's house. After Julien had departed, Madame de Rênal was filled with remorse. Her conscience suffered because of her adultery and she became extremely religious.

Julien did not get on well at the seminary, for he found it full of hypocrites. The students did not like him and feared his sharp intelligence. His only friend was the Abbé Pirard, a highly moral man.

One day Julien went to help decorate the cathedral and by chance found Madame de Rênal there. She fainted, but he could not help her because his duties

THE RED AND THE BLACK by Stendhal. Published by Liveright Publishing Corp.

called him elsewhere. The experience left him weak and shaken.

The Abbé Pirard lost his position at the seminary because of his opposition to the local bishop; he had supported the Marquis de La Mole, who was engaged in lawsuits against the bishop. When the Abbé Pirard left the seminary, the marquis obtained a living for him in Paris. He also hired Julien as his secretary.

Julien was thankful for his chance to leave the seminary. On his way to Paris he called secretly upon Madame de Rênal. At first she repulsed his advances, conscious of her great sin. But at last she yielded once again to his pleadings. M. de Rênal became suspicious and decided to search his wife's room. To escape discovery, Julien jumped out the window, barely escaping with his life.

Finding Julien a good worker, the marquis entrusted him with many of the details of his business. Julien was also allowed to dine with the family and to mingle with the guests afterward. He found the Marquise de La Mole to be extremely proud of her nobility. Her daughter, Mathilde, seemed to be of the same type, a reserved girl with beautiful eyes. Her son, the Comte de La Mole, was an extremely polite and pleasant young man. However, Julien found Parisian high society boring. No one was allowed to discuss ideas.

Julien enjoyed stealing volumes of Voltaire from the marquis' library and reading them in his room. He was astonished when he discovered that Mathilde was doing the same thing. Before long they began to spend much of their time together, although Julien was always conscious of his position as servant and was quick to be insulted by Mathilde's pride. The girl fell in love with him because he was so different from the dull young men of her own class.

After Julien had spent two nights with her, Mathilde decided that it was degrading to be in love with a secretary. Her pride was an insult to Julien. Smarting,

he planned to gain power over her and, consequently, over the household.

Meanwhile the marquis had entrusted Julien with a diplomatic mission on behalf of the nobility and clergy who wanted the monarchy reestablished. On this mission Julien met an old friend who advised him how to win Mathilde again. Upon his return he put his friend's plan into effect.

He began to pay court to a virtuous lady who was often a visitor in the de La Mole home. He began a correspondence with her, at the same time neglecting Mathilde. Then Mathilde, thinking that Julien was lost to her, discovered how much she loved him. She threw herself at his feet. Julien had won. But this time he would not let her gain the upper hand. He continued to treat Mathilde coldly as her passion increased. In this way he maintained his power.

Mathilde became pregnant. She was joyful, for now, she thought, Julien would know how much she cared for him. She had made the supreme sacrifice; she would now have to marry Julien and give up her place in society. But Julien was not so happy as Mathilde over her condition, for he feared the results when Mathilde told her father.

At first the marquis was furious. Eventually, he saw only one way out of the difficulty; he would make Julien rich and respectable. He gave Julien a fortune, a title, and a commission in the army. Overwhelmed with his new wealth and power, Julien scarcely gave a thought to Mathilde.

Then the Marquis received a letter from Madame de Rênal, whom Julien had suggested to the marquis for a character recommendation. Madame de Rênal was again filled with religious fervor; she revealed to the marquis the whole story of Julien's villainy. The marquis immediately refused to let Julien marry his daughter.

Julien's plans for glory and power were ruined. In a fit of rage he rode to Verrières, where he found Madame de Rênal at church. He fired two shots at her before he was arrested and taken off to prison. There he promptly admitted his guilt, for he was ready to die. He had his revenge.

Mathilde, still madly in love with Julien, arrived in Verrières and tried to bribe the jury for the trial. Fouqué arrived and begged Julien to try to escape. But Julien paid no attention to the efforts his friends made to help him.

Tried, he was found guilty and given the death sentence, even though his bullets had not killed Madame de Rênal. In fact, his action had only rekindled her passion for him. She visited him and begged him to appeal his sentence. The two were as much in love as they had been before. When M. de Rênal ordered his wife to come home, Julien was left again to his dreams. He had lost his one great love — Madame de Rênal. The colorless Mathilde only bored and angered him by her continued solicitude.

Julien went calmly to his death on the appointed day. The faithful Fouqué obtained the body in order to bury it in a cave in the mountains, where Julien had once been fond of going to indulge in his daydreams of power.

A woman had loved a famous ancestor of Mathilde with an extreme passion. When the ancestor was executed, the woman had taken his severed head and buried it. Mathilde, who had always admired this family legend, did the same for Julien. After the funeral ceremony at the cave, she buried Julien's head with her own hands. Later, she had the cave decorated with Italian marble.

Madame de Rênal did not go to the funeral. But three days after Julien's death she died in the act of embracing her children.

# THE RED BADGE OF COURAGE

*Type of work:* Novel
*Author:* Stephen Crane (1871-1900)
*Type of plot:* Impressionistic realism
*Time of plot:* Civil War
*Locale:* A Civil War battlefield
*First published:* 1895

### Principal characters:

HENRY FLEMING, a young recruit
JIM CONKLIN, a veteran
WILSON, another veteran

## Critique:

Most war stories are epic histories of generals and victories or defeats. In *The Red Badge of Courage* we follow only the personal reactions of a soldier; we do not even know what battle is being fought or who the leaders are. We know only that Henry Fleming was motivated, not by the unselfish heroism of more conventional and romantic stories, but first by cowardice, then by fear, and finally by egoism. The style of narrative of the novel belongs to a late period in English prose fiction. The stream of Henry's thought tells a story, and the reader must perceive the hero's environment through the subjective consciousness of the young man. This novel set the pattern for the treatment of war in modern fiction.

## The Story:

The tall soldier, Jim Conklin, and the loud soldier, Wilson, argued bitterly over the rumor that the troops were about to move. Henry Fleming was impatient to experience his first battle, and as he listened to the quarreling of the seasoned soldiers he wondered if he would become frightened and run away under gunfire. He questioned Wilson and Conklin, and each man stated that he would stand and fight no matter what happened.

Henry had come from a farm, where he had dreamed of battles and longed for army life. His mother had held him back at first. When she saw that her son was bored with the farm, she packed

his woolen clothing and with a warning that he must not associate with the wicked kind of men who were in the military camps sent him off to join the Yankee troops.

One gray morning Henry awoke to find that the regiment was about to move. With a hazy feeling that death would be a relief from dull and meaningless marching, Henry was again disappointed. The troops made only another march. He began to suspect that the generals were stupid fools, but the other men in his raw regiment scoffed at his idea and told him to shut up.

When the fighting suddenly began, there was very little action in it for Henry. He lay on the ground with the other men and watched for signs of the enemy. Some of the men around him were wounded. He could not see what was going on or what the battle was about. Then an attack came. Immediately Henry forgot all his former confused thoughts, and he could only fire his rifle over and over; around him men behaved in their strange individual manner as they were wounded. Henry felt a close comradeship with the men at his side who were firing at the enemy with him.

Suddenly the attack ended. To Henry, it seemed strange that the sky above should still be blue after the guns had stopped firing. While the men were recovering from the attack, binding wounds, and gathering equipment, another surprise attack was launched from the enemy line. Unprepared and tired from the first fighting, the men retreated in panic. Henry, sharing their sudden terror, ran, too.

When the fearful retreat had ended, the fleeing men learned that the enemy had lost the battle. Now Henry felt a surge of guilt. Dreading to rejoin his companions, he fled into the forest. There he saw a squirrel run away from him in fright. The fleeing animal seemed to vindicate in Henry's mind his own cowardly flight; he had acted according to nature whose own creatures ran from danger. Then, seeing a dead man lying in a clearing, Henry hurried back into the retreating column of wounded men. Most were staggering along in helpless bewilderment and some were being carried on stretchers. Henry realized that he had no wound and that he did not belong in that group of staggering men. There was one pitiful-looking man, covered with dirt and blood, wandering about dazed and alone. Everyone was staring at him and avoiding him. When Henry approached him, the young boy saw that the soldier was Jim Conklin. He was horrified at the sight of the tall soldier. He tried to help Jim, but with a wild motion of despair Jim fell to the ground dead. Once more Henry fled.

His conscience was paining him. He wanted to return to his regiment to finish the fight, but he thought that his fellow soldiers would point to him as a deserter. He envied the dead men who were lying all about him. They were already heroes; he was a coward. Ahead he could hear the rumbling of artillery. As he neared the lines of his regiment, a retreating line of men broke from the trees ahead of him. The men ran fiercely, ignoring him or waving frantically at him as they shouted something he could not comprehend. He stood among the flying men, not knowing what to do. One man hit him on the head with the butt of a rifle.

Henry went on carefully, the wound in his head paining him a great deal.

He walked for a long while until he met another soldier, who led Henry back to his regiment. The first familiar man Henry met was Wilson. Wilson, who had been a terrible braggart before the first battle, had given Henry a packet of letters to keep for him in case he were killed. Now Henry felt superior to Wilson. If the man asked him where he had been, Henry would remind him of the letters. Lost was Henry's feeling of guilt; he felt superior now, his deeds of cowardice almost forgotten. No one knew that he had run off in terror. Wilson had changed. He no longer was the swaggering, boastful man who had annoyed Henry in the beginning. The men in the regiment washed Henry's head wound and told him to get some sleep.

The next morning Wilson casually asked Henry for the letters. Half sorry that he had to yield them with no taunting remark, Henry returned the letters to his comrade. He felt sorry for Wilson's embarrassment. He felt himself a virtuous and heroic man.

Another battle started. This time Henry held his position doggedly and kept firing his rifle without thinking. Once he fell down, and for a panicky moment he thought that he had been shot, but he continued to fire his rifle blindly, loading and firing without even seeing the enemy. Finally someone shouted to him that he must stop shooting, that the battle was over. Then Henry looked up for the first time and saw that there were no enemy troops before him. Now he was a hero. Everyone stared at him when the lieutenant of the regiment complimented his fierce fighting. Henry realized that he had behaved like a demon.

Wilson and Henry, off in the woods looking for water, overheard two officers discussing the coming battle. They said that Henry's regiment fought like mule drivers, but that they would have to be used anyway. Then one officer said that probably not many of the regiment would live through the day's fighting. Soon after the attack started, the color bearer was killed and Henry took up the flag, with Wilson at his side. Although the regiment fought bravely, one of the commanding officers of the army said that the men had not gained the ground that they were expected to take. The same officer had complimented Henry for his courageous fighting. He began to feel that he knew the measure of his own courage and endurance.

His outfit fought one more engagement with the enemy. Henry was by that' time a veteran, and the fighting held less meaning for him than had the earlier battles. When it was over, he and Wilson marched away with their victorious regiment.

# THE RED ROOM

*Type of work:* Novel
*Author:* August Strindberg (1849-1912)
*Type of plot:* Realistic satire
*Time of plot:* 1870's
*Locale:* Stockholm and X-köping, a provincial town in Sweden
*First published:* 1879

Principal characters:
  ARVID FALK, a writer
  CHARLES NICHOLAS FALK, his brother, a businessman
  MRS. CHARLES NICHOLAS FALK
  SELLÉN, a painter
  LUNDELL, a practical painter
  OLLE MONTANUS, a philosopher and sculptor
  YGBERG, a philosopher
  REHNHJELM, a would-be actor
  LEVIN, a post-office clerk
  NYSTRÖM, a schoolmaster
  SMITH, a publisher
  FALANDER, an actor
  AGNES (BEDA PETTERSON), a young actress
  STRUVE, a journalist
  BORG, a young doctor

*Critique:*

A biting satire leveled against contemporary Swedish society, *The Red Room* was Strindberg's first published novel. The story deals with the fortunes of a group of young Swedish intellectuals and artists trying to get along in Stockholm of the 1870's. The intellectuals and artists, dedicated to their tasks and to honest appraisals of the society about them, are constantly tricked, defeated, and victimized by the insensitive bourgeois world in which they live. They are constantly faced with poverty (although there are a few examples of unpredictable and temporary success when the artist happens, quite by chance, to catch the public fancy), scorn, or indifference. By the end of the novel, all the artists have either gone mad, committed suicide, or sold out to the commercial society. Various institutions are also satirized: the government agency where a large staff does no work, the newspaper that makes or breaks reputations to suit its purpose without regard to factual accuracy, the Parliament that endlessly debates inconsequential matters, the charitable organization out of touch with reality.

*The Story:*

Arvid Falk, a young government worker who wanted to be a poet, told Struve, a journalist, some facts concerning the waste and inadequacy of a government department where he, Arvid, had worked. Struve worked this material into an exposé for a newspaper that was looking for sensational stories. Arvid was discharged for giving out the information.

Arvid's brother, Charles Nicholas, a flax merchant, liked to feel that he was supporting Arvid by lending him money, offering him cigars, and inviting him to dinner. He could not believe that Arvid, despite certain unconventional opinions, would give out such information for publication. Charles Nicholas was a rising merchant, but his favorite cronies were a beaten clerk named Levin and an apathetic schoolmaster named Nyström. Levin and Nyström would flatter Charles Nicholas and write him fulsome verses of appreciation for the small sums of money he lent them. Charles Nicholas had a young wife who slept until noon every day and aspired to become a social and civic leader.

Arvid visited his friends: Sellén and Lundell, who were painters; Rehnhjelm, who ardently desired to be an actor, and Olle Montanus and Ygberg, who spent all day arguing the fine points of philosophy. All were serious about their art or their arguments, and all were poor. Although the practical Lundell made a living by doing magazine illustrations, the group had little money; frequently they were forced to combine their credit or pawn some of their clothes in order to scrape together enough money for dinner.

Out of a job, Arvid brought some of his verses to Smith, a successful publisher who offered Arvid the job of writing about Ulrica Eleonora, a Swedish historical personage, and doing hack work on other trite and uninteresting subjects. Arvid tried to do the work, in which he had no interest at all, but was unable to complete his dull assignments. He joined his friends in the Red Room, a café where they gathered, argued, and spent as little money as possible.

Arvid finally got a job on a newspaper. As a reporter on the affairs of Parliament he did his work successfully, although he was privately outraged at the time wasted in interminable and senseless discussions. Most of the Swedes, however, were proud of their new, more democratic Parliament.

About this time Sellén had succeeded in getting a picture hung in the Academy show. At first it was pointed out as an example of the new decadent, Bohemian art, and as such was criticized by one of the papers. For reasons having nothing to do with art, another paper defended Sellén's painting, and he became a hotly debated and highly successful young man. For the moment all the members of this Bohemian group were working; they were able to pay for their drinks at the Red Room and recover the overcoats they had pawned.

When a group of unscrupulous men organized a marine insurance company called Triton, Charles Nicholas Falk was pleased and flattered to be a member of their board. At the same time his wife was pleased to be on a committee organized to erect a large crèche for a church. Charles Nicholas helped to forward his wife's social ambitions by making a large donation for the crèche, but he made the donation with shares of the marine insurance company. When Mrs. Falk was accepted by society, she made visits to the homes of poor people and tried to convert them to believing in her church. She had little success and assumed that the poor people were simply ignorant and uncouth. Later, when the marine insurance company was proved to be a hoax and collapsed, the project for the crèche, along with Mrs. Falk's social aspirations, had to be abandoned.

In the meantime, Rehnhjelm had gone to the town of X-köping and joined a theatrical company. He played only minor parts and the theater manager took advantage of him, but he felt that he was learning the profession. He was impressed by Falander, a suave older actor, and he fell in love with Agnes, a sixteen-year-old ingénue. His love for Agnes was pure and idealistic; and he did not know that she had long been Falander's mistress. When he finally and belatedly discovered this fact, he thought he would commit suicide in his despair at the wickedness in the world. Instead, he returned to Stockholm and the security offered by his wealthy family.

Arvid became a successful journalist and his poems were published at last. He moved from paper to paper every so often in the hope that each would offer him the opportunity to report the news as honestly as he saw it, but the papers were interested only in versions of news or scandal that would fit their particular needs. Frustrated in his efforts, Arvid became friendly with Borg, a cynical and iconoclastic doctor, and he fell in love with Beda Petterson, a young girl who worked in a Stockholm café. The vogue for Sellén's work had ended and he was again poor. In the meantime Lundell had become a society portrait painter. One night Borg found Arvid in a low dive with two representatives of a paper even lower than the conventional papers Arvid had found so unprincipled. Arvid had gone raving mad. Borg took him on a ship voyage under treatment for his nervous breakdown.

When Arvid recovered and returned to Stockholm, he found that the old group at the Red Room had broken up.

Olle Montanus, unable to work except as a stonemason, had finally committed suicide. Sellén's painting had again become fashionable. Charles Nicholas had, strangely enough, emerged unscathed from the Triton disaster and was about to establish a bank. Arvid discovered that Beda Petterson and Rehnhjelm's Agnes were really the same woman, a kind of symbol for the faithless woman whose only allegiance is a physical connection to some man. None of his living friends or associates retained any semblance of the idealism and honesty that had once motivated all their actions and conversations. Arvid himself became a conventional schoolmaster, married a schoolmistress, and studied numismatics in his spare time. Only Borg, the skeptic who expected nothing, remained unchanged.

# THE RED ROVER

*Type of work:* Novel
*Author:* James Fenimore Cooper (1789-1851)
*Type of plot:* Historical romance
*Time of plot:* Mid-eighteenth century
*Locale:* Newport, Rhode Island and the Atlantic Ocean
*First published:* 1827

*Principal characters:*
HARRY WILDER, formerly Henry Ark, actually Henry de Lacy
THE RED ROVER, captain of the *Dolphin*
DICK FID, and
SCIPIO AFRICA, seamen, Harry Wilder's friends
GERTRUDE GRAYSON, General Grayson's daughter
MRS. WYLLYS, her governess

## Critique:

Cooper, who knew the sea quite well, wrote this novel to repeat the success of *The Pilot.* His characters, as is customary with him, are types, and there is little character development. The plot is simple and plausible until the end of the story, when Cooper unravels the mystery surrounding Henry Ark and the Red Rover by proving improbable relationships among the characters. However, few novels of the sea contain a better record of life and work aboard a sailing ship.

## The Story:

While in the town of Newport, Rhode Island, Harry Wilder saw in the outer harbor a ship, the *Dolphin,* which interested him greatly. He decided to try to secure a berth on her for himself and his two friends, Dick Fid and Scipio Africa, a Negro sailor. His determination was strengthened after meeting a stranger who in effect dared him to try to obtain a berth there. That night the three men rowed out to the ship lying at anchor, in order to give the vessel a closer inspection. Hailed by the watch on deck, Wilder went aboard her. There he learned that he had been expected and that if he were interested in sailing with her, he might go to see the captain. The captain was the mysterious, mocking stranger whom Wilder had met that afternoon in the town. But before Wilder signed on as a member of the ship's crew, the captain revealed the true nature of the ship and admitted that he himself was the Red Rover, the scourge of the sea. Wilder, who had formerly been an officer in the British Navy, was given the post of second in command. He persuaded the captain to sign on Dick and Scipio as well. He then returned to shore to settle his affairs in the town. The other two men remained aboard the *Dolphin.*

At the same time the *Royal Caroline,* a merchantman trading along the coast and between the colonies and England, lay in the inner harbor ready to embark on the following day. Two ladies, Gertrude Grayson and her governess, Mrs. Wyllys, were to take passage on her to Charleston, South Carolina, Gertrude's home. Wilder met the ladies as if by chance and tried to dissuade them from sailing aboard the *Royal Caroline.* He hinted that the *Royal Caroline* was unsafe, but his words were discredited by an old seaman who insisted that there was nothing wrong with the ship. The ladies decided to sail in spite of Wilder's warnings. Then the master of the *Royal Caroline* fell from a cask and broke his leg, and a new captain had to be found immediately. The Red Rover sent a message ordering Wilder to apply for the vacant position. He did, and was immediately hired.

The voyage of the *Royal Caroline* began with difficulties which continued as time went on. They were not long out of port when a ship was sighted on the horizon. It continued to keep its distance in approximately the same position, so that all aboard the *Royal Caroline* suspected that it was following them. In trying to outdistance the other ship, Wilder put on all sail possible, in spite of the threatening weather. A storm struck the ship and left her foundering in heavy seas. When Wilder commanded the crew to man the pumps, they refused and deserted the sinking ship in one of the boats. Only Wilder and the two women were left aboard the helpless *Royal Caroline*. Hoping to make land, they embarked in a longboat, but the wind blew them out to sea. They were sighted and picked up by the *Dolphin*.

Gertrude and Mrs. Wyllys were not long aboard the *Dolphin* before the true state of affairs became apparent to the women in spite of the kindly treatment afforded them. Mrs. Wyllys realized also that Roderick, the cabin boy, was in reality a woman. But this mystery was nothing when compared with that of Harry Wilder.

Dick Fid told the story of Harry Wilder's past history to the two ladies and the Red Rover, thus explaining the affection Wilder, Dick, and Scipio held for each other. Some twenty-four years earlier, Dick and Scipio had found a child and a dying woman, apparently a nurse, aboard an abandoned ship. After the woman died, the two seamen took care of the boy. They had only one clue to follow in their efforts to locate the child's relatives. This was the name Ark of Lynnhaven which had been painted on a ship's bucket and which Scipio had tattooed on Dick's arm. But there was no ship of that name in any port registry, and so the search for the child's relatives was abandoned.

As Dick finished his story, another ship was sighted. It was the *Dart*, a British naval vessel on which Wilder, Dick, and Scipio had previously sailed. Wilder wanted the Red Rover to flee, but the captain had another plan for dealing with the *Dart*. After showing British colors, the Red Rover was invited by Captain Bignall of the *Dart* to come aboard his

ship. There the pirate captain learned that Henry Ark, alias Harry Wilder, was absent from the *Dart* on a dangerous secret mission. The Red Rover realized that he had betrayed himself to his enemy. He went back to the *Dolphin* and then sent Wilder, Dick, Scipio, and the two women to the *Dart*.

Wilder had informed the Red Rover that once aboard his own ship, the *Dart*, he would be duty bound to reveal the true nature of the *Dolphin*. But in telling Captain Bignall his story, Wilder begged for mercy for both the master and the crew of the pirate ship. Bignall agreed and sent Wilder back to the *Dolphin* with lenient terms of surrender. The Red Rover refused them and told Wilder that if there were to be a fight Captain Bignall would have to start it. As the *Dart* attacked the pirate ship, a sudden storm gave the *Dolphin* an unexpected advantage. Its crew boarded the *Dart*, killed Captain Bignall, and captured the ship. The crew of the *Dolphin* demanded the lives of Wilder, Dick, and Scipio as traitors, and the Red Rover handed them over to the crew. When the chaplain who was aboard the *Dart* came forward to plead for their lives, he saw the tattoo on Dick's arm. He told the story of the *Ark of Lynnhaven* and revealed that Harry Wilder must be the son of Paul de Lacy and Mrs. Wyllys, who had kept the marriage a secret because of parental disapproval and later because of Paul's death. Mrs. Wyllys then begged for the life of her son, whom she had thought dead all these years. The Red Rover dismissed his crew until the next morning, when he would announce his decision concerning the fate of the prisoners.

The next morning, the Red Rover put his crew and all the gold aboard the *Dolphin* into a coaster and sent them ashore. The crew of the *Dart*, Wilder, Dick, Scipio, and the women were put aboard the *Dart* and told to sail off. When they were some distance away, they saw the *Dolphin* catch fire and burn. None had been left aboard her but the Red Rover and Roderick. Some aboard the *Dart* thought they saw a small boat putting off from the burning ship, but none could be sure because of the billowing smoke.

Twenty years later, after the colonies had won their independence from England, the Red Rover, a veteran of the Revolutionary War, reappeared in New-port and made his way to the home of Captain Henry de Lacy, who had previously called himself Henry Wilder. Admitted, he identified himself as the long-lost brother of Mrs. Wyllys. Shortly thereafter the Red Rover, pirate and patriot, died.

# REDBURN

*Type of work:* Novel
*Author:* Herman Melville (1819-1891)
*Type of plot:* Adventure romance
*Time of plot:* Mid-nineteenth century
*Locale:* New York, the Atlantic Ocean, and England
*First published:* 1849

Principal characters:
WELLINGBOROUGH REDBURN, a young lad on his first voyage
CAPTAIN RIGA, master of the *Highlander*
HARRY BOLTON, a young English prodigal

## Critique:

*Redburn,* like much of Herman Melville's work, was based on his own life. The background of the Redburn family is very similar to that of the Melville family after the father's death. The trip on a merchant vessel is clearly based on a similar round trip to Liverpool which Melville himself had made while still in his teens. The incident of the guidebook, for instance, and the guidebook itself, are taken directly from Melville's own experience. Again, like other of Melville's books, *Redburn* is authentic in its treatment of sailors and sea life. Melville saw seafaring life through the eyes of a common sailor who learned his trade the hard way and wrote his novel from the seaman's point of view. Also, we find in *Redburn* the beginnings of the philosophical elements that made *Moby Dick,* Melville's masterpiece, one of the great novels of all time.

## The Story:

Wellingborough Redburn's father had died, leaving the mother and children poorly provided for, even though the father had been a highly successful merchant and at one time a wealthy man. When Redburn was in his middle teens, he decided to take some of the burden off his mother by going to sea. Given an old gun and a hunting jacket by an older brother, young Redburn left his home along the Hudson River and went to New York to seek a berth on a ship.

A college friend of his older brother aided Redburn in finding a berth on a ship bound for Liverpool. Unfortunately the friend had emphasized the fact that Redburn came from a good family and had wealthy relatives; consequently, Captain Riga, master of the *Highlander,* was able to hire the young lad for three dollars a month. Having spent all his money, and unable to get an advance on his wages, Redburn had to pawn his gun for a shirt and cap to wear aboard ship.

During his first few days out of port Redburn thought that he had made a dreadful mistake in going to sea. His fellow sailors jeered at him as a greenhorn; he made many silly mistakes; he became violently seasick; and he discovered that he did not even have a spoon with which to take his portion of the food from the pots and pans in which it was sent to the forecastle. Most horrifying of all was the suicide of a sailor who dived over the side of the ship in a fit of delirium tremens.

As the thirty-day cruise to Liverpool from New York wore on, Redburn learned how to make himself useful and comfortable aboard the ship. When he went aloft alone to release the topmost sails, he earned a little respect from his fellow seamen, although they never did, throughout the voyage, let him forget that he was still a green hand and had signed on as a "boy." Redburn found the sea fascinating in many ways; he also found it terrifying, as when the *Highlander* passed a derelict schooner on which three corpses were still bound to the railing.

For Redburn one of the liveliest incidents of the voyage was the discovery of a little stowaway on board the *High-lander*. The small boy had been on board the vessel some months before, when the father had been a sailor signed on for a trip from Liverpool to New York. The father had since died, and the boy had stowed himself away in an effort to return to England. Everyone on the ship, including the usually irascible Captain Riga, took a liking to the homesick stowaway and made much of him.

Redburn had little in common with his fellow crew members, most of whom were rough fellows many years older than he. Through them, however, he received an education quite different from that which he had learned in school. At first he tried to talk about church and good books to them, but he soon discovered that such conversation only irritated them into more than their usual profanity and obscenity. Redburn thought they were not really very bad men; they had never had the chance to be good men. Most of all, he disliked them because they looked upon anyone who could not follow the seaman's trade as a fool.

A long, low skyline in the distance was Redburn's first glimpse of Ireland. He met his first true European when an Irish fisherman hailed the *Highlander* and asked for a line. When he had hauled fifteen or so fathoms of the line into his boat, the Irishman cut the line, laughed, and sailed away. Even though the rope was not Redburn's, he, boylike, felt that the man had played a scurvy trick.

When the *Highlander* arrived at Liverpool, Redburn decided that the English city was not a great deal different from New York. Sailors and ships, he found, were the same in one place as in another, with a few notable exceptions. His trips into the city, away from the waterfront, and excursions into the Lancashire countryside convinced him that he, as an alien, was not welcome. People distrusted him because of his ragged clothing, and he had no money to purchase a new outfit, even though Captain Riga had advanced him three dollars, one month's pay, upon the ship's arrival in port.

Redburn's greatest disappointment came when he tried to use for his excursions an old guidebook he had brought from his father's library. The guidebook, almost half a century old, was no longer reliable, for streets and structures it mentioned were no longer in existence. Redburn felt that the whole world must have changed since his father's time; he saw in the unreliable guidebook a hint that as the years passed the habits and ideals of youth had to be charted anew. Each generation, he learned, had to make its own guidebook through the world.

While in Liverpool, Redburn met Harry Bolton, a young Englishman of good family but a prodigal son. Bolton said that he had shipped on two voyages to the East Indies; now he wanted to emigrate to America. With Redburn's help Harry Bolton was enrolled as a "boy" on the *Highlander* for its return trip to New York. The two boys, traveling on Bolton's money, made a quick excursion to London before the ship sailed, but they were back in Liverpool within forty-eight hours. Redburn saw little of England beyond the port where he had arrived.

On the return trip to America the ship carried a load of Irish emigrants. Redburn quickly felt sorry for them but at the same time superior to the miserable wretches crowded between decks. The steerage passengers suffered a great deal during the voyage. Their quarters were cramped at best, and during heavy weather they could not remain on deck. For cooking they had a stove placed on one of the hatches, one stove for five hundred people. Worst of all, an epidemic of fever broke out, killing many of the emigrants and one of the sailors.

Bolton had a miserable trip, and Redburn was sorry for him, too. The English boy had lied in saying he had been at sea before. Because he could not bear to go aloft in the rigging, he, in place of Redburn, became the butt of all the jokes and horseplay that the crew devised.

After the ship reached America, however, the voyage seemed to both Redburn and Bolton to have been a good one. They

ants had resorted to terrorizing the land-lords with tar buckets, rifles, and calico hoods. To mask their greed for land, they claimed that their activities were carried on in the name of liberty, equality, and justice.

Because it would be dangerous to visit Ravensnest openly Hugh and his uncle disguised themselves as a watch peddler and an organ grinder, acquired a broken German accent, and started for Ravens-nest. On the boat to Albany they met Seneca Newcome, who, thinking that they might make good Injins. invited them to Ravensnest. They got off at Albany and went from there to Troy. In that city they made the acquaintance of the Rev. Mr. Warren and his daughter Mary. In his new role as an organ grinder Hugh invented a false history for himself and his uncle, a story accepted by the Warrens. Hugh soon learned that the Warrens lived at Ravensnest, where Mr. Warren was an Episcopal clergyman, and that Mary was a close friend of Hugh's sister Patt. Mary proved to be a charming, well-bred girl in striking contrast to Opportunity Newcome, who was also present at the inn. After Seneca Newcome joined the group the conversation turned from Opportunity's preten-tious learning to anti-rentism. Mary and her father argued gracefully and well in marked contrast to Seneca's and Oppor-tunity's ill-constructed logic.

After a journey by train and carriages Hugh and his uncle arrived in Ravens-nest. Still in their new roles as a ped-dler and an organ grinder, they traveled about the area to see for themselves how matters stood. At the tavern where they stopped overnight, they heard two men arguing over anti-rentism. While a law-yer took a mild stand against it, Hall, a mechanic, stood firmly against it and the greed behind it.

After a day's walk the travelers arrived at Ravensnest manor. They decided, however, to retain their disguises and visit the two old men on the place, the Indian, Susquesus, and the colored serv-ant, Jaap. While they were at the hut

of these faithful old retainers, Hugh's grandmother, Mrs. Ursula Littlepage, his sister Patt, Mary Warren, and his uncle's two wards, Henrietta Coldbrook and Anne Marston, rode up. None penetrated the disguises. After the others had gone Susquesus revealed that he knew who Hugh and his uncle were, but he prom-ised secrecy.

The two also visited the Miller farm where they learned that Tom Miller was hostile to anti-rentism and that a farm-hand of his strongly favored it. The farmhand, Joshua Brigham, was extreme-ly greedy, Miller pointed out. While they were at the Miller farm, the five women again rode up, and Uncle Ro showed them some watches. Mrs. Littlepage, who wished to buy a very expensive watch for Mary, told them that they could receive payment for the watch at the manor.

That evening, still dressed as peddlers, they went to the Littlepage home. Hugh, asked to play his flute, performed very well, but when the flute was passed around his grandmother recognized it. When she drew her grandson aside he confessed to the deception. Soon he and his uncle were reunited witn Mrs. Little-page and Patt, who also promised se-crecy. Later that evening Hugh slept in the Miller house next to Joshua Brigham. Drawn into a discussion on anti-rentism, the farmhand, thinking Hugh shared his sentiments, told of his plans for robbing the Littlepages of their land. He also re-vealed that the Injins were to hold a meeting the next day.

On the following day Hugh and his uncle, riding in a wagon to the meeting at the town of Ravensnest, were stopped on the way by a gang of hooded Injins who wanted to know their business. In-terrupted by the appearance of Mr. War-ren and Mary, the hoodlums disappeared into the bushes. The Littlepages, trying to pacify the hiding Injins by expressing mild anti-rentist sentiments, provoked Mr. Warren to argue with them, where-upon the Injins came out of hiding. The Injins then drove Uncle Ro and Mr.

Warren to the meeting, leaving Hugh to drive Mary. On the way he disclosed to her his true identity and motives.

At the meeting house the imported lecturer began to rant about liberty, equality, and justice, accused the Littlepage family of standing for slavery, aristocracy, and injustice, and declared that they were no better than other folks. When he had finished, Hall, the mechanic, got up to speak. He said that the true aristocrats of America were demagogues and newspaper editors, that the Littlepages had as much right to their ways as he did to his, and that if the Littlepage property should be divided, that of the tenants should be too. His speech was interrupted by several Injins who came whooping into the meeting house. Most of the people fled, but Mary, Hall, and the Littlepages remained, comporting themselves with dignity.

The Injins ran wild stealing calico and wagons from their own sympathizers. After seeing the Warrens off, Hugh and his uncle got into their wagon and rode toward the manor. They could see a party of armed men following them. On the way they met some anti-renters who had been deprived of their wagon. They walked alongside, still talking about the virtues of anti-rentism. Suddenly a group of real Indians appeared in the road. Surprised, Uncle Ro forgot his German accent, and the anti-renters, realizing who their companions were, ran into the bushes. The Littlepages learned that the Indians had come from Washington and were seeking Susquesus, the old Onondaga who lived at Ravensnest manor. When the terrorist Injins appeared, the real Indians let out a war whoop and the Injins ran. Two, Joshua Brigham and Seneca Newcome, were captured but were soon released. The Littlepages invited the Indians to stay in an old farmhouse at the manor. When Hugh and his uncle arrived home, everyone knew who they really were, and there was great rejoicing.

That night the Indians held a conference on the lawn in which Susquesus was the center of attention. The Indians spoke about the old days, the coming of the white man, and the different types of men with force, eloquence, and reserve. Hugh felt that they were as much gentlemen in their own way as he and Uncle Ro were in theirs.

Later that night Hugh, looking from his bedroom window, saw Opportunity Newcome riding toward the house. The ostensible purpose of her visit was to tell him that the Injins were trying to get a legal charge against him and that they were planning arson. He immediately warned Mary to keep an eye out for trouble and then went to tell the Indians to do the same.

A short time later Mary signaled to him as he was patrolling the grounds. She said that two Injins were setting fire to the kitchen. Hugh rushed to the kitchen window and fired a shot into the air as the men came out. He clubbed one over the head and fell grappling with the other. Hugh might have been overpowered if Mary had not come to his aid. At that moment the Indians, attracted by the shot, arrived on the scene. The prisoners turned out to be Joshua Brigham and Seneca Newcome. A short time later a few Injins set fire to a load of hay and then ran off, the Indians close at their heels.

Sunday morning was peaceful. The Littlepages went to church and sat in the canopied pew that the tenants resented. After church, following a brief meeting down the road, three anti-renters presented Hugh with a petition to remove the canopy; he refused. On the way home Opportunity coyly asked Hugh to release her brother, but he was noncommittal. After leaving her he learned that the canopy had been torn down and placed over the Miller pigpen. On arriving home he was told that Seneca had tried to escape arson charges by proposing to each of the four young women at the manor.

Later that day a final ceremony was held in honor of Susquesus. The peace pipe was passed around, and Jaap, the colored companion of Susquesus, was invited to make a speech. He was interrupted, however, by the appearance of a large group of Injins. While the Littlepages waited to see what was intended, Opportunity rode up, drew Hugh into the house, and told him that these Injins were not afraid of Indians. She said that Hugh was standing over an earthquake if he did not release her brother. Hugh was called outside again when it was discovered that the Injins had surrounded the Warrens. Mr. Warren and Mary maintained their composure, however, and managed to go free. The Injins were duly warned about the ferocity of the Indians, and the ceremony was continued. The Indians told how the white men broke their laws for selfish reasons and hid their shame under calico hoods, while the red men upheld their laws even at great personal sacrifice. The Injins were humiliated by this speech. While they were listening, Jack Dunning, the business agent, arrived with the sheriff and a posse to drive off the Injins. But by this time the Injins had lost public support and were thoroughly disgraced. Taking advantage of the confusion, Opportunity released her brother and Joshua Brigham, and the two were never seen in that part of the country again. The Supreme Court upheld the rights of the landlords and the anti-rent wars ended.

Uncle Ro gave a good portion of his estate to Mary when she and Hugh were married. Hugh heard that Opportunity Newcome intended to sue him for breach of promise, but nothing ever came of that threat.

# THE RELAPSE

*Type of work:* Drama
*Author:* Sir John Vanbrugh (1664-1726)
*Type of plot:* Social satire
*Time of plot:* Seventeenth century
*Locale:* England
*First presented:* 1696

*Principal characters:*
SIR NOVELTY FASHION, LORD FOPPINGTON, a London fop
YOUNG FASHION, his brother
LOVELESS, a gentleman
AMANDA, his wife
WORTHY, a gentleman of the town
SIR TUNBELLY CLUMSEY, a country squire
MISS HOYDEN, Sir Tunbelly's daughter
COUPLER, a matchmaker
BERINTHIA, a comely widow

## Critique:

The Relapse, Or, Virtue in Danger was written as a sequel to Colley Cibber's Love's Last Shift because in Vanbrugh's opinion the latter play did not present an accurate picture of human nature. Lord Foppington is Cibber's Sir Novelty Fashion elevated to the peerage. The Relapse was a huge success, and for more than fifty years it held the London stage, sometimes running in more than one theater at a time. Historically, the play is important because it helped to break up the formulas followed in the artificial comedy of manners. Vanbrugh has been accused of irreligion, which is probably not wholly true, and of licentiousness, which is probably accurate.

## The Story:

In the country Loveless and Amanda led a quiet life after a stormy period of marriage troubles. Because Loveless had to go to London rather frequently and because she had reason to doubt his fidelity, Amanda was apprehensive. But Loveless assured her he was temptation-proof; going to London provided a test of his reform.

Young Fashion and his servant Lory called on Sir Novelty Fashion, the new Lord Foppington, young Fashion's elder brother. Lord Foppington had recently bought a title. Since he was the eldest son, he had plenty of money, although he spent too much as it was. Young Fashion, on the contrary, was destitute. He was minded to join the army as a last resort, but at Lory's suggestion he resolved to humble himself to ask the new lord to pay his debts. But Lord Foppington was busy with the tailor and the shoemaker and hardly spared his brother a word. Although Lord Foppington was on the point of going out, he did invite his brother to stay and have a home dinner by himself.

Angered by his brother's attitude, young Fashion determined on revenge. Coupler, a matchmaker who providentially came in, had a plan. Coupler had arranged a marriage between Lord Foppington and Miss Hoyden, wealthy daughter of Sir Tunbelly Clumsey. Lord Foppington was to pay the matchmaker two thousand pounds, but he was afraid the new lord would evade the money agreement. It was decided that young Fashion was to go to Sir Tunbelly's house and, pretending to be his brother, marry Miss Hoyden. Coupler, in turn, was to receive a fee of five thousand pounds. Young Fashion agreed to the plan, after a hard time fighting off Coupler's amorous advances.

Loveless and Amanda were installed in their London lodgings and Loveless had already been to the theater. In a con-

3160

fidential mood he told his wife of seeing a beautiful woman in the audience, a woman so handsome he had been unable to keep his eyes off her. Amanda was alarmed, but he told her he admired the woman only in an aesthetic way. Berinthia, Amanda's widowed friend, came to call. To Loveless' surprise, she was the woman he had admired in the theater. Because he pretended to be indifferent to Berinthia's charms, Amanda invited her to stay with them while they were in London.

Lord Foppington also came to call and was quite smitten with Amanda's beauty. Resolving to make a conquest at once, he drew her aside and declared his love. Amanda slapped his face. Loveless, seeing the fracas, wounded Lord Foppington with his sword. Although the wound was not serious, the surgeon pretended that it was, in order to increase his fee. As Lord Foppington was being carried out, Worthy entered and was also attracted by Amanda's charms. After the men had all left, Berinthia had a long talk with Amanda about men and love.

Young Fashion determined to make one more attempt before taking revenge on his brother. Once again he told Lord Foppington of his debts and asked for money to settle them. Lord Foppington refused haughtily, and in the ensuing quarrel young Fashion tried to fight a duel with his brother. Lord Foppington contemptuously refused to fight and left. Resolved to do his worst, young Fashion set out for Coupler's house.

Loveless made love to Berinthia and finally seized her. He left, however, when they were interrupted by Worthy's arrival. Worthy was in love with Amanda. Because Berinthia had once been his mistress, he asked her help in his suit. Berinthia's plan was to let Amanda become jealous of her erring husband; in her anger she would be an easier prey. When Amanda returned, Berinthia told her that Loveless was pursuing a strange woman.

Armed with a letter from Coupler,

young Fashion called at Sir Tunbelly's house. When he knocked, Sir Tunbelly quickly locked Miss Hoyden in her room with her old nurse and sent armed peasants to the gate. Young Fashion was cordially received, however, when he explained that he was Lord Foppington. Miss Hoyden, ripely nubile, was all atwitter.

Although the nurse was supposed to be a chaperone, she was an indulgent one, and she allowed young Fashion to talk privately with Miss Hoyden. Sir Tunbelly wanted to defer the wedding for a while to allow time to invite the guests, but young Fashion did not dare wait so long. For a small bribe, since Miss Hoyden was more than willing, the nurse made arrangements for Bull, the chaplain, to marry them secretly in the morning. And, since they were to be married so soon, she saw no harm in their staying together that night. The following morning the complaisant Bull performed the ceremony.

When Berinthia and Amanda again discussed the subject of love, Berinthia skillfully played on Amanda's doubts of Loveless' fidelity. According to plan, Worthy then arrived to say that Loveless would be out until very late, and that while waiting for Loveless he would play cards with the ladies. Artful Berinthia withdrew to her chamber and left Worthy and Amanda alone. In her bedroom, meanwhile, Berinthia received the erring Loveless. Putting out the candles, he seized Berinthia and dragged her into the closet. She shouted for help, but she was careful to scream very softly.

Lord Foppington arrived at Sir Tunbelly's house to claim his bride. Taken for an impostor, he was set upon and bound, and young Fashion declared he had never seen the man before. A neighbor identified Foppington, however, and young Fashion fled precipitately. Miss Hoyden decided to keep still about her marriage to young Fashion and to marry again, this time the real Lord Foppington.

Back in London, Coupler showed young Fashion a letter. Lord Foppington had married Miss Hoyden but would wait until they returned to Lord Foppington's own bed to consummate the marriage. Young Fashion had to wait until the couple came to town to regain his Miss Hoyden. Fortunately, the parson of Fat-goose Living had just died and young Fashion had the disposition of the post. By promising the living to Bull, young Fashion persuaded him that he should tell the truth about the secret marriage.

Meanwhile Berinthia, trying to arouse Amanda's jealousy to the point where she would accept Worthy as a lover, arranged to have Amanda present at a masquerade. Loveless was there in the company of Berinthia, who was masked. Convinced that her husband had a mistress, Amanda received Worthy in her home, but in spite of his best efforts she retained her virtue.

Lord Foppington invited the whole company to come and honor his new bride. Young Fashion appeared also and declared that Miss Hoyden was married to him. Sir Tunbelly was thunderstruck and Lord Foppington was contemptuous of his younger brother's story. True to their agreement, the nurse and Bull backed him up. When it was learned that young Fashion was Lord Foppington's brother, Sir Tunbelly withdrew his opposition and accepted his son-in-law. Lord Foppington met the new turn of events as gracefully as he could. Miss Hoyden, having learned that her first husband was Lord Foppington's brother, had no complaint to make, just so long as she was married to someone.

# R. E. LEE

*Type of work:* Biography
*Author:* Douglas Southall Freeman (1886-1953)
*Time:* 1807-1870
*Locale:* Mostly the Confederate States of America
*First published:* 1934-1935

Principal personages:
GENERAL ROBERT E. LEE
MARY CUSTIS LEE, his wife
GENERAL WINFIELD SCOTT, U.S.A.
PRESIDENT JEFFERSON DAVIS, C.S.A.
THOMAS JONATHAN ("STONEWALL") JACKSON,
JAMES LONGSTREET,
JAMES EWELL BROWN STUART,
RICHARD STODDERT EWELL,
AMBROSE POWELL HILL, and
JUBAL ANDERSON EARLY, Generals of the Confederacy
GENERAL ULYSSES S. GRANT, U.S.A.

By heritage, education, profession, and talent Douglas Southall Freeman was ideally fitted to write the definitive biography of Robert Edward Lee. The son of a Confederate veteran, a Doctor of Philosophy in history from Johns Hopkins University, editor of the Richmond *News Leader,* whose "chief avocation" was "the study of military history" and whose prose style was fascinating, he accepted in 1915 a publisher's invitation to tell the life story of the South's best beloved hero. It seems that Douglas Freeman's ambition to compose such a book was born in 1903, when as a youth of seventeen in the company of his father he attended a reunion of Confederate veterans in Petersburg, Virginia. Incidentally, the elder Freeman lived to see his son's work come from the press. At first the biographer expected to write only a single volume, but a wealth of compelling material, much of it scarcely tapped, expanded his number to four. Even then he had not exhausted the accumulations of his research, with the result that, after completing the work originally planned, he brought out *Lee's Lieutenants,* a three-volume "Study in Command." As a title for his monumental

production Dr. Freeman chose the general's autograph: *R. E. Lee.*

Volume I, containing thirty-six chapters, covers a period of fifty-five years, from Lee's birth on January 19, 1807, to the beginning of the War between the States in 1861 and the early months of 1862. It takes its reader with never flagging interest through the West Point years, marriage, gradual rise in the United States Army, the Mexican War, the capture of John Brown, "The Answer He Was Born to Make," and the early, unsuccessful operations in western Virginia. Concerning Lee's momentous decision, which has entailed much dispute by many persons, the author states: "The spirit of Virginia had been alive in his heart every hour of his life. . . . He was a United States officer who loved the army and had pride in the Union, but something very deep in his heart kept him mindful that he had been a Virginian before he had been a soldier."

Volume II, of thirty-five chapters, recounting the Seven Days' Battles east of Richmond against McClellan, Second Manassas against Pope, the Sharpsburg Campaign in Maryland with McClellan again the adversary, and the Battle of

Fredericksburg against Burnside, all in 1862, concludes with the victory over Hooker at Chancellorsville and the death of Stonewall Jackson in May, 1863. Through these pages painstaking, absorbing military analysis continues.

Volume III, twenty-nine chapters in length, proceeds from the beginning of the Gettysburg Campaign through that fateful conflict with the full power of Dr. Freeman's critical study. Then comes the "hammer and rapier" matching of Grant against Lee in 1864, with such battles as the Wilderness, Spotsylvania Courthouse, and Cold Harbor, the historian's expositions being precise but never tiresome. Grant crosses the James, and the long, encircling blue lines outside Petersburg are held in check by Lee's thin gray battalions for nearly ten months, with the unique Battle of the Crater furnishing a new, strange story for the history of war. The reader lives with freezing, starving Southern veterans to the end of the winter of 1864-1865.

The first eleven chapters of Volume IV relate the close of the war in Virginia with the surrender at Appomattox Courthouse. The next sixteen chapters picture General Lee—body, mind, and soul—as he turns to civilian pursuits and works sincerely and consistently for peace and reconciliation. He maintains his dignity and grandeur as college president at Lexington, until his death on October 12, 1870. The final chapter, "The Pattern of a Life," is Freeman's masterpiece. Epitomizing Lee's career and character, it can be designated properly by one term only: a classic.

R. E. Lee was a labor of love. For nineteen years, from its inception in 1915 to its publication in 1934-1935, the author, discarding apocryphal and legendary tales, scrupulously winnowed and used documented facts. Averring that he was "fully repaid by being privileged to live, as it were, for more than a decade in the company of a great gentleman," Dr. Freeman adds in his foreword: "There were no 'secrets' and no scandals to be exposed or explained. . . . Neither was there any occasion to attempt an 'interpretation' of a man who was his own clear interpreter." The reader enjoys the biography as he shares the author's uplift of spirit.

Though detailed, the narrative is never boring. Minor, no less than major, incidents are recorded delightfully; for instance, Lieutenant Lee's riding double on horseback with a brother officer along Pennsylvania Avenue in Washington; kissing a little boy whom he mistook for his own son; picking up under shellfire a small sparrow and putting it back in a tree from which it had fallen; smiling upon hearing a colored attendant explain that he had not been shot because he stayed back where the generals stayed.

Dr. Freeman would have transcended human ability if he had never erred in his minutiae. Few and inconsequential, however, are such slips as entitling the Right Reverend John Johns "Bishop of Virginia" in 1853, whereas at that time he was Assistant Bishop, and calling Colonel David A. Weisiger "Daniel" Weisiger. Generally Freeman's accuracy of research and transcription equals his natural stylistic charm. Moreover, R. E. Lee retains freshness and vigor throughout its length. Nor have verbal mannerisms become so patent in it as the author's often repeated "doubtless" in his later George Washington.

Promptly upon the appearance of the first two volumes, R. E. Lee was awarded a Pulitzer Prize, and, in the years which have followed, neither the scholar nor the mere average reader has been prone to dispute the judges' logic. Definitely this life of an unspotted American hero is the *magnum opus* of an unexcelled American biographer.

# REMEMBRANCE OF THINGS PAST

*Type of work:* Novel
*Author:* Marcel Proust (1871-1922)
*Type of plot:* Psychological realism
*Time of plot:* Late nineteenth, early twentieth centuries
*Locale:* France
*First published:* 1913-1927

> *Principal characters:*
> MARCEL, the narrator
> MARCEL's GRANDMOTHER, a kind and wise old woman
> M. SWANN, a wealthy broker and esthete
> MME. SWANN, formerly a cocotte, Odette de Crécy
> GILBERTE, their daughter, later Mme. de Saint-Loup
> MME. DE VILLEPARISIS, a friend of Marcel's grandmother
> ROBERT DE SAINT-LOUP, her nephew, Marcel's friend
> BARON DE CHARLUS, another nephew, a Gomorrite
> MME. VEDURIN, a vulgar social climber
> THE PRINCE and PRINCESS DE GUERMANTES, and
> THE DUKE and DUCHESS DE GUERMANTES, members of the old aristocracy

## Critique:

Remembrance of Things Past is not a novel of traditional form. Symphonic in design, it unfolds without plot or crisis as the writer reveals in retrospect the motifs of his experience, holds them for thematic effect, and drops them, only to return to them once more in the processes of recurrence and change. This varied pattern of experience brings together a series of involved relationships through the imagination and observation of a narrator engaged in tracing with painstaking detail his perceptions of people and places as he himself grows from childhood to disillusioned middle age. From the waking reverie in which he recalls the themes and characters of his novel to that closing paragraph with its slow, repeated echoes of the word *Time,* Proust's novel is great art distilled from memory itself, the structure determined entirely by moods and sensations evoked by the illusion of time passing, or seeming to pass, recurring, or seeming to recur. The title shows Proust's two-fold concern as a novelist: time lost and time recalled. To the discerning reader it is plain that for Proust the true realities of human experience were not contained in a reconstruction of remembered scenes and events but in the capture of physical sensations and moods re-created in memory. The seven novels which make up *Remembrance of Things Past* are *Swann's Way, Within a Budding Grove, The Guermantes Way, Cities of the Plain, The Captive, The Sweet Cheat Gone,* and *The Past Recaptured.*

## The Story:

All his life Marcel found it difficult to go to sleep at night. After he had blown out the light, he would lie quietly in the darkness and think of the book he had been reading, of an event in history, of some memory from the past. Sometimes he would think of all the places in which he had slept—as a child in his great-aunt's house in the provincial town of Combray, in Balbec on a holiday with his grandmother, in the military town where his friend, Robert de Saint-Loup, had been stationed, in Paris, in Venice during a visit there with his mother.

He remembered always a night at Combray when he was a child. M. Swann, a family friend, had come to dinner. Marcel had been sent to bed early, where he lay for hours nervous and unhappy until at last he heard M. Swann leave. Then his mother had come upstairs to comfort him.

For a long time the memory of that night was his chief recollection of Combray, where his family took him to spend a part of every summer with his grandparents and aunts. Years later, while drinking tea with his mother, the taste of a small sweet cake suddenly brought back all the impressions of his old days at Combray.

He remembered the two roads. One was Swann's way, a path that ran beside M. Swann's park where the lilacs and hawthorns bloomed. The other was the Guermantes way, along the river and past the chateau of the Duke and Duchess de Guermantes, the great family of Combray. He remembered the people he saw on his walks. There were familiar figures like the doctor and the priest. There was M. Vinteuil, an old composer who died broken-hearted and shamed because of his daughter's friendship with a woman of bad reputation. There were the neighbors and friends of his grandparents. But best of all he remembered M. Swann, whose story he pieced together slowly from family conversations and village gossip.

M. Swann was a wealthy Jew accepted in rich and fashionable society. His wife was not received, however, for she was his former mistress, Odette de Crécy, a cocotte with the fair, haunting beauty of a Botticelli painting. It was Odette who had first introduced Swann to the Vedurins, a vulgar family that pretended to despise the polite world of the Guermantes. At an evening party given by Mme. Vedurin, Swann heard played a movement of Vinteuil's sonata and identified his hopeless passion for Odette with that lovely music. Swann's love was an unhappy affair. Tortured by jealousy, aware of the vulgarity and pettiness of the Vedurins, determined to forget his unfaithful mistress, he went to Mme. de Sainte-Euvert's reception. There he heard Vinteuil's music again. Under its influence he decided, at whatever price, to marry Odette.

After their marriage Swann drifted more and more into the bourgeois circle of the Vedurins. When he went to see his old friends in Combray and in the fashionable Faubourg Saint-Germain, he went alone. Many people thought him both ridiculous and tragic.

On his walks Marcel sometimes saw Mme. Swann and her daughter, Gilberte, in the park at Combray. Later, in Paris, he met the little girl and became her playmate. That friendship, as they grew older, became an innocent love affair. Filled also with a schoolboyish passion for Mme. Swann, Marcel went to Swann's house as much to be in her company as in Gilberte's. But after a time his pampered habits and brooding, neurasthenic nature began to bore Gilberte. His pride hurt, he refused to see her for many years.

Marcel's family began to treat him as an invalid. With his grandmother, he went to Balbec, a seaside resort. There he met Albertine, a girl to whom he was immediately attracted. He met also Mme. de Villeparisis, an old friend of his grandmother and a connection of the Guermantes family. Mme. de Villeparisis introduced him to her two nephews, Robert de Saint-Loup and Baron de Charlus. Saint-Loup and Marcel became close friends. While visiting Saint-Loup in a nearby garrison town, Marcel met his friend's mistress, a young Jewish actress named Rachel. Marcel was both fascinated and repelled by Baron de Charlus; he was not to understand until later the baron's corrupt and depraved nature.

Through his friendship with Mme. de Villeparisis and Saint-Loup, Marcel was introduced into the smart world of the Guermantes when he returned to Paris.

One day, while he was walking with his grandmother, she suffered a stroke. The illness and death of that good and unselfish old woman made him realize for the first time the empty worldliness of his smart and wealthy friends. For comfort he turned to Albertine, who came to stay with him in Paris while his family was away. But his desire to be humored and indulged in all his whims, his suspicions of Albertine, and his petty jealousy, finally forced her to leave him and go back to Balbec. With her, he had been unhappy; without her, he was wretched. Then he learned that she had been accidentally killed in a fall from her horse. Later he received a letter, written before her death, in which she promised to return to him.

More miserable than ever, Marcel tried to find diversion among his old friends. They were changing with the times. Swann was ill and soon to die. Gilberte had married Robert de Saint-Loup. Mme. Vedurin, who had inherited a fortune, now entertained the old nobility. At one of her parties Marcel heard a Vinteuil composition played by a musician named Morel, the nephew of a former servant and now a protegé of the notorious Baron de Charlus.

His health breaking down at last, Marcel spent the war years in a sanitarium. When he returned to Paris, he found still greater changes. Robert de Saint-Loup had been killed in the war. Rachel, Saint-Loup's mistress, had become a famous actress. Swann was also dead, and his widow, remarried, was a fashionable hostess who received the Duchess de Guermantes. Prince de Guermantes, his fortune lost and his first wife dead, had married Mme. Vedurin for her money. Baron de Charlus had grown senile.

Marcel went to one last reception at the Princess de Guermantes' lavish house. Meeting there the daughter of Gilberte de Saint-Loup, he realized how time had passed, how old he had grown. In the Guermantes library, he happened to take down the novel by George Sand which his mother had read to him that remembered night in Combray, years before. Suddenly, in memory, he heard again the ringing of the bell that announced M. Swann's departure and knew that it would echo in his mind forever. He saw then that everything in his own futile, wasted life dated from that far night in his childhood, and in that moment of self-revelation he saw also the ravages of time among all the people he had ever known.

# REMEMBRANCE ROCK

*Type of work:* Novel
*Author:* Carl Sandburg (1878-    )
*Type of plot:* Historical chronicle
*Time of plot:* 1607-1945
*Locale:* England and America
*First published:* 1948

*Principal characters:*
> ORVILLE BRAND WINDOM, former Justice of the United States Supreme Court
> OLIVER BALL WINDROW, a woodcarver and philosopher
> MARY WINDLING, a young Puritan
> JOHN SPONG, whom she married
> REMEMBER SPONG, their daughter
> ORTON WINGATE, a sojourner in Plymouth
> PETER LADD, a seaman and gambler
> RESOLVED WAYFARE, a follower of Roger Williams
> ORDWAY WINSHORE, a Philadelphia printer
> ROBERT WINSHORE, his older son
> JOHN LOCKE WINSHORE, his younger son
> MARINTHA (MIM) WILMING, a dressmaker's assistant
> OATES ELWOOD, friend of Robert and Locke
> ANN, his sister, Locke's wife
> OMRI WINWOLD, an ex-gambler
> JOEL WIMBLER, an abolitionist
> RODNEY WAYMAN, Mibs' husband, a Confederate officer
> MILLICENT (MIBS), their daughter
> BROOKSANY, his wife

## Critique:

Remembrance Rock, a first novel published when its writer was 70, is a work almost as sprawling and formless as the land it celebrates. The pattern is simple: three stories dealing with the settling of Plymouth, the American Revolution, and the Civil War, set between a prologue and an epilogue which have for background Washington in the years of World War II. Imperfect as a novel, the book is nevertheless a great American document, presenting in human terms and in the idiom of Sandburg's "swift and furious people" the growth of the American dream through more than three centuries of our national history. Remembrance Rock has been called a saga, a chronicle, a sermon, a collection of Chaucerian tales, a miscellany on folk themes; and it is all of these. By means of fable, paean, symbol, and style that ranges from the grave, proud language of Bunyan and Defoe to the downright slangy and boisterous, Sandburg has projected a poet-historian's testament of American life. The result is a narrative as passionate and affirmative as the tough and mystic eloquence of his poetry. Unity of theme is provided by characters recurring in the major episodes and by the symbolic reappearances of a bronze plaque bearing an inscription of Roger Bacon's Four Stumbling Blocks to Truth: 1) The influence of fragile or unworthy authority. 2) Custom. 3) The imperfection of undisciplined senses. 4) Concealment of ignorance by ostentation of seeming wisdom.

## The Stories:

The rock stood in the cedar-shaded garden of former Supreme Court Justice Orville Brand Windom, a giant boulder about which he had scattered earth from Plymouth, Valley Forge, Gettysburg, the Argonne. The justice was old, with a deep and brooding concern for the American land, its history, its people. Some of his ideas he spoke to the world in a radio broadcast he made in 1944. Others he recorded in three chronicles of the living past that his grandson, Captain Raymond Windom, veteran of Okinawa, found in a locked box after the old man's death. These tales, like the antique bronze plaque inscribed with Roger Bacon's Four Stumbling Blocks to Truth, were Justice Windom's legacy of wisdom and love to his grandson, his grandson's wife, and their son, Joseph Stilwell Windom.

## I

Red-haired Oliver Ball Windrow, the woodcarver, had on one side of his face the look of a poet and dreamer, on the other a countenance of wrath and storm. A seeker and questioner, he loved Mary Windling, a girl only half his age and a member of the Separatist congregation that worshipped secretly at Scrooby, and for her he made a small plaque of bronze, on which he inscribed Roger Bacon's Four Stumbling Blocks to Truth, to wear on a silver cord around her neck.

Mary liked his sudden whims and strange humors, but in the end she married a young workman named John Spong. This happened in 1608, just before the Scrooby congregation escaped to Holland. For twelve years Mary Spong and her husband lived in Leyden. Infrequent news came from England. Windrow had wed Matilda Bracken, the devoted mute who kept his house. Then, in 1620, he and his two daughters died of smallpox. Mary's sadness for her old friend was lessened by promises and fears surrounding plans of the Puritans to try their fortunes in the new world.

The Spongs and their daughter Remember were passengers aboard the *Mayflower* when it sailed. Little Remember had only one memory of Plymouth. One day, while she was playing on the wharf, some boys began to torment her. Another boy came with an ax handle and beat them off. She forgot to ask his name.

Mary Spong, dying during that first terrible winter in the wilderness, gave her daughter the tarnished keepsake Windrow had made years before. Remember grew up in Plymouth, a cluster of houses between forest and sea, and those gaunt years of hardship and toil helped to shape her strong body, her resolute will, her sober decorum that hid deep passions. Her father grew grim and silent as time passed. He disliked Orton Wingate, a sojourner in Plymouth, a man whose face showed peace and calm on one side, turmoil on the other. But Wingate was Remember's friend and came to sit with her from time to time. She knew without his saying that she could have had him for her husband. Restless, uncertain of her own mind, she waited.

Sometimes she rebelled against the harsh Puritan laws, as when she concealed Hode Latch, a convicted drunkard for whom constables were searching, and then she was afraid that she was damned. Perhaps Peter Ladd sensed that wild streak in her when he came courting. He was a young seaman who drifted into Plymouth, steadied himself for a while, and then fell once more into dissolute ways. When Remember refused him, he went away to make his fortune in the slave trade. Two years later he was drowned in a wreck off the Virginia capes.

Roger Williams, free-thinking preacher, lived in Plymouth for a time. Several years later he was shaking the colonies with his liberal beliefs and teachings. A new age was beginning when Williams, a fugitive, built his own town beside Narragansett Bay, but Remember Spong could not know how far-reaching were to be his challenges to usages of authority and custom. She feared him most because he revealed the rebel in herself. For that reason she was of two minds about Resolved Wayfare, a newcomer to the colony in 1638. Wayfare had crossed the ocean to learn for himself the meaning of Roger Williams' message. He was also the boy, grown to manhood, who had defended Remember on the Plymouth wharf.

After he saved John Spong's life during a blizzard, Remember nursed the young man back to health. During that time there was a battle of wills between them. He wanted her to go with him to Providence, but she, like her father, held that the teachings of Roger Williams were of Satan. Although Wingate's wisdom and the cruel lashing of an unmarried mother finally convinced her of the folly and blindness of custom, she could not quite make up her mind to go with Wayfare on his journey. Yet she walked with him some distance into the forest, and before they parted she gave him the bronze keepsake she had from her mother. Knowing that they would meet again, they vowed to be true as long as grass would grow or water flow. That was the solemn promise between them.

## II

In March, 1775, Ordway Winshore, master printer, left Philadelphia to visit his sons in New York and Boston. Below rusty hair, his face on one side promised peace, on the other wrath and doom—a face half serious, half comic, making him a man easy to confide in. Among his fellow travelers were two young British lieutenants, Francis and George Frame. During a tavern halt Francis Frame broke his hand by striking a blacksmith who had cursed King George. The Philadelphia printer felt that the war was beginning.

Winshore spent two days in New York with Locke, his younger son, a typesetter for Henry Tozzer, printer of Independence leaflets. Locke reported that his brother Robert was deep in the activities of Massachusetts patriots. He also hinted at Robert's romance with a dressmaker's assistant.

Another passenger in the coach to Boston was Marintha Wilming, to whom George Frame paid marked attention. Winshore liked her, not knowing, however, that she was the girl his older son loved.

Not far from Boston, Robert Winshore helped some Sons of Liberty to tar and feather Hobart Reggs, a prosperous Tory who had informed on a British deserter. Sapphira, Reggs' daughter, accidentally saw his face during the tarring.

Boston, Winshore found, was a seething, sullen city filled with British troops, Tories, Rebels, and neutrals. At the dress shop where Marintha Wilming worked there was much talk of Ann Elwood, an innocent young girl who had been tricked into a false marriage by a Grenadier sergeant. Winshore met Marintha—Mim— again in Robert's company and visited the house where she lived with her aunt. He also encountered Isaiah Thomas, printer of the *Massachusetts Spy* and Robert's employer, and in Henry Knox's bookstore he met Mary Burton, whom he, a widower, was to marry a short time later. One day, at the dress shop, Sapphira Reggs recognized Robert. When Lieutenant George Frame attempted to arrest him at the home of Mim's aunt, Robert escaped. Fleeing, he lost the old bronze plaque which had come to him from a great-granduncle and which he wore on a chain under his shirt.

Robert was with the Minute Men when the British marched on Lexington. Darius, Mim's brother, was killed in the fighting, and Lieutenant George Frame was crippled for life. Robert ventured into Boston to tell Mim of her brother's death, but the girl, distracted by his news and George Frame's injuries, declared that she wanted to forget him and his rebel violence.

Locke became a military courier. In Philadelphia, Winshore and his new wife read Paine's *Common Sense*. Robert and Oates Elwood, Ann's brother, marched with Benedict Arnold toward Quebec until they became ill with fever and were forced to turn back. The British evacuated Boston. Robert was invalided home. Locke and Elwood, carrying messages from General Greene to General Washington, spent a night with the Winshores in Philadelphia. Robert was there, a messenger at the Continental Congress. There was no time for Locke to tell his family that he had secretly married Ann Elwood. The next night, while riding to New

York, Locke was shot by British scouts. Mim Wilming, working in a Philadelphia dress shop, delivered the shroud for his burial. Meeting Robert for the first time since the fighting at Lexington, she told him that she believed at last in the patriots' cause.

The years moved ahead with dates and names—July 4, 1776, and the Unanimous Declaration, Christmas night and Trenton, Valley Forge. Near Morristown, Ann Winshore gave birth to a son named after his dead father. Mim, nursing the sick and wounded at Bethlehem, became ill with putrid fever. Ordway Winshore drove through the British lines in Quaker clothes to take her back to his house and nurse her there. When word came that Robert had died at Valley Forge, she showed his father the plaque she had found after Robert's flight from arrest. Winshore told her it was hers to keep.

Summer came, and with it the British left Philadelphia. The Winshores hung out the flag which had been hidden under Mim's mattress during her illness. One day Oates Elwood arrived with his sister and her baby. Mim told Winshore that his grandson, born in 1777, the Year of the Three Gallows, would see many dawns. He was the future.

### III

Omri Winwold had been many things —tavern chore boy, mill worker, lawyer's clerk, gambler. He was a man of easy manners but deep reserves, his brick-dust beard covering a face peacefully calm on one side, seamed with turmoil on the other. The person who understood him best was a distant cousin, Brooksany Wimbler, whose husband Joel was an abolitionist harness-maker in Arpa, New York.

For years Omri had dreamed of a farm in Illinois, and in 1836 he headed west by wagon with his wife Bee and their infant son, Andrew Marvel. Near Arpa, where he stopped to say goodbye to the Wimblers, he deserted his sluttish wife, taking the child with him, after she had behaved shamelessly with a bachelor mover. The Wimblers knew nothing of his plans, but they believed that he had continued his journey west.

All America seemed moving westward by highway and canal. Millicent Wimbler was a baby in arms when her parents went with a large party of neighbors to found the antislavery community of New Era, Illinois. Her childish nickname, Mibs, stuck, even after she grew into a beautiful young woman with a will of her own. She had two admirers. One was Hornsby Meadows, instructor at New Era College and a crusading abolitionist. The other was Danny Hilton, a farmer and contractor. She went to church and to antislavery lectures with Hornsby, to dances and the Lincoln-Douglas debate in nearby Galesburg with Danny, but she would have neither. Hornsby finally married Fidelia Englehart, a village teacher. Danny went to Chicago. Then, in 1859, Rodney Wayman and his friend Nack Doss rode into New Era. Wayman was a cattle buyer from Atlas, Illinois. A Southerner, he had been a banjo player in a traveling minstrel show, a miner in California. Mibs married him without her parents' consent two weeks later.

In Pike County, meanwhile, Omri Winwold had prospered. Taking a gambler's chance on a charge of bigamy, he had married Sarah Prindle, a neighbor's daughter. After her death he married her sister, Anne Moore, a widow. By 1857 his roomy farmhouse held eight children, from Andrew Marvel, who was twenty-two, to Robert, who was seven—a good muster, Omri felt, after his unsettled early years. In 1852, during a business trip to St. Louis, he ran into Bee again and also met her husband, Henry Flack. The husband never knew the truth about Omri and Bee. After Bee ran away to San Francisco and Anne Winwold died, Omri and Flack, both lonely, became close friends. When Rodney Wayman brought his bride home to Atlas, and Mibs and Omri had established their kinship, letters passed once more between Omri and

3171

Brooksany.

Storm clouds were gathering. John Brown raided Harper's Ferry. Clayborn Joel Wayman was born a few months before Lincoln was elected. Rodney was buying horses in Texas with Nack Doss when the war began. Both became captains in the Confederate Army. Doss was killed in a raid in Mississippi. Captured at Chickamauga, Rod was sent to the military prison at Camp Morton. Omri's boys who were old enough joined up. Rodney Wayman, Junior, was born that first year of the war, but his father never had word of him; he had escaped from Camp Morton and rejoined the troops. Joel Wimbler, commissioned in the commissary service, was furloughed home and lay dying in New Era. Brooksany died a few days after her husband. Going through their things, Mibs found in a trunk an ancient bronze plaque with Roger Bacon's Four Stumbling Blocks to Truth inscribed on it in antique script. She hung the keepsake around her neck, under her dress.

At Fredericksburg, Rod was again wounded and taken prisoner. While he lay in a barn hospital, Colonel Hornsby Meadows died on the floor next to him.

Rod lived in the filth and stench of Johnson's Island until Mibs came to get him, an exchanged prisoner. One night they went to have supper with Omri, and Rod lost some of his deep bitterness when he saw the younger Winwolds maimed and crippled in the war. Andrew Marvel, brevetted brigadier general, lacked an arm. Milton was paralyzed by a bullet in his spine. Holliday, starved in a prison camp, was dead.

The fighting ended, but deeper grief hung over the land when Lincoln's body was brought back to Springfield for burial. Mibs felt, however, that their days of storm and travail were almost over. Across the wide land the arch of union, strength, and love still held firm.

Captain Raymond Windom and his wife knew that they, too, had seen years of crisis and destiny. To them it seemed only fitting that other earths, symbols of hardship and storm and stars coming after the storm, should be buried at the base of Remembrance Rock—gravel from Anzio, sand from Utah Beach in Normandy, black volcanic ash from Okinawa.

# RENÉE MAUPERIN

*Type of work:* Novel
*Authors:* Edmond (1822-1896) and Jules (1830-1870) de Goncourt
*Type of plot:* Domestic tragedy
*Time of plot:* Nineteenth century
*Locale:* France
*First published:* 1864

*Principal characters:*

RENÉE MAUPERIN, a sensitive, talented girl in her late teens
HENRI MAUPERIN, her brother
MADAME DAVARANDE, her sister
MONSIEUR MAUPERIN, Renée's father
MADAME MAUPERIN, his wife
NAOMI BOURJOT, Renée's friend and fiancée of Henri Mauperin
MADAME BOURJOT, her mother and lover of Henri Mauperin
MONSIEUR DENOISEL, family friend of the Mauperins
DE VILLACOURT, shabby heir of an old French family

## Critique:

For those readers who prefer the analysis of "a slice of life," this novel is the Goncourt brothers' best work of fiction. In it the authors have presented a detailed and careful study of a middle-class French family during the middle of the nineteenth century. The younger people are products of their parents' later lives, for we are told that older generation was one which had originally believed in the revolutionary movements of the late eighteenth century but had in mature years become conservative owners of property. Perhaps nowhere in literature has the lingering death of a victim of any disease been as carefully delineated as has the death of Renée Mauperin, whose slow and sad departure from this life consumes at least a fourth of the chapters of the novel and is, to the sensitive reader, almost excruciating.

## The Story:

Renée Mauperin's father had served under the first Napoleon and had battled for the liberal forces until he had become a husband and father, with the responsibilities that such a position had forced upon him. After acquiring a family he had ceased being a scholar and political figure, in favor of the more financially reliable career of sugar refiner. His wife was a very proper woman, one who wished to see her children married well and respectably, that she might enjoy her old age in satisfaction of a job well done.

The children of the Mauperins, at least the oldest two, were model children, so well disciplined and quiet that they failed to excite the interest of their father. Renée, the third child, born late in in his life, was Mauperin's favorite. Renée was a lively youngster from the beginning, a lover of horses and action, a vivacious creature who was demonstrative in her affection, and an artistic but spirited personality. While these qualities endeared her to her father, they made her the bane of her mother's existence. The oldest daughter had dutifully married and become the respectable Madame Davarande, but Renée, who had already dismissed summarily a dozen suitors of good family and fortune, showed no inclination to accept any who came seeking her hand.

Almost as great a worry to Madame Mauperin was her son, on whom she doted. Henri Mauperin was a political economist and a lawyer; he was also a cold and calculating fellow, though his mother, in her excessive love for him, failed to realize just how selfish he was. She thought that he had never given a thought to marriage and chided him for his lack of interest. She felt that at the age of thirty he should have settled down.

Not knowing his plans, Madame Mauperin arranged to have him often in the company of Naomi Bourjot. Naomi was the only daughter of a very rich family known to the Mauperins for many years. The only difficulty lay in convincing her father that Henri, who had no title, was a suitable match for his daughter. Henri himself had seen that such was to be the great difficulty, and he had undertaken to gain the aid of Madame Bourjot in his suit. His method of securing her aid was to become her lover.

Through the medium of an amateur theatrical, Naomi, Renée, and Henri were placed in one another's company, although Naomi had to be forced into the venture by her mother. Madame Bourjot realized that Henri wanted to marry her daughter, but she had no idea that he was in love with the girl. It was only Henri's portrayal of Naomi's lover on the stage that revealed the true state of his affections. Rather than lose him altogether, Madame Bourjot, as Henri had anticipated, resolved to help him win her daughter and the family fortune, although tearful and bitter scenes preceded that decision. Through the efforts of his wife, Naomi's father reluctantly consented to the marriage if Henri Mauperin could gain the government's permission to add "de Villacourt" to his name.

In the meantime Naomi had discovered that Henri and her mother had been lovers. Although she loved Henri, she was dismayed by what she had learned. Even so, because of her parents, she had to go through with the marriage. Naomi's only consolation was to tell what she knew to Renée, who was horrified to learn of her brother's actions. When she confronted him with the story, he made no attempt to deny the facts; all he did was tell her curtly and angrily that the affair was none of her business.

A short time later, when, superficially, the antagonism between Renée and her brother had been smoothed over, she accompanied him to the government offices where he received permission to make the addition to his name. While she was waiting for him, she overheard two clerks saying that the real de Villacourt family had not really died out and that one member, a man, was still alive; the clerks even mentioned the address. Her knowledge gave Renée an opportunity for revenge, although she had no idea what might happen if she put her plan into action. What she did was to take a copy of the newspaper announcing that the title "de Villacourt" was to be given to Henri Mauperin and send it to the real de Villacourt, a villainous lout who immediately planned to kill the upstart who dared to appropriate his title.

The real de Villacourt journeyed to Paris and learned that, penniless as he was, he had no legal means to regain his title. Then he went to the apartment of Henri Mauperin and attempted to beat the young man. Henri, no coward, immediately challenged the man to a duel. The arrangements were made by Monsieur Denoisel, a friend of the Mauperin family for many years. He also served as Henri's second in the affair. Henri shot de Villacourt and thought the duel was over, but the man was not fatally wounded. Calling Henri back, he shot and killed him. To Denoisel was given the unhappy duty of reporting to all concerned Henri's untimely death. The one who seemed to take the news hardest was Renée. No one expected her to make so much of her brother's death, since they had never been close.

One day, in a conversation, Denoisel remarked that someone had sent the newspaper clipping to de Villacourt. Renée, fearful that she had been discovered as the author of her brother's death, had a heart attack. For many months she lay ill, apparently with no desire to live. Even the realization, after many weeks, that she had not revealed her guilt made no difference in her recovery. Her father called in the best specialists he could find, but they only remarked that some terrible shock had caused her condition. When told that she had recently lost a brother, they said that his death was probably not the real cause of her illness.

In spite of all efforts on her behalf, Renée Mauperin wasted away and finally died. Nor was the tragedy of the Mauperins yet finished. They lost their third child, Madame Davarande, a few months afterward, when she died in childbirth. Childless and alone, the elder Mauperins traveled abroad, hoping thereby to ease their grief and loneliness.

# THE REPUBLIC

*Type of work:* Philosophic dialogue
*Author:* Plato (427-347 B.C.)
*Time:* Fifth century B.C.
*Locale:* The Piraeus, Greece
*First transcribed:* Fourth century B.C.

Principal personages:
SOCRATES, the Athenian philosopher
CEPHALUS, an old man
POLEMARCHUS, his son
THRASYMACHUS, a Sophist
GLAUCON, and
ADEIMANTUS, Plato's brothers

The *Republic* is Plato's masterpiece, not only because it presents a fascinating defense of the author's conception of the ideal state, but also because it gives us the most sustained and convincing portrait of Socrates as a critical and creative philosopher. Other dialogues, such as the *Phaedo* and the *Apology,* may be superior as studies of the personality and character of Socrates, but the *Republic* is unexcelled as an exhibition of the famed Socratic method being brought to bear on such questions as "What is justice?" and "What kind of state would be most just?"

Although the constructive arguments of this dialogue come from the mouth of Socrates, it is safe to assume that much of the philosophy is Platonic in origin. As a rough reading rule, we may say that the method is Socratic, but the content is provided by Plato himself. Among the ideas which are presented and defended in the *Republic* are the Platonic theory of Ideas—the formal prototypes of all things, objective or intellectual—the Platonic conception of the nature and obligations of the philosopher, and the Platonic theory and criticism of poetry. But the central concern of the author is with the idea of justice in man and the state. The pursuit of this idea makes the *Republic* the longest of the dialogues with the exception of the *Laws.*

The dialogue is a discussion between Socrates and various friends while they are in the Piraeus for a festival. The discussion of justice is provoked by a remark made by an old man, Cephalus, to the effect that the principal advantage of being wealthy is that a man near death is able to repay what he owes to the gods and men, and is thereby able to be just in the hope of achieving a happy afterlife. Socrates objects to this conception of justice, maintaining that whether a person should return what he has received depends on the circumstances. For example, a man who has received dangerous weapons from his friends while sane should not, if he is just, return those weapons if his friend, while mad, demands them.

Polemarchus amends the idea and declares that it is just to help our friends and return to them what they are due, provided they are good and worthy of receiving the good. Enemies, on the other hand, should have harm done to them for, as bad, that is what they are due.

Socrates compels Polemarchus to admit that injuring anyone, even a wicked man, makes him worse; and since no just man would ever sanction making men worse, justice must be something other than giving good to the good and bad to the bad.

Thrasymachus then proposes the theory that justice is whatever is to the interest of the stronger party. His idea is that justice is relative to the law, and the law is made by the stronger party according to his interests. In rebuttal, Socrates maneuvers Thrasymachus into saying that sometimes rulers make mistakes.

3176

If this is so, then sometimes the law is against their interests; when the law is against the interests of the stronger party, it is right to do what is not to the interest of the stronger party.

The secret of the Socratic method is evident from analysis of this argument. The term "interest" or "to the interest of" is ambiguous, sometimes meaning what a man is interested in, what he wants, and at other times what he could want if he were not in error, as when we say, "But although you want it, it is not really to your interest to have it." Socrates adroitly shifts from one sense of the expression to the other so that Thrasymachus apparently contradicts himself. In this indirect way Socrates makes it clear both to the "victim" and to the onlookers that the proponent of the claim—in this case, Thrasymachus—has not cleared it of all possibility of misinterpretation.

Socrates then goes on to say that justice must be relative to the needs of those who are served, not to the desires of those who serve them. The physician, for example, as physician, must make the health of the patient his primary concern if he is to be just.

Socrates suggests that their understanding of justice would be clarified if they were to consider a concrete case, say the state: if by discussion they could come to understand what a state must be in order to be just, it might be possible to generalize and to arrive at an idea of justice itself.

Beginning with an account of what a state would have to be in order to fulfill its functions as a state, Socrates then proceeds to develop the notion of an ideal state by asking what the relations of the various groups of citizens to each other should be.

Every state needs three classes of citizens: the Guardians, who rule and advise the rest; the Auxiliaries, who provide military protection for the state; and the Workers, the husbandmen and other providers of food, clothing, and such useful materials.

In a just state these three classes of citizens function together, each doing its own proper business without interfering with the tasks of the other classes.

Applying this idea to the individual person, Socrates decides that a just man is one who gives to each of his functions its proper task, relating them to each other in a harmonious way. Just as the state has three distinct elements, the governing, the defending, and the producing bodies, so the individual person has three corresponding elements, the rational, the spirited, and the appetitive. By the spirited element Plato means the passionate aspect of man's nature, his propensity to anger or other irrational emotions. He so uses the term anger that he allows for what we call righteous indignation, the passionate defense of reason against desire. The rational element is the discerning and calculating side of man's nature, and it is what enables man to be wise and judicious. The appetitive side of man is his inclination to desire some things in preference to others.

A just man, then, is one who keeps each of the three elements of his nature doing its proper work with the rational element in command. A person is brave, says Socrates in the dialogue, if his spirited element remains always in the service of reason. He is wise if he is governed by reason, for reason takes into account the welfare of the entire person; and he is temperate if his spirit and appetite work harmoniously under the guidance of reason.

In order to discover those citizens best suited to be Guardians, Socrates proposed that the ideal state educate all its citizens in music and gymnastics, continually observing them to decide upon the sort of occupation for which they would best be fitted. He also argued that the Guardians and Auxiliaries should have no private property, and that they each should share a community of wives and children.

These obvious communal features of the ideal state have led many critics to dismiss Plato's construction as unacceptable. But it is well to remember that in the dialogue Socrates tells his listeners that he is not concerned about the practicality of his state; the conception of the state is constructed merely to bring out the nature of justice.

In considering the education of the Guardians, Socrates builds the conception of the philosopher as the true aristocrat or rational man, the ideal ruler for the ideal state. The philosopher is a lover of wisdom, and he alone manages to keep appetite and spirit in harmony with reason. Consequently, the Guardians of the state should be educated as philosophers, supplementing their training in arithmetic, geometry, astronomy, and music with training in the philosophic skills of dialectic. But the prospective Guardians should not be allowed to undertake philosophic education until they are old enough to take it seriously, not as mere amusement. After his philosophic training the prospective Guardian should take part in the active life of his times, so that at fifty he can assume political power with some knowledge of the actual matters with which he shall be concerned.

In connection with his discussion of the philosopher, Socrates introduced his famous myth of the cave. Men are like prisoners in a cave that faces away from the light. Unable to see themselves or anyone else because they are shackled, the men observe only the shadows of things on the wall in front of them, not realizing that the reality is something quite different from the shadows. The philosopher is like a man who leaves the cave, comes to know things as they really are, and returns reluctantly to help the shackled men who think that shadows make up the true world.

The philosopher comes to know reality through a study of the Ideas or Forms of particular things. The world of our experience is like the world of shadows, but the world of Ideas is the true reality.

For every class of objects, such as beds (Socrates' example), there is an Idea-bed, a form shared by all particular beds. The man who studies only the individual beds made by carpenters, or only the pictures of beds made by artists, knows only copies of reality (and, in the case of the imitative artist, only copies of copies); but the philosopher, making the effort to learn the Idea itself, comes closer to reality.

Socrates objects to poetry and to art whenever they are imitative, which they usually are. Although he admits that some poetry can be inspiring in the patriotic training of the Guardians, he stresses the point that imitative art is corrupting because it is misleading Physical things, after all, are merely copies of the Forms, the Ideas; hence they are one step removed from reality. But works of art are copies of physical things; hence they are at least two steps removed from reality. Furthermore, the artist paints only a single aspect of a thing; hence, strictly speaking, art is three steps removed from reality. It is on this account, as well as because of the immoral effect of the poetic style of all but the most noble poets, that Socrates recommends that imitative poets be banned from the state.

The *Republic* closes with Socrates' reaffirmation of his conviction that only the just man is truly happy, for only he harmonizes reason, appetite, and spirit by loving wisdom and the Form of the Good. The soul is immortal, he argues, because the soul's illness is injustice; yet injustice itself does not destroy a soul. Since the soul cannot be destroyed by any illness other than its own, it must be immortal. Socrates concludes by using a myth about life after death to show that the just and wise man will prosper both in this life and "during the journey of a thousand years."

# RESURRECTION

*Type of work:* Novel
*Author:* Count Leo Tolstoy (1828-1910)
*Type of plot:* Social criticism
*Time of plot:* Late nineteenth century
*Locale:* Russia
*First published:* 1899

> Principal characters:
> PRINCE DMÍTRI IVÁNOVITCH NEKHLÚDOFF, a gentleman
> KATERÍNA MIKHÁELOVNA MÁSLOVA (KATÚSHA), a prostitute
> VALDEMAR SÍMONSON, and
> VÉRA DOÚKHOVA, political prisoners

## Critique:

*Resurrection (Voskraeseniye)* is characteristic of one of Russia's foremost novelists because of its rich visual record of people and settings, its deftness in presenting the vices of petty officialdom, the humor of small people who want to seem great, and the hollowness of ritualistic orthodoxy. For Tolstoy, evil begins when one ceases to listen to his conscience and becomes self-centered. The public theme of the novel concerns the shortcomings of social organizations. The personal theme, which involves the need for forgiveness, takes a form characteristic of Tolstoy: human failure revealed by a sin committed in semi-ignorance, followed by a long and soul-strengthening atonement.

## The Story:

Katerína Máslova, better known as Katúsha, was being led out of prison to attend her own trial for murder. Born illegitimate, she had been taken in by Sophia and Mary Ivánovna, well-to-do sisters who cared for her and began to educate her. When she was sixteen Katúsha was seduced by her guardians' nephew, Prince Dmítri Ivánovitch Nekhlúdoff. When she learned that she was to become a mother, Katúsha went to stay with a village midwife. When her child was born it was taken to the foundling hospital, where it soon died. After various tribulations Katúsha became a prostitute. When she was twenty-six she was accused of complicity in the murder of a Siberian merchant, the charge on which she was to be tried.

While Katúsha was being led into court, Nekhlúdoff, her seducer, lay in bed considering his position. Although he had been having an affair with a married woman, he was almost engaged to marry Princess Mary Korchágin. He thought also of how he had given away some of his lands to the peasants. When Nekhlúdoff arose, he was reminded that he had to serve that day as a juror in the criminal court.

In court, Nekhlúdoff was astonished to see that the defendant was Katúsha, falsely accused of helping to rob and poison the merchant from Siberia. The trial was disgusting because of the self-interest of the officials, who were vain, stupid, and more concerned with formalities than with the fair judgment of the accused.

When Nekhlúdoff was a student at the university he would spend his summers with his aunts, and it was there that he first came to know and to like Katúsha. He gave her books to read and eventually fell in love with her. When he next returned, three years later, military life had made him depraved and selfish, and he seduced her. The next day he gave her some money and left for his regiment. When he returned after the war, he learned that she had become pregnant and had gone away. Somewhat relieved, he had tried to forget her.

Now, at the trial, Nekhlúdoff saw Katúsha with a mixture of loathing and pity. At first he was afraid that his relation to her would be discovered, but Katúsha did not recognize him; then he began to feel remorse for the life to which he had driven her. Because of a careless legalistic oversight by the jury, the innocent Katúsha was sentenced to four years at hard labor in Siberia. Moved by his uneasy conscience, Nekhlúdoff went to a lawyer to discuss the possibility of an appeal.

Later, when Nekhlúdoff was with the Korchágins, he realized that their life was empty and degenerate, and he felt the need to cleanse his soul. He determined that he would marry Katúsha and give up his land.

When Nekhlúdoff went to the prison and revealed himself to Katúsha, the girl treated him coldly. She seemed proud of her occupation as a prostitute, because it alone gave some meaning to her otherwise empty life. The next time he visited her, she behaved coarsely to him, and when he said that he wanted to marry her, she became angry with him and returned to her cell.

On his next visit to the prison Nekhlúdoff was told that Katúsha could not be seen because she had become drunk on vodka bought with money he had given her. He then went to see Véra Doúkhova, a revolutionist acquaintance who had sent him a note from the prison. He was surprised at the inordinate pride Véra took in the sacrifices she had made for the revolutionary cause. Véra told him to get Katúsha into the prison hospital as a nurse, so that conditions would be better for her. Nekhlúdoff arranged to have Katúsha transferred.

By this time Nekhlúdoff was no longer joyful at the prospect of marrying Katúsha. Still determined to go through with his plan, however, he started out on a journey to settle his estates in anticipation of his departure for Siberia. At Panóvo he saw the miserable conditions of the people. He saw Matróna Khárina, Katúsha's aunt, and learned about the death of his child at the foundling hospital. He gave up his title to the land at Panóvo and arranged for the peasants to have communal holdings in it, an act which brought him great joy.

Nekhlúdoff then went to St. Petersburg. His chief reason was to appeal Katúsha's case to the Senate and to try to secure the release of Lydia Shoústova, an innocent prisoner who was Véra Doúkhova's friend. In St. Petersburg he came within the aristocratic circle of his aunt, Katerína Ivánovna Tchársky, who claimed to be interested in evangelism but who had no pity for the unfortunate of the world. Nekhlúdoff went to see various prominent people on the business which had taken him to St. Petersburg. The next day he learned that Lydia Shoústova had been released.

Katúsha's case was put before the Senate. Because one of the senators styled himself a Darwinian and thought that Nekhlúdoff's morality in the case was disgusting, the girl's sentence was upheld. On the same day Nekhlúdoff met an old friend, Selénin, now a public prosecutor, an intelligent, honest man but one who had been drawn into the tangled web of "correct" society and its standards. Nekhlúdoff began to see the same principle at work in all official circles: condemn some who might be innocent in order to be assured of catching the truly guilty.

Back in Moscow, Nekhlúdoff went to see Katúsha to have her sign a petition to the emperor. During his visit he felt love taking hold of him once more. Katúsha also loved Nekhlúdoff, but she felt that marriage to a woman like herself would be bad for him.

While Nekhlúdoff was preparing for his journey to Siberia with Katúsha, he began to study and to think about the nature of criminal law. Although he began to read much on the subject, he could not find the answer to his desire to know by what right some people punish others. He also began to feel that the only reasonable kinds of punishment were corporal and capital, which were unfortunate but at least effective, while imprisonment was simply unfortunate.

On the long march to Siberia, Nekhlú- doff followed the prisoners and saw Ka- túsha whenever possible. He also saw the horrible conditions of the exiles. Nekhlú- doff began to have a new love for Ka- túsha, a feeling composed of tenderness and pity. He also learned to understand the point of view of the revolutionists, since Katúsha had been allowed to travel with the political prisoners. One of these, Valdemar Símonson, fell in love with Katúsha. He told Nekhlúdoff that he wished to marry the girl but that she wanted Nekhlúdoff to decide for her. Nekhlúdoff said that he would be pleased to know that Katúsha was well cared for. When she learned of his answer, Katúsha would not speak to Nekhlúdoff.

At a remote town in Eastern Siberia, Nekhlúdoff collected his mail and learned that Katúsha's sentence to hard labor had been commuted to exile in a less remote region of Siberia. When he went to tell Katúsha the news, he realized how much he wanted to have a family. Katúsha said that she preferred to stay with Si- monson; however, she refused to say that she loved him. She told Nekhlúdoff that he would have to live his own life.

Nekhlúdoff felt that he was not needed any longer and that his affair with Ka- túsha was ended. He saw that evil existed because those who tried to correct it were themselves evil, and that society had per- severed, not because of systems of pun- ishments, but because of human pity and love. Because he realized that the Sermon on the Mount could indeed be a practical law, that night Nekhlúdoff's new life be- gan.

# THE RETURN

Type of work: Novel
Author: Walter de la Mare (1873-1956)
Type of plot: Fantasy
Time of plot: Nineteenth century
Locale: England
First published: 1910

Principal characters:
ARTHUR LAWFORD, a middle-aged Englishman
SHEILA, his wife
ALICE, their teen-age daughter
THE REVEREND BETHANY, a rector
HERBERT HERBERT, a bookish recluse
GRISEL HERBERT, his sister

## Critique:

As a literary apprentice, Walter de la Mare took himself into a world of fancy, in an effort to escape the dull world about him. He became a master in writing fiction and poetry that carry his readers into a no-man's land of knowledge somewhere between the real and the unreal. He took this area consciously, believing that it is modern man's one hope of escaping from excessive realism. This novel, written early in his career, is a splendid example of de la Mare's use of the imaginative experience as a reality more profound than the ordinary, unimaginative variety. De la Mare has been severely criticized for not indulging himself in a more prevalent temper, that of literary realism, but his own forte has been recognized by a sufficient number of discriminating adult readers and by a sympathetic government, which gave him a pension in 1908 because of his contributions to serious literature.

## The Story:

Late one September evening Arthur Lawford, who was recovering from an attack of influenza, was walking in an ancient churchyard. There he found the grave of a man named Nicholas Sabathier, who had killed himself in 1739. Suddenly tired, Lawford stopped to rest and fell asleep. When he awoke, he felt very strange and quite recovered from his illness. Indeed, he felt so well that he practically ran home.

Going up to his room to dress for dinner, Lawford lit a candle and prepared to shave. He stopped in horror when he saw that his whole physical being had changed; he was now lean-faced and dark, an entirely different person. The only thing that could have happened, he thought, was that his nap in the churchyard had changed him into someone else, perhaps the occupant of the grave, Sabathier. Still thankful that he retained his own mind, Lawford tried to think what to do. As he stood undecided, his wife came to call him to dinner. When she came into the room, she was horrified and refused at first to believe the person she saw was her husband.

The Lawfords called in the rector, the Reverend Bethany, who was also horrified. He was willing to believe, however, that something had happened to Lawford and that the person he saw was no impostor. The three decided to wait until a week had passed before doing anything drastic.

Sheila Lawford refused to stay with her husband at night; he seemed too much a stranger to her in his new shape. She tried to get him to remain in his room, but he found it necessary to go out in the evening. On one of his rambles at dusk he met an old woman who had been a schoolfriend of his mother's. She failed to recognize him in his new shape, even though he prompted her by telling her where she had known his mother. She did say he looked somewhat like the late Mrs. Lawford.

On another of his rambles, this time back to the same churchyard, Lawford met a strange man named Herbert Herbert. They talked over the grave of Nicholas Sabathier, and Lawford hinted at his own history. Herbert seemed interested and asked Lawford to come to tea the following day. When they shook hands to part, light fell on Lawford's face for the first time. As it did, Herbert gave an obvious start.

When Lawford went to tea the next day, Herbert told him that his was the face of Nicholas Sabathier, whose picture was in a book Herbert owned. The book also contained an autobiography of Sabathier which revealed him as a man very fond of women. Tea was served by Grisel Herbert, the host's sister. Seeing the look of fear on Lawford's face when he left, she ran after him with the book her brother had mentioned. The two went for a walk, during which Lawford felt that he wrestled with an alien spirit and won out over it.

Alice, Arthur's daughter, returned home from school. When she accidentally met her father, the shock caused her to faint. Her mother tried to make her believe it was someone else, a doctor. Alice went to her father in secret and told him that she knew him and hoped all would turn out well in the end. Sheila, after several arguments with her changed husband, finally decided to go away for a few days, leaving Lawford alone in the big house to wrestle with his problem. Although he hoped to throw off the spirit that had taken possession of him, he feared that it might conquer him entirely.

Lonely after his wife had gone, Law-

ford turned to the Herberts, of whom neither the rector nor anyone else had previously heard. He spent several days and nights with his new friends. Lawford felt that he was getting better, that he was conquering whatever had taken hold of him. Grisel seemed especially helpful.

One night Lawford went back to the house alone. There he had fearful dreams and once again had a spiritual battle with something he could not name. The following day he went to see the Herberts, who took him on a picnic. They walked many miles until, as they came over a hill, Lawford saw a village. The village awakened strange memories in him, horrible memories. He turned to Grisel and told her that she knew what memories they were; she made no denial.

The next day Grisel and Lawford went out together for a long walk, during which they revealed their mutual feeling that they had come to love each other, as they felt, in another life. It seemed as if through them Nicholas Sabathier and a woman he loved were talking to one another. At last Grisel told Lawford that he was pursuing a dream that could never reach reality. They returned to the Herberts' house, where Grisel told her brother, who seemed not in the least surprised, that Nicholas Sabathier had come to say goodbye for a while. They made their farewells. Lawford, somewhat returning to himself, remarked that he had never appreciated life before his strange adventure.

Lawford went back to his own house. It was locked. Going in quietly, he listened to a conversation between his wife and some friends she had entrusted with the secret of his change. The friends, in spite of what her eyes had seen, and which one of them had also seen, plus the picture and account of Sabathier, which Sheila had found in the house, refused to believe what had happened. They advised her to have him placed in an asylum as mad or else into prison as an impostor. Lawford, standing in the hall, overheard the whole conversation. When they left, he remained, still silent, in the house.

That evening was the eve of St. Michael and All Angels, the same night on which Nicholas Sabathier had killed himself in 1739. As he sat in the quiet house, Lawford felt himself returning to his original condition. Unexpectedly, he was visited by the old lady whom he had met on his walk, the woman who had known his mother at school. She had come to see him in order to assure herself that the man she had met was not Lawford. This evening she immediately recognized him as her schoolfriend's son, with almost no resemblance to the stranger who had accosted her. When she left, she made some ambiguous remarks which left Lawford wondering if she had not, in some fashion, learned more than she revealed. At any rate, he decided that he was sufficiently himself once more to write to his wife and let her know of the change. He sat down to write, but because of what he had overheard earlier in the evening he was unable to put into words what he wanted to say. Fatigued, he fell asleep over the table.

As Lawford slept, the rector came into the room, recognized him as his own parishioner again, and sat down to watch over the sleeping man. Before long the rector was also sound asleep.

# THE RETURN OF THE NATIVE

*Type of work:* Novel
*Author:* Thomas Hardy (1840-1928)
*Type of plot:* Romantic tragedy
*Time of plot:* Mid-nineteenth century
*Locale:* Egdon Heath, in southern England
*First published:* 1878

Principal characters:
DIGGORY VENN, a reddleman
DAMON WILDEVE, proprietor of the Quiet Woman Inn
THOMASIN YEOBRIGHT, betrothed to Wildeve
MRS. YEOBRIGHT, Thomasin's guardian
CLYM YEOBRIGHT, Mrs. Yeobright's son
EUSTACIA VYE, a designing woman

## Critique:

In this novel Thomas Hardy created two strong and opposing forces: Egdon Heath, a somber tract of wasteland symbolic of an impersonal fate, and Eustacia Vye, a beautiful young woman representing the opposing human element. Throughout the book Eustacia struggles against the Heath, but in vain. Of course, her failure to overcome her environment would seem to prove Hardy's view that man is not the master of his fate. But in attempting to minimize the importance of the individual in this life, Hardy has created in the character of Eustacia Vye a person of great strength and marked individuality. Indeed, the reader, contemplating her, feels that Eustacia herself, not fate alone, is responsible for her tragic end.

## The Story:

Egdon Heath was a gloomy wasteland in southern England. Against this majestic but solemn, brooding background a small group of people were to work out their tragic drama in the impersonal presence of nature.

Fifth of November bonfires were glowing in the twilight as Diggory Venn, the reddleman, drove his van across the Heath. Tired and ill, Thomasin Yeobright lay in the rear of his van. She was a young girl whom Diggory loved, but she had rejected his proposal in order to marry Damon Wildeve, proprietor of the Quiet Woman Inn. Now Diggory was carrying the girl to her home at

Blooms-End. The girl had gone to marry Wildeve in a nearby town, but the ceremony had not taken place because of an irregularity in the license. Shocked and shamed, Thomasin had asked her old sweetheart, Diggory, to take her home.

Mrs. Yeobright, Thomasin's aunt and guardian, heard the story from the reddleman. Concerned for the girl's welfare, she decided that the wedding should take place as soon as possible. Mrs. Yeobright had good cause to worry, for Wildeve's intentions were not wholly honorable. Later in the evening, after Wildeve had assured the Yeobrights, rather casually, that he intended to go through with his promise, his attention was turned to a bonfire blazing on Mistover Knap. There old Cap'n Vye lived with his beautiful granddaughter, Eustacia. At dusk the girl had started a fire on the Heath as a signal to her lover, Wildeve, to come to her. Though he had intended to break with Eustacia, he decided to obey her summons.

Eustacia, meanwhile, was waiting for Wildeve in the company of young Johnny Nunsuch. When Wildeve threw a pebble in the pond to announce his arrival, Eustacia told Johnny to go home. The meeting between Wildeve and Eustacia was unsatisfactory for both. He complained that she gave him no peace. She, in turn, resented his desertion. Meanwhile Johnny Nunsuch, frightened by strange lights he saw on the Heath, went back to Mistover Knap to ask Eustacia to let her servant accompany him home, but he kept silent when he came upon Eustacia and Wildeve. Retracing his steps, he stumbled into a sand pit where stood the reddleman's van. From the boy, Diggory learned of the meeting between Eustacia and Wildeve. Later, he overheard Eustacia declare her hatred of the Heath to Wildeve, who asked her to run away with him to America. Her reply was vague, but the reddleman decided to see Eustacia without delay to beg her to let Thomasin have Wildeve.

Diggory's visit to Eustacia was fruitless. He then approached Mrs. Yeobright, declared again his love for her niece, and offered to marry Thomasin. Mrs. Yeobright refused the reddleman's offer because she felt that the girl should marry Wildeve. She confronted the innkeeper with vague references to another suitor, with the result that Wildeve's interest in Thomasin awakened once more.

Shortly afterward Mrs. Yeobright's son, Clym, returned from Paris, and a welcome-home party gave Eustacia the chance to view this stranger about whom she had heard so much. Uninvited, she went to the party disguised as one of the mummers. Clym was fascinated by this interesting and mysterious young woman disguised as a man. Eustacia dreamed of marrying Clym and going with him to Paris. She even broke off with Wildeve, who, stung by her rejection, promptly married Thomasin to spite Eustacia.

Clym Yeobright decided not to go back to France. Instead he planned to open a school. Mrs. Yeobright strongly opposed her son's decision. When Clym learned that Eustacia had been stabbed in church by a woman who thought that Eustacia was bewitching her children, his decision to educate these ignorant people was strengthened. Much against his mother's wishes, Clym visited Eustacia's home to ask her to teach in his school. Eustacia refused because she hated the Heath and the country peasants, but as the result of his visit Clym fell completely in love with the beautiful but heartless Eustacia.

Mrs. Yeobright blamed Eustacia for Clym's wish to stay on the Heath. When bitter feeling grew between mother and son, he decided to leave home. His marriage to Eustacia made the break complete. Later Mrs. Yeobright relented somewhat and gave a neighbor, Christian Cantle, a sum of money to be delivered in equal portions to Clym and Thomasin. Christian foolishly lost the money to Wildeve in a game of dice. Fortunately, Diggory won the money from Wildeve, but, thinking that all of it belonged to Thomasin, he gave it to her. Mrs. Yeobright knew that Wildeve had duped Christian. She did not know that the reddleman had won the money away from the innkeeper, and she mistakenly supposed that Wildeve had given the money to Eustacia. Meeting Eustacia, she asked the girl if she had received any money from Wildeve. Eustacia was enraged by the question and in the course of her reply to Mrs. Yeobright's charge she said that she would never have condescended to marry Clym had she known that she would have to remain on the Heath. The two women parted angrily.

Eustacia's unhappiness was increased by Clym's near-blindness, a condition brought on by too much reading, for she feared that this meant she would never get to Paris. When Clym became a woodcutter, Eustacia's feeling of degradation was complete. Bored with her life, she went by herself one evening to a gipsying. There she accidentally met Wildeve and again felt an attachment for him. Seeing Eustacia and Wildeve together, the reddleman told Mrs. Yeobright of the meeting and begged her to make peace with Eustacia for Clym's sake. She agreed to try.

But Mrs. Yeobright's walk at noon across the hot, dry Heath to see her son and daughter-in-law proved fatal. When she arrived in sight of Clym's house, she saw her son from a distance as he entered the front door. Then, while she rested on a knoll near the house, she saw another man entering, but she was too far away to recognize Wildeve. After resting for twenty minutes, Mrs. Yeobright went on to Clym's cottage and knocked. No one came to the door. Heartbroken by what she considered a rebuff by her own son, Mrs. Yeobright started home across the Heath. Overcome by exhaustion and grief, she sat down to rest and a poisonous adder bit her. She died without knowing that inside her son's house Clym had been asleep, worn out by his morning's work. Eustacia did not go to the door because, as she later explained to her husband, she had thought he would answer the knock. The real reason for Eustacia's failure to go to the door was fear of the consequences, should Mrs. Yeobright find Eustacia and Wildeve together.

Clym awoke with the decision to visit his mother. Starting out across the Heath toward her house, he stumbled over her body. His grief was tempered by bewilderment over the reason for her being on the Heath at that time. When Clym discovered that Eustacia had failed to let his mother in and that Wildeve had been in the cottage, he ordered Eustacia out of his house. She went quietly because she felt in part responsible for Mrs. Yeobright's death.

Eustacia took refuge in her grandfather's house, where a faithful servant thwarted her in an attempt to commit suicide. In utter despair over her own wretched life and over the misery she had caused others, Eustacia turned to Wildeve, who had unexpectedly inherited eleven thousand pounds and who still wanted her to run away with him. One night she left her grandfather's house in order to keep a prearranged meeting with the innkeeper, but in her departure she failed to receive a letter of reconciliation which Thomasin had persuaded Clym to send to her. On her way to keep her rendezvous with Wildeve she lost her way in the inky blackness of the Heath and either fell accidentally or jumped into a small lake, and was drowned. Wildeve, who happened to be near the lake when she fell in, jumped in to save her and was drowned also.

(Originally *The Return of the Native* ended with the death of Eustacia and of Wildeve; but in order to satisfy his romantic readers, in a later edition Hardy made additions to the story. The faithful Diggory married Thomasin. Clym, unable to abolish ignorance and superstition on the Heath by teaching, became in the end an itinerant preacher.)

# THE REVENGE OF BUSSY D'AMBOIS

*Type of work:* Drama
*Author:* George Chapman (c. 1559-1634)
*Type of plot:* Tragedy of blood
*Time of plot:* Sixteenth century
*Locale:* Paris
*First presented:* c. 1610

> Principal characters:
> CLERMONT D'AMBOIS, brother of Bussy d'Ambois, a soldier of fortune recently murdered
> BALIGNY, Clermont's brother-in-law
> CHARLOTTE, Clermont's sister
> MONTSURRY, Bussy's murderer
> TAMYRA, his wife
> THE DUKE OF GUISE
> HENRY III, King of France
> MAILLARD, Baligny's lieutenant

## Critique:

The Revenge of Bussy d'Ambois is a portrait of Chapman's ideal tragic hero. All other elements of the play are subordinated to the revelation of the character and philosophy of Clermont d'Ambois. Clermont, with his stoic idealism, is indeed an interesting and compelling figure. Unfortunately, however, his character is not one that lends itself well to the dramatic situation. He is essentially a man of reflection, not of action; he lacks the tragic flaw upon which the plot might be developed. As a result, Chapman wrote a superb character study, but a poor drama.

## The Story:

Clermont d'Ambois had vowed to avenge the murder of his brother. Although he doubted the virtue of repaying violence with violence, he had made a solemn promise to Bussy's ghost. His sister Charlotte, unambiguous in her feelings, was impatient for immediate revenge, and her marriage to Baligny had been made under the stipulation that he, too, pledge himself to effect the death of Montsurry, Bussy's murderer. Tamyra, the wife of Montsurry and former mistress of Bussy, had returned to her husband, but she made no secret of her hatred of him and her desire for his death. But the design of these people was obstructed by the cowardly Montsurry, who had barricaded himself in his home.

Clermont, who insisted on a fair duel and who would allow no one else to discharge his duty, had instructed Baligny to deliver his challenge. Baligny's entrance to Montsurry's home was accomplished with the help of a decayed nobleman, the Marquess Renel. Renel, visiting Montsurry on business, bribed the guards to admit Baligny. When Baligny entered, Montsurry was terrified and refused to accept the proffered challenge. Baligny left the challenge with Tamyra, who promised to make her husband read it.

This plot was not the only one in which Baligny was involved. A treacherous man, he based his actions on the belief that troubles for others meant blessings for himself. Wearing a different mask for every acquaintance, he was able to gain men's confidence and thus discover their dissatisfactions and sow the seeds of further discontent. In dealing with King Henry III, he expounded the doctrine that any evil done out of loyalty to a king was justified. Such a philosophy being agreeable to King Henry, Baligny had become his trusted agent. In talking to the Duke of Guise, on the other hand, he expressed the belief that conspiracy was sometimes defensible.

The principal object of jealousy in the court at this time was the Guise faction.

King Henry was fearful and jealous of the increasing influence of the Duke of Guise, and Baligny strove to increase his distrust. Guise's closest friend was Clermont d'Ambois, whom Guise not only admired but endeavored to emulate. He saw in Clermont a valor equal to Bussy's and, more important, a profound knowledge of life. Clermont's principles of restraint, unworldliness, and stoic acceptance guided the actions of the powerful duke. Because of the close relationship between the two men, jealousy of Guise was often extended to include Clermont. Thus Baligny was able to convince King Henry of the advantage of getting rid of Clermont. He suggested that Clermont be invited to visit Cambrai and there, away from his friends at court, be arrested.

Baligny induced Clermont to go to Cambrai on the pretext of reviewing a muster of the king's troops. In his conversation with Clermont, Baligny attempted to weaken Clermont's tie with Guise by criticizing the latter for his part in the St. Bartholomew Massacre. But Clermont was one man on whom the schemer's efforts were wasted because he was convinced of Guise's virtue.

While Clermont was being entertained by his sister in Cambrai, he received an anonymous letter informing him of the betrayal and of Baligny's complicity in it. Refusing to think evil of his sister's husband, he dismissed the letter as false. Charlotte, who could think of little but avenging Bussy's death, regarded the message as an effort further to enfeeble Clermont's weak will in carrying out his duty.

Maillard, Baligny's lieutenant, had been instructed by the king to apprehend Clermont. When Maillard came to Charlotte's house, ostensibly for the purpose of accompanying Clermont on a tour, the latter asked him if he were charged to arrest him. Maillard's obvious signs of guilt convinced Clermont that earlier presentiments he had felt about the journey had been justified. Clermont offered to let Maillard take him peacefully, but Maillard denied that any intrigue was afoot. Although quite certain of the consequences, Clermont, with characteristic acceptance of fate, followed Maillard.

It was planned that Clermont be taken while he was reviewing the troops. Two soldiers disguised as lackeys were to lead him into an ambush, where several men would seize him. But Clermont's strength exceeded even the estimate of his attackers. The disguised soldiers succeeded only in unhorsing him. Afoot, he easily beat them off and drove straight through the ambush. He ran until, exhausted, he fell to the earth and was captured.

Believing that outer circumstances had no power to touch the inner man without his will, he accepted his capture with little concern. His only worry was that he would be unable to keep an appointment with his mistress, the Countess of Cambrai, and his one request was that a message be sent to her. Other people, however, did not accept his internment with so much complacency. Upon receiving his message, the countess sent him jewels that she hoped would effect his release and vowed that she would cry until her eyes poured out. When the Duke of Guise heard the news, he rushed to King Henry and spoke so passionately and eloquently of Clermont's virtues that the weak-willed king, unable to answer Guise, ordered that Clermont be released.

After his release Clermont went to the house of the Duke of Guise. There he again met Bussy's ghost, who chided him for not having exacted the revenge. Guise, who had been implicated in Bussy's murder, felt that the ghost should thunder threats against him, but Clermont asserted that the duke had fully compensated for his error. Guise was also worried about a plot against him; he believed that his efforts at propagating the Catholic cause were endangered. Clermont wanted him to retire from his plans, but Guise regarded withdrawal as an abandonment of France.

A plot was indeed threatening the Duke of Guise; King Henry, with Baligny's encouragement, had ordered his murder. The king, in addition to his long-standing jealousy of Guise, had been angered at having his hand forced over Clermont. As the duke was on his way to visit the king, Henry's men stepped from behind an arras and killed him.

With the assistance of Tamyra, Clermont gained access to Montsurry's house. There he found Charlotte, disguised as a man. She had planned to kill Montsurry herself but had been stopped by the ghost. When Clermont drew his sword, Montsurry at first refused to defend himself and did so only after Clermont offered to let Tamyra stab him. Although Montsurry at last gained sufficient courage to conduct himself courageously in the duel, Clermont succeeded in killing him. Soon after Clermont had fulfilled his duty to his brother, he received the news that the Duke of Guise had been killed by the king's men. The death of his friend and patron was a severe blow to Clermont, whose life had been centered around his relationship with the powerful duke. Believing that his purpose in this world was now destroyed, he took his own life.

# THE REVENGER'S TRAGEDY

*Type of work:* Drama
*Author:* Cyril Tourneur (c. 1575-1626)
*Type of plot:* Tragedy of blood
*Time of plot:* The Renaissance
*Locale:* A city in Italy
*First presented:* c. 1607

Principal characters:
VENDICE, the revenger, often disguised as Piato
HIPPOLITO, his brother, sometimes called Carlo
CASTIZA, their sister, a near victim of Lussurioso's lust
GRATIANA, their mother, a widow
THE DUKE, the lecherous ruler of an Italian principality
LUSSURIOSO, his legitimate son
SPURIO, his illegitimate son
THE DUCHESS, his recent bride
AMBITIOSO,
SUPERVACUO, and
THE THIRD SON, the Duchess' sons by an earlier marriage
ANTONIO, an Italian nobleman, the Duke's final successor.

## Critique:

There has been considerable scholarly wrangling over the relative dates and even the authorship of the two plays associated with the name of Cyril Tourneur; but today they are both ascribed to him, and *The Revenger's Tragedy* is held to be the earlier. The tragedy of blood, with its themes of betrayal and revenge, had its vogue during the entire Elizabethan period beginning with Kyd's *The Spanish Tragedy* as far back as 1585, and helped bring about the closing of the theaters in 1642. With Webster, Tourneur represents the final stage of this dramatic genre. The plot of this play is melodramatic; murder is piled upon murder and horror upon horror to a point at which the reader is driven either to revulsion or to a refusal to take the play seriously. Yet the overdrawn plot is redeemed by the splendor of the language. John Addington Symonds described *The Revenger's Tragedy* as "an entangled web of lust, incest, fratricide, rape, adultery, mutual suspicion, hate, and bloodshed, through which runs, like a thread of glittering copper, the vengeance of a cynical plague-fretted spirit."

## The Story:

As the Duke, accompanied by his new wife and his two sons, passed through the city in the glare of torches, they were watched by Vendice, the revenger. In his hand he carried the skull of his dead betrothed, poisoned by the Duke when she had resisted his lecherous advances. To the hate engendered by this horrible murder had been added further incentive to revenge: the death of Vendice's father at the hands of this same decadent ruler. Now his brother Hippolito added fresh fuel to the flame by reporting that he had been asked by Lussurioso, the Duke's heir and a man as depraved as his father, to employ a procurer in order to ensnare their sister Castiza. Vendice's nimble brain at once saw the possibility of revenge in this situation; he disguised himself, took on the role of a panderer, and was presented to Lussurioso under the name of Piato, thus gaining access to the ducal household.

The sons of the newly married Duchess were as evil as their stepbrothers. The youngest had recently raped the wife of Antonio, a highly respected nobleman, and that poor lady had committed suicide. But when the young villain was brought to trial and sentenced, the Duke put off his execution and merely ordered that he be kept in prison. His older brothers promised to find a way to help him escape. Meanwhile, their depraved mother was revealing her love for Spurio, the Duke's illegitimate son and a man who hated his father for his own illegitimate birth. He accepted the Duchess' advances, since adultery with her would avenge him on his father.

In pursuance of his plan, Vendice undertook Lussurioso's commission, and, still disguised, went to tempt the virtue of his sister Castiza. His delight was great when she spurned Lussurioso's suit, but this delight was soon turned to horror when their mother tried to persuade her daughter to yield. Vendice rightly felt that, were it not for gold and women, there would be no damnation.

Having returned to the palace with news of his mission, Vendice found out from Hippolito that the Duchess and Spurio had been seen together and were planning an assignation for that very night. Taking quick advantage of this news, he informed Lussurioso; the latter, ostensibly eager to protect his father's honor but really wishing to get rid of his hated half-brother, went with Vendice to the Duke's bedchamber and stabbed the man sleeping in the bed with the Duchess. This man, however, proved to be the Duke himself and not Spurio. But the surprise was to Vendice's advantage, for Lussurioso, whose blows had not killed the Duke, was led to prison under sentence of death.

The Duchess' sons, eager to eliminate their stepbrothers, attempted the trick of urging the Duke to mercy, in the expectation that their pleas would have the opposite effect. The crafty ruler, however, saw through their game and surprised them by granting their request and sending them to release Lussurioso. But Ambitioso and Supervacuo determined to reverse the Duke's orders and then pretend that their errand of mercy had been too late. What they did not know was that Lussurioso had already been released through a prior order of the Duke's. When they informed the gaoler that it was the Duke's command that "their

brother" was to die, the gaoler, having now only the Duchess' youngest son in custody, naturally executed him. Thus the first of the villains was disposed of.

Meanwhile, Vendice's plot was going forward apace. The Duke had commanded him, still in the disguise of the panderer Piato, to bring him a woman in some secluded spot. Knowing that the Duchess and Spurio were to meet in a lodge in the palace grounds, Vendice selected this spot and brought to it the skull of his betrothed decked out, in some manner, in rich attire. On the fleshless mouth of the skull he had smeared the same poison that the Duke had used to kill her. In a scene of unmitigated horror, the Duke kissed the poisoned skull; his own teeth and mouth were consumed by the vitriol, while Vendice and Hippolito, holding their daggers against him, compelled him to spend his last agonized moments of life in watching the meeting of his wife and his illegitimate son. So the second stage of the revenge was finished.

Before the meeting with his supposed mistress-to-be, the Duke had given word that he was riding off on an undisclosed journey; hence no one knew where he was nor made an attempt to find him. Lussurioso, meanwhile, had resolved to dismiss Piato, whom he had come to regard as an inefficient panderer, and he ordered Hippolito, whom he knew to have a brother unknown to the court, to bribe that brother to kill Piato. Thus Vendice was in the strange position of being hired to murder himself. Again his quick wit saw how advantage could be taken of this fantastic situation: he and Hippolito resolved to dress the still undiscovered body of the Duke in the clothes discarded by Piato; a dagger thrust into the corpse would then account for the Duke's death. While this macabre scheme was in preparation, they had their family affairs to settle—that was, to punish their mother because she had urged their sister to yield to Lussurioso. But they were so moved by her sincere repentance that they spared her life and returned to the ducal palace to complete their plot.

The Duke's corpse, now dressed in the old clothes of Piato, was still lying in the lodge. It was the brothers' plan to show it to Lussurioso, tell him the manner of his father's death, and then kill him. But Lussurioso spoiled the plan by coming, not alone as they had expected, but with a group of courtiers. So the best they could do was to point out the form of the supposed Piato lying on a couch, say that he was drunk, and then stab him on Lussurioso's command. The son immediately discovered the true identity of the corpse, but was sufficiently deceived to absolve the brothers of any guilt in his father's death. He was hardly grief-stricken, for this death made him the duke. He gave three orders as the new ruler: to search for Piato, the suspected murderer; to hold revels in honor of his accession to the title; and to banish the Duchess. After he had left the lodge, the Duchess' two remaining sons resolved to take advantage of the revels to murder him.

Vendice, Hippolito, and other disaffected nobles also determined to take advantage of the revels and to do away with the new ruler. Having heard that a masque was to be a part of the entertainment, they planned to copy the masquers' costumes and, having thus got into the hall of state, to assassinate Lussurioso. As the duke and his nobles sat at a table and argued over the ominous portent of a comet blazing in the sky, Vendice, Hippolito and two other lords, in the fantastic costumes of masquers, entered and performed their dance. At its conclusion they drew their swords and killed Lussurioso and his companions.

Hardly had they left the scene when Ambitioso, Supervacuo, Spurio, and a fourth noble came into the hall, dressed in the same costumes and bent upon the same bloody errand. Finding Lussurioso and his companions already dead, the would-be murderers fell out among themselves over the succession to the dukedom, and Spurio killed Ambitioso, only to fall himself at the hand of the noble who had accompanied them. When Antonio and the guards burst in, they naturally assumed that the masquers whom they found there had been the murderers, nor could the surviving lord convince them otherwise. But Lussurioso was not yet quite dead. It was his dying voice that had summoned Antonio, and now he had to undergo the last agony of having Vendice whisper in his ear the full story of the revenge.

The ducal line having now been wiped out, Antonio was proclaimed the ruler. It was now that Vendice's bitter wit betrayed him; he could not resist telling the new duke that he and his brother had been the avengers. Instantly Antonio ordered them to execution, not wishing to condone their actions even though he had benefited from them. Further, he knew that the men who had murdered the old Duke and his family might well murder him. Vendice accepted his sentence calmly; his task was accomplished, and it was time for him to die.

# THE REVOLT OF THE ANGELS

Type of work: Novel
Author: Anatole France (Jacques Anatole Thibault, 1844-1924)
Type of plot: Fantasy
Time of plot: Early twentieth century
Locale: France
First published: 1914

Principal characters:
MAURICE D'ESPARVIEU, a lazy young man
ARCADE, his guardian angel
MONSIEUR JULIEN SARIETTE, a librarian
MADAME GILBERTE DES AUBELS, Maurice's mistress

Critique:

Anatole France was a revolutionary. Opposed to the Church and the state, he wrote many bitter novels ridiculing those institutions. The Revolt of the Angels is one of the most abusive satires of this century. It is a fantasy, telling the story of an angel who read so widely in the field of science that he lost his faith in God. He aroused thousands of angels, and they planned to take over the Kingdom of Heaven for Satan. In this satire France attacked almost every established institution in the world, but in his desire to ridicule he often sacrificed sincerity and thus effectiveness. His greatest personal conviction, as reflected in this satire, was his love for and his faith in the little people of the world. This factor is the greatest positive quality of the novel.

The Story:

Because their fabulous library was so large and valuable, the d'Esparvieu family employed Monsieur Julien Sariette to look after the three hundred thousand volumes. The books were the most precious charge that Sariette had ever had, and he guarded them as if they were jewels. There were rare first editions, some with notations in the handwriting of famous men of history. There were several unpublished manuscripts written on sheepskins and sycamore tablets. It was no more difficult to steal an emerald than to borrow one of those precious books or manuscripts from Sariette.

One morning he entered the library to find many of the books in complete disorder. Some of the finest specimens were among the desecrated books, and for a time the old librarian could not comprehend what his eyes saw. But he was even more disturbed when he realized that some of the books were gone. When he reported the theft to his master, he was told that he had probably left them lying carelessly around. Sariette was completely upset.

For more than two months the thefts continued. Locks were changed, and a detective was employed, but all precautions failed. Sariette hid himself in the library one night, and what he saw there frightened him more than ever. He had fallen asleep. When he awoke, he saw that the room was filled with a queer, phosphorescent light. A book he held in his hand opened, and he could not close it. When he tried to force it shut, the book leaped up and struck him over the head, knocking him unconscious.

From that time on Sariette could neither sleep nor eat. He was at the point of insanity when young Maurice d'Esparvieu, who lived in the garden pavilion and who had not heard of the losses, asked him why so many of the books from the library were piled in his rooms. Sariette rushed to the pavilion.

THE REVOLT OF THE ANGELS by Anatole France. Translated by Mrs. Wilfrid Jackson. By permission of the publishers, Dodd, Mead & Co., Inc. Copyright, 1914, by Dodd, Mead & Co., Inc. Renewed, 1942, by Mrs. Wilfrid Jackson.

There lay his precious books, scattered around but all complete. He carefully carried them back into the house and put them on the shelves again.

The books continued to disappear each night and appear in the pavilion the next morning. Sariette knew no more than he did before. One day a fine talcum scattered on the floor revealed a strange footprint. Some thought it the print of a fairy, others that of a small, dainty woman.

While these events were disrupting the peace of the d'Esparvieu household, Maurice was having a love affair with Madame Gilberte des Aubels. While she was visiting him in his pavilion one evening, they were startled by the sight of a nude man who suddenly appeared. Gilberte, thinking him a burglar, offered him her money and jewels, but the stranger announced in a calm voice that he was Arcade, Maurice's guardian angel. He explained his appearance by telling them that angels could take human form when they pleased. He had come to the earth at Maurice's birth, but had remained invisible, as all good guardian angels do. Because Maurice was a lazy young man, Arcade had found time heavy on his hands, and he had gone into the d'Esparvieu library to find something to read. He had studied the great books on philosophy, theology, and science, and the scientific approach to the creation of the universe had impressed him so much that he had decided to assume human form and lead the angels into revolt against God.

In his explanation to Gilberte and Maurice he acknowledged that God existed, but he denied that He was the creator of the universe. Arcade now considered God, or Ialdabaoth, as He was called in Heaven, as only one of the strong men of that kingdom. Ialdabaoth and Satan had battled for the supremacy of that beautiful and rich land, and Ialdabaoth had won. Now there were many other angels on earth who had also assumed human form, thus disobeying Ialdabaoth, and they too were ready to revolt. Arcade was determined to join the rebel angels and lead them to victory against Ialdabaoth.

Gilberte and Maurice were shocked They begged Arcade to renounce his wicked ways and return to God, but he was firm in his decision. Not wishing to leave his angel in a nude state, Maurice secured some clothes for him before Arcade left the pavilion.

Arcade found many revolutionary angels to plan with him for the final battle. There was Prince Istar, the chemist, who spent his time manufacturing bombs. Zita was a female angel, as willing to go to war as any of the males. Théophile was not a revolutionary and did not want to go to war against Ialdabaoth. Théophile was a fallen angel who had succumbed to the lust he felt for a mortal woman, but he still believed in God and would not join in plans for the revolt. While they were gathering recruits, most of the angels enjoyed the pursuits of mortal men. Many of them took lovers; Arcade seduced Gilberte in Maurice's pavilion, after Maurice had brought the angel home with him. Arcade tried to enlist the help of Sophar, an angel who had become a Jewish banker named Max Everdingen, but Sophar would not give them money for the revolution. He offered to sell them munitions, however, and to finance the purchases at his bank.

While the angels were preparing for the final attack, Gilberte and Maurice continued their affair, for Maurice had forgiven Arcade and Gilberte. Sariette, among his books, was happy because Arcade, busy with the revolution, no longer stole the precious volumes. But through a mishap, *Lucretius*, one of the most precious of the rare editions, was taken from the library and lost. This final blow drove Sariette to madness.

At last all was in readiness for the revolt. Hundreds of thousands of rebel angels joined Arcade and presented themselves to Satan, asking him to lead them into the battle against Ialdabaoth. Satan asked them to wait until the next day for his answer. That night he had a dream. He dreamed that he led the rebels against Ialdabaoth, and that they were victorious. Satan was crowned king, and he banished Ialdabaoth as He had banished Satan millions of years ago. But Satan dreamed that as he received the praises of mankind and the angels, he became like the other God, Ialdabaoth, and lost his sympathy for humanity.

Satan awoke from his dream, and called the leaders of the angels around him. He told them that they would not conquer Heaven, that one war always brings on another because the vanquished seek constantly to regain what they have lost. He told them that he did not want to be God, that he loved the earth and wanted to stay on earth and help his fellow men. And he told the angels that they had done much already to destroy God on earth, for they had been slowly destroying ignorance and superstitions concerning the false religion taught by God. Satan told the angels to stay on earth to spread the doctrine of love and kindness; in this way they would triumph over God and bring peace to heaven and earth.

# THE REVOLT OF THE MASSES

*Type of work:* Essay on political science
*Author:* José Ortega y Gasset (1883-1955)
*First published:* 1930

Among the few modern Spaniards known beyond his national boundaries is Ortega y Gasset, professor of metaphysics, literary critic and journalist, and a representative of the school that believes in the rule of an intellectual aristocracy or small group of superior men, not the privileged caste of the old feudal nobility.

Born in Madrid, José Ortega y Gasset sought in Malaga the thorough training of a Jesuit college, then took his doctorate in philosophy at the Central University of Madrid in 1904. Further study in Germany preceded his teaching career in Madrid. When Rivera became dictator, Ortega, a critic of the monarchy, stopped teaching and began to write for the influential *El Sol*. In 1923 he founded the *Revista de Occidente*, the leading Spanish intellectual publication until Franco drove its editor out of Spain in 1936. Later Ortega traveled widely, lecturing in Buenos Aires, Paris, and the United States. Returning to Spain, he died in Madrid in 1955.

*The Revolt of the Masses* had its seeds in an earlier book, *España invertebrada* (1922), in an article titled "Masas" in *El Sol* (1926), and in several lectures delivered in Argentina in 1928. As he wrote in a footnote to the title of the first chapter: "My purpose now is to collect and complete what I have already said, and so to produce an organic document concerning the most important fact of our time."

Repetition and interpolated material weaken the structural unity of the book, and the colloquial style may grate on the reader before the final pages. Nevertheless, the work is seminal and provocative. Ortega advocates a European confederation with judicial and political unity, an "integration, not a lamination," of nations, ultranational rather than international, where a new liberalism and a totalitarian form will each correct the excesses of the other. The resulting equilibrium, he promises, would produce a new faith.

In his final paragraph, Ortega acknowledges that the present-day situation results from basic defects in European culture, but he postpones any consideration of that problem, and so the work is incomplete. However, for the Buenos Aires edition of 1938, Ortega added a prologue for French readers and an epilogue for English readers, in which he denied the accusation that his theme was the decadence of Spain since 1580. He is no pessimist. While he does look back on the good old days, he insists that a return to the past is impossible for modern man. Stressing the advances and improvements of today, he asserts that if anything superior is eventually evolved, it will be based on technical knowledge and liberal democracy.

Ortega's main thesis is that among human beings there are two types of individuals: the excellent or superior man, who makes demands on himself, and the common man, who is content with what he is. The development and activities of these types are shown against the perspective of Western history.

Greece and Rome evolved from rural communities and became cities. The ancients, concerned with their past, were unconscious of a future. Gradually the State came into existence, built in the Middle Ages by the feudal nobles. The State was relatively small. Ortega quotes the economist Werner Sombart for the statement that Europe, from 700 to 1800, never had a population of more than 180,000,000. Each state was directed by its superior individuals, without whom humanity would cease to preserve its essentials. The mass man accepted higher authority, and in general followed the orders of a select minority.

The first divergence came when the

bourgeoisie adopted gunpowder, which the nobles never thought of using, and with it won battles against the nobility. Eventually a middle class took over the State and made it so powerful that "state intervention" has become a symbol of danger. What were once privileges are now rights, even though the masses attack the institutions by which these rights are sanctioned.

During the nineteenth century the population of Europe rose to 460,000,-000, and part of it overflowed to settle in the Americas. In Ortega's view, however, those who look with astonishment at the rapid growth of the New World should turn their eyes to Europe, where the population increase has been even more spectacular.

Nietzsche foresaw a "flood tide of Nihilism rising." Actually, the world as it was organized during the nineteenth century automatically created a new type of man, provided with formidable appetites and powerful means of satisfying them. The nineteenth cenury left these new men to their own devices. Believing in direct action, they intervened violently in everything. Having been previously guided by others, these "barbarian products of modern civilization" determined to govern the world for and by themselves, and in their self-satisfaction, according to Ortega, they now threaten the degeneration of human culture.

In tracing the development of the mass man, Ortega repeats his assertion that the civilization of the nineteenth century can be summed up under two headings: Liberal democracy and technology. Modern technical advance represents the coöperation of Capitalism and Experimental Science. The scientist is likely to become a mass man, a primitive, since he confines his knowledge to so small an area. There was a time, the author asserts, when men could be divided into the learned and the ignorant, but today even those learned in science are frequently ignorant of the inner philosophy of the science they cultivate.

Ortega discusses historians, or "philol-ogists," as he calls them, who turn their attention to sources instead of the future. The author does not believe in absolute determinism of history, because in his view the past does not tell us what to do, but what to avoid. Life is now greater in scope than ever before, presenting a greater choice. Circumstances offer a dilemma for the mass man to decide, but he has no concept of the future. In the Mediterranean countries, where the triumph of the masses has made its greatest advance, the mass man lives for the moment, with no consideration for future existence.

Life has become world-wide in character, but time and space cannot be easily obliterated. The "purchasing power of life" has been broadened. Man believes himself capable of creation without knowing what to create. Power has brought insecurity. Liberal democracy based on technical knowledge is the highest type of public life yet known. The perfect organization of the nineteenth century gave the impression that it represented natural things, and therefore should belong to everybody; but all that it represents had earlier beginnings.

According to Ortega, bolshevism and fascism are examples of retrogression in politics, because they handle rational elements in an anti-historical, even archaic, way. Consequently, the political hope of Europe lies in contemporaneous men who abhor archaic and primitive attitudes.

Ortega does not believe in the "decadence of Europe," a legend begun by intellectuals who felt themselves stifled by their nationality and who longed to borrow from other literatures, or by politicians similarly motivated. If there should be a decadence among European nations, the result, he argues, would be the creation of a United States of Europe. There is no one else to "rule," by which Ortega means "to control public opinion." New York and Moscow represent two sections of European order. Writing in 1929, Ortega believed that Russia would need centuries before she could aspire to rule, but that she would never succeed if there was in Europe a political union with a new Western moral code and a new inspirational program of life.

In one important sense, the title of this work is misleading, in the light of recent history. The author is not referring to either actual revolt—*rebelión* is the Spanish word he uses—or the Marxian proletariat. What he had in mind was the mass man whose claim to the right to act is, in effect, a rebellion against his own destiny. Since that is what he is doing at the present time, Ortega y Gasset considered his efforts a revolt of the masses.

# REYNARD THE FOX

*Type of work:* Folk tale
*Author:* Unknown
*Type of plot:* Fable
*Time of plot:* Tenth century
*Locale:* Germany
*First transcribed:* Twelfth century

Principal characters:
    REYNARD, the fox
    NOBLE, the lion, King of Beasts
    ISEGRIM, the wolf
    TIBERT, the cat
    BRUIN, the bear
    OTHER ANIMALS AND BIRDS

## Critique:

Second in popularity only to the fables of Aesop is the old Germanic tale of *Reynard the Fox*. Originally a folk comedy, it became through the ages a subtle satire on the customs and institutions of the Middle Ages, indeed on all ages. Here we see that cunning always conquers force, that one who lives by his wits will never suffer. We grudgingly admire the villainous hero even while we hope that he will get his just punishment. The fable is undoubtedly of Oriental origin, passing into the Germanic folk tradition early in the Middle Ages. The earliest extant version is that of Heinrich der Glichesäre in the twelfth century. Goethe gave the tale its best-known form in his *Reineke Fuchs*.

## The Story:

When Noble, the great Lion-king, held court during the Feast of the Pentecost, all the animals told the king of their grievances against Reynard the Fox. The list of sins and crimes was almost as long as the list of animals present. First to complain was Isegrim the wolf, whose children had been made blind by the crafty fox. Panther told how Reynard had promised the hare that he would teach him his prayers, but when the hare had stood in front of Reynard as he was instructed, Reynard had grabbed him by the throat and tried to kill him. To Chanticleer the cock Reynard had gone disguised as a monk, saying that he would

never eat flesh again. But when Chanticleer relaxed his vigilance over his flock and believed the villain, Reynard had grabbed his children and eaten them.

So the complaints went on, with only Tibert the cat and Grimbard the brock speaking in Reynard's defense. These two reminded the king of the crimes committed by the complainers, but the king was stern; Reynard must be brought to court to answer for his sins. Bruin the bear was sent to bring the culprit in. Bruin was strong and brave, and he promised the king that he would not be fooled by Reynard's knavery or flattering tongue.

When Bruin arrived at Reynard's castle and delivered the king's message, Reynard welcomed the bear and promised to accompany him back to court. In fact, Reynard said that he wished they were already at court, for he had abstained from meat and eaten so much of a new food, called honeycombs, that his stomach was swollen and uncomfortable. Bruin fell into the trap and begged to be taken to the store of honey. Reynard pretended to be reluctant to delay their trip to court, but at last he agreed to show Bruin the honey. The wily fox led Bruin into a trap in some tree trunks, where the poor bear was set upon by humans and beaten unmercifully. He escaped with his life and sadly made his way back to court, mocked by the taunts of his betrayer.

Enraged at the insult to his personal

3200

messenger, the king sent Tibert the cat to tell Reynard to surrender himself at once, under penalty of death. But Tibert fared no better. He was tricked into jumping into a net trap by the promise of a feast on mice and rats. He too escaped and returned to the court, no longer a defender of the traitorous Reynard. The next time the king sent Grimbard the brock to bring the fox in. He too was warmly received by Reynard and his wife, and he too received Reynard's promise to accompany him to court. This time the evil fox actually kept his promise, confessing all his sins to the brock as they journeyed.

At court, Reynard was confronted by all his accusers. One by one they told of his horrible crimes against them. Reynard defended himself against them all, saying that he was a loyal and true subject of the king and the object of many lies and deceits. The king, unmoved, sentenced Reynard to death. On the gallows, the fox confessed his sins, saying that he was the more guilty because he did not steal from want since money and jewels he had in great plenty. Hearing Reynard speak of his treasure, the greedy king wanted it for himself, and he asked Reynard where the jewels were hidden. The fox said that he would gladly tell him the hiding place, for the treasure had been stolen in order to save the king's life. Crafty Reynard told a slippery story about a treasure which the other animals were going to use to depose the king and make Bruin the ruler in his place. In order to save the life of his sovereign, Reynard had stolen the treasure from the traitors and now had it in his possession. The foolish king, believing the smooth liar, ordered Reynard released from the gallows and made a favorite at court. Bruin the bear and Isegrim the wolf were arrested for high treason.

Reynard said that he himself could not show the king the treasure because he had to make a pilgrimage to Rome to ask the pope to remove a curse from him. For his journey he was given the skin of the bear and the shoes of the wolf, leaving those two fellows in terrible pain. The king then put his mail around Reynard's neck and a staff in his hand and sent him on his way. Kyward the hare and Bellin the ram accompanied Reynard on the pilgrimage. They stopped at the fox's castle to bid his wife goodbye, and there Reynard tricked the hare, killed him, and ate all but the head. That he sent back to the king by the ram, that stupid animal thinking he was carrying a letter for the monarch. The king was so furious that he gave the ram and all his lineage to the wolf and the bear to atone for the king's misjudgment of them.

Again complaints against the fox poured into the king's ear. At last he determined to lay siege to Reynard's castle until the culprit was captured. This time there would be no mercy. But Grimbard the brock hurried to the castle and warned Reynard of the plot. The crafty fellow went immediately to the court to plead his case before the king.

On the way he again confessed to the brock that he was guilty of many sins, but he made them seem mild in comparison with those of the animals now accusing him. To the king also he confessed that he had sinned, but he denied the worst of the crimes laid to his doing. His plea was that he would not have surrendered voluntarily had he been so guilty. His words were so moving that most of his accusers kept silent, fearing that the king would again believe Reynard and punish those who would condemn him. Only the wolf and the bear held fast to their accusations. With the help of his aunt, the ape, Reynard once more excused himself in the king's eyes and made the monarch believe that it was the injured who were the guilty. Again Reynard talked of lost jewels of great value, jewels which he would search for and present to the king.

Only Isegrim the wolf would not accept Reynard's lies. He challenged the fox to a fight. Reynard would have been hard put to fight with the wolf except that Isegrim's feet were still sore from Reynard's taking of his shoes some time before. Also, the ape shaved off Reynard's fur and covered him with oil so that the wolf could not get hold of him. Even so, Isegrim would have defeated him had he not listened to Reynard's oily promises of all the rewards Isegrim would receive were he to let Reynard go. At last the king stopped the fight and ordered all the animals to a great feast. There he for gave Reynard all his sins after taking the scamp's promise that he would commit no more crimes against his fellow animals. The king made Reynard high bailiff of the country, thus setting him above all the others. From that time on the mighty of the forest would bow to the cunning of the weak.

# RHADAMISTUS AND ZENOBIA

*Type of work:* Drama
*Author:* Prosper Jolyot de Crébillon (1674-1762)
*Type of plot:* Romantic tragedy
*Time of plot:* About A.D. 60
*Locale:* Artanissa, capital of Iberia
*First presented:* 1711

*Principal characters:*
RHADAMISTUS, King of Armenia
ZENOBIA (ISMENIA), his wife
PHARASMANES, King of Iberia, Rhadamistus' father
ARSAMES, Rhadamistus' brother
HIERO, Armenian ambassador, Rhadamistus' confidant
MITHRANES, captain of the guards of Pharasmanes
HYDASPES, Pharasmanes' confidant
PHENICE, Zenobia's confidante

## Critique:

*Rhadamistus and Zenobia* contains elements of greatness but lacks firmness and symmetry of structure as well as vigor of style. Now and then a line reminds one of Shakespeare, but the more revealing comparison is to Voltaire, Crébillon's rival and enemy. Voltaire's *Zaïre* is in many respects a better play; the action is continuous and the exposition is effectively simple—yet *Rhadamistus and Zenobia,* for all its static presentation of background material in the first act, is more successful at creating the tragic sense, the realization of the self-defeating character of human passion. Few members of a contemporary audience would tolerate Crébillon's play on the stage; the lengthy expository passages, the unmotivated antipathies, the awkward and precipitous close—all are distasteful. But for the reader the play still offers passages of quiet force and power, and within the faulty whole there are parts to be remembered.

## The Story:

Zenobia, wife of Rhadamistus, was the prisoner of Pharasmanes, King of Iberia. When Phenice, her companion, attempted to persuade her that she should accept the love Pharasmanes was offering her in the hope that she would become his queen, Zenobia, who had been using the name Ismenia, revealed that she could not accept Pharasmanes because the king was her uncle and the father of Rhadamistus. Zenobia explained that her father, Mithridates, had reared Rhadamistus as if the boy were his own son; but when Pharasmanes invaded the Armenian kingdom of Mithridates, Mithridates turned against Rhadamistus and refused to allow him to marry Zenobia as Rhadamistus had expected. Rhadamistus had then attacked the kingdom of Mithridates and had driven the king into exile. Zenobia, to protect her father, had offered to wed Rhadamistus; only after the wedding had she learned that Rhadamistus had murdered her father. In rage, Rhadamistus had then attacked his bride and thrown her into the Araxes. Believing her dead, he had no knowledge of her rescue. Zenobia ended her account by telling Phenice that Rhadamistus had been killed by his own father, who had been jealous of his son's rise to power. The most compelling reason against marrying Pharasmanes, Zenobia told Phenice, was that she was in love with Rhadamistus' brother and Pharasmanes' son, Arsames.

When Arsames came to Zenobia from a campaign in Albania, he asked her whether she intended to marry Pharas-

RHADAMISTUS AND ZENOBIA by Prosper Jolyot de Crébillon, from CHIEF RIVALS OF COR-NEILLE AND RACINE. Translated by Lacy Lockert. By permission of the publishers, Vanderbilt University Press. Copyright, 1956, by Lacy Lockert.

manes that day, as he had heard. He declared his love for her and his jealousy of his father. Zenobia assured him that she would not marry Pharasmanes, but she also declared that she could never consider marriage with Arsames. Arsames, knowing Zenobia only as Ismenia, was forced to accept her decision.

Pharasmanes appeared and criticized Arsames for returning to Iberia without permission. When Arsames declared that he came in support of his father to meet the invasion planned by Corbulo on behalf of Rome and Syria, Pharasmanes dismissed the excuse and forbade his son to profess love for Ismenia or ever to see her again. Pharasmanes, having dismissed Arsames, warned Ismenia that he would not tolerate refusal. In desperation, Zenobia appealed to Phenice to tell the Roman ambassador of her plight.

But Rhadamistus still lived. Tortured by repentance, knowing himself to be the murderer of Zenobia's father, and believing himself to be the murderer of his wife, he arrived in Iberia as the representative of Rome and the Roman choice for king of Armenia. Rhadamistus told his companion Hiero how he had been wounded by Pharasmanes' soldiers and how Corbulo had rescued him. Rhadamistus, vowing revenge on his father, had joined forces with Corbulo and been appointed Roman ambassador. Hiero told Rhadamistus that the Armenians, fearing Pharasmanes, hoped to persuade Arsames to become their king.

When Pharasmanes entered, Rhadamistus told him that Nero did not choose to have Pharasmanes become king of Armenia. Pharasmanes answered that Rome had better get its legions together, for he was determined to invade Armenia. He then supported his claim to the throne by referring to his brother, Mithridates, and to his son, Rhadamistus. Rhadamistus, who had managed to keep his identity hidden from his father, then angered Pharasmanes by declaring that the king should not expect to be heir to those he had murdered. Only Rhadamistus' status as ambassador kept Pharasmanes from ordering him seized.

Arsames, not recognizing Rhadamistus, refused to join with him in a revolt against Pharasmanes; but he urged the ambassador to take Ismenia from Iberia. Arsames also told Rhadamistus of his love for Ismenia, which for some hidden reason she could not return. Rhadamistus, who had no way of knowing that Ismenia and Zenobia were the same, agreed to help Ismenia.

When Zenobia came to Rhadamistus he recognized her immediately, but only his outcry made her realize that the ambassador was the husband who had tried to murder her. Rhadamistus, throwing himself at her feet, blamed himself for all his deeds, and Zenobia, partly from duty and partly from pity, forgave him his crimes.

Zenobia, who thought herself guilty because of her love for Arsames, could not wholly condemn Rhadamistus. When Arsames again told her of his love, she revealed that Rhadamistus was alive and that he was her husband. Rhadamistus interrupted the conversation and gave way to angry jealousy when he learned that Zenobia had revealed his identity. Zenobia remonstrated with him, pointing out that she would never have admitted her love for Arsames had not Rhadamistus' anger prompted her. Rhadamistus, ashamed of his outburst, begged their forgiveness.

Pharasmanes, fearing that Arsames was in league with the Romans, for he had seen his son talking to the Roman ambassador, arrested Arsames and sent his soldiers to capture the envoy. His anger was further aroused when he observed that the ambassador had taken Ismenia with him. He pursued Rhadamistus and wounded him with his sword. Arsames' grief stirred Pharasmanes strangely; he felt that somehow he had done a terrible act. Rhadamistus, dying, appeared before Pharasmanes and by a reference to Mithridates made his identity known to his father. Pharasmanes, realizing at last the fatal consequences of his jealousy and his lust for power, directed Arsames to take the Armenian throne. Sacrificing his own love for Zenobia as punishment for having killed his son, Pharasmanes relinquished Zenobia to Arsames and told them to flee from him lest his jealousy once again lead him to slay one of his own offspring.

# RICEYMAN STEPS

*Type of work:* Novel
*Author:* Arnold Bennett (1867-1931)
*Type of plot:* Social criticism
*Time of plot:* 1919
*Locale:* Riceyman Steps, a suburb of London
*First published:* 1923

Principal characters:
HENRY EARLFORWARD, a bookseller
MRS. VIOLET ARB, owner of a nearby shop
ELSIE, maid for both Earlforward and Mrs. Arb
JOE, Elsie's friend

## Critique:

Riceyman Steps is a novel both amusing and tragic. Bennett's gifts for satire, for ironic comment and incident, and for character development, combine in this novel to create an excellent comedy of manners. But, as in all of Bennett's work, the note of tragedy is, in the last analysis, the important one and it is not absent in *Riceyman Steps*. Henry Earlforward and his wife, as well as Elsie and Joe, are the victims of selfishness and greed.

## The Story:

Henry Earlforward owned a bookstore left to him by his uncle, T. T. Riceyman. It was cluttered, dusty, badly lighted. Earlforward lived in a back room of the shop, the upstairs of the building being filled with old books.

One night Elsie, his cleaning girl, came into the shop. She told Henry that she also worked for Mrs. Arb, who owned the confectioner's shop next door, and that Mrs. Arb had sent her for a cookbook. Henry found one containing recipes for making substantial meals out of practically no food at all. A little later Elsie returned and said that Mrs. Arb thanked him, but the book was too expensive.

His curiosity aroused, he himself went to Mrs. Arb's shop. Even though he marked down the price of the book, Mrs. Arb still refused to buy it. Henry became more interested, for it was clear that Mrs. Arb was no spendthrift. The following Sunday they went for a walk, and from then on they became close friends.

At last Violet Arb sold her shop and agreed to marry Henry. When Violet asked him about a wedding ring, he seemed surprised, for he had supposed the one she already owned would do. He got a file, sawed off the ring, sold it, and bought another, all without really spending a penny. They were married one morning and for a honeymoon spent the day in London.

They visited Madame Tussaud's Waxworks and the Chamber of Horrors. Henry, who had thought the wedding breakfast expensive enough, was distressed at being forced to spend more money. He wondered if he had been deceived, if Violet were not a spendthrift after all. He began to complain about his lame foot. Violet was dismayed; she had wanted to see a motion picture. But Henry could not be persuaded to change his mind. He did not, he said, want a painful leg on his wedding day.

When they passed by the shop that night, Henry thought the place was on fire. It was glowing with light, and men were working inside. Violet explained that the men had been engaged to clean the dirty, cluttered shop. She had planned the work as her wedding gift to him, but he had spoiled the surprise by coming home before the men had finished their task. Henry showed Violet a safe that he had bought to safeguard her valuables and her money.

Violet soon discovered that miserly Henry would not light a fire, would have no electric light, would eat practically nothing. On their first morning together she cooked an egg for him but he refused to eat it. Later Elsie ate it in secret. At another time Violet had Elsie cook steaks, but Henry would not touch them. There was an argument in which Violet called him a miser who was starving her to death. He left the room and his steak. That night Elsie ate it.

When Violet discovered that Elsie had eaten the steak, there was another row. But Elsie began to eat more and more when nobody was there to observe her. The girl was half-starved in the miserly household. To stop Elsie's thefts of food, Henry went to bed, called Elsie to his room, announced he was seriously ill, and asked if she thought it right to steal food while he lay dying. Elsie was glum and frightened.

A short time later Henry actually became ill. Elsie, in defiance of the Earlforwards, managed to get Dr. Raste to examine Henry. The doctor said that the sick man would have to go to the hospital. Then the doctor discovered that Violet was also ill. At first Henry refused to go to the hospital, but Violet finally persuaded him to go. When the doctor called the next morning, it was Violet, however, who went to the hospital. Henry stayed at home in the care of Elsie.

In the meantime Elsie had been hoping for the return of Joe, her sweetheart. He had been employed by Dr. Raste, had been ill, and had wandered off. Elsie was sure he would return some day.

One night Elsie wanted to send a boy to the hospital to inquire about Violet.

When she asked Henry for sixpence for the messenger, he said she could go herself. Not wanting to leave him, she picked up his keys, went downstairs, and opened the safe. Amazed to find so much money there, she borrowed sixpence and put an I. O. U. in its place. Then she dashed out to find a boy to carry her note. When she came back, she found Joe waiting for her. He was shabbily dressed and sick.

Elsie quietly carried Joe up to her room and took care of him, taking pains so that Henry would not suspect his presence in the house. When Joe began to improve, he told her he had been in jail. Elsie did not care. She continued to take care of Henry, promising him that she would never desert him. The hospital informed them that Violet was to have an operation. That night Elsie went next door to the confectioner's shop. Mrs. Belrose, the wife of the new proprietor, telephoned the hospital and was told that Violet had died because her strength had been sapped through malnutrition.

Henry seemed to take the news calmly enough, but he grew steadily worse. Dr. Raste came again and said that he must go to a hospital, but Henry refused. Without Elsie's knowledge, he got up and went downstairs, where he discovered with dismay Elsie's appropriation of the sixpence. He sat down at his desk and began to read his correspondence.

Elsie was in her room taking care of Joe. To the neighbors the house seemed quite dark. Accordingly, Mrs. Belrose insisted that her husband go over to inquire about the sick man. He discovered Henry's body lying in the shop.

A relative came from London and sold the shop to Mr. Belrose. Joe recovered and went back to work for Dr. Raste. Because Elsie intended to marry Joe, she also went to work for Dr. Raste.

# RICHARD THE SECOND

*Type of work:* Drama
*Author:* William Shakespeare (1564-1616)
*Type of plot:* Historical tragedy
*Time of plot:* Fourteenth century
*Locale:* England
*First presented:* c. 1595

*Principal characters:*
RICHARD II, King of England
JOHN OF GAUNT, Duke of Lancaster, Richard's uncle
EDMUND LANGLEY, Duke of York, another uncle of Richard
HENRY BOLINGBROKE, Duke of Hereford, son of John of Gaunt
DUKE OF AUMERLE, son of the Duke of York
THOMAS MOWBRAY, Duke of Norfolk
EARL OF NORTHUMBERLAND, supporter of Bolingbroke

*Critique:*

One of Shakespeare's best-known historical plays, *The Tragedy of King Richard the Second* is his first truly independent work in this form. Its concentration on blank verse reveals the influence of Marlowe, but the character of Richard himself clearly indicates the course the playwright will follow in creating his later tragedies of character. Revealing, as it does, Shakespeare's patriotic feelings, this play is among his most eloquent and contains many lines frequently quoted.

*The Story:*

During the reign of Richard II, two young dukes, Henry Bolingbroke and Thomas Mowbray, quarreled bitterly; and in the end the king summoned them into his presence to settle their differences publicly. Although Bolingbroke was the oldest son of John of Gaunt, Duke of Lancaster, and therefore a cousin of the king, Richard was perfectly fair in his interview with the two men and showed neither any favoritism.

Bolingbroke accused Mowbray, Duke of Norfolk, of mismanaging military funds and of helping to plot the murder of the dead Duke of Gloucester, another of the king's uncles. All these charges Mowbray forcefully denied. At last Richard decided that to settle the dispute the men should have a trial by combat at Coventry, and the court adjourned there to witness the tournament.

Richard, ever nervous and suspicious, grew uneasy as the contest began. Suddenly, just after the beginning trumpet sounded, the king declared that the combat should not take place. Instead, calling the two men to him, he banished them from the country. Bolingbroke was to be exiled for six years and Mowbray for the rest of his life. At the same time Richard exacted promises from them that they would never plot against him. Still persistent in his accusations, Bolingbroke tried to persuade Mowbray to plead guilty, before he left England, to the charges against him. Mowbray, refusing to do so, warned Richard against the cleverness of Bolingbroke.

Not long after his son had been banished, John of Gaunt, Duke of Lancaster, became ill and sent for Richard to receive his dying advice. Although the Duke of York pointed out that giving advice to Richard was too often a waste of time, John of Gaunt felt that perhaps a dying man would be heeded while a living one would not. From his deathbed he criticized Richard's extravagance, for mishandling of public funds had almost impoverished the nation. John of Gaunt warned Richard also that the kingdom would suffer for his selfishness.

Richard paid no attention to his uncle's advice. After the death of John of Gaunt, the king seized his lands and wealth to use for capital in backing his Irish wars.

His uncle, the aged Duke of York, attempted to dissuade the king from these moves because of Bolingbroke's anger and influence among the people. York's fears were soon confirmed. Bolingbroke, hearing that his father's lands had been seized by the king's officers, used the information as an excuse to terminate his period of banishment. Gathering about him troops and supplies, he landed in the north of England. There other unruly lords, the Earl of Northumberland and his son, Henry Percy,· known as Hotspur, Lord Ross, and Lord Willoughby joined him.

Richard, heedless of all warnings, had set off for Ireland to pursue his foreign war. He left his tottering kingdom in the hands of the weak Duke of York, who was no match for the wily Bolingbroke. When the exiled traitor reached Gloucestershire, the Duke of York visited him at his camp. Caught between loyalty to Richard and his despair over the bankrupt state of the country, York finally yielded his troops to Bolingbroke. Richard, returning to England and expecting to find an army of Welshmen under his command. learned that they, after hearing false reports of his death, had gone over to Bolingbroke. Moreover, the strong men of his court, the Earl of Wiltshire, Bushy, and Green, had all been executed.

Destitute of friends and without an army, the sorrowing Richard took refuge in Flint Castle, where Bolingbroke went pretending to pay homage to the king. Making his usurped titles and estates his excuse, Bolingbroke took Richard prisoner and carried him to London. There Richard broke completely, showing little interest in anything, philosophizing constantly on his own downfall. Brought before Bolingbroke and the cruel and unfeeling Earl of Northumberland, Richard was forced to abdicate his throne and sign papers confessing his political crimes. Bolingbroke, assuming royal authority, ordered Richard imprisoned in the Tower of London.

During a quarrel among the young dukes of the court, the Bishop of Carlisle announced that Mowbray had made a name for himself while fighting in the Holy Land, had then retired to Venice, and had died there. When Bolingbroke affected great concern over that news, the Bishop of Carlisle turned on him and denounced him for his part in depriving Richard of the throne. Nevertheless, Bolingbroke, armed with numerous legal documents he had collected to prove his rights, ascended the throne. Richard predicted to the Earl of Northumberland that Bolingbroke would soon distrust his old aide because the nobleman had had practice in unseating a king. Soon afterward Richard was sent to the dungeons at Pomfret Castle and his queen was banished to France.

At the Duke of York's palace the aging duke sorrowfully related to his duchess the details of the coronation procession of Henry IV. When the duke discovered, however, that his son Aumerle and other loyal followers of Richard were planning to assassinate Henry IV at Oxford, York immediately started for the palace to warn the new monarch. The duchess, frantic because of her son's danger, advised him to reach the palace ahead of his father, reveal his treachery to the king, and ask the royal pardon. She herself finally pleaded for her son before the king and won Aumerle's release.

Having punished the conspirators, Henry IV grew uneasy at the prospect of other treasonable activities, for while Richard lived there was always danger that he might be restored to power. Henry IV, plotting the death of the deposed monarch, suggested casually to Sir Pierce Exton, a faithful servant and courtier, that he murder Richard at Pomfret.

There in his dungeon Richard quarreled with his keeper, according to Exton's plan, and in the struggle that ensued the knight drew his sword and struck down his unhappy prisoner. He then placed Richard's body in a coffin, carried it to Windsor Castle, and there presented it to Henry IV. Distressed over the news of mounting insurrection in the country, King Henry pretended innocence of the murder of Richard and vowed to make a pilgrimage to the Holy Land to atone for the death of his fallen cousin.

# RICHARD THE THIRD

*Type of work:* Drama
*Author:* William Shakespeare (1564-1616)
*Type of plot:* Historical chronicle
*Time of plot:* Fifteenth century
*Locale:* England
*First presented:* c. 1593

*Principal characters:*
EDWARD IV, King of England
RICHARD, Duke of Gloucester, his brother
GEORGE, Duke of Clarence, another brother
QUEEN ELIZABETH, wife of Edward IV
LADY ANNE, widow of Edward, Prince of Wales, son of Henry VI;
    afterward married to Richard III
QUEEN MARGARET, widow of Henry VI
EDWARD, Prince of Wales, young son of Edward IV
RICHARD, Duke of York, another young son of Edward IV
THE DUKE OF BUCKINGHAM, accomplice of the Duke of Gloucester
LORD HASTINGS, a supporter of Prince Edward
LORD STANLEY, Earl of Derby
SIR WILLIAM CATESBY, a court toady
HENRY TUDOR, Earl of Richmond, afterward King Henry VII

*Critique:*

The Tragedy of King Richard the Third is the last in the series of history plays which Shakespeare wrote depicting the strife between the Houses of York and Lancaster. Like *Richard the Second,* this play is patterned after the work of Marlowe with great emphasis on blank verse rather than on prose and songs. A tragedy of blood, *Richard the Third* is full of the traditional violence and murder, yet it manages to evoke a surprising amount of sympathy for its hero-villain, especially in the last scenes of the drama.

*The Story:*

After the conclusion of the wars between the Houses of York and Lancaster, Edward IV was firmly established on the throne once again. Before long, however, his treacherous brother Richard, the hunchbacked Duke of Gloucester, resumed his own plans for gaining the throne. Craftily he removed one obstacle in his path when he turned the king's hatred against the third brother, the Duke of Clarence. Telling the king of an ancient prophecy that his issue would be disinherited by one of the royal line whose name began with the letter G, Richard directed suspicion against the Duke of Clarence, whose name was George. Immediately Clarence was arrested and taken to the Tower. Richard, pretending sympathy, advised him that the jealousy and hatred of Queen Elizabeth were responsible for his imprisonment. After promising every aid in helping his brother to secure his freedom, Richard, as false in word as he was cruel in deed, gave orders that Clarence be stabbed in his cell and his body placed in a barrel of malmsey wine.

Hoping to insure his position more definitely, Richard then made plans to marry Lady Anne, widow of Prince Edward, son of the murdered Henry VI. The young Prince of Wales had also been slain by Richard and his brothers after the battles had ended; Lady Anne and Queen Margaret, Henry's widow, were the only remaining members of the once powerful House of Lancaster still living in England. Intercepting Lady Anne at the funeral procession of Henry VI, Richard attempted to woo her. In spite of her hatred and fear of her husband's murderer, she was finally persuaded to

3211

accept an engagement ring when Richard insisted that it was for love of her that he had murdered the Prince of Wales.

Richard went to the court, where Edward IV lay ill. There he affected great sorrow and indignation over the news of the death of Clarence, thus endearing himself to Lord Hastings and the Duke of Buckingham who were friends of Clarence. Insinuating that Queen Elizabeth and her followers had turned the wrath of the king against Clarence and thus brought about his death, Richard managed to convince everyone except Queen Margaret, who knew well what had really happened. Openly accusing him, she attempted to warn Buckingham and the others against Richard, but they ignored her.

Edward IV, meanwhile, ailing and depressed, tried to make peace among the enemy factions in his realm, but before this end could be accomplished he died. His son, Prince Edward, was sent for from Ludlow to take his father's place. At the same time Richard imprisoned Lord Grey, Lord Rivers, and Lord Vaughan, followers and relatives of the queen, and subsequently had them executed.

Queen Elizabeth, frightened, sought refuge for herself and her second son, the young Duke of York, with the Archbishop of Canterbury. Richard, upon hearing of the queen's action, pretended much concern over the welfare of his brother's children and set himself up as their guardian. Managing to remove young York from the care of his mother, he had him placed in the Tower, along with Prince Edward. He announced that they were under his protection and that they would remain there only until Prince Edward had been crowned.

Learning from Sir William Catesby, a court toady, that Lord Hastings was a loyal adherent of the young prince, Richard contrived to remove the influential nobleman from the court. He summoned Hastings to a meeting called supposedly to discuss plans for the coronation of the new king. Although Lord Stanley warned Hastings that ill luck awaited him if he went to the meeting, the trusting nobleman paid no attention but kept his appointment with Richard in the Tower. There, in a trumped-up scene, Richard accused Hastings of treason and ordered his immediate execution. Then Richard and Buckingham dressed themselves in rusty old armor and pretended to the lord mayor that Hastings had been plotting against them; the lord mayor was convinced by their false protestations that the execution was justified.

Richard, with Buckingham, plotted to seize the throne for himself. Buckingham, speaking in the Guildhall of the great immorality of the late King Edward, hinted that both the king and his children were illegitimate. Shocked, a citizens' committee headed by the lord mayor approached Richard and begged him to accept the crown. They found him, well coached by Buckingham, in the company of two priests, with a prayer book in his hand. So impressed were they with his seeming piety, that they repeated their offer after he had hypocritically refused it. Pretending great reluctance, Richard finally accepted, after being urged by Buckingham, the lord mayor, and Catesby. Immediate plans for the coronation were made.

Lady Anne, interrupted during a visit to the Tower with Queen Elizabeth and the old Duchess of York, was ordered to Westminster to be crowned Richard's queen. The three women heard with horror that Richard had ascended the throne, and they were all the more suspicious of him because they had been refused entrance to see the young princes. Fearing the worst, they sorrowed among themselves and saw only doom for the nation.

Soon after his coronation Richard suggested to Buckingham that the two princes must be killed. When Buckingham balked at the order, Richard refused to consider his request for elevation to the earldom of Hereford. Proceeding alone to secure the safety of his position, he hired Sir James Tyrrel, a discontented nobleman, to smother the children in their sleep.

Then, to make his position still more secure, Richard planned to marry Elizabeth of York, his own niece and daughter of the deceased Edward IV. Spreading the news that Queen Anne was mortally ill, he had her secretly murdered. He then removed any threat from Clarence's heirs by imprisoning his son and by arranging a marriage for the daughter whereby her social position was considerably lowered.

But all these precautions could not stem the tide of threats that were beginning to endanger Richard. In Brittany, the Earl of Richmond, Henry Tudor, gathered an army and invaded the country. When news of Richmond's landing at Milford reached London, Buckingham fled from Richard, whose cruelty and guilt were finally becoming apparent to his closest friends and associates. Buckingham joined the forces of Richmond, but shortly afterward he was captured and executed by Richard.

In a tremendous final battle the armies of Richmond and Richard met on Bosworth Field. There, on the night before the encounter, all the ghosts of Richard's victims appeared to him in his sleep and prophesied his defeat. At the same time they foretold the coming victory and success of the Earl of Richmond. These predictions held true, for the next day Richard, fighting desperately, was slain in battle by Richmond, after crying out the offer of his ill-gotten kingdom for a horse, his own having been killed under him. The duke mounted the throne and married Elizabeth of York, thus uniting the houses of York and Lancaster and ending the feud of those noble families forever.

# RIGHT YOU ARE—IF YOU THINK SO

*Type of work:* Drama
*Author:* Luigi Pirandello (1867-1936)
*Type of plot:* Expressionistic parable
*Time of plot:* Early twentieth century
*Locale:* A small Italian town, the capital of a province
*First presented:* 1917

>    *Principal characters:*
>        LAMBERTO LAUDISI, an observer of human nature
>        PONZA, secretary to the provincial councilor
>        SIGNORA FROLA, his mother-in-law
>        SIGNORA PONZA, his wife
>        COMMENDATORE AGAZZI, a provincial councilor
>        AMALIA, his wife
>        DINA, their daughter
>        THE PREFECT
>        CENTURI, a police commissioner

## Critique:

Pirandello's *Così è—se vi pare!*—which has been given such varied English titles as *Right You Are—If You Think So*, *Right You Are If You Think You Are*, and *It Is So! (If You Think So)*—develops one of Pirandello's favorite themes: the relativity of truth. Laudisi, who mocks the determination of the townspeople to pry out the secret of Signora Frola and the Ponzas and who several times vainly tries to stop them, serves as the author's spokesman and the explicator of his theme. Despite the philosophic nature of this theme, the drama is an eminently actable one.

## The Story:

There was much talk in the small capital of an Italian province about the peculiar family arrangements of old Signora Frola and her daughter, the wife of Ponza, a newly appointed secretary to the provincial councilor, Commendatore Agazzi. Why was Signora Frola living by herself in a fine apartment next door to the Agazzis and not with her daughter and her son-in-law? Why were Ponza and his wife living in fifth-floor tenement rooms on the edge of town? Why did Ponza visit the old lady every evening and sometimes during the day, but always by himself? Why did Signora Frola never visit her daugher, and why did her daughter, whom no one except Ponza ever saw, never visit her? Why would the old lady not even permit Signora Agazzi and her daughter to pay a social call?

While the enigma was being discussed by Agazzi, his family, and several visitors in the Agazzi parlor, Signora Frola came in to apologize for having refused to admit the Agazzis when they came calling, and also to explain why she lived apart from her daughter. She did not want to interfere, she said, in the home life of her daughter and Ponza. She lived by herself it was true, but she was not unhappy about it; and she kept in contact with her daughter even though there were no face-to-face visits. Signora Frola had hardly left when Ponza—a fierce, nervous, even sinister-looking man—came in to explain about his poor mother-in-law. The truth was she was mad. Actually, her daughter had been dead for four years and he had married again two years later. But he had prevailed upon his second wife to humor the old woman by carrying on shouted conversations from a fifth-floor balcony and writing notes to be let down in a basket from the balcony to the old woman on the ground.

No sooner had Ponza gone than Signora Frola returned. Though the company at first denied it, she knew what Ponza had been telling them. The sad truth was, however, that *he* was the mad one. The real truth, which she wished she did not have to tell, was that when he married her young and innocent daughter he so frightened her with his passionate attentions that she had to be put into an institution for a while. When she finally returned, Ponza himself was in such a nervous state that he could not be convinced that she was his wife; and she was prevailed upon to pretend that she was a second wife taking the place of the one he had lost.

Before long a plot was hatched to have Signora Frola and Ponza confront each other in the presence of Agazzi and the others in order that the truth might be uncovered. Lamberto Laudisi, the brother-in-law of Agazzi, even from the beginning of the gossipy, inquisitorial discussion, had been of the opinion that the private domestic lives of the Ponzas and Signora Frola were their own affair and should remain so. They were harming no one; they were not seeking anyone's aid; they should be let alone. But Laudisi was overruled. Agazzi left and came back shortly to get some papers which he had purposely left in his study so that he might bring Ponza back with him to get them. As they came in, Ponza heard a piano in the next room playing a tune which had been a favorite with his wife Lena. Signora Frola was playing, and when she stopped her voice could be heard through the doorway. She was discussing her daughter's cherished melody in such a way as to suggest that Lena was still alive. When she confronted Ponza a moment later in the study, he furiously insisted that Lena was dead, that he was now married to Julia, and that the piano which Lena used to play had been smashed to pieces long ago.

While he was frenziedly shouting at her, she was occasionally glancing about at the others in the room as if to call attention to his piteous state and to her forbearance in humoring him. After bursting into tears, Ponza suddenly ordered her out of the room and she soon left, sobbing. When she had gone, Ponza immediately grew calm again and explained the reason for his actions. The old woman, he said, was so convinced of his madness that he had to pretend to be mad. Now he must go and see her. Laudisi, who had earlier insisted that truth is a relative thing and that what is one person's truth is not necessarily another's, laughed at the confusion of the Agazzis and their visitors. Now, he mocked, they had the truth they had wanted!

Still the puzzle remained: who was telling the truth and who was lying, either knowingly or unknowingly? Earlier someone had suggested that documents such as a marriage certificate for the second marriage, or the letters which the second—or first—Signora Ponza wrote to the old woman, might be secured to prove who was right. One of those interested, Commissioner Centuri, arrived with some data which he had uncovered and which might yet clear up the puzzle; but the data turned out to be as inconclusive as the information already at hand.

A chance remark that Signora Ponza might as well be in another world since no one had ever seen her made Laudisi wonder whether there really *was* a Signora Ponza.

Still another solution to the enigma was suggested. Let Ponza go and get his wife so that she might be seen by everybody, to prove that she existed, and let her be questioned by the prefect himself in the presence of everyone so that the truth might be generally known. Ponza left after he had been assured that his wife and his mother-in-law would not be compelled to face each other. But in his absence the old woman returned to say that, since she could not live her own life in peace, she would leave town and not come back. To pacify her, the pre-

3215

fect pretended to believe her version of the truth, though he had earlier said he believed Ponza's. When Ponza returned with a heavily veiled woman dressed as if she were in deep mourning, he was shocked and angry to see his mother-in-law, since he had been assured that she would not be there. Signora Ponza, to quiet the clamor, asked Ponza to take the old woman away. Both Ponza and his mother-in-law went out weeping and with their arms about each other's waists.

Now the truth would finally come out: Signora Ponza would tell the entire group the whole truth. But again and for the final time the decision was left to each of her hearers: she was the daughter of Signora Frola; she was also the second wife of Ponza, and, for herself, she was nobody. When the prefect insisted that she must be one or the other of the two women, she answered that she was the person she was believed to be. Hearing that reply, Laudisi, saying that everybody now knew the truth, burst out laughing.

# LE RIME OF PETRARCH

*Type of work:* Poetry
*Author:* Francesco Petrarch (1304-1374)
*First transcribed:* After 1327

Of the 366 poems included in the collection which Petrarch made of his poetry, 317 are sonnets, twenty-nine *canzoni*, nine *sestine*, seven *ballate*, and four madrigals. According to the introduction by Theodor E. Mommsen to Anna Maria Armi's translation of the sonnets and songs, the collection has no definite title but is sometimes called the *Rime* or *Canzoniere*. Petrarch called the collection *Rerum vulgarium fragmenta*, calling attention to the fact that the brief poems were written, not in Latin, but in the vernacular.

The comparison between Dante and Petrarch is inevitably made when one considers the sonnets and songs of Petrarch, for both were Italians writing in the vernacular; both centered their poems about some gracious lady suddenly discovered, idealized, and praised throughout a lifetime; and both became giants of Italian literature. Dante wrote his *Vita Nuova* about Beatrice Portinari, whom he met when he was nine and she was eight and whom he continued to worship as the ideal woman and to celebrate in his poetry even after her death. Petrarch's ideal woman was Laura, possibly Laura de Noves, whom he met in 1327, in his twenty-second year.

Like Dante, Petrarch kept his passion at a distance—one might say at a poetic distance—from the woman who charmed him; and cynics can add that that is the secret of enduring poetic love. When one reads the poems of either Dante or Petrarch, however, it is difficult to believe that the love is merely an excuse for poetry; somehow in the midst of creative passion, something of human passion burned as well to supply the warmth which survives the centuries. It may be that this enduring emotion can be attributed to those distant ladies who set the poets to writing immortal poetry, but it is more reasonable to suppose that poetic genius worked in both cases to turn a sudden fancy into a lifelong poetic enterprise.

Naturally, critics have wondered who Laura was, or whether she was. Even Petrarch's contemporaries were not certain, and some of them contended that the Laura of the poems was an invention, an ideal based on no model whatsoever. Petrarch denied the charge; but, more significantly, the poems also deny it by the force of their feeling and imagery. One sympathizes with Petrarch, who pointed out that it would be madness to spend years writing hundreds of poems about an entirely imaginary woman.

For both Dante and Petrarch the idealization process took them beyond earth to heaven. That is, neither Beatrice nor Laura, as a poetic figure, is merely mortal, physical woman as she ideally could be; she is also spiritually significant, by her person and manner a being who symbolizes the highest values to which the human soul can hope to attain. Dante made Beatrice an inspiration even in Paradise and used her as the central guiding figure of the latter half of *The Divine Comedy*. In writing of the painter Simon, Petrarch comments:

> But certainly Simon saw paradise
> Wherein this gentle lady had her place;
> There he saw her and portrayed in such
> guise
> That is the witness here of her fair face.
> (From LXXVII)

Later, writing more explicitly of Laura after her death, Petrarch speaks of "Seeing her now on such intimate term/With Him who in her life had her heart's right," and, in the same sonnet, he concludes:

LE RIME OF PETRARCH, from SONNETS AND SONGS. Translated by Armi. Excerpts reprinted by permission of the publishers, Pantheon Books Inc. Copyright, 1946, by Pantheon Books Inc.

For fairer than before, my inner eye
Sees her soar up and with the angels fly
At the feet of our own eternal Lord.
(From CCCXLV)

It has been traditional to divide the sonnets and songs into two major parts, the one including poems written while Laura was living, and the other including those poems written after her death. Petrarch first saw her on April 6, 1327, and she died on the same day of the year, in 1348, from the plague.

Poem III of the collection tells us of the first meeting:

It was the day when the sun's rays turned white
Out of the pity it felt for its sire,
When I was caught and taken by desire,
For your fair eyes, my lady, held me quite.

In V Petrarch works the syllables of the name "Laura" into his verse in order to describe what happens when his sighs call her with the name that Love wrote on his heart: "Cosi LAUdare e REverire insegna/La voce stessa . . ." ("Thus to LAUd and REvere teaches and vows/The voice itself . . .")

In VI appears one of Petrarch's numerous puns of Laura's name, when he writes of Love as holding the bridle of his desire and thus being directed "Only to reach the laurel and its sour fruit . . ." ("Sol per venir al lauro . . .") Again, in the following poem, he speaks of the "love of laurel." It was in part because of such puns that Petrarch was accused of inventing the character "Laura."

These plays with words were the least of Petrarch's accomplishments in the sonnet form. He was so adept at using the fourteen lines to express a complete idea or image with its emotional correlate that poets have taken him as a model ever since. A full appreciation of the poet comes only from the reading of his poetry; only then does one understand what other poets have envied in Petrarch's work. Since he wrote in Italian, it follows that to know his poetry one must know Italian—or, at the very least, something of the flow and sound of the language. Then it is possible, by comparing an English translation to the original, to sense the beauty which results from sensitive use of the sound and sense of language within the sonnet form.

Attention to form alone will not yield full knowledge of Petrarch's power in poetry. Poets and artists generally like to think that form alone is what counts—and for an obvious reason: the poet gives the form to the material he finds: since he wants credit, he turns attention to form. But what the poet forgets, when he talks this way, is that he selects material, understands it from his perspective, and in using it for his purposes forces a recognition of its power as material. So it is with Petrarch. He writes in the tradition of love poetry, but he chose to do so; and the advantage he gained is that he writes of his beloved from a poignant distance. In making Laura unobtainable, he secured her forever in his poetry. Not that it is a simple matter to sing doleful songs of romantic longing, but there is an advantage, after all, in being able to give the imagination full rein while touching the sympathies of the reader who, even across centuries, regrets that Petrarch did not finally possess his Laura:

A rain of bitter tears falls from my face
And a tormenting wind blows with my sighs
Whenever toward you I turn my eyes,
Whose absence cuts me from the human race. (From XVII)

Much of Petrarch's poetry is concerned with the shortness of life, the inevitableness of death, the end of all that is fair and young on earth; and these matters are, of course, related to Laura. Thus the poetry before her death has a great deal in common with the poetry written afterward—the difference being that regret and speculation have now taken the place of fear for her loss. Before her death Petrarch amused himself with poetically metaphysical imagery by which he claimed that Laura would outshine stars and draw the angels to her, but after her death the poetic amusement is either absent or tempered by a sober recognition of the fact of death; and if Laura is the favorite of anyone in heaven, it is because of her spirit for which he shows reverent respect. We are reminded of Donne by the following image:

To count the constellations one by one
And to pour in a goblet all the seas
Was perhaps my intention when I took
This small sheet to relate such mys-
teries. . . .          (From CXXVII)

Not all the poems are about Laura. Petrarch writes of Italy at war, of nature, of God and the love of God, of life and death and other matters of universal concern. But even these poems have a human dimension which would be lost were they not fixed within the context of the Laura poetry. Perhaps it is because Petrarch had the heart and wit to be a love poet that we can attend with respect to his thoughts about matters that concern us all.

After Laura's death Petrarch wrote a sonnet of lament, CCLXVII, which begins, "Alas! the lovely face, the eyes that save/Alas! the charming countenance and proud!" and in the following poem he asks, "What shall I do? What do you counsel, Love?/It is now time to die./And I have waited longer that I would./My lady died and did my heart remove. . . ." The long song ends:

Flee the clearness, the green,
Do not go near where there is song and
laughter,
Canzone, follow after
Weeping: you are not fit for merry
folk,
A widow, without comfort, in black
cloak.

Petrarch's lamentations gradually change character as one reads toward the end of the collection. Grief gives way to reflection, and reflection turns his thoughts to spiritual love—thus to the love of God. Laura becomes the symbol of what man should strive for, even though in life she was desirable as woman. Because "Death quelled the sun wonted to overwhelm" him, and "Dust is the one who was my chill and spark," he is able to write, "From this I see my good," and "I find freedom at last, bitter and sweet/And to the Lord whom I adore and greet,/Who with his nod governs the holy things,/I return, tired of life, and with life sated." (From CCCLXIII)

Although translation does not always succeed in reproducing the finely-wrought rhythms of Petrarch's verse, the best has the great virtue of coming as close to the form, sound, and even syntax of the original as one could hope for. On that account, an appreciation of the original becomes possible, even for those who do not understand Italian.

# THE RIME OF THE ANCIENT MARINER

*Type of work:* Poem
*Author:* Samuel Taylor Coleridge (1772-1834)
*Type of plot:* Ballad fantasy
*Time of plot:* Late medieval period
*Locale:* A voyage around the Horn into the Pacific and thence home
*First published:* 1798

Principal characters:
THE ANCIENT MARINER
A HERMIT
A WEDDING GUEST

## Critique:

According to Coleridge, his aim in writing *The Ancient Mariner* was to make the supernatural seem real. For the poem he chose as his verse form the old four-line ballad stanza and an archaic style. Especially noteworthy is the division of the poem into parts, each part ending with a striking sentence which serves as a high point in the story.

## The Story:

Three young gallants on their way to a wedding were stopped by an old gray-headed sailor who detained one of them. The Ancient Mariner held with his glittering eye a young man whose next of kin was being married in the church nearby and forced him to listen, against his will, to the old seaman's tale. The Ancient Mariner told how the ship left the home port and sailed southward to the equator. In a storm the vessel was blown to polar regions of snow and ice.

When an albatross flew out of the frozen silence, the crew hailed it as a good omen. The sailors made a pet of the albatross and regarded it as a fellow creature. One day the Ancient Mariner killed the bird with his crossbow. The superstitious sailors believed bad luck would follow.

Fair winds blew the ship northward until it reached the equator, where it was suddenly becalmed and lay for days without moving. The thirsty seamen blamed the Ancient Mariner and hung the dead albatross about his neck as a sign of his guilt.

In the distance a ship appeared, a skeleton ship which moved on the still sea where no wind blew. On its deck Death and Life-in-Death were casting dice for the crew and the Ancient Mariner. As a result of the cast, Death won the two hundred crew members, who dropped dead one by one. As the soul of each dead sailor rushed by, the Ancient Mariner was reminded of the whiz of his crossbow when he shot the albatross. Life-in-Death had won the Ancient Mariner, who must now live on to expiate his sins. Furthermore, the curse lived on in the eyes of the men who died accusing him. One night the Ancient Mariner, observing the beauty of the water snakes around the ship, blessed these creatures in his heart. The spell was broken. The albatross fell from his neck into the sea.

At last the Ancient Mariner was able to sleep. Rain fell to quench his thirst. The warped vessel began to move, and the bodies of the dead crew rose to resume their regular duties as the ship sailed quietly on, moved by a spirit toward the South Pole.

The Ancient Mariner fell into a trance. He awoke to behold his own country, the very port from which he had set sail. Then the angelic spirits left the dead bodies of the crew and appeared in their own forms of light. Meanwhile, the pilot on the beach had seen the lights and he rowed out with his son and a holy Hermit to bring the ship in to harbor.

Suddenly the ship sank, but the pilot pulled the Ancient Mariner into his boat. Once ashore, the old man asked the Hermit to hear his confession and give him penance. The Ancient Mariner told the Wedding Guest that at uncertain times since that moment, the agony of his guilt returned and he must tell the story of his voyage to one who must be taught love and reverence for all things God has made and loved.

The merry din of the wedding had ceased, and the Wedding Guest returned home a sadder and a wiser man.

# THE RING AND THE BOOK

*Type of work:* Poem
*Author:* Robert Browning (1812-1889)
*Type of plot:* Dramatic monologues
*Time of plot:* Seventeenth century
*Locale:* Italy
*First published:* 1868-1869

*Principal characters:*
PIETRO COMPARINI, an aged Roman
VIOLANTE, Pietro's wife
POMPILIA, the Comparini's adopted daughter
GUIDO FRANCESCHINI, Pompilia's husband
GIUSEPPE CAPONSACCHI, a priest

## Critique:

This poem reveals Browning's deep perceptive and poetic powers at their greatest heights. Based upon a murder trial in the city of Florence in 1698, the poem attempts to probe the inner motivations of the people involved in that old, sordid tale of passion and crime. A series of dramatic characterizations and episodes carries the reader to the magnificent conclusion. Pompilia and Caponsacchi are among Browning's most notable creations. Too long to be one of the widely read poems of Browning, yet too penetrating to be disregarded by any of his admirers, *The Ring and the Book* is written with tremendous power of language.

## The Story:

Count Guido Franceschini, descended from an ancient house of Aretine, had married Pompilia Comparini, a young and beautiful Roman girl. Unhappy with her husband, the young wife fled back to Rome in the company of a young priest, Giuseppe Caponsacchi. Guido and four accomplices followed her, and on Christmas night he found his wife at the home of her parents, Pietro and Violante. He murdered the seventy-year-old man and woman and fatally wounded seventeen-year-old Pompilia.

The aged parents were laid in the church where the people of Rome came to stare and to speculate. The Comparini had been childless until somehow Violante had tricked Pietro into thinking that she had given birth to the child she had secretly bought. It was Violante's mischief which had led to evil, asserted the Roman people. She had spied Guido, of a noble family, and had persuaded him to take Pompilia for his wife. Then all three, parents and daughter, had moved to his estate in Arezzo and there learned of Guido's poverty. Leaving Pompilia behind, the Comparini returned to Rome. Back in Rome, Violante confessed to Pietro that she had bought the child from a prostitute, and by disowning her parentage the aged couple denied Guido his dowry rights. Pompilia, meanwhile, wrote a letter to the archbishop in Rome, telling him that since her parents' departure life in Arezzo had become unbearable. In Arezzo, Pompilia had begun a flirtation with Caponsacchi, the Roman gossipers related, and at last had run away with him. As the guilty pair neared Rome, Guido overtook them and brought them to Rome and to the Pope. The couple declared themselves innocent and disavowed love letters which Guido claimed had passed between them. When the court treated the case as a slight marriage quarrel, Guido returned to Arezzo and the taunts of his townsmen. Soon afterward news reached him that Pompilia, who had returned to the Comparini, had given birth to a son. Then Guido took four men, went to Rome, killed the parents, and left Pompilia dying. The Romans excitedly awaited the trial, for Caponsacchi would be one of the witnesses.

Another group of spectators in Rome

took a different view of the murderer and his wife. Pompilia had been a blessing to her foster parents, no matter how she came to them. They had considered it a blessing when Guido married their daughter, only to reach horrible disillusionment when they went to Arezzo and saw his cruelty and poverty. She was Guido's victim, these gossips said.

The tribunal tried to determine the truth in the case. Pietro and Violante had been poor, struggling creatures. When the mother of Pompilia was with child, Violante had bargained with her for the baby and deceived her husband by pretending that it was she who was pregnant. Her act was judged criminal. When Guido came to Rome to find a wife to bear him sons, and a dowry to pay his debts, Pietro and Violante gave him their daughter so that she could rise in name and fortune. When they learned that Guido was penniless, they cried that they had been cheated. Meanwhile it was Pompilia who suffered between the rival factions of parents and husband. She was tricked by Guido to trace letters to Caponsacchi, which were offered at the trial. But Guido's friends claimed that he could not have so mistreated his young wife, that she must have written the letters herself.

Guido told his own story. His family had once been wealthy and great, but in his lifetime they had known only poverty. His brothers were priests; he alone remained to carry on the Franceschini name. His brother Paul, a priest in Rome, had advised him that Pompilia would make a suitable wife. He was to give the girl his name and state in return for her dowry and her son. But Pompilia shirked her wifely duties from the first. One day she caught the eye of Caponsacchi at the opera. Afterward Caponsacchi's way to church led him past Guido's house, past Pompilia's window. Then one night Pompilia drugged Guido and all the servants and fled with her priest to the inn where Guido located them. He found some letters Caponsacchi had exchanged with her, letters

which she claimed had been forged. He brought them to court to have his marriage annulled, but the court upheld the marriage and sent Caponsacchi away for a short confinement. Pompilia returned to Pietro and Violante and there she had a child which Guido believed Caponsacchi's. He had no other course, he said, but to go to Rome and cleanse his family name, and he threw himself upon the justice of the court.

Caponsacchi took the stand to describe his first sight of Pompilia at the opera. Not long after he received a letter, signed by Pompilia, confessing love and asking him to come to her window. Suspecting the letter to be a forgery, he answered it with a refusal. He received more letters. At last he became curious and went to stand outside Guido's house. Pompilia, seeing him, rebuked him for his unseemly letters to her, a married woman. They decided that they were victims of Guido's plot. Pompilia begged Caponsacchi to take her to her parents in Rome. His heart softening at her plight, he arranged for her to go away with him.

Pompilia, Caponsacchi said, had been victimized by her cruel husband. The testimony of dying Pompilia upheld what Caponsacchi had said. At the time of her marriage she had been only thirteen years old. She had been brought to Arezzo, to an impoverished home where Guido's brother had tried to seduce her. For three years she lived in misery. Then she received letters from Caponsacchi. She tried to understand the mystery, knowing that somehow she was being tricked, but finally she sent for the priest because she had decided to seek help from the outside world.

The testimony of others followed, some in defense of Guido, others exposing his carefully laid plot to rid himself of Pompilia. Testimony of Pompilia's innocence was also presented. The Pope, condemning Guido for the crime, pronounced Pompilia innocent of guilt and told the court of the tremendous burden of justice that a Pope must carry on his shoulders. Guido and his four accomplices were sentenced to be hanged.

Humbled and fearful of death, Guido made one last plea for his life. Pride and self-love colored his statements as he confessed his crime but rationalized his motive. He was to be pitied; he wanted to live. He pleaded for mercy which was not granted.

# RING ROUND THE MOON

*Type of work:* Drama
*Author:* Jean Anouilh (1910-    )
*Time:* 1912
*Locale:* The Auvergne, France
*First presented:* 1947

*Principal characters:*
    HUGO, a young man about town
    FREDERIC, his twin brother
    MADAME DESMERMORTES, their aunt
    DIANA MESSERSCHMANN, engaged to Frederic
    MESSERSCHMANN, her millionaire father
    LADY DOROTHY INDIA, Madame Desmermortes' niece and Messer-
        schmann's mistress
    ISABELLE, a ballet dancer
    HER MOTHER, a teacher of the pianoforte
    ROMAINVILLE, Isabelle's patron
    PATRICE BOMBELLES, Messerschmann's traveling secretary, secretly in
        love with Lady India
    CAPULAT, Madame Desmermortes' faded companion

Jean Anouilh likes to divide his plays into three categories of material and treatment, and to date he has maintained a fairly even balance of productivity among the classifications he has designated. Included in his *pièces noires,* as he calls his more somber dramas, are those based on themes taken from classic Greek sources or from history: *Legend of Lovers,* the retelling in a modern setting of the Orpheus and Eurydice story; *Antigone,* a thinly veiled allegory of France during the German occupation; *Medea,* and *The Lark,* which deals with the martyrdom of Joan of Arc. On the evidence of these plays it would be possible to make out a good case proving that Anouilh is the leading tragic dramatist of his generation in France; however, he is better known in this country and in England for his *pièces roses* and *pièces brillantes,* his lighter works of tender feeling, artifice, and wit which do not fall into any of the conventional classifications of drama. Neither comedy, farce, fantasy, nor romance, they contain elements of all four. *Ring Round the Moon,* listed among the *pièces brillantes,* is a typical example.

*Ring Round the Moon* is the title given by Christopher Fry to his adaptation of Anouilh's *L'Invitation au Château.* Although this version in English has consid-

erable merit and unmistakable charm in its own right—a Cinderella theme treated in the manner of Oscar Wilde—Fry has caught little more than the mannered grace and brittle style of the original. His treatment, aptly described as "A Charade with Music," is a work of surface brilliance, poetic overtones, and sly wit, and as an engaging divertissement it provides an entertaining evening in the theater. Anouilh's play, on the other hand, is more serious in its ironic implications, depth of feeling, and insight into the muddled human situation, matters presented against a background that seems always on the point of dissolving into the make-believe atmosphere of a fairy tale.

This effect is characteristic of Anouilh's art, for he holds that the primary business of the theater is to create an illusion and a mood. The world of his plays is a moon-struck region of imagination and invention in which the logic of things as they happen is seldom the daylight logic of the actual or the commonplace. In spite of the fact that this world is as circumscribed and meticulously detailed as Proust's, it lends itself to effects of unabashed theatricality appropriate to a Cloud-Cuckoo-Land in which the fantastic becomes the real, art is also artifice, and no clear line divides the rueful from the comic. Since Giraudoux no writer has been more successful in combining the irresponsible with the serious, the improbable with the real. Such stock situations as the confusion of identical twins, contrived or ridiculous misunderstandings between lovers, affections abruptly transferred, and the play within a play abound in Anouilh's dramas because he dares to be original in an old-fashioned way. He works within a stage tradition that goes back through the comedy of manners and the *commedia dell' arte* to Plautus, Terence, and Menander.

A twofold theme of deception and self-deception provides the dramatic motivation in *Ring Round the Moon*. The setting is the fifteenth-century chateau of Madame Desmermortes, the time those almost forgotten days before World War I when everyone had plenty of money—except the poor—and there was an international society, when aristocratic elderly ladies had genteel companions and wealthy elderly men had traveling secretaries, and when fabulous balls were common. An assemblage of guests has gathered at the chateau for such a gala occasion. They include Madame Desmermortes' nephews, Hugo and Frederic; Messerschmann, a millionaire industrialist of obscure origins; Diana, his daughter; Romainville, a patron of the arts; Lady Dorothy India, Madame Desmermortes' niece and Messerschmann's mistress, and Patrice Bombelles, the millionaire's secretary, with whom Lady India is involved in a secret love affair.

Hugo and Frederic are identical twins, alike in every respect except that Frederic has a heart and Hugo does not. Frederic is engaged to Diana, who is as heartless as Hugo and obviously the wrong person for Frederic to marry. Unable to see reason, he has followed a blind path wherever love has led; his latest folly is sleeping in the rhododendron bushes under Diana's window. Not realizing that he himself is in love with Diana, Hugo is determined to end his guileless brother's romance. To this end he hires Isabelle, a dancer in the corps de ballet at the Paris

Opera, politely blackmails Romainville into passing her off as his niece, and introduces her as a guest invited to the ball. For a fee and the dress he has provided, Isabelle is to make herself the center of attention, so much so, in fact, that Hugo will appear to be in love with her. At the same time she is supposed to make Frederic think that she is in love with him in order to draw that young man to her and away from Diana.

Even before the ball matters begin to go awry. To the consternation of Madame Desmermortes' proper butler, Isabelle's vulgar mother also arrives and is recognized by Capulat, Madame Desmermortes' companion, as an old school friend. To explain her presence, the mother tells Capulat that Hugo and Isabelle are really in love and that the young man has brought the girl to the ball under the pretense that she is Romainville's niece in order to conceal her true identity. Informed of this circumstance by her companion, Madame Desmermortes decides to take a hand in the masquerade; she dresses Isabelle's mother in finery and introduces her as prominent in society.

From these materials Anouilh has constructed a plot in which irony and nonsense are only a part of the thematic design, not the ultimate effect of the play. With compassion and insight he shows in brief glimpses the reverse side of the illusions by which humanity lives, for his real theme is the isolation of the lonely and the loving and the attempts of men and women to find understanding among themselves, happiness in money or in love. Messerschmann and Isabelle stand on a common footing when the millionaire, urged on by his jealous daughter, offers Isabelle money to leave the ball, and the dancer refuses. They end by tearing up the money in an angry, despairing rejection of material values. Then Messerschmann, remembering his peace and contentment in the days when he was a tailor in Cracow, goes off to break the Bourse and so lose his great fortune. His failure—for his flurry on the exchange more than doubles his wealth—is as ironic in its consequences as Isabelle's pretended suicide when, according to Hugo's plan, she throws herself in the lake on the chateau grounds; it is Hugo, not Frederic, who pulls her out, and it is to heartless Hugo that she turns in the misery of not being loved.

In the end worldly, shrewd old Madame Desmermortes sets these confused matters straight. Frederic discovers the true nature of Diana and finds in Isabelle an innocence and gentleness of heart to match his own. Hugo realizes that he has secretly wanted Diana all the while, after Madame Desmermortes makes him see that they were really made for each other. Even Messerschmann's future holds a promise of happiness. Believing that he has lost all his money, Lady India forgets Bombelles and swears that she will follow Messerschmann to Siberia if need be.

As stylized as a quadrille, touching even in its absurdity, Anouilh's play reveals not only the human capacity for error, self-deception, cruelty, and guilt but also man's striving toward goodness and love, within the confines of a limited but imaginatively conceived world in which illusion and reality stand back to back to shape a metaphor of life.

# RIP VAN WINKLE

*Type of work:* Tale
*Author:* Washington Irving (1783-1859)
*Type of plot:* Regional romance
*Time of plot:* Eighteenth century
*Locale:* New York State
*First published:* 1819-1820

Principal characters:
RIP VAN WINKLE, a henpecked husband
DAME VAN WINKLE, his wife

*Critique:*

"Rip Van Winkle," like "The Legend of Sleepy Hollow," first appeared in *The Sketch Book of Geoffrey Crayon, Gent.,* and with these romantic, almost fantastic, tales Irving made his earliest and most favorable impression upon the English and American reading publics. He was living in England when he wrote these tales, but it is easy to see that the fascination of the American landscape was with him there. "Rip Van Winkle" is said to be based on a common European legend, transferred to American soil; that is, Otmar's tale of "Peter Klaus" in the *Volkssagen.*

*The Story:*

Along the reaches of the Hudson, not far from the Kaatskill mountains, there was a small, antique Dutch town. The mountains overshadowed the town and there were times when the good Dutch burghers could see a hood of clouds hanging over the crests of the hills.

In that small town lived a man named Rip Van Winkle. He was beloved by all his neighbors, by the children and the dogs, but at home his life was made miserable by his shrewish wife. Though he was willing to help anyone else at any odd job that might be necessary, it was impossible for him to keep his own house or farm in repair. He was descended from a good old Dutch family, but he had none of the fine Dutch traits of thrift or energy.

He spent a great deal of his time at the village inn, under the sign of King George III, until his wife chased him from there. Then he took his gun and his dog Wolf and headed for the hills. Wolf was as happy as Rip to get away

from home. When Dame Van Winkle berated the two of them, Rip raised his eyes silently to heaven, but Wolf tucked his tail between his legs and slunk out of the house.

One fine day in autumn Rip and Wolf walked high into the Kaatskills after squirrels. As evening came on, he and his dog sat down to rest a while before starting home. When Rip started down the mountainside, he heard his name called.

A short, square little man with a grizzled beard had called Rip to help carry a keg of liquor. The little man was dressed in antique Dutch clothes. Although he accepted Rip's help in carrying the keg, he carried on no conversation. As they ascended the mountain, Rip heard noises that sounded like peals of thunder. When they reached a sort of amphitheater near the top, Rip saw a band of little men, dressed and bearded like his companion, playing ninepins. One stout old gentleman, who seemed to be the leader, wore a laced doublet and a high-crowned hat with a feather.

The little men were no more companionable than the first one had been, and Rip felt somewhat depressed. Because they seemed to enjoy the liquor from the keg, Rip tasted it a few times while they were absorbed in their game. Then he fell into a deep sleep.

On waking, he looked in vain for the stout old gentleman and his companions. When he reached for his gun, he found only a rusty flintlock. His dog did not answer his call. He tried to find the amphitheater where the little men had played, but the way was blocked by a rushing stream.

The people he saw as he walked into town were all strangers to him. Since most of them, upon looking at him, stroked their chins, Rip unconsciously stroked his and found that his beard had grown a foot long.

The town itself looked different. At first Rip thought the liquor from the keg had addled his head, for he had a hard time finding his own house. When he did locate it at last, he found it in a state of decay. Even the sign over the inn had been changed to one carrying the name of General Washington. The men gathered under the sign talked gibberish to him, and they accused him of trying to stir up trouble by coming armed to an election. When they let him ask for his old cronies, he named men who the loungers told him had moved away, or else they had been dead these twenty years.

Finally an eager young woman pushed through the crowd to look at Rip. Her voice started a train of thought and he asked who she was and who her father had been. When she claimed to be Rip Van Winkle's daughter Judith, he asked one more question about her mother. Judith told him that her mother had died after breaking a blood vessel in a fit of anger at a Yankee peddler. Rip breathed more freely.

Although another old woman claimed that she recognized him, the men at the inn only winked at his story until an old man, a descendant of the village historian, vouched for Rip's strange tale. He assured the men that he had it as a fact from his historian ancestor that Hendrick Hudson with his crew came to the mountains every twenty years to visit the scene of their exploits, and that the old historian had seen the crew in antique Dutch garb playing at ninepins just as Rip had related.

Rip spent the rest of his life happily telling his story at the inn until everyone knew it by heart. Even now when the inhabitants of the village hear thunder in the Kaatskills, they say that Hendrick Hudson and his crew are playing ninepins. And many a henpecked husband has wished in vain for a draught of Rip Van Winkle's quieting brew.

# THE RISE OF SILAS LAPHAM

*Type of work:* Novel
*Author:* William Dean Howells (1837-1920)
*Type of plot:* Domestic realism
*Time of plot:* Nineteenth century
*Locale:* New England
*First published:* 1885

*Principal characters:*
SILAS LAPHAM, a self-made manufacturer
MRS. LAPHAM, his wife
PENELOPE, and
IRENE, his daughters
TOM COREY, the Laphams' friend
MR. ROGERS, Mr. Lapham's former partner

## Critique:

According to many critics, *The Rise of Silas Lapham* is the most important book William Dean Howells ever wrote. Howells, a prolific though never a brilliant writer, attempted to deal conscientiously with the everyday experiences of rather ordinary people. By presenting character and situation in a straightforward manner, he wrote novels characterized chiefly by their moral atmosphere and authentic domestic realism.

## The Story:

Silas Lapham was being interviewed for a Boston paper. The journalist was secretly mocking Lapham's way of life, but Lapham, content with his success, paid little attention to his interviewer as he proudly exhibited a photograph of his two daughters and his wife. He told how he had been brought up in a large family, how he had gone West with his brothers, how he had returned, bought a stage route, married the village schoolteacher and finally hit upon making paint from a mineral his father had discovered on his farm.

The story of his success was a story of determination and hard work. During the Civil War his wife had kept the paint works going and after the war he had taken a man named Rogers as a partner for a short time.

After the interview Lapham and his wife drove out to see the site of a house they were building in a more fashionable part of Boston. Although both looked with pride upon the place soon to be their residence, they pretended not really to want the house at all. They merely suggested the new home would be a greater advantage for Penelope and Irene when their friends came to call.

But neither Penelope nor Irene anticipated with any great joy their coming change of living. They said they felt the present house was more convenient to the horsecars. Secretly, both realized that their parents were awkward in social life. At the same time they themselves had never been brought up to feel comfortable in the presence of people whose families had been accustomed to wealth for generations.

One day, as Mr. and Mrs. Lapham were dismounting from their carriage, Lapham's former partner appeared unexpectedly. Rogers had furnished money to help Lapham get started, but later Lapham had crowded Rogers out. Lapham insisted that what he had done had merely been good business. But Mrs. Lapham maintained that she never felt quite right about what had happened to Rogers, and seeing him again took all the happiness out of her plans for the new house.

The next time the family ventured out to visit the partly-completed house, Irene was surprised by the arrival of Tom Corey, a young man who had shown some interest in her. Immediately Mr. Lapham took over the occasion, and by his bragging greatly embarrassed his

3230

daughters.

That evening young Corey talked to his father about the Laphams. Bromfield Corey did not agree with his son's easy acceptance of the Laphams, but he did not object when his son announced his intention to apply for a position in Lapham's firm.

Young Corey visited Lapham in his office in order to ask for a job. Lapham was so pleased that he invited Corey to go with him to Nantasket where Mrs. Lapham and the girls were expecting Lapham for the weekend. At the Nantasket cottage the girls and their mother could not understand what had brought young Corey for the weekend visit. They had thought Lapham's bragging would have kept him away forever.

That evening Lapham discussed Corey with his wife. Mrs. Lapham contended that Corey was interested not in the paint but in Irene. Her husband commented that unless the young man were interested in the paint he would never get a chance to be interested in Irene. When Lapham said he intended to give the young man a chance, Mrs. Lapham warned him that he was playing with a situation which was bound to bring trouble.

Tom Corey's mother was concerned when she heard what her son had done. She admitted she would not object if he made a fortune from the paint business, but she did not want him to fall in love with either of the Lapham girls.

After Corey entered Lapham's employ, he was invited frequently to the Lapham home, for Irene was beginning to fall in love with him. Bromfield Corey grew more and more curious about the Laphams. He decided that he would encourage his wife to give a dinner for them in the autumn.

The cost of the new house worried Mrs. Lapham, and she asked her husband to stop his lavish spending. She learned he had given a substantial loan to Rogers, his former partner.

When Mrs. Corey returned from Bar Harbor, she debated a long time about giving a dinner party for the Laphams. In the first place, the Laphams were newcomers. On the other hand, she wanted to give public recognition of the new connection between her son and the Lapham family. She finally decided to give a formal dinner early in the season, before her more prominent friends returned to the city.

On the night of the dinner the Laphams tried to appear at ease. Penelope had refused to attend, thus causing her mother considerable embarrassment. Lapham watched the other men carefully, feeling sure he had not made too many social blunders. The next day, however, he was not so sure, for he had taken too much wine at dinner.

At the office Lapham sought out Corey and mentioned with embarrassment his behavior of the night before. He offered Corey his liberty to seek another job, a position among gentlemen, but Corey refused to go, saying that Lapham's tipsy talk had been only an unfortunate accident. When they parted, Corey insisted that Lapham's conduct had been proper and entertaining.

That night, feeling that he had actually patronized Lapham, Corey resolved to go to his employer and apologize. Lapham was out, but Penelope received Corey. At the end of a long talk he stammeringly confessed his love for her. In great confusion he left without waiting to speak to Lapham.

The next day Mrs. Lapham informed her husband that Corey had been coming to see Penelope all the time. She could only imagine what the shock would do to Irene. They felt, however, that Penelope would never permit Corey to become her suitor, for Penelope was convinced he belonged to Irene.

Irene was informed of the situation by her mother that evening. Immediately she carried to her sister's room every memento of Corey's attentions she possessed. After a few days Lapham took her to his boyhood village in Vermont.

Corey called on the Laphams to present his explanation, saying that he had cared more for Penelope all the time. Penelope refused to give him any satisfaction. She said she owed more to her sister's hurt feelings.

At the same time Lapham's finances were troubling him greatly. People who owed him money were unable to pay; his own creditors were pressing him. Lapham determined to take a trip west to inspect some mills held as security for his loan to Rogers. When he returned he was even more concerned. Rogers had drawn him into a trap with his securities, for a railroad controlled the value of the property. Lapham decided it would be necessary to sell the new house unfinished. Learning of Lapham's difficulties, Corey offered to lend his employer thirty thousand dollars, but Lapham rejected the offer.

Lapham's affairs took a turn for the worse. An added blow was the destruction of the unfinished Back Bay house. Wandering through the house one night, he decided to test one of the chimneys and made a fire from blocks and shavings the workmen had left scattered about. He thought the fire had burned out before he left. That night the house burned to the ground. The insurance policy had expired a week before.

Determined to raise money by selling everything he could, Lapham visited his competitors who were working on a new mineral paint. They were willing to merge with him if he could raise money to help develop their plant. While he was trying to secure a loan, he learned from Rogers that some English gentlemen were interested in buying the property which Rogers had put up as security and which Lapham had thought valueless. Lapham refused to sell the mills however, because he believed a sale would be unethical as long as the railroad controlled their value.

He asked for time to think over the proposition. Shortly afterward the railroad forced him to sell the mills at a ruinous figure. Lapham felt that his honesty, which had kept him from selling the property to the Englishmen, had been unjustly abused. Rogers claimed Lapham had made it impossible for him to recover his losses. Lapham was now ruined, for he could not raise capital to merge with the rival paint firm.

Tom Corey was determined to marry Penelope in spite of her father's impending ruin. He did marry her after Lapham went into bankruptcy, and his family accepted her for their own sake as well as for his. Irene, who had returned as soon as she heard of her father's troubles, was pleased with her sister's happiness.

Lapham managed to save a part of his fortune, but more important to him was the belief that he had acted honestly in all his business dealings.

# THE RIVALS

*Type of work:* Drama
*Author:* Richard Brinsley Sheridan (1751-1816)
*Type of plot:* Comedy of manners
*Time of plot:* Eighteenth century
*Locale:* Bath, an English watering place
*First presented:* 1775

> *Principal characters:*
> CAPTAIN JACK ABSOLUTE (ENSIGN BEVERLEY), a young officer in love with Lydia
>     Languish
> SIR ANTHONY ABSOLUTE, his father
> FAULKLAND, his friend, in love with Julia
> BOB ACRES, a country squire
> SIR LUCIUS O'TRIGGER, a fiery Irishman
> LYDIA LANGUISH, an heiress
> MRS. MALAPROP, her aunt
> JULIA MELVILLE, her cousin

## Critique:

One of the most popular of the English comedies of manners, *The Rivals* is most successful in character portrayal. All the great characters are here — Mrs. Malaprop, whose misuse of words gave the word malapropism to the language; Bob Acres, the bumptious but lovable country squire trying to behave like a gentleman; romantic Lydia Languish with her head stuffed with nonsense from current novels. The play is Sheridan's satire on the pretentiousness and sentimentality of his age, satire which in many respects is applicable to our own day.

## The Story:

To beautiful and wealthy young Lydia Languish, who had been brought up on romantic novels, the only lover worth considering was one whose position in life was in complete contrast to her own. To this end she had fallen in love with a penniless young ensign named Beverley. But to this same Beverley, her aunt, Mrs. Malaprop, raised serious objections. Her antipathy to young Mr. Beverley was partly aroused by letters which the ensign had written to Lydia, letters which made uncomplimentary references to her aunt's age and appearance. Mrs. Malaprop had some moments of extreme discomfiture, when she wondered whether she did resemble the she-dragon to which Beverley had compared her.

Mrs. Malaprop herself had fallen hopelessly in love with a quixotic Irishman named Sir Lucius O'Trigger, who presumably returned her affection. Sir Lucius, who had never seen Mrs. Malaprop, had been hoodwinked by a maidservant into believing that the romantic creature with whom he was exchanging love letters was Lydia herself.

The situation was further complicated by the fact that Beverley was in reality young Captain Jack Absolute, the son of Sir Anthony Absolute, and as wealthy and aristocratic as Lydia herself. Jack very early sensed that he would get nowhere if he wooed the romantic Lydia in his own person, and so he assumed a character more nearly resembling the heroes of the novels with which Lydia's pretty but silly head was stuffed.

Nor did Jack's friend, Faulkland, fare any better in his own romantic pursuit of Lydia's cousin, Julia Melville. In fact, it might be thought that he fared worse, for unlike Jack, he was forever placing imaginary obstacles between himself and his beloved. Whenever they were separated, Faulkland imagined all kinds of horrible catastrophes which might have

THE RIVALS by Richard Brinsley Sheridan. Published by The Macmillan Co.

befallen her, and when he found that she was alive and well he tormented himself with the thought that she could not be in love and remain so happy. At last Jack Absolute lost patience with his friend's ridiculous behavior, and even Julia became a little tired of her lover's unfounded jealousy. This curious love tangle reached a crisis when Sir Anthony Absolute informed his son that he had selected the woman for him to marry, threatening, if he refused, to cut him off without a penny. Not having the faintest idea as to the identity of the woman his father had picked out for him, and conjuring up pictures of some homely heiress his father intended to force on him against his will, Jack rebelled. He declared that, whatever the consequences, he would have nothing to do with his father's choice.

Having been quite a connoisseur of pretty women in his youth, and being not exactly immune to their charms in his old age, Sir Anthony Absolute was not the man to saddle his son with an unattractive wife. He had made an agreement with Mrs. Malaprop for the bestowal of her niece's hand upon his son. Mrs. Malaprop, in turn, was only too glad to save Lydia from a foolish marriage to Beverley. But when Jack refused to marry anyone not of his own choosing, Sir Anthony flew into a rage and insisted that the marriage take place regardless of what the lady might be like.

By chance, however, Jack discovered that the girl Sir Anthony had selected as his bride was Lydia Languish, the identical girl he himself had been wooing as Ensign Beverley. He immediately assured his father that he would be willing to marry anyone of his choosing. Sir Anthony, not used to such tractability on Jack's part, became suspicious and a little worried. Nevertheless, he made arrangements for his son to meet his bride-to-be, thus placing Jack in a neat dilemma.

Jack realized that Lydia would have none of him as Sir Anthony Absolute's son. Finally the supposed Ensign Beverley pretended to Lydia that in order to gain access to her aunt's house, he would be forced to pose as Jack Absolute.

Lydia had another suitor in the person of Bob Acres, a wealthy country squire and a neighbor of Sir Anthony, who had ambitions to become a man about town. Before Sir Anthony proposed his son as a husband for her niece, Mrs. Malaprop had favored Bob Acres as a likely candidate for Lydia's hand. When Acres discovered he had a rival in Ensign Beverley, he was disheartened. Encouraged by his friend, Sir Lucius O'Trigger, he challenged Beverley to a duel. Never having seen young Beverley, he was forced to give the challenge to the ensign's friend, Jack Absolute, to deliver.

The great crisis in Jack's love affairs came when he was forced to face Lydia in the company of his father. With his true identity revealed, Lydia's dreams of a romantic elopement with a penniless ensign vanished. She dismissed Jack from her life forever. Chagrined by his abrupt dismissal, Jack accepted with positive gusto another challenge to a duel from Sir Lucius O'Trigger. Sir Lucius named the place as King's Mead Fields at six o'clock that very evening, when he had an appointment to act as a second to his friend, Acres, in a duel with a certain Ensign Beverley.

When Lydia learned that Jack had involved himself in a duel on her account, he became a different person in her eyes, and she hurried with her aunt to King's Mead Fields in an effort to halt the duel. Meanwhile Sir Lucius O'Trigger had alarmed Acres with his bloodthirsty stories of dueling, so that when Acres recognized his opponent as his old friend, Jack Absolute, he heaved a distinct sigh of relief.

With the arrival of Lydia and Mrs. Malaprop, the whole situation was quickly explained. Sir Lucius, much to his chagrin, was forced to realize that the writer of tender love letters to whom he addressed his own impassioned correspondence was not Lydia but Mrs. Malaprop. Faulkland was content to accept Julia's love for the whole-hearted thing it was. Lydia at last saw Ensign Beverley and Jack Absolute as the same person with whom she was in love. And Bob Acres, happy because he would not be forced to fight a duel with anyone, ordered fiddles and entertainment for all in the fashionable parlors of Bath.

# RIVER OF EARTH

*Type of work:* Novel
*Author:* James Still (1906-    )
*Type of plot:* Regional romance
*Time of plot:* Early twentieth century
*Locale:* Kentucky
*First published:* 1940

Principal characters:

BRACK BALDRIDGE, a Kentucky mountaineer
ALPHA BALDRIDGE, his wife
BRACK'S OLDEST BOY, the narrator
EULY, the narrator's sister
GRANDMOTHER MIDDLETON, Alpha's mother
UNCLE JOLLY, Alpha's brother

## Critique:

It is obvious that James Still is a poet as well as a novelist, for his words almost sing as he describes the Kentucky hills and the people who inhabit them. He tells the story of the *River of Earth* through the words of a very young boy, and through the eyes of that boy shows us the tiny, barren farms; the smoky, sooty mining towns; the bat-filled schoolhouses; the local jails where a prisoner could have company for as many days as he wished. Although the boy did not understand all that he saw and heard, he makes us understand what the author is trying to say—that life flows as a river flows and that the cycle of life is never finished but goes on and on.

## The Story:

When the mines closed in March, there was very little food left in the house. It was still a long time before the garden crops would be ready, and Alpha wanted Brack to tell his two cousins, Harl and Tibb Logan, to leave the house and find food for themselves. But the father said that as long as he had food in his house, he would never turn his blood kin away. Then Uncle Samp came to live with them, and the mother saw her four children getting hungrier and leaner. Knowing that the kin would leave if there were no place for them to sleep, she calmly set fire to the house, first moving the children and the skimpy furniture to the smokehouse.

All spring, while the family lived in the smokehouse, they ate less and less and waited for the first vegetables. When the beans were almost ready and the whole family dreamed of having their stomachs full, three men came from the mining town to beg food for their families. Unable to turn down starving people, Brack sent the men into his garden. When they came out, the boy saw that they had taken every bean from the patch. He turned away, wanting to cry.

In May, Brack took the boy with him when he went to help a neighbor deliver a colt. The boy expected to get the colt for his own, as his father's fee, but the neighbor's son told him that no Baldridge was going to get the colt, that the Baldridges were cowards, and that after their Grandpa Middleton had been killed by Aus Coggins no Baldridge had done anything about it. The boy fought with the neighbor's son. When the fight was over, they found that the colt was dead.

One day Uncle Jolly arrived and brought them a pair of guineas from Grandmother Middleton. Uncle Jolly spent as much time in jail as out. It was said that he was avenging Grandpa's death by tormenting Aus Coggins—cutting his fences, breaking his dam, and

RIVER OF EARTH by James Still. By permission of the author and the publishers, The Viking Press, Inc. Copyright, 1940, by James Still.

doing other mischief.

Soon after Uncle Jolly left, Brack wanted to move the family down to Blackjack, for the mines were going to open again. The mother did not want to go because the smoky valley would be a bad place for her sickly baby. But she resigned herself to her husband's wishes.

In the middle of August the boy and his sister Euly started to school. They were anxious to learn to read and write, the boy especially, for he did not want to be a miner. He hoped that some day he could be an animal doctor, as his father had always wanted to be. But it seemed to the boy and Euly that the most important thing they learned in school was how to smoke bats out of the building.

In late September the boy was sent to stay with his Grandmother Middleton while Uncle Jolly served a term in jail. He was to stay with her only until Uncle Luce came, but the corn was husked and the other grain harvested before Uncle Luce arrived. The boy was astonished at his grandmother's ability to do heavy work, for she was very old. When she learned that Uncle Jolly had been sentenced to two years in the state penitentiary, she asked the boy to stay with her during the winter. As soon as the crops were in she spent a great deal of time in bed. She spent hours telling him about her children and her husband. It was easy to see that Jolly was her favorite.

In January Uncle Jolly came home. There had been a fire at the penitentiary, and Jolly had been so brave in helping to fight the fire that the governor had pardoned him. Grandmother Middleton said nothing when Uncle Jolly told her that he had started the fire.

Uncle Jolly also brought the news that the boy's family had moved at last to Blackjack, but there was no other word of his family. Visitors were scarce in the hills.

Spring and summer passed pleasantly for the boy. In October Uncle Jolly was in jail again, this time for fighting. Uncle Toll came to bring Grandmother Middleton the news and he took the boy back to Hardin Town with him. They found Jolly content to be in jail except that he was lonesome. Uncle Toll begged him not to break out, for one more jail-break would send him to the penitentiary for a long time. Toll left the boy at the jail so that Uncle Jolly would not break out for lack of companionship. The boy slept in the hall outside his uncle's cell. When Uncle Jolly thought he would have to break out of jail or die, he stole the keys from the deputy and told the boy to take the key of Jolly's cell to his mother and ask her to keep it until the remaining days of the sentence were served. In that way the boy went back to his family.

In March the family moved from Blackjack again, this time to a little rented farm on a hillside. There the baby died of croup. Another garden was planted, and in the summer they had a funeral for the baby. The boy saw more relatives than he had known he had. At the end of summer Brack decided to go back to the mines and moved his family to Blackjack and into a house with windows.

Uncle Samp and Harl and Tibb Logan came back to live with the family. Harl and Tibb worked in the mine, but Uncle Samp had never worked and did not intend to start now. Soon the mines began to close down, and men everywhere were laid off again. Brack was kept on, with only one or two days of work each week.

Harl and Tibb, angry because they were laid off, dynamited one of the veins. At first it was thought that they were trapped in the mine and had died, but Uncle Samp and Brack rescued them. They left the Baldridge house after Harl and Tibb were kicked out by the mine boss and Uncle Samp married a fortune-teller.

Food was scarce again, and the mother sickly most of the time, her stomach swollen terribly. In March Uncle Jolly

3237

brought Grandmother Middleton's body to the house. The old lady had died at last, and Jolly was taking her to her old home to be buried. While they were sitting with the body in the front room of the house, the boy noticed his father looking constantly at the closed door behind which the mother had been taken by a neighbor woman. In the morning the boy knew what his father had been waiting for and why his mother had been so swollen. As he stood looking at the tracks the wagon had made as it carried his grandmother's body away for the last time, he heard a baby begin to cry.

# THE RIVET IN GRANDFATHER'S NECK

*Type of work:* Novel
*Author:* James Branch Cabell (1879-1958)
*Type of plot:* Social satire
*Time of plot:* 1896-1927
*Locale:* Litchfield, not to be found on the map of Virginia
*First published:* 1915

### Principal characters:

COLONEL RUDOLPH MUSGRAVE, a Southern gentleman
MISS AGATHA MUSGRAVE, his sister
PATRICIA STAPYLTON MUSGRAVE, his wife
JOHN CHARTERIS, a novelist
ANNE CHARTERIS, his wife
MRS. CLARICE PENDOMER. Charteris' former mistress

## Critique:

The Rivet in Grandfather's Neck, James Branch Cabell's third novel and the fourteenth volume in the Storisende Edition of his works, deals with the American descendants of Count Manuel of Poictesme. Subtitled "A Comedy of Limitations," the book satirizes the American South and its adherence to the code of chivalry. The title is taken from Hans Christian Andersen's fairy tale of "The Shepherdess and the Chimney Sweep," in which two porcelain figures who are in love attempt to escape after the shepherdess' grandfather, a porcelain Chinese figure with a nodding head, promises her to a wooden satyr. The shepherdess is frightened by the outside world, and they return. The grandfather had been broken while pursuing them, and his neck was riveted so that he could no longer nod agreement to the satyr's proposal. In the novel Musgrave interprets this tale as an allegory about human limitations: everyone has a figurative rivet in his neck, and this signifies the action one cannot perform. Although the outmoded code by which Musgrave lives is satirized, the author also perceived that this code was not without grace and charm. The manner matches the matter. Cabell was an urbane stylist who seems closer to the English wits than to any American writer.

## The Story:

Colonel Rudolph Musgrave, family head of the Musgraves of Matocton in Litchfield, was forty years old in 1896. He was a consummate Southern gentleman: an aristocrat, a scholar, a lover, and an indifferent businessman. A bachelor, he lived with his sister Miss Agatha, who let nothing interfere with his comfort. His small income from his position as librarian of the Litchfield Historical Society was augmented by his genealogical research for people who were trying to establish a pedigree, and the brother and sister lived quite comfortably on his earnings.

Both, however, had inherited Musgrave weaknesses. She tippled, and he fell in love with many women. The colonel had a streak of chivalry in his nature which prompted him to make gallant gestures of renunciation for the sake of the lady in question. His most recent act of chivalry, which had provided Litchfield with amusing gossip, occurred when he had been overheard by Anne Charteris —whom he had loved and lost to the selfish novelist, John Charteris—while he was reprimanding her husband for siring a child by Mrs. Pendomer. Anne, who blindly worshiped her husband, had misunderstood the situation, and she had supposed that Musgrave was the guilty party. Musgrave had accepted the blame in order to save Anne from learning that her husband was a philanderer. Privately, Musgrave delighted in the episode.

The Musgraves were visited by Patricia Stapylton, the twenty-one-year-old daughter of a second cousin once removed who had eloped with an overseer. Roger Stapylton, the overseer, had become wealthy in the North, and Patricia was engaged to marry Lord Pevensey. Although Musgrave tried to impress Patricia with his most formal manner, she was not at all awed by him and immediately punctured his reserve. He spent a good deal of time with her, however, and once he read to her "The Shepherdess and the Chimney Sweep."

Musgrave, acting according to his code of honor, fell in love with Patricia and tried to renounce her; but she saw through his performance and jilted the Englishman. During the dinner at which their engagement was to be announced, Musgrave discovered that Patricia had fallen in love with Joe Parkinson. Musgrave made his grand gesture by announcing her engagement to the younger man. But Patricia jilted Parkinson and Musgrave married her.

At first their marriage was very happy, even though Patricia was troubled by her husband's reserve. Stapylton offered Musgrave a remunerative position in his business, but Musgrave refused it. Then Musgrave tried to make some quick money in the stock market but promptly lost all his savings. After that they lived on Patricia's allowance, which was rather small because Stapylton was displeased by their refusal to leave Litchfield.

Patricia had inherited a deformed pelvis from her mother, who died in childbirth. When Patricia became pregnant the doctors gave her the choice between losing the child or her life. Without telling her husband anything about the matter, she decided to have the child because she knew how much Musgrave wanted a son. Though she survived the birth of her son, she was never completely well afterward and had to have a series of operations. The son was named Roger after her father, and Stapylton settled almost all his money on the child.

Tensions began to develop between the Musgraves. Miss Agatha and Patricia had never got along well together because the spinster resented Patricia's role in Musgrave's life. Patricia, still young and lively, found her husband's formality increasingly annoying. Also, she was annoyed by his ineptness with money.

The crisis in their relationship came with the death of Miss Agatha. During one of her drinking spells Miss Agatha had wandered out into a storm and caught pneumonia. When she died she was attended only by the colored maid, Virginia, and Musgrave rebuked his wife for leaving the sick woman alone. Patricia said some bitter things about Miss Agatha and insisted that Virginia hated all the Musgraves because Musgrave's uncle had fathered her son, who had been lynched by a mob for becoming involved with a white woman. Patricia declared that Virginia frequently was the only one present when a Musgrave died. Musgrave insisted that this claim was nonsense. The quarrel ended bitterly and their relationship was never quite the same afterward.

When their son was five, the Musgraves gave a house party at Matocton, the Musgrave ancestral estate. Among the guests were Anne and John Charteris. Patricia, finding Charteris a pleasing contrast to her husband, let him persuade her to run off with him. On his part, Charteris enjoyed the adoration of women and had been involved in many affairs. Though a successful novelist, he was not independently wealthy, and so he had always remained with Anne because she had a great deal of money. Now he was prepared to leave his wife because he thought he had found a richer woman.

Musgrave, discovering the plan, informed Charteris that Patricia had very little money of her own. Charteris then told Patricia that he could not take her away, giving her many hypocritical reasons for his change of heart.

Patricia was told by her doctor that her heart was weak and that she would not live long. Although she kept her own counsel, she was now determined to seek happiness with Charteris, and so she persuaded him to go through with their original plan. Charteris borrowed money from his wife to finance his desertion.

Musgrave, learning that Charteris and Patricia were going through with the elopement, attempted to dissuade Charteris by telling him that they were actually half-brothers. According to Musgrave's code of honor, no gentleman would steal his brother's wife. Charteris was unmoved by the news. The next morning Musgrave met the lovers as they were departing and struck Charteris. Patricia, realizing that Charteris was a coward, broke with him.

A few days later Charteris was murdered by a jealous husband. On this occasion, for once, he was innocent. The newspaper with the story was brought to Patricia by Virginia, and Patricia died of a heart attack.

Anne Charteris, who had never seen through her husband, continued to adore him. Some five years after his death she met Musgrave in the cemetery where both Patricia and Charteris were buried. Musgrave had Mrs. Pendomer's son with him. At first Anne was outraged by Musgrave's lack of taste in being seen in the company of his illegitimate child, but as she looked at the boy she realized that Charteris was the boy's real father. Although Musgrave tried to maintain the deception, Anne finally realized that her husband had been a scoundrel. There was now nothing to stand between Anne and Musgrave; they recognized, however, that their loyalties to their dead mates were too strong to let them marry.

In 1927, Colonel Rudolph Musgrave died dreaming of his first meeting with Patricia.

# ROAN STALLION

Type of work: Poem
Author: Robinson Jeffers (1887-1962)
Type of plot: Symbolic melodrama
Time of plot: 1920's
Locale: Carmel Coast, California
First published: 1925

Principal characters:
    CALIFORNIA, a farm wife
    JOHNNY, her husband
    CHRISTINE, their daughter

## Critique:

Roan Stallion is a powerful and highly symbolic narrative poem. Jeffers is a decentralist who believes that the only salvation for man lies in his escaping from himself and his fellow men to a communion with nature. In this poem he employs the roan stallion as a symbol of the rejection of man and the embracing of the natural life. It is a brutal story, but its difficult theme is handled with delicacy and power.

## The Story:

California was the daughter of a Scottish father and a Spanish and Indian mother. From her mother she had inherited a dark beauty and a passionate nature. When she was still very young she married a farmer, Johnny, and at twenty-one her features were already beginning to show the marks of hard work.

Johnny spent much of his time away from the farm drinking and gambling. One evening he brought home a splendid roan stallion he had won. It was shortly before Christmas, and California, pleased with his good fortune, decided to go into town to buy some Christmas presents for her young daughter, Christine. Johnny delayed her departure in the morning so that it was quite late before she could hitch their old mare to the buggy and set out for Monterey. By nightfall, when she was ready to return home, a heavy rainstorm had started. The water was high when she reached the ford. Before trying to cross in the darkness, she lashed the presents around her body and hoped that they would keep dry. Refusing to cross the swollen stream, the mare floundered back to shore. California soothed the mare and tried once more to guide her across the ford, but the animal was still frightened. Desperate, California prayed for light. Suddenly the heavens lit up brilliantly and she saw in them the face of a child over whom hovered angels. The mare, startled by the light, scrambled back to shore. Sobbing, California climbed out of the buggy, fastened the presents securely to her back, and mounted the horse. By the light of the heavens she was able to guide the mare across the stream and reach home safely.

California thought she hated the roan stallion, but she could not forget the magnificent beast. When she told young Christine of the miraculous light at the ford and described the birth of Christ, she could hardly restrain herself from identifying God and the stallion. She knew that outside Johnny was mating the stallion with a neighbor's mare.

That evening Johnny went down the valley to the home of a neighbor. After Christine was asleep, California stole out to the stable. She leaned against the fence, listening to the far-off cries of the coyotes and watching the moon rise over the hill. Once before she had seen God. If she were to ride to the top of the hill, perhaps she might see Him again. She hurried down to the corral. The stallion heard her as she approached. She ca-

ROAN STALLION by Robinson Jeffers. By permission of the author and Random House, Inc. Published by The Modern Library, Inc. Copyright, 1925, by Boni & Liveright, Inc., 1935, by The Modern Library, Inc.

ressed his flanks, wishing that nature had not made it impossible for him to possess her. Then she sprang upon his back and reveled in the feel of his muscles as he galloped up the hillside. At the top they halted, and she tethered him lightly to a tree. Overwhelmed by his majesty and her desire, she threw herself at his feet.

The following night California could not bear the thought of being with Johnny. He had brought home some wine and, half drunk, he ordered her to drink some. Revolted at the thought of the night ahead, California stole to the door, opened it, and fled. Excited by the prospect of a chase, Johnny called to his dog to help him. When California heard them approaching, she crawled under the fence into the corral, the dog close behind her. The stallion plunged, frightened by the snarling, snapping dog. Johnny climbed into the corral, where the fierce stallion trampled him to death.

In the meantime Christine had awakened. Frightened by the lonely house, she made her way to the corral. When she saw her father's body she ran back to the house for the rifle. California took the gun and shot the dog. While she watched, the stallion struck again at Johnny's body. Then, prompted by a remnant of fidelity to the human race, she raised the rifle and shot the stallion. It was as though she had killed God.

# ROB ROY

*Type of work:* Novel
*Author:* Sir Walter Scott (1771-1832)
*Type of plot:* Historical romance
*Time of plot:* 1715
*Locale:* Northumberland and Glasgow
*First published:* 1818

Principal characters:
MR. WILLIAM OSBALDISTONE, of the firm of Osbaldistone & Tresham
FRANK OSBALDISTONE, his son
SIR HILDEBRAND OSBALDISTONE, Frank's uncle
RASHLEIGH OSBALDISTONE, his son
SIR FREDERICK VERNON, a Jacobite
DIANA VERNON, his daughter
ROB ROY MACGREGOR CAMPBELL, a Scottish outlaw

## Critique:

Rob Roy MacGregor Campbell is not the hero of this novel; he is the man behind the scenes. The novel itself concerns the fortunes of Frank Osbaldistone and his adventures with Rob Roy, the Scottish Robin Hood. Scott, as he usually does, manipulates Scottish history to suit his purpose. The story is told by Frank Osbaldistone, writing to his friend, Tresham. Always a popular Waverley novel, it has been dramatized several times and was the subject of an opera by Flotow.

## The Story:

Frank Osbaldistone was recalled from France where he had been sent to learn his father's mercantile business. Disappointed in his son's progress, the angry parent ordered the young man to Osbaldistone Hall, home of his uncle, Sir Hildebrand Osbaldistone, in northern England. His father gave him fifty guineas for expenses and instructions to learn who among Sir Hildebrand's sons would accept a position in the trading house of Osbaldistone and Tresham.

On the road Frank fell in with a traveler named Morris, who was carrying a large sum of money in a portmanteau strapped to his saddle. That evening they stopped at the Black Bear Inn, in the town of Darlington, where they were joined at dinner by Mr. Campbell, a Scotsman. Campbell was Rob Roy, the Scottish outlaw. The next morning Campbell and Morris left together, and at a secluded spot along the road the men were halted and a highwayman robbed Morris of his saddlebag. Frank, meanwhile, rode toward Osbaldistone Hall. As he neared the rambling old mansion, he saw a fox hunt and met Diana Vernon, Sir Hildebrand's niece. Outspoken Diana told Frank that his cousins were a mixture of sot, gamekeeper, bully, horse-jockey, and fool, these characteristics being mixed in varying proportions in each man. Rashleigh, she said, was the most dangerous of the lot, for he maintained a private tyranny over everyone with whom he came in contact.

It was Rashleigh, however, who was prevailed upon to accept Frank's vacant position. The cousins disliked each other. One night, while drinking with the family, Frank became enraged at Rashleigh's speech and actions and struck him. Rashleigh never forgot the blow, although to all intents and purposes he and Frank declared themselves friends after their anger had cooled.

Shortly after Frank's arrival he was accused of highway robbery and he went at once to Squire Inglewood's court to defend himself and to confront his accuser, who turned out to be Morris. Rob Roy, however, appeared at the squire's court of justice and forced Morris to confess that Frank had not robbed him.

When Rashleigh departed to go into

business with Frank's father, Frank became Diana's tutor. Their association developed into deep affection on both sides, a mutual attraction marred only by the fact that Diana was by faith a Catholic and Frank a Presbyterian.

One day Frank received a letter from his father's partner, Mr. Tresham. The letter informed him that his father, leaving Rashleigh in charge, had gone to the continent on business, and that Rashleigh had gone to Scotland, where he was reported involved in a scheme to embezzle funds of Osbaldistone and Tresham.

Frank, accompanied by Andrew Fairservice, Sir Hildebrand's gardener, set off for Glasgow in an attempt to frustrate Rashleigh's plans. Arriving in the city on Sunday, they went to church. As Frank stood listening to the preacher, a voice behind him whispered that he was in danger and that he should not look back at his informant. The mysterious messenger asked Frank to meet him on the bridge at midnight. Frank kept the tryst and followed the man to the Tolbooth prison. There he found his father's chief clerk, Mr. Owen, who had been arrested and thrown into prison at the instigation of MacVittie and MacFin, Glasgow traders who did business with his father. Frank learned that Campbell had been his mysterious informant and guide, and for the first time he realized that Campbell and Rob Roy were one and the same.

Shortly thereafter Frank saw Morris, MacVittie, and Rashleigh talking together. He followed them and when Morris and MacVittie departed, leaving Rashleigh alone, Frank confronted his cousin and demanded an explanation of his behavior. As their argument grew more heated, swords were drawn, but the duel was broken up by Rob Roy, who cried shame at them because they were men of the same blood. Rob Roy considered both men his friends. Frank learned also that his father's funds were mixed up with a Jacobite uprising, in which Sir Hildebrand was one of the plotters. He suspected that Rashleigh had robbed Morris on information supplied by Rob Roy.

Frank and Andrew were arrested by an officer on their way to meet Rob Roy, and the officer who searched Frank discovered a note which Rob Roy had written to him. On the road the company was attacked by Scotsmen under the direction of Helen, Rob Roy's wife, who captured or killed all the soldiers. Helen, a bloodthirsty creature, ordered the death of Morris, who had fallen into the hands of the Highlanders. In the meantime, Rob Roy had also been captured but had made his escape when one of his captors rode close to Rob Roy and surreptitiously cut his bonds. Rob Roy threw himself from his horse into the river and swam to safety before his guards could overtake him.

With a Highland uprising threatening, Frank thought he had seen Diana for the last time. But he met her soon afterward riding through a wood in the company of her father, Sir Frederick Vernon, a political exile. She gave him a packet of papers which Rashleigh had been forced to give up; they were notes to the credit of Osbaldistone and Tresham. The fortune of Frank's father was safe.

In the Jacobite revolt of 1715, Rashleigh became a turncoat and joined the forces of King George. At the beginning of the revolt Sir Hildebrand had made his will, listing the order in which his sons would fall heir to his lands. Because Rashleigh had betrayed the Stuart cause, he substituted Frank's name for that of Rashleigh in the will. Sir Hildebrand was captured by the royal forces and imprisoned at Newgate, where he died. His four sons died in various ways and Frank inherited all the lands and properties belonging to Sir Hildebrand. When Frank went to Osbaldistone manor to take over, Rashleigh showed up with a warrant for Diana and her father. But he obtained no end that he desired, for he was killed in a fight with

Rob Roy. Frank became the lord of Osbaldistone Hall. At first Frank's father did not like the idea of having his son marry a Papist, but at last he relented and Frank and Diana were married.

# ROBIN HOOD'S ADVENTURES

*Type of work:* Folk tales
*Author:* Unknown
*Type of plot:* Adventure romance
*Time of plot:* Thirteenth century
*Locale:* England
*First published:* c. 1490

> *Principal characters:*
> ROBIN HOOD, Earl of Huntingdon
> LITTLE JOHN,
> FRIAR TUCK,
> WILL SCARLET,
> A TINKER, and
> A COOK, of the Band of Merry Men
> THE SHERIFF OF NOTTINGHAM
> SIR RICHARD OF THE LEA, Robin Hood's friend

## Critique:

Robin Hood, legendary outlaw, is a folk hero who has been celebrated in ballad and tale since the Middle Ages. The first collection of ballads dealing with his exploits was published about 1490. This book, printed by Wynkyn de Worde, was titled *The Lytel Geste of Robin Hood*. These adventure stories tell of Robin Hood's courage, skill at archery, and daring deeds in support of the poor. Nowadays Robin himself is known chiefly as a children's hero, but he has served as the prototype for a great many heroes of romantic fiction.

## The Story:

Robin Hood, before he became an outlaw, was the rightful Earl of Huntingdon. Because the times were so corrupt, his father had been dispossessed of his estates and young Robin was driven into the forest. His method of protest was to organize a band of outlaws in Sherwood Forest and prey upon the rich to give to the poor.

The reason for his outlawry was this: a great archer, he was on his way to a shooting match in Nottingham. Some of the king's foresters met him in Sherwood Forest and mocked his youth. Because one of the foresters wagered that he could not slay a deer, Robin Hood killed one of the king's stags. The penalty for his deed was death. When the foresters gave chase, Robin was forced to hide in the forest.

There he found other landless, hunted men and became their leader.

One day, seeking adventure, Robin Hood encountered a tall stranger at a bridge. Calling his merry men after the stranger had tumbled him into the stream, Robin and his companions soon overcame the stranger. Then a shooting match took place between the two. Robin Hood won the match, and the stranger good-naturedly acknowledged defeat and joined Robin's band. The outlaws called him Little John because he was so big.

The Sheriff of Nottingham, angered because Robin flouted his authority, sent out a warrant for his arrest. This warrant was carried by a Tinker into the forest. When the Tinker met Robin Hood, however, he failed to recognize the fugitive because Robin was disguised. Robin took the Tinker to the Blue Boar Inn, got him drunk, and stole the warrant. Later the Tinker met Robin in the forest and fought with him. Robin Hood won the bout, and the Tinker happily joined the other merry men in Robin's band.

The Sheriff of Nottingham grew more and more enraged by Robin's boldness. When the king rebuked him for not capturing the outlaw, the sheriff devised still another plan. Knowing that Robin Hood prided himself on his skill in archery, the sheriff proclaimed a shooting match in Nottingham Tower. There he hoped to catch Robin Hood and his men. They outwitted him, however, for they went to the match in disguise. As a tattered stranger, Robin won the golden arrow given as a prize. After he returned to Sherwood Forest, he sent the sheriff a note of thanks for the prize. This act infuriated that officer even more.

Now the band of outlaws lay low in the forest for a time. At last Robin Hood sent one of his men to learn the sheriff's next plan. When he was captured, the band set out to rescue him. As he was being dragged forth to be hanged, Little John leaped into the cart and cut the prisoner's bonds. The other outlaws ran from their hiding places and overcame the sheriff's men.

Next Robin Hood bought some meat and took it to Nottingham to sell to the poor at half price. Disguised as a butcher, he was thought by most people to be either a foolish peasant or a wealthy nobleman in disguise. When Robin Hood offered to sell him a herd of cattle at a ridiculously low price, the sheriff gleefully accepted the offer. Then Robin took the sheriff to Sherwood Forest, took his money, showed him the king's deer, and told him that there stood his herd.

As a lark Little John went to the Fair at Nottingham Town, where he treated all the people to food and drink. When he was asked to enter the sheriff's service, because of his great size, Little John decided such employment might be fun. He found life in the sheriff's household so pleasant that he stayed six months, until he gradually grew bored and became arrogant toward the steward. The steward called the cook to fight Little John. Both men ate such a huge meal before fighting that neither could win. Finally they decided to stop because they did not really dislike each other. Then Little John persuaded the cook to join the Band of Merry Men.

On another day Robin Hood and his men went out to find Friar Tuck of Fountain Dale, supposedly a rich curate. Spying a strange monk singing and feasting beside a brook, Robin joined him. When Robin wished to go across the water, he persuaded the man to carry him on his back. On the return trip the monk, who was in reality Friar Tuck, dumped Robin into the water. After another great fight, with Robin the victor, the friar joyfully joined the outlaw band.

Having heard of Robin's prowess and fascinated by stories told about him and his men, the queen invited him to come to London. In an attempt to outwit the king she proposed an archery match at which she would put up three archers against his best three. If her team won, the king was to issue a pardon of forty days to certain prisoners. The king accepted the wager. The queen's archers were Robin Hood, Little John, and Will Scarlet, all in disguise. Naturally, the outlaws won, although Will Scarlet was bested in his match. When the king learned that the queen's archers were Robin Hood and two of his men, he was angry, and they escaped capture only with the queen's help. The others returned safely to Sherwood Forest, but Robin Hood met with many dangerous adventures on the way. During his journey he encountered Sir Richard of the Lea, a knight whom he had once aided, and Sir Richard advised him to return to London and throw himself on the queen's mercy. She persuaded the king to give Robin Hood safe escort back to Sherwood Forest and so pay the wager of the shooting match.

King Richard the Lion-Hearted, returning from the Crusades, decided to seek out Robin Hood and his outlaw band. With six others, all disguised as friars, Richard encountered Robin and his men and bested them. Richard then revealed himself and pardoned Robin and his men. Robin he restored to his rightful honors as the Earl of Huntingdon.

Several years later, on a visit to Sherwood Forest, Robin Hood became so homesick for his old life that he gave up his title and returned to live with the outlaws. His action infuriated John, the new king, and the Sheriff of Nottingham. They sent their men to capture the outlaws and during the fighting the sheriff was killed. Robin Hood, ill and much depressed by this bloodshed, went to Kirkley Abbey, where his cousin was prioress, to be bled. She was a treacherous woman and had him bled too long, so that he lay dying. At last Little John, having pulled down bolts and bars to get to Robin, reached his leader's bedside. As Robin Hood lay dying in Little John's arms, he asked for his bow and arrows and said that he wished to be buried wherever his arrow fell. Then Robin shot an arrow through the window of the priory. Little John marked its flight and Robin was buried beneath the ancient oak that was his last target. His merry men disbanded after his death, but the stories of their brave deeds and the prowess of Robin Hood live on even to this day.

# ROBINSON CRUSOE

*Type of work:* Novel
*Author:* Daniel Defoe (1660-1731)
*Type of plot:* Adventure romance
*Time of plot:* 1651-1705
*Locale:* An island off the coast of South America, and the Several Seas
*First published:* 1719

*Principal characters:*
ROBINSON CRUSOE, a castaway
FRIDAY, his faithful servant

## Critique:

The *Life and Strange Surprising Adventures of Robinson Crusoe* as Defoe called his novel, is read as eagerly today as when it was first published. At times the narrative seems too detailed, since the routine of Crusoe's life on the island was much the same. But Defoe knew the theatrical device of timing, for no sooner do we begin to tire of reading the daily account of his hero's life than a new situation breaks the monotony of Crusoe's life and of our reading. The book has attained a high place in the literature of the world, and justly so.

## The Story:

Robinson Crusoe was the son of a middle-class English family. Although his father desired that Robinson go into some business and live a quiet life, Robinson had such longing for the sea that he found it impossible to remain at home. Without his parents' knowledge he took his first voyage. The ship was caught in a great storm, and Robinson was so violently ill and so greatly afraid that he vowed never to leave the land again should he be so fortunate as to escape death.

But when he landed safely, he found his old longing still unsatisfied, and he engaged as a trader, shipping first for the coast of Africa. The ship on which he sailed was captured by a Turkish pirate vessel, and he was carried a prisoner into Sallee, a Moorish port. There he became a slave, and his life was so unbearable that at the first opportunity he escaped in a small boat. He was rescued by a Portuguese freighter and carried safely to Brazil. There he bought a small plantation and began the life of a planter.

When another English planter suggested they make a voyage to Africa for a cargo of slaves, Robinson once more gave way to his longing and sailed again. This voyage was destined to be the most fateful of all, for it brought him his greatest adventure.

The ship broke apart on a reef near an island off the coast of South America, and of the crew and passengers only Robinson was saved. The waves washed him ashore, where he took stock of his unhappy plight. The island seemed to be completely uninhabited, and there was no sign of wild beasts. In an attempt to make his castaway life as comfortable as possible, he constructed a raft and brought away food, ammunition, water, wine, clothing, tools, sailcloth, and lumber from the broken ship.

He first set up a sailcloth tent on the side of a small hill. He encircled his refuge with tall, sharp stakes and entered his shelter by means of a ladder which he drew up after him. Into this area he carried all of the goods he had salvaged, being particularly careful of the gunpowder. His next concern was his food supply. Finding that there was little which had not been ruined by rats or by water, he ate sparingly during his first days on the island.

Before long, having found some ink and a quill among the things he had brought from the ship, he began to keep a journal. He also added the good and evil of his situation and found that he had much for which to thank God. He began to make his shelter permanent.

Behind his tent he found a small cave which he enlarged and braced. With crude tools he made a table and a chair, some shelves, and a rack for his guns. He spent many months on the work, all the time able to find wild fowl or other small game which kept him well supplied with food. He also found several springs and so was never in want for water.

His life for the next twenty-four years was spent in much the same way as his first days upon the island. He explored the island and built what he was pleased to call his summer home on the other side of it. He was able to grow corn, barley, and rice. He carefully saved the new kernels each year until he had enough to plant a small field. With these grains he learned to grind meal and bake coarse bread. He caught and tamed wild goats to supply his larder and parrots for companionship. He made better furniture and improved his cave, making it even safer from intruders, whom he still feared, even though he had seen no sign of any living thing except small game and fowl and goats. From the ship he had brought also three Bibles, and he had time to read them carefully. At a devotional period each morning and night, he never failed to thank God for delivering him from the sea.

In the middle of Robinson's twenty-fourth year on the island, an incident occurred which altered his way of living. About a year and a half previously he had observed some savages who had apparently paddled over from another island. They had come in the night and gorged themselves on some other savages, obviously prisoners. Robinson had found the bones and the torn flesh the next morning and had since been terrified that the cannibals might return and find him. Finally a band of savages did return. While they prepared for their gruesome feast, Robinson shot some of them and frightened the others away. Able to rescue one of the prisoners, he at last had human companionship. He named the man Friday after the day of his rescue, and Friday became his faithful servant and friend.

After a time Robinson was able to teach Friday some English. Friday told him that seventeen white men were prisoners on the island from which he came. Although Friday reported the men well-treated, Robinson had a great desire to go to them, thinking that together they might find some way to return to the civilized world. He and Friday built a canoe and prepared to sail to the other island, but before they were ready for their trip another group of savages came to their island with more prisoners. Discovering that one of the prisoners was a white man, Robinson managed to save him and another savage, whom Friday found to be his own father. There was great joy at the reunion of father and son. Robinson cared for the old man and the white man, who was a Spaniard, one of the seventeen of whom Friday had spoken. A hostile tribe had captured Friday's island, and thus it was that the white men were no longer safe.

Robinson dispatched the Spaniard and Friday's father to the neighboring island to try to rescue the white men. While waiting for their return, Robinson saw an English ship one day at anchor near shore. Soon he found the captain of the ship and two others, who had been set ashore by a mutinous crew. Robinson and Friday and the three seamen were able to retake the ship, and thus Robinson was at last delivered from the island. He disliked leaving before the Spaniard and Friday's father returned, and he determined to go back to the island some day and see how they had fared. Five of the mutinous crew chose to remain rather than be returned to England to hang. And so Robinson and Friday went to England, Robinson returning to his homeland after an absence of thirty-five years. He arrived there, a stranger and unknown, in June of 1687.

But he was not through with adventure. When he visited his old home, he found that his parents had died, as had all of his family but two sisters and the two children of one of his brothers.

Having nothing to keep him in England, he went to Lisbon to inquire about his plantation. There he learned that friends had saved the income of his estate for him and that he was now worth about five thousand pounds sterling. Satisfied with the accounting, Robinson and Friday returned to England, where Robinson married and had three children.

After his wife died, Robinson sailed again in 1695 as a private trader on a ship captained by his nephew and bound for the East Indies and China. The ship put in at his castaway island, where he found that the Spaniards and the English mutineers had taken native wives from an adjoining island, so that the population was greatly increased. Robinson was pleased with his little group and gave a feast for them. He also presented them with gifts from the ship.

After he had satisfied himself that the colony was well cared for, Robinson and Friday sailed away. On their way to Brazil some savages attacked the ship and Friday was killed. From Brazil Robinson went around the Cape of Good Hope and on to the coast of China. At one port, after the sailors had taken part in a massacre, Robinson lectured them so severely that the crew forced their captain, Robinson's nephew, to set him ashore in China, as they would have no more of his preaching. There Robinson joined a caravan which took him into Siberia. At last he reached England. Having spent the greater part of fifty-four years away from his homeland, he was glad to live out his life in peace and in preparation for that longer journey from which he would never return.

# RODERICK RANDOM

*Type of work:* Novel
*Author:* Tobias Smollett (1721-1771)
*Type of plot:* Picaresque romance
*Time of plot:* Eighteenth century
*Locale:* England
*First published:* 1748

Principal characters:
RODERICK RANDOM, an adventurer
TOM BOWLING, his uncle
STRAP, Tom's friend and companion
MISS WILLIAMS, an adventuress
NARCISSA, Roderick's sweetheart

## Critique:

*The Adventures of Roderick Random* is unique in being the first English novel to describe with any detail life on a British warship. For this material Smollett drew upon his own experience as a ship surgeon. There is little structure to the book. The success of the novel lies in Smollett's ability to narrate and describe incident after incident and to keep his readers interested and, usually, amused. The central character of Roderick Random is used, as in a picaresque novel, to unite the incidents into a story and to provide a reason for the development of the climax. Roderick's adventures provide an opportunity for satire on the follies and affectations of the age

## The Story:

Although Roderick Random came from a wealthy landowning family of Scotland, his early life was one of vicissitudes. Roderick's father had married a servant in the Random household, and for that reason he had been disowned without a penny. Soon after Roderick's birth his mother died. When his father disappeared, heartbroken, the grandfather was prevailed upon to send the lad to school for the sake of the family's reputation.

At school Roderick was the butt of the masters, although a great favorite with the boys his own age. His whippings were numerous, for he could be used as a whipping boy when something had gone wrong and the real culprit could not be determined. In Roderick's fourteenth

year, however, there was a change in his fortunes. His mother's brother, Tom Bowling, a lieutenant in the navy, came to visit his young nephew.

Lieutenant Bowling remonstrated with his nephew's grandfather over his treatment of Roderick, but the old man was firm in his refusal to do anything beyond what necessity dictated for the offspring of the son whom he had disinherited. When the grandfather died, he left Roderick nothing. Tom Bowling sent the lad to the university, where Roderick made great progress. Then Tom Bowling became involved in a duel and was forced to leave his ship. This misfortune cut off the source of Roderick's funds and made it necessary for him to leave the university.

Casting about for a means of making a livelihood, Roderick became a surgeon's apprentice. He proved to be so capable that before long his master sent him to London with a recommendation to a local member of Parliament, who was to get Roderick a place as surgeon's mate in the navy.

Securing a place on a man-of-war was a difficult task. To keep himself in funds, Roderick worked for a French chemist in London. In the shop he met Miss Williams, with whom he fell in love, but much to his chagrin he discovered one day that she was a prostitute trying to better her fortune. Soon afterward Roderick was accused of stealing and was dismissed by his employer. While he was leading a precarious existence, waiting for his navy warrant, he learned that Miss Williams lived in the same lodging-house. He won the ever-lasting gratitude of the young woman by acting as her doctor while she was ill.

One day, while walking near the Thames, Roderick was seized by a press-gang and shanghaied aboard the man-of-war *Thunder*, about to sail for Jamaica. Roderick, who had found friends on the ship, was made a surgeon's mate.

The voyage to Jamaica was a terrible one as the commanding officer, Captain Oakhum, was a tyrant who came very close to hanging Roderick and another surgeon's mate because one of the ship's officers claimed he had heard them speak-ing ill of both the surgeon and the cap-tain. Thinking that Roderick's Greek notebook was a military code, the captain threatened again to hang him as a spy.

After seeing action against the Spanish at Cartagena, Roderick secured a billet as surgeon's mate aboard the *Lizard,* a ship returning to England with dis-patches. On the way the captain died and Lieutenant Crampley, an officer who greatly disliked Roderick, took command of the ship. Crampley, being a poor of-ficer, ran the ship aground off the Sussex coast. The crew robbed and tried to kill Roderick when they reached the shore, but an old woman befriended him, cured him of his wounds, and found him a place as footman with a spinster gentle-woman who lived nearby.

Roderick spent several months in her service. He found his way into his em-ployer's good-will by his attention to his duties and by showing a knowledge of literature, even to the extent of explain-ing passages from Tasso's Italian poetry to her. The spinster had a niece and a nephew living with her. Narcissa, the niece, was a beautiful girl of marriage-able age to whom Roderick was immedi-ately attracted. Her brother, a drunken, fox-hunting young squire, was deter-mined that she should marry a wealthy knight in the neighborhood.

One day Roderick prevented the girl's brutal suitor from forcing his attentions on her and beat the man severely with a cudgel. While he was deliberating on his next move, he was taken prisoner by a band of smugglers who for their own safety carried him to Boulogne in France. There Roderick found his uncle, Tom Bowling, and assured him that he would be safe if he returned to England, for the man Bowling believed he had killed in a duel was very much alive.

Roderick set out for Paris in company with a friar who robbed him one night and left him penniless. Meeting a band of soldiers, Roderick enlisted in the army of King Louis XIV and saw service at the battle of Dettingen. After the battle his regiment went into garrison and Roder-ick unexpectedly met a boyhood com-panion, Strap, who was passing as Mon-sieur D'Estrapes and who was friendly with a French nobleman. Strap be-friended Roderick and secured his release from onerous service as a private in the French army.

Strap and Roderick schemed for a way to make their fortunes and finally hit upon the idea of setting up Roderick as a wealthy gentleman. They hoped that he would marry, within a short time, some wealthy heiress.

The two men went to Paris, where Roderick bought new clothes and became acquainted with the ways of a man about town. Then they went to London. There Roderick quickly became ac-quainted with a group of young men who were on the fringe of fashionable society.

Roderick's first attempt to become inti-mate with a rich woman was a dismal failure, for she turned out to be a woman of the streets. On the second attempt he met Melinda, a young woman of fortune, who won many pounds from him at cards and then refused to marry him because he did not have an inde-pendent fortune of his own. Finally one of Roderick's friends told him of a cousin, Miss Snapper, who was a wealthy heiress. The friend promised that he would help Roderick in his suit in return for Roderick's note for five hundred pounds, due six months after the marriage.

Falling in with this suggestion, Roderick immediately started out for Bath in company with the young woman and her mother. On the way he saved them from being robbed by a highwayman, a deed which established him in the good graces of both mother and daughter. At Bath, Roderick squired the young woman about day and night. Although she was crippled and not good-looking, the thought of her fortune was greater in his mind than her appearance. Besides, she was an intelligent and witty young woman.

All went well with the plan until Roderick caught sight of Narcissa, the young girl he had known while he was employed as a footman by her aunt. Realizing that he was in love with her, he promptly deserted Miss Snapper.

Narcissa soon revealed to Roderick that she returned his love. The young squire, her brother, had no objections to Roderick because he thought that Random was a wealthy man. Unfortunately Roderick's former love, Melinda, arrived in Bath and caught the attention of Narcissa's brother. At a ball she spread evil reports about Roderick because he had left her. The result was that Roderick first fought a duel with Lord Quiverwit, one of Narcissa's admirers, and then saw his Narcissa spirited away by her brother. The only thing that kept Roderick's hope alive was the fact that he knew Narcissa loved him and that her maid, the Miss Williams whom Roderick had long before befriended, was eternally grateful to him and would help him in any way which lay in her power.

Returning to London, Roderick again met his uncle, Tom Bowling, who had been appointed to take a merchant ship on a mysterious trip. He proposed to take Roderick with him as ship surgeon, and he gave Roderick a thousand pounds with which to buy goods to sell on the voyage. He also made out a will leaving all his property to Roderick in case he should die.

The mysterious trip proved to be a voyage to the Guinea Coast to pick up Negro slaves for the Spanish American trade. The slaves and the cargo, including the goods shipped by Roderick, were sold at a handsome profit. While their ship was being prepared for the return voyage, Roderick and his uncle spent several weeks ashore, where they were entertained by people they met and with whom they did business. One of their acquaintances was a rich Englishman known as Don Rodrigo, who invited them to visit him on his estate. During their stay it was discovered that the man was Roderick's father, who had gone to America to make his fortune after having been disinherited because of his marriage to Roderick's mother.

The voyage back to England was a happy one. Roderick was full of confidence, for he had made a small fortune out of the voyage and had expectations of quite a large fortune from the estates of his father and his uncle. He immediately paid his addresses to Narcissa, who accepted his offer of marriage in spite of her brother's opposition. They were married shortly afterward and went to live in Scotland on the Random estate, which Roderick's father had bought from his bankrupt elder brother.

# ROGUE HERRIES

*Type of work:* Novel
*Author:* Hugh Walpole (1884-1941)
*Type of plot:* Historical chronicle
*Time of plot:* 1730-1774
*Locale:* England
*First published:* 1930

*Principal characters:*
FRANCIS HERRIES, the Rogue
MARGARET HERRIES, his first wife
MIRABELL STARR, his second wife
DAVID HERRIES, his son
DEBORAH HERRIES, his daughter
ALICE PRESS, his mistress
SARAH DENBURN, David's wife

*Critique:*

*Rogue Herries* is the first novel of a tetrology which traces in detail the story of an English family over a period of two hundred years. The story of the Herries becomes also the story of England through the Georgian, Victorian, and modern periods, largely upon the domestic level of morals and manners. There is a growing complexity to the novel as new generations appear and succeed one another, but Hugh Walpole keeps the narrative within bounds by relating the action to the descendants of the notorious Rogue Herries. Throughout there is a fairly successful capturing of the flavor of the period.

*The Story:*

In the year 1730 Francis Herries brought his family from the roistering life of Doncaster to live in a long-deserted family house—called Herries—at Rosthwaite not far from Keswick in Cumberland. In addition to his wife and three children, he brought along the most recent of his many mistresses, Alice Press, who, under pretense of being the children's governess, had actually been unkind and overbearing with them and insolent to their mother. The family rested for a period at the Keswick inn, and met Francis' oldest brother and his wife. After an uncomfortable journey on horseback over a scarcely discernible road, the party reached Herries.

Francis Herries had led a life of dissipation. His respectable relatives, of whom there were a great many, looked on him as the black sheep of the family and avoided him. His wife Margaret he had married more for pity than for love. But she had brought him some money. The one person whom Francis really loved was his son David. And David returned his love.

One day Francis, now tired of Alice Press, came upon her berating his wife. Although he did not love Margaret, he loved Alice less. He tried from that day to make Alice leave the house, but she refused. When he took David to Keswick to a fair, they saw Alice Press. Furious, Francis told Alice that she must not return to Herries. At last he began to shout, announcing that Alice was for sale. People were shocked and astounded. Then a man threw down a handful of silver. Francis picked up a token piece and walked away. David felt that his father was possessed of a devil.

Francis became notorious throughout the district for his escapades and before long acquired the epithet of Rogue Herries. One Christmas night, at a feast in a friend's house, he was challenged to a duel by young Osbaldistone. Francis had won money from him gambling in Keswick and had also paid some attention to a young woman that Osbaldistone fancied. In the course of the duel, Francis had the advantage. Then, when Francis' guard was down, Osbaldistone slashed him from temple to chin. The resulting scar marked Rogue Herries for the rest of his life.

One evening in the spring following, Francis came in from working on his land and found Margaret ailing. They had never had any warmth of feeling between them, but even in the moment of her death she felt that he would be at a loss without her. After making David promise never to leave his father, she called for Francis and died in his arms.

In 1745 Francis had a strange adventure. After a long walk through the hills near his home, he lay down to rest and fell sound asleep. When he awoke he was bound hand and foot. His mysterious captor untied his bonds after questioning him as to his identity and led him to a cave where he saw several desperate-looking men and a lovely young girl. One of the men gave him a cross and chain which the girl's mother had left for him at her death. Years before, he had seen her shuddering with cold by the roadside and had given her his cloak. Fascinated now by the girl, he talked kindly to her and learned that her name was Mirabell Starr. The men with whom she lived were thieves and smugglers.

In November Francis took David to Carlisle. The Young Pretender had landed in Scotland and was marching toward London. At an inn in Carlisle, Francis saw Mirabell with a young man of her own age. He was jealous, for he knew that he loved Mirabell despite the great difference in their ages. He also saw that an ugly man of considerable age was jealous of Mirabell's lover. During the siege of the city all able men were pressed into service. When Carlisle fell to the Pretender's forces, the city became quiet once more. On a dark night Francis, out for a walk, saw Mirabell and the young man walking ahead of him. He also saw the ugly man of the inn approach the pair. He yelled a warning too late. The boy Harry dropped dead. Mirabell escaped in the darkness.

In the summer of 1756 David and his sister Deborah attended a ball in Keswick. At the dance Deborah fell in love with a young clergyman. When they arrived home next day, they were met by their father, who explained to them that Mirabell had arrived and had promised to marry him. After her hard life on the roads Mirabell had come to offer herself to Francis in return for food and protection.

In 1758 David was thirty-eight. On a business trip he met and fell in love with a girl named Sarah Denburn, a frank, friendly girl of more than average beauty. Her uncle-guardian intended her for another man, but David carried her off one night after killing his rival.

For about two years David and Sarah lived at Herries. Mirabell hated Sarah. At last David bought a house not far off and moved with his wife to it. Deborah went to Cockermouth to wed her clergyman. Alone with his young wife, Francis unsuccessfully tried to teach her to read and write and to love him. Mirabell had something of the gipsy in her. One day she ran away. From then on most of Francis' life was devoted to traveling over England looking for Mirabell.

Meanwhile David and Sarah, settled at Uldale, had three children and became well established in the community. Sarah loved the society of the people of Uldale and David prospered.

After many years of wandering, Francis at last saw Mirabell again among a troupe of players in Penrith. She promised to meet him after the play, but did not. Francis searched the town in vain. As he returned to his inn, he fell ill of an old ailment, a fever, and was forced to stay there for six months.

When at last he returned home, he found Mirabell waiting for him. She explained that she could not desert the acting company on that fateful night because the leader, her lover, had threatened to kill himself if she deserted him, and his death would have left his children friendless orphans. But at last he had run away with a younger woman, and Mirabell had come back to Francis once more for protection. She tried to make him understand that the only man she had ever truly loved was the boy killed in Carlisle.

In 1774 an old woman from a nearby village came in to cook for Francis and Mirabell, for at last Mirabell was going to have a baby. Francis, stricken again by his fever, was in bed in the next room as Mirabell gave birth to a daughter and died. Francis, in a final spasm of vigor, rose from his bed and then fell back, he thought, into Mirabell's arms. He too was dead. Only the new-born child and the old woman were alive in the house on that stormy winter night.

# THE ROMAN ACTOR

*Type of work:* Drama
*Author:* Philip Massinger (1583-1640)
*Type of plot:* Tragedy of intrigue
*Time of plot:* First century
*Locale:* Rome
*First presented:* 1626

*Principal characters:*
PARIS, the Roman actor
DOMITIAN, Emperor of Rome
DOMITIA, his wife
ARETINUS, Domitian's spy
PARTHENIUS, Domitian's freedman

## Critique:

The Roman Actor depicts the degeneracy of imperial Rome under the tyrant Domitian. In contrast to the general corruption stand Paris, the actor, and two senators of Stoic persuasion. The most original and impressive element of the play is the character of Paris. Unfortunately, the plot revolves around Domitian, a much less interesting character, while Paris is forced awkwardly into the central action. Paris, in defending the theater of Rome, is Massinger's spokesman for the Stuart theater.

## The Story:

During the reign of Domitian, there was little public support for the theater. The people, accustomed to circuses and involved in their own licentious practices, found the drama tame by comparison; thus most actors made a bare livelihood. One troupe of actors, however, prospered, because of the special affection Domitian had for its leading member, Paris. But Paris also had his enemies in the inner circles around the emperor, the most notable being Aretinus, Domitian's spy, who believed he and other leaders had been satirized in a production by the players. While Domitian was involved in a military campaign, Aretinus took the opportunity to have Paris and his fellow actors arrested.

At a session of the Senate they were charged with treason. Paris' defense was in the form of a general vindication of the theater, in which he eloquently testified to the uplifting effect of drama through its revelation of evil and its attempt to inspire honorable action. As he finished his speech, news was brought of Domitian's return from his conquest of the Chatti and the Daci; thus the release of the actors was assured.

The people's praise of Domitian for his victory was exceeded only by his self-praise. In a characteristic gesture, he celebrated his return by having his captives tortured and slain. Although his despotism and his brutality were causing unrest among the people, few dared speak against him.

Among those who welcomed the emperor were several women who vied for his favor. All were greeted with contempt, except the beautiful Domitia. She had been the wife of a senator, Lamia, until one of Domitian's men had forced her husband, under threat of death, to sign a bill of divorce. She, ambitious for position, had been agreeable to the change as long as she could be Domitian's wife, not his strumpet. Now he bestowed on her the title of Augusta.

Aretinus had kept a watchful eye on signs of discontent during his ruler's absence. Now he informed Domitian of opposition to his poisoning of Agricola his execution of Paetus Thrasea, his incest with his niece Julia, and his intended marriage to Domitia. Prominent among the malcontents were three senators—

3259

Rusticus, Sura, and Lamia. Domitian resolved to have revenge first on Lamia.

After Domitia had been established in the imperial palace as his wife, the emperor ordered Lamia brought to him. Domitian gave lavish thanks to the senator for the gift of his wife, declaimed the joys of living with Domitia, and at an appropriate moment had Domitia sing a song from the window above them. After Lamia had time to experience fully his mental anguish, Domitian ordered his execution.

In compliance with one of the emperor's first orders on arriving in Rome, the actors presented a play. *The Cure of Avarice* was chosen at the request of Parthenius, Domitian's freedman, who hoped that the dramatization would help turn his father from his miserly habits. But the obdurate old man was unimpressed. Domitian then tried to convince him of the foolishness of his practices, but to no avail. Finally, piqued, Domitian ordered the old man's death. Despite the long and faithful service of Parthenius, the emperor refused to hear his plea for his father's life.

The next to satisfy Domitian's lust for blood were the senators Rusticus and Sura, who had criticized the emperor for his execution of the Stoic philosopher, Paetus Thrasea. In hopes of hearing their cries for mercy, Domitian had them tortured. Sustained by their Stoic principles, however, the two men refused to show any sign of pain and mocked him for his impotence against them. Even after he had ordered them killed, the experience unsettled him and gave him his first doubts of his omnipotence.

Domitia, to cheer up her husband after this ordeal, had a play presented in which Paris acted the part of a rejected lover. As the drama progressed, she became increasingly agitated, until at the point of Paris' threatened suicide she jumped from her seat to stop him.

This unusual behavior immediately aroused the suspicions of the women of the court. Having been replaced by Domitia in the emperor's favor, and having been treated like servants by Domitia, these women had been awaiting a chance to discredit her. Their suspicions were confirmed when they discovered that she had sent a letter to Paris requesting that he meet her. Aretinus, the ubiquitous spy, was also aware of this situation; he saw in it a chance not only to gain further power but to triumph over Paris. In a petition signed by him and the women, Domitian was notified of his wife's behavior. Although refusing at first to believe the accusation, he agreed to observe the meeting between his wife and Paris.

At this meeting, Domitia, after finding that hints of her feelings failed to elicit the desired response in Paris, openly stated her love for him. Loyalty to Domitian kept Paris from succumbing to her enticements, however, and her threats and her bribes left him unmoved. Finally, after she begged for a brotherly kiss, he weakened. At that moment Domitian arrived on the scene. Enraged by her infidelity, but still too much ruled by the power of her beauty to kill her immediately, Domitian had his wife placed under guard in her chamber. Aretinus, expectant of reward for informing on the pair, was put to death instead. The palace women, for their efforts, were cast into a dungeon.

Left alone with Paris, Domitian protested his aversion to killing him. At Domitian's request, they acted out a play called *The False Servant,* with Paris playing the part of the servant, Domitian acting as the wronged husband. In the scene in which the husband discovers the treachery of his servant, Domitian drew his sword and killed Paris. The emperor, feeling in honor bound to kill a man he much admired, believed he, at least, had provided a fitting end.

Domitia's hold on her husband was so great that she was soon restored to grace. Far from being remorseful, however, she openly mocked Domitian for his weakness in loving her and refused ever again to respond to his love. Finally, after an especially vicious taunting, he gained courage to place her name in his book of condemned people.

A further source of irritation to him was an astrologer's prediction of his imminent death. According to the prophecy, the astrologer himself would be eaten by dogs before Domitian would die. In order to shift the course of events, the emperor gave orders that the astrologer be burned. As the soldiers prepared to burn him, a heavy rain put out the fire, and dogs burst upon them and devoured the body.

Filled with fear by this happening, Domitian surrounded himself by tribunes and awaited the hour of five, at which time his death had been predicted.

Meanwhile, Domitian's book having been stolen by Domitia, she, Parthenius, and the women of the court found their names on the condemned list. With others, they decided on immediate action. By falsely telling Domitian that the hour of five was passed, Parthenius drew him away from his guard, and all the conspirators fell upon him and ended the life of a tyrant.

# THE ROMANCE OF A SCHOOLMASTER

*Type of work:* Novel
*Author:* Edmondo de Amicis (1846-1908)
*Type of plot:* Social criticism
*Time of plot:* Nineteenth century
*Locale:* Italy
*First published:* 1876

Principal characters:

EMILIO RATTI, a young schoolmaster
PROFESSOR MEGARI, his adviser and friend
FAUSTINA GALLI, a young schoolteacher whom Ratti loves
GIOVANNI LABACCIO, a schoolteacher and Ratti's friend
CARLO LERICA, another friend, a teacher

## Critique:

*The Romance of a Schoolmaster* was a product of the author's later years, when he was convinced that socialism offered the only palliative for his country's ills. In this novel he found fault with the lower and middle classes for being harsher toward their inferiors than the upper class was to people below it. The novel is also a timeless study of the vicissitudes of the teacher in the elementary school, the type of teacher recruited from a shallow culture and the lower classes. In the novel the teacher's hardships, his low pay, his pettifogging enemies, the lack of social position, and his lack of a cultural background are all vividly drawn. When the novel appeared in Italy, it was bitterly criticized because of the author's attacks on the system and officials of the Department of Public Instruction.

## The Story:

The unexpected death of Emilio Ratti's father plunged the family into poverty, and Emilio, at seventeen, found it necessary to look for some way to make his own living. At his mother's suggestion, and with financial help from a wealthy family named Goli, he entered a normal school located in the town where the Rattis resided. The young man felt a real call to the teaching profession; the love and sympathy he felt for his young brothers and sisters had given him an interest in the welfare and training of small children.

His mother's death came on the day Emilio learned of his appointment to the normal school. As a result, he spent his first months there in relative solitude, reading and studying during the hours when he was not required to be in classes. His only friends were his roommates. One was Carlo Lerica, a thirty-year-old ex-corporal of grenadiers who had left the army to go into elementary teaching. The other was a quiet, compromising chap in his mid-twenties, Giovanni Labaccio. His only other friend was Professor Megari. Emilio believed that the professor had a genuine liking for him, even though he did not let it show among the other students.

When Emilio finished his course at the normal school, the professor admitted his sympathy for the young man and showed him a note written by Emilio's mother on her deathbed, a note asking this faculty member to do what he could for her son. Professor Megari, thinking that the letter might inspire Emilio in his career, gave the letter to him.

Emilio's first post was at an elementary school in Garasco, not far from the city of Turin, in the northern part of Italy. There the new teacher spent his first professional year, a year not without its tribulations. He inadvertently made an enemy of the local priest's cook, a spiteful woman who did everything she could to harm his reputation with the parents of his pupils and with the local authorities, mostly because he refused to bow to her in the street. During that first year Emilio tried to keep discipline and order in his room and motivate his students by kindness and affection for them. He learned, however, that the rather brutal peasant youngsters took his attitude for weakness and disliked him for being so easygoing At the annual inspection the school inspector for the province advised Emilio to keep his affection for his pupils but not to let it show, lest they continue to take advantage of him. Emilio was leaving Garasco at the end of the year, his position being only a temporary one, and he resolved to change his methods when he changed his location.

The following year Emilio taught at Piazzena, a small village on the plains. Inadvertently, he found himself regarded in the area as a member of the opposition to the political group in office, largely because he had secured his position through an influential gentleman of the neighborhood. The first year in Piazzena went by without any but the usual petty incidents of a schoolteacher's existence, and at its end Emilio was congratulated by the provincial inspector. In the second year, however, the village was thrown into open war over the treatment of a young woman who taught girls in the elementary school. The local priest accused her of teaching the girls to go against the principles of the Church. When those charges failed to arouse her or the village, he accused her of immorality. Emilio, knowing how unjust the priest's accusations were, was among those who sided with the young woman. After a long battle, in which the school authorities and the courts became involved, the teacher's good name was vindicated and the priest was forced to pay her an indemnity and to apologize in print. The battle was enough to convince Emilio that he no longer wanted to remain in the community. He did not request to have his two-year contract renewed.

Emilio's next post was in Altarana, situated in the Occidental Alps. There he ran into a new problem. Because the government decreed that all children should be sent to school, there was a good deal of resentment on the part of the peasants and their children. Try as he would to keep the children in attendance, Emilio fought a losing battle. Both the parents and youngsters preferred to have the children work in the fields.

In spite of his difficulties Emilio stayed in Altarana six years, hoping that by the end of that time his study and experience would enable him to get a post in the municipal school system in Turin. The pay was better in the city and teaching was not completely subject to the whims of pettifogging authorities who tried to keep money from the schools and to harass the teachers for not being friends to every faction and individual.

Faustina Galli, a new teacher for girls, arrived in Altarana. She had been chosen by one of the village officials because of her beauty, and the man who chose her hoped to have an affair with her. When she proved to be impervious to his solicitations or his threats, Emilio, impressed with her virtue and beauty, fell in love with her. But Faustina, having the responsibility of a crippled father to look after, rejected his attentions. Disappointed and despairing of ever getting ahead in his profession, Emilio turned to liquor. He almost lost his post, but his old friend and adviser, Professor Megari, interceded in his behalf and also showed him the folly of his drinking.

In his last year at Altarana, Emilio learned what had happened to his roommates at the normal school. The ex-corporal of grenadiers, Carlo Lerica, had encountered many difficulties, but Giovanni Labaccio had made a name for himself by insinuating himself into everyone's graces. He finally married a rich woman older than he and retired from teaching. After his retirement he turned against the profession from which he had risen and accused the teachers of thinking only of money, rather than their professional responsibilities.

Emilio's next village post was in Camina, where he spent two more years. There he had numerous small adventures and the usual troubles with the local authorities and parents, but he was learning to put up with them as one of the conditions of his profession. From there he went to Bossolano, where he spent his final year as a teacher in a village school. At the end of that year he felt that he had served his apprenticeship and had put in enough study to compete successfully for a post in Turin. He took the examinations in the city, along with more than two hundred other candidates. He was successful, as was his old classmate, Carlo Lerica. Not only did they pass the examination, but they were appointed immediately to posts. To add to his joy, Emilio discovered that Faustina Galli was also teaching in Turin. From her he learned that her father had died, and she gave him reason to hope that she was at last ready to return his love.

# THE ROMANCE OF LEONARDO DA VINCI

*Type of work:* Novel
*Author:* Dmitri Merejkowski (1865-1941)
*Type of plot:* Historical romance
*Time of plot:* 1494-1519
*Locale:* Italy and France
*First published:* 1902

> *Principal characters:*
> LEONARDO DA VINCI, Renaissance artist
> GIOVANNI BELTRAFFIO, his pupil
> CESARE BORGIA, Leonardo's patron
> MONNA CASSANDRA, a sorceress
> FRANCESCO MELZI, another pupil of Leonardo
> MONNA LISA GIOCONDA, model for a portrait by Leonardo

### Critique:

This novel presents a vivid picture of the glittering Italian Renaissance. The royal courts, the Vatican, the quiet countryside, the studios of artists, an alchemist's workshop, and many other scenes serve as a backdrop for the story of the later years of the famed painter and thinker, Leonardo da Vinci. Almost all the great figures of the age pass through the pages of the novel as they cross the path of Leonardo. More than a fictionalized biography, it is also the history of a culture, for Merejkowski has depicted the religious and political struggles of the age as well as its adventure, romance, and bravado.

### The Story:

In 1494 the fear of the coming of the Antichrist prophesied in the New Testament began to make itself felt in Italy. Greek and Roman statues, which had recently been excavated and accepted as supreme works of art by such men as Leonardo da Vinci, were considered by the common people as actual pagan deities returning to prepare the world for the reign of the Antichrist.

Leonardo da Vinci had become a member of the court of Duke Moro in Milan. Besides acting as chief architect for the duke, he interested himself in teaching his pupils, Giovanni Beltraffio and Andrea Salaino, and in working on whatever caught his fancy. Most of the money he received from the duke's treasury went to buy pieces of amber with bugs imbedded in them, old shells, live birds that he studied and then freed, and other curious objects which distracted his attention and kept him from completing his painting, *The Last Supper.*

The student Giovanni was attracted to Monna Cassandra, a beautiful girl who lived in the neighborhood. Unknown to him, she was a practicer of the black arts and a favorite of suspected witches.

The Duke of Milan called upon the King of France to help protect and support his dukedom. But Louis XII of France soon proved false to his friendship with the duke and overran the duchy. The French forces used a clay statue of a mounted warrior, which Leonardo had not yet cast in bronze, as a target for a shooting contest, and a flood caused the walls on which *The Last Supper* was painted to bulge and crack. Realizing that these two works of art could never be finished, Leonardo decided to leave Milan and go to the court of Cesare Borgia, son of Pope Alexander VI.

As Borgia's adviser, Leonardo designed many pieces of war equipment and machinery which Borgia used in his attempt to seize all of Italy for the pope. None of

Leonardo's pupils approved of his working for Borgia, whose cruelties and vices made him hated all over Italy.

One day one of Leonardo's students, a blacksmith named Zoroastro da Peretola, had gone against his orders and had tried to fly in Leonardo's only partly completed airplane. Falling from a considerable height, he received such a jolt that his mind was never again sound.

Leonardo left Borgia's services and, with the help of his friend Machiavelli, received a commission from the city of Florence to plan a system of waterways which would divert the course of the Arno River. Because Machiavelli had underestimated the expense of the work, Leonardo was soon in trouble with the authorities. The canal project was abandoned and Leonardo was asked instead to paint a large picture depicting the battle of Anghiari. At that time Michelangelo was also working in Florence, and a great jealousy had grown up between admirers of the two artists. Leonardo tried to make friends with Michelangelo, but the passionate artist would have nothing to do with the mild Leonardo. Raphael, at that time only a young man, was friendly with both artists. His works were more popular with artistically-minded Pope Leo X than those of either of the older men.

During his stay in Florence, Leonardo had begun the portrait of a young married woman of the town named Monna Lisa Gioconda. As she sat for him, day after day, he would amuse her by telling her stories as he worked, or converse with her on any subject in order to keep her interested in the dull task of posing. As the months passed, Monna Lisa and Leonardo were more and more drawn to each other. Both were essentially secretive persons who seemed to understand each other intuitively. Months passed into years, and still Monna Lisa came to the studio to pose. No one suspected anything improper of the meetings, but it became a source of amusement in Florence that the gentle artist, who had never before taken an interest in women, seemed to be in love. Monna Lisa's sudden death shocked Leonardo to the bottom of his soul. He had hoped to finish her portrait, to finish this one work at least, but with Monna Lisa's death his hopes fell. He had tried to show in her face the mystery of the universe, for he had found that the mystery of Monna Lisa and the mystery of the universe were one.

Because of the trouble over the canal and the unfinished picture of the battle of Anghiari, Leonardo da Vinci was dismissed from the service of the city of Florence. He returned to Milan to serve under the new ruler of that city, Louis XII of France. There Giovanni Beltraffio again met Monna Cassandra. One day she promised to show him the answers to his deepest questions. He was to meet her late that same night. As Giovanni left her, he was shocked to see in her face the expression of the White She-Demon, a specter which had haunted him since childhood.

But before the time for their meeting Monna Cassandra was taken prisoner by the Most Holy Inquisition. Thinking her completely innocent, Giovanni visited all his old friends in an effort to secure her release. The more he tried to help her, however, the more convinced he became that there were indeed evil spirits who inhabited the forms of human beings, and that the White She-Demon was one of them. Unable to prevent Monna's death, Giovanni walked about the streets disconsolately. Suddenly he realized that the strange odor he had been smelling was the scent of burning flesh. Monna and one hundred and twenty-nine others accused as witches were being burned at the stake. Terror-stricken, he almost lost his mind. Later, still haunted by the White She-Demon, he committed suicide.

The loss of his favorite pupil would have been a more terrible blow to Leonardo if Francesco Melzi had not recently joined his group of students. Francesco Melzi, who was to be the true and faithful friend of the old artist, helped him through the final years of his life, especially in that trying period when the death of Louis XII left Leonardo without a patron. But the new French king, Francis I, soon afterward called Leonardo da Vinci to Paris. In 1516 Leonardo and his small group left Italy for France; the artist was never to see his home country again.

In France he was well treated in spite of his inability to finish anything he began. He took up the Monna Lisa portrait again, and almost finished it to his satisfaction from memory. One day King Francis visited him in his studio. Seeing the portrait, the king purchased it but agreed that Leonardo could keep his beloved portrait until he died.

King Francis did not have long to wait. A few years later Leonardo, old and weak, grew sick and died. His faithful pupil, Francesco Melzi, saw to it that Leonardo received the rites of the Church before his death. He also arranged to have the artist buried in a style which, he hoped, would forever still the whispering tongues that called Leonardo a disciple of the Antichrist to come.

# THE ROMANCE OF THE FOREST

*Type of work:* Novel
*Author:* Mrs. Ann Radcliffe (1764-1823)
*Type of plot:* Gothic romance
*Time of plot:* Seventeenth century
*Locale:* France and Savoy
*First published:* 1791

Principal characters:
ADELINE, a victim of intrigue
PIERRE DE LA MOTTE, her benefactor, a fugitive from justice
MADAME DE LA MOTTE, his wife
LOUIS, their son
THEODORE PEYROU, a young soldier
THE MARQUIS DE MONTALT, a villainous nobleman
ARNAUD LA LUC, a cleric and scholar
CLARA, his daughter
PETER, a loyal servant

## Critique:

One of the most popular writers of her day, Mrs. Radcliffe made her name practically synonymous with the tale of mystery and terror. To her the Gothic novel was a work of the romantic imagination, the background usually a ruined castle or abbey whose secret passages and moldy dungeons contributed much to the action and atmosphere of her story. Unlike others among the Gothic romancers, she did not descend to the supernatural for the sake of ghastly horror. Her situations, exaggerated and extreme as they appear to the modern reader, were always accounted for in some logical fashion. Her plots were awkward, her character drawings stilted and sentimentalized, but her novels achieved a remarkable vitality because of her skill with effects of atmosphere and suspense.

## The Story:

On a dark and tempestuous night Pierre de la Motte left Paris to escape his creditors and prosecution by the law. Descended from an ancient house, he was a man whose passions often proved stronger than his conscience. Having dissipated his own fortune and that of his wife, he had engaged in various questionable schemes which brought him at last to disgrace and made necessary his flight with only the small wreck of his once considerable property. Leaving Paris

with his wife and two faithful servants, he hoped to find a refuge in some village of the Southern Provinces. The departure was so sudden that there had been no time for the harried parents to say farewell to their son Louis, on duty with his regiment in Germany.

Several leagues from the city Peter, the coachman, lost his way while driving across a wild heath. Seeing in the distance the lighted window of a small, ancient house, La Motte dismounted and walked to the dwelling in the hope of securing directions from its inmates. A grim-visaged man opened the door at his knock and ushered him into a desolate apartment, the door of which was abruptly locked behind him. Over the howling of the wind La Motte could hear rough voices close at hand and the muffled sobbing of a woman.

The door was at last unlocked and the forbidding ruffian reappeared, dragging by the hand a beautiful girl of about eighteen. Putting a pistol to La Motte's breast, the man offered him his choice between death or taking the girl with him. When the girl begged him to take pity on her, La Motte, moved by her tears as much as by his own danger, readily assented. Other men appeared and the prisoners, now blindfolded, were taken on horseback to the edge of the heath. There La Motte and the girl were put into his carriage. Followed by the threats and curses of the wild crew, Peter drove rapidly away. The agitated girl, thrust so strangely into the company of La Motte and his wife, gave her name only as Adeline. Not wishing to add to her distress, they did not pursue their questioning. Madame de la Motte was filled with pity for the unfortunate creature.

Several days later the travelers reached the vast forest of Fontanville. The sun was setting when they saw against the ruddy sky the towers of an ancient abbey. Awed by the solemn beauty of the ruins, they proceeded on their way, but at no great distance a carriage wheel broke, overturning the vehicle. Not wishing to spend the night in the open, they returned to the abbey. During their explorations they discovered a suite of apartments still habitable and of more modern date than the rest of the structure. In spite of his wife's misgivings, La Motte decided to make the secluded abbey his place of refuge.

Peter, dispatched to a nearby village for provisions and furniture, returned with the report that the ruins were the property of a nobleman living on a distant estate. The country people also claimed that a mysterious prisoner had once been confined there, and although no one knew his fate his ghost was supposed to haunt the scenes of his imprisonment. For seventeen years the natives of the region had not dared to approach the old abbey.

La Motte was well pleased with all that he heard, and before long he and his household had made their rude quarters as comfortable as possible. La Motte spent most of his mornings out of doors, either hunting or fishing, his afternoons and evenings with his family. Sometimes he read, but more often he sat in gloomy silence. Adeline alone had power to enliven his spirits when he grew moody and depressed. Having fully recovered from her terrifying experience, she had become a girl of sweet, lively disposition and diligent habits. After a time she began to look upon Madame de la Motte as a mother, and to her benefactress she confided the story of her life.

She was the only child of the poor but reputable Chevalier de St. Pierre. Her mother being dead, she had been reared in a convent, it being her father's intention that she should take the veil. On her refusal, he rebuked her for her obstinacy, but at last named a day to take her from the convent. Much to her dismay, she was not taken to his magnificent house in Paris but to that lonely house on the heath. There she was turned over to the care of brutal keepers. Only the arrival of La Motte, she believed, had saved her from an unknown but terrible fate.

After a month passed in his forest refuge, La Motte regained a measure of his tranquility and even cheerfulness, much to the delight of his wife and their ward. Then his mood suddenly changed. Preyed upon by some guilty secret or deep remorse, he avoided his family and spent many hours alone in the forest. Peter, the faithful servant, tried to follow his master on more than one occasion, but La Motte always eluded his follower and at one particular place disappeared as if the trees and rocks had swallowed him. About that time, also, Peter brought from the village a report that a stranger was in the neighborhood inquiring for his master. Greatly disturbed, La Motte remembered a trapdoor he had observed in one of the decaying chambers of the abbey. Thinking that it might lead to a place of hiding, he explored the passageway to which the trapdoor gave access and came finally to a room containing a large chest of ancient design. Throwing open the lid, he was horrified to find inside a human skeleton. Although he told them nothing about the gruesome remains in the chest, he insisted that his family join him in the hidden apartments he had discovered.

The next day, venturing out of hiding, La Motte saw a stranger in the abbey. He returned quickly to his place of concealment. But their provisions were running low, and at last it was decided that Adeline should reconnoiter the ruins to learn whether the supposed officer of the law had gone away. In the cloisters she encountered a young man in military uniform. Although she tried to flee, he overtook her and demanded to know the whereabouts of Pierre de la Motte. Adeline's relief was as great as her joy when the stranger's identity was revealed. He was Louis de la Motte, whose filial affection had drawn him to his father's side.

Unfortunately, his coming was to destroy completely Madame de la Motte's liking and esteem for Adeline. At times in the past she had been moved to jealousy, suspecting that La Motte went to keep assignations with his lovely ward when he disappeared so mysteriously into the forest, but she had tried to put such unworthy thoughts out of her mind. Now, seeing her son's growing fondness for the girl, she became unkind in her manner toward her. Aware of the mother's coldness and dislike, Adeline spent much of her time in the forest, where she composed poems inspired by the beauty of the landscape and her own gentle melancholy.

One day, while she sang some stanzas of her own composition, a strange voice echoed her. Startled to find a young man in hunter's dress close at hand, she would have fled in fright if the stranger had not paused respectfully on seeing her agitation. Adeline decided to refrain for a time from walking so far from the abbey. On her return Madame de la Motte added to her confusion by greeting her suspiciously.

About a month later a party of horsemen arrived at the abbey during a violent midnight storm. When La Motte ignored their knocking, they pushed the decayed door from its hinges and stalked into the hall. Adeline, overcome by fear for her benefactor, fainted. She revived to find the young man of the forest in the room. From the conversation she learned that his name was Theodore Peyrou and that his older companion, a chevalier of haughty demeanor, was the Marquis de Montalt, the owner of the abbey, who was staying at his hunting lodge on the edge of the forest. La Motte, who had fled when the knocking began, returned to the room. Immediately he and the marquis regarded each other in great confusion, and the nobleman put his hand threatingly upon his sword. He agreed, however, when La Motte requested a private discussion in another room. Madame de la Motte overheard enough of their conversation to realize that there was some secret between the two men.

The marquis and his retinue departed early in the morning. Returning the next day, the nobleman, after inquiring for La Motte, paid courteous attention to Adeline. When he and La Motte had disappeared into the forest on an errand of their own, Theodore remained with the ladies. Adeline realized suddenly that she was falling in love with the young man, an officer in a regiment commanded by the marquis.

Louis de la Motte prepared to return to his regiment. The marquis continued to visit the abbey almost every day. Adeline, meeting Theodore in the forest, received hints of some mysterious danger. He promised to meet her again the next evening, but when Adeline went to meet him he failed to appear. The marquis had suddenly ordered him to return to duty.

That night Adeline dreamed that she was in a strange chamber of the abbey, where a cloaked guide conducted her to a coffin covered with a pall. When her guide lifted the covering, she saw a dead man lying within, blood gushing from his side. Awaking, she slept no more that night.

The next day the marquis came for dinner and consented with reluctance to sleep at the abbey. A rearrangement of the private apartments being necessary to accommodate the guests, Adeline retired to a small chamber usually occupied by Madame de la Motte's maid. Behind an arras she uncovered a door which led into the chamber she had seen in her dream.

A rusted dagger lay on the floor and in a moldering bed she found a small roll of manuscript. On her return to her room she heard voices coming from the room below and to her horror recognized the impassioned accents of the marquis as he declared his intention to make her his own. She retired in great distress of mind, to be aroused again when the nobleman, in evident alarm, left the abbey unceremoniously before daybreak.

Later that same morning the marquis returned and over Adeline's protests declared his suit. When she turned to La Motte for aid, he assured her that he was unable to help her, since his safety depended upon the nobleman's favor. So great was Adeline's despair that she almost forgot the manuscript she had found in the abandoned room. She read enough of it, however, to realize that the despairing document had been written by the mysterious prisoner of the abbey, a victim of the cruel Marquis de Montalt. From Peter she learned also that the suit of the marquis was false; his wife was still living.

At last, to save the helpless girl from her suitor's evil design, Peter promised to take her to his native village in Savoy. She was to meet the servant at an old tomb in the forest, but when she arrived at the place of meeting a strange horseman appeared and in spite of her struggles carried her to the marquis' hunting lodge. There he again pressed his suit upon her. When he finally withdrew, she managed to escape through a window. Theodore, who had returned from his regiment when he learned of the marquis' evil designs, joined her in her flight. In a carriage which he had waiting they drove all night in the direction of the frontier. At an inn where they stopped for some refreshment they were overtaken by officers who tried to arrest Theodore in the king's name. Resisting, he received a saber cut in the head. He had almost recovered from his wound when the Marquis de Montalt appeared and ordered his men to seize Theodore on a charge of treason. Theodore, snatch-ing up a sergeant's cutlass, wounded the marquis. During the confusion Adeline was hustled into a chaise and driven back to the abbey, where La Motte locked her in her room. Anxious for word of Theodore, she was told a short time later that the young officer had been returned under arrest to his regiment.

By the time the marquis was able to travel, his passion for Adeline had turned to hate, and La Motte was instructed to do away with the girl. The unscrupulous nobleman's hold over La Motte was strong, for that unhappy man, driven to desperation by his lack of funds, had during his early days at the abbey held up and robbed the marquis, whom he mistook for a chance traveler in the forest. Although he was completely in the other's power, La Motte refused to stain his hands with blood. Instead, he ordered the faithful Peter to take Adeline to Leloncourt, in Savoy, where she would be safe from the marquis' agents. When her flight was revealed, the nobleman had La Motte arrested for highway robbery and imprisoned.

Shortly after her arrival in Leloncourt Adeline became ill. Arnaud La Luc, a scholarly clergyman, took her into his home for nursing and during her convalescence she formed a close friendship with his daughter Clara. So deep was her grief over Theodore that she never mentioned him to her new friends. Then La Luc's health began to fail, and she and Clara accompanied him to the Mediterranean seacoast. There Adeline encountered Louis de la Motte and learned that he was on his way to Leloncourt on an errand for Theodore. To her great surprise, it was revealed that the man she knew as Theodore Peyrou was in reality the son of Arnaud La Luc. The travelers immediately hastened to Vaceau, where the young officer was being held under sentence of death.

La Motte, meanwhile, had been taken to Paris for trial on the charges brought against him by the marquis. The prisoner was in despair when an unexpected witness appeared in his behalf. The man was

Du Bosse, one of the ruffians hired to dispose of Adeline while she was held prisoner in the lonely house on the heath. His story started an investigation which revealed that Adeline was the natural daughter of the Marquis de Montalt, who had never seen the girl before he met her at the ruined abbey. In the past one of his agents had always played the part of her father. The marquis was arrested and Adeline was summoned to Paris for his trial. With the arrest of the man she had always considered her father other of the marquis' activities came to light. He had also ordered the murder of his older brother, whose skeleton La Motte had found in the abbey. The confederate also testified that Adeline was not the nobleman's natural daughter but his older brother's child, an heiress whom he had tried to conceal from the world. The manuscript Adeline had found provided further documentary evidence of her uncle's villainy. He was sentenced to death for his crimes.

The extent of the marquis' evil designs being known, Theodore received a royal pardon and was restored to his military rank. Pierre de la Motte was sentenced to exile in England, and Adeline provided for his comfort and that of his wife in their old age. Her father's skeleton she buried with all respect in the vault of his ancestors. A short time later she and Theodore married and went to live at Leloncourt. Clara married Monsieur Verneuil, Adeline's distant kinsman, who had been helpful to her and the La Lucs during the time of their distress over Theodore and La Motte. Before many years had passed Louis de la Motte came with his bride to a house nearby, and there in Leloncourt the three deserving couples lived out their lives in happiness and prosperity.

# ROMANCE OF THE THREE KINGDOMS

*Type of work:* Novel
*Author:* Lo Kuan chung (c. 1320 c. 1380)
*Type of plot:* Historical romance
*Time of plot:* Third century
*Locale:* China
*First transcribed:* Fourteenth century

Principal characters:

LIU PEI, a distant descendant of the royal family of the Han dynasty and the founder of the Shu Han Kingdom

KUAN Yü, Liu Pei's sworn brother, later apotheosized by Chinese as the God of War

CHANG FEI, the sworn brother of Liu and Kuan, a blunt soldier of great prowess

CHU-KO LIANG. prime minister to Liu Pei and to his weakling successor

TS'AO TS'AO. founder of the Wei Kingdom, noted for his unscrupulous resourcefulness

SUN CH'ÜAN, founder of the Wu Kingdom

CHOU Yü, Sun Ch'üan's brilliant military commander, perpetually piqued by Chu-ko Liang's superior intelligence

CHAO YÜN, a brave general of the Shu Han Kingdom

Lü Po, an unprincipled and matchless warrior famous for his romantic involvement with the beauty Tiao Shan

SSU-MA I, founder of the all-powerful Ssu-ma family in the Wei Kingdom

CHIANG WEI, Chu-ko Liang's successor

*Critique:*

The colorful events of the period of the Three Kingdoms. beginning with the rise of the Yellow Turban rebels under the last emperors of the Eastern Han dynasty and ending with the unification of China under the first Chin Emperor, have always fascinated the Chinese. Lo Kuan-chung. who made use of official history as well as oral traditions in the composition of this great dynastic romance. permanently fixed the popular image of the period. In this respect he is not unlike Homer, who rendered a similar service for the Greeks. It is not too much to say that the *Romance of the Three Kingdoms* (*San-kuo chih yen-i*) has been for centuries the most popular book in China, beloved alike by literati and populace. Lo Kuan-chung wrote from the point of view which believes Liu Pei to be the rightful successor to the Han throne, but while his treatment of the major personages of Shu Han is al-ways sympathetic, he seldom stoops to vilify the equally colorful heroes of Wei and Wu. Even Ts'ao Ts'ao, always the caricature of a villain on the Chinese stage, is a more complex and subtle character in the book than most careless readers would allow. In making Chu-ko Liang his hero, a man of unexcelled intelligence who nevertheless attempts the impossible out of his devotion to Liu Pei and his cause, Lo Kuan-chung has given his history a tragic meaning of the most disturbing kind.

*The Story:*

When the Yellow Turban rebellion was finally quashed, the many soldiers of fortune who took part in its suppression seized power for themselves, thus precipitating the downfall of the Eastern Han dynasty. Among these the most shrewd and successful politician was Ts'ao Ts'ao, who had already attracted a

ROMANCE OF THE THREE KINGDOMS by Lo Kuan-chung. Translated by C. H. Brewitt-Taylor. By permission of the publishers, Charles E. Tuttle Co., Rutland, Vt. Copyright, 1925, by Kelly & Walsh, Ltd. Renewed. All rights reserved. Copyright, 1959, by Charles E. Tuttle Co.

large following of able counselors and warriors. After the systematic elimination of his many rivals, such as Tung Cho, Lü Po, Yüan Shao, and Yüan Shu, he ruled over North China as the King of Wei, subjecting the Han Emperor and his court to great indignity.

Liu Pei, who also rose to fame during the Yellow Turban rebellion, was for a long time doing very poorly, in spite of the legendary prowess of his sworn brothers, Kuan Yü and Chang Fei. It was not until he sought out Chu-ko Liang and made him his prime minister that his fortunes began to improve. In time he ruled over Szechwan as the King of Shu Han.

While Liu Pei was beginning to mend his fortunes, the only man who blocked Ts'ao Ts'ao's territorial ambitions was Sun Ch'üan, who had inherited from his father and older brother the rich kingdom of Wu, south of the Yangtze. When Ts'ao Ts'ao finally decided to cross the Yangtze and subdue Wu, Sun Ch'üan and Liu Pei formed an alliance, and the combined strategy of their respective military commanders, Chou Yü and Chu-ko Liang, subjected Ts'ao Ts'ao's forces to a crushing defeat. After this victory Liu Pei went to Szechwan and the precarious power balance of the Three Kingdoms was established.

The friendly relationship between Shu and Wu did not last long. Kuan Yü, entrusted with the vital task of governing the province of Hupeh, adjacent to the Wu territory, had antagonized Sun Ch'üan, and in the subsequent military struggle he was killed. Liu Pei now vowed to conquer Wu; against the sage advice of Chu-ko Liang, who wanted to conciliate Wu so as to counter their more dangerous common enemy, Wei, he led a personal expedition against Wu and suffered a disastrous defeat. Liu Pei died soon afterward.

Liu Pei's son and successor was a moronic weakling. Out of loyalty to his late master, however, Chu-ko Liang was determined to serve him and improve the fortunes of Shu. He made peace with Wu and led several expeditions against Wei. These campaigns ended in a stalemate. Overburdened with work and handicapped by the lack of able generals (of the "Five Tiger Warriors" of Liu Pei's day, only Chao Yün had remained, an old fighter as intrepid as ever), Chu-ko Liang could no longer direct his campaigns with his usual brilliance. Moreover, the Wei commander, Ssu-ma I, whose family had become increasingly powerful in the Wei court following the death of Ts'ao Ts'ao, was in many ways his shrewd match. Finally Chu-ko Liang died of physical exhaustion.

By that time the Ssu-mas had usurped the power of Wei and had subjected Ts'ao Ts'ao's descendants to as much cruelty and torture as Ts'ao Ts'ao and his immediate successor had subjected the Han emperors. Wu and Shu had both weakened. Even though Chiang Wei, the Shu general, tried bravely to stem the tide, he was overwhelmed by the numerical strength of the invading Wei forces, under the command of T'eng Ai and Chung Hui. Soon after the death of Chiang Wei, the kings of Shu and Wu surrendered. Ssu-ma Yen, Ssu-ma I's grandson, now ruled China as the first Emperor of Chin.

# THE ROMANTIC COMEDIANS

Type of work: Novel
Author: Ellen Glasgow (1874-1945)
Type of plot: Humorous satire
Time of plot: 1920's
Locale: Richmond, Virginia
First published: 1926

Principal characters:
JUDGE GAMALIEL BLAND HONEYWELL, a widower of sixty-five
ANNABEL, his second wife, a girl of twenty-three
MRS. UPCHURCH, Annabel's mother
EDMONIA BREDALBANE, the judge's sister
AMANDA LIGHTFOOT, the judge's childhood sweetheart

## Critique:

The Romantic Comedians presents the age-old problem of the old man who marries a young girl. But symbolized in these two people is the struggle between two diverse eras in American culture. The man represents the faded Victorianism of the American South in the last third of the nineteenth century. The girl represents the generation of Southern Americans in the decade after the first World War. Since Ellen Glasgow's purpose was to present the new South, the novel succeeds because it reflects the forces which pervade that section of our country today.

## The Story:

As Judge Honeywell walked home from church on the first Easter morning after his wife's death, he was surprised by his own reactions to the Virginia springtime. He felt quite young, for sixty-five, and life with his wife, now dead, seemed so remote as never to have happened. In fact, he felt relieved, for his first wife had seldom let him lead an existence of his own.

The judge looked after Mrs. Upchurch and her daughter Annabel in a friendly way because they were kinswomen of his late wife. But shortly after that memorable Easter morning he began to think of twenty-three-year old Annabel in quite another way. His changed attitude began because he was secretly sorry for her.

She had been engaged to a young man who had left her almost at the altar. It had hurt her bitterly, as the judge and her mother knew.

As time passed the judge found himself thinking more and more of Annabel Upchurch and of Amanda Lightfoot, his childhood sweetheart. Unfortunately, the judge's sister, Mrs. Bredalbane, tried to convince him that falling in love with Amanda would be the sensible thing for him to do. The judge, like most men, promptly closed his mind to Amanda and began thinking more of Annabel, who had asked the judge if he would help her to open a flower shop.

Soon the judge had purchased a house with a large garden for Mrs. Upchurch and her daughter, so that Annabel might practice landscape gardening. When he told the girl, he added that he only expected the reward of seeing her happy. But when she left, he kissed her.

By the time that Mrs. Upchurch and Annabel were settled in their new home, the judge knew he was in love with the girl, who was more than forty years younger than he. He bought new clothes and had his hair and beard trimmed to lessen the amount of gray which had appeared. He felt that he could give Annabel everything she needed—love, tenderness, security, and wealth.

The number and quality of the judge's

gifts soon made apparent to Annabel and her mother what was in the old man's mind. Annabel thought at first that it would be more suitable for him to marry her mother. But, as she informed her mother, marrying an older man was certainly better than living in an atmosphere of shabby gentility. Annabel decided to visit Amanda Lightfoot. Knowing that Amanda had never married because she had been in love with the judge, Annabel wished to find out if the older woman still loved him. If she did not, Annabel decided, she herself would marry him. But the older woman almost refused to say anything at all. Annabel was disappointed but secretly relieved. When she arrived home, Judge Honeywell was waiting with a present for her, a sapphire bracelet. Before he left the house he told her he loved her, and she accepted him.

After the marriage the judge and Annabel traveled in Europe and in England. The judge felt that he was as fine a man as he had been at thirty-five, although his nerves were jarred a little when some one occasionally referred to Annabel as his daughter. That she often danced with young men did not bother him. He felt no envy of their youth: after all, she was his wife.

The judge was glad to be back in his home in Virginia after the honeymoon. His dyspepsia soon disappeared after he began to eat familiar cooking once more, and he felt at peace to be living in the familiar old house which had not been refurnished in over thirty years.

The couple dined out frequently and went to many dances. The judge, after noting how silly his contemporaries appeared on the dance floor, abstained from any dancing, but he encouraged Annabel to enjoy herself. He always went with her, not from jealousy but because he felt that he had to keep up with her life. It cost him a great deal of effort, for on those evenings he sometimes thought that he had never before known what fatigue was really like.

At home, Annabel had brought changes into the house. While he did not approve, the judge said nothing until she tried to change the furniture in his own room. She learned then, although it cost him a ring she had admired, that he would not let her meddle with his own privacy.

When the judge came down with bronchitis, Annabel proved an able and attentive nurse. During his convalescence, however, she found it difficult to remain at home reading night after night. He, noticing her restlessness, told her to begin going out again, even though he could not go with her. When Annabel went out, her mother or the judge's sister would come to have dinner and stay with him during the evening.

The passing weeks brought in Annabel a change which many people noticed. Noted for her boisterous spirits and lack of reticence, she surprised them by becoming more vague about her comings and goings. At the same time they complimented the judge on how happy she seemed. The compliments made the old gentleman content, for, as he said, Annabel's happiness was what he wanted most.

Slowly the judge began to feel that all was not right in his home. Annabel was distant in her manner. When he talked with his sister and Annabel's mother, both reassured him of the girl's devotion. Still, he knew something was not right. He received proof one day when he found Annabel kissing a young man. Dabney Birdsong belonged to an old family in the community. Annabel had resolved to have him, cost what it might. To the judge, his greatest sorrow was that it might be only an infatuation which would not make Annabel happy. The girl, on the other hand, thought if she did not have Dabney she would die.

Annabel and her lover ran away and went to New York. The judge followed them to the city. Unable to understand his young wife, he felt sorry for her because she defied convention, and he thought that he himself was to blame for what had happened. After a talk with Annabel he left New York, defeated, to return to Virginia.

The rain and the draughty train gave the judge a cold which turned into influenza, and he was in bed for several weeks in a serious condition. During his convalescence he discovered that spring had once more arrived. With the stirring in nature, he felt a resurgence of life in his weary body. Like many an old man before him, the season of freshness and greenery gave him the feeling of youth that he had had on the previous Easter Sunday morning. He found himself beginning to look with new, eager interest at the young nurse who was attending him during his illness.

# THE ROMANTIC LADIES

*Type of work:* **Drama**
*Author:* Molière (Jean Baptiste Poquelin, 1622-1673)
*Type of plot:* Comedy of manners
*Time of plot:* Seventeenth century
*Locale:* Paris
*First presented:* 1659

Principal characters:
LA GRANGE, and
DU CROISY, young men of Paris
MAGDALEN, and
CATHOS, the romantic ladies
THE MARQUIS DE MASCARILLE, La Grange's valet
VISCOUNT JODELET, Du Croisy's valet
GORGIBUS, Magdalen's father and Cathos' uncle

*Critique:*

When *The Romantic Ladies* (*Les Précieuses Ridicules*) was first presented in Paris, it was the fashion for people of fashionable society to talk in affected, ultra-sentimental style. Molière, using his rapier-like pen to lampoon this custom, made the people of Paris see themselves as they appeared to others, and before long they mended their foolish ways of speech. The play had instant success, for not only did it deal with a subject near to the hearts of pleasure-loving Paris but also it was a true comedy, delicate and subtle in its effects. This one-act play deserves a place with Molière's best.

*The Story:*

Gorgibus had taken his daughter Magdalen and his niece Cathos from their country home for a stay in Paris. There La Grange and Du Croisy, calling on them to propose marriage, were greatly disgusted by the affectation displayed by the young ladies, for the girls had adopted manners prevalent everywhere in France, manners which were a combination of coquetry and artificiality. With the help of their valets, La Grange and Du Croisy determined to teach the silly young girls a lesson. One of the valets in particular, Mascarille, loved to pass for a wit; he dressed himself as a man of quality and composed songs and verses.

Gorgibus, meeting the two prospective suitors, inquired into their success with his niece and his daughter. The evasive answers he received from them led him to discuss the affair with the two ladies. He had to wait some time for them, while they were busily engaged in painting their faces and arranging their hair. When they were finally ready to receive him, he was enraged by their silly conversation.

He had expected them to accept the two young men, who were both wealthy and of good family, but the romantic ladies explained that they would only spurn suitors so direct and sincere. Also, much to the disgust of the two girls, the young men had proposed at their first meeting. They wanted lovers to be deceiving. A lover also must be pensive and sorrowful, not joyful and healthy, as La Grange and Du Croisy had been. In addition, a young lady must refuse her lover's pleas in order to make him miserable. If possible, there should also be adventures: the presence of rivals, the scorn of fathers, elopements from high windows. Another fault the girls found with the two young men was that they were dressed simply, with no ribbons or feathers on their clothing. Poor Gorgibus thought his daughter and niece out of their minds. He was convinced of this when they asked him to call them by other names, for their own were too vulgar. Cathos would be called Amintha and Magdalen renamed Polixena. Gorgibus knew only one thing after this foolish conversation—either the two girls would marry quickly or they would both become nuns.

Even the girls' maid could not understand the orders they gave her, for they talked in such riddles that no one could rightly understand their meaning. She announced that a young man was in the parlor, come to call on the two ladies. The caller was the Marquis De Mascarille, in reality La Grange's valet. The girls were enchanted with Mascarille, for he was a dandy of the greatest and most artificial wit. His bombastic puns were so affected that the girls thought him the very soul of cleverness. He pretended to all sorts of accomplishments and acquaintances. On the spot he composed terrible verses and songs, which he sang out of key and in a nasal tone. He claimed to have written a play that would be acted at the Royal Theater. He drew their attention to his beautiful dress, complete with ribbons, feathers, and perfume. Not to be outdone, the ladies boasted that although they knew no one in Paris, as yet, a friend had promised to make them acquainted with all the fine dandies of the city. They were a perfect audience for the silly valet pretending to be a marquis. They applauded each verse, each song, each bit of shallow wit.

The Viscount Jodelet, in reality Du Croisy's valet, joined the group. He claimed to be a hero of the wars, in command of two thousand horsemen. He had the girls feel the scars left by deadly wounds he had received. The two scoundrels were hard put to outdo each other in telling the foolish girls ridiculous tales. When they talked of their visits with dukes and countesses, the girls were fascinated by their good connections. Running out of conversation, the two valets then asked the girls to arrange a party. They sent for musicians and other young people in order to have a proper dance. Mascarille, not being able to dance, accused the musicians of not keeping proper time, and Jodelet agreed with him.

The dance was in full swing when La Grange and Du Croisy appeared upon the scene. Raining blows upon them and calling them rogues, they fell upon the two impostors. Mascarille and Jodelet tried to pretend this scene was all a joke, but their masters continued to beat them. When other servants appeared and began to strip the clothes from the two pretenders, the girls screamed in horror. La Grange and Du Croisy berated them for receiving servants better than they received masters. They told the girls that if they loved the two scoundrels so well, they must love them without their masters' finery. Taking all the outer apparel from the rogues, La Grange and Du Croisy ordered them to continue the dance.

Gorgibus, having heard on the streets of Paris of his ladies' scandal, appeared and soundly berated the pranksters for the disgrace they had brought upon his house. All Paris, all France even, would laugh at the joke, for the young people at the dance were now spreading the news up and down the streets and in the cafés. Gorgibus was furious with La Grange and Du Croisy for their trick, but knew the stupid girls deserved the treatment they had received. He sent the two valets packing and ordered the romantic ladies to hide themselves from the world. Then he cursed folly, affectation, and romantic songs, the causes of his horrible disgrace.

# THE ROMANY RYE

*Type of work:* Novel
*Author:* George Henry Borrow (1803-1881)
*Type of plot:* Simulated autobiography
*Time of plot:* Nineteenth century
*Locale:* England
*First published:* 1857

Principal characters:
LAVENGRO, a scholar gipsy
ISOPEL BERNERS (BELLE), his companion
JASPER PETULENGRO, a gipsy
JACK DALE, a horse-trader
MURTAGH, an Irishman and Lavengro's childhood friend
THE COACHMAN

## Critique:

The Romany Rye continues without a break the story of *Lavengro*. The novel is a collection of stories about the people Lavengro met, together with his many side remarks and observations on gipsy customs, English fairs, religion, and literature. *The Romany Rye* is unevenly written, but its pictures of English life in the first half of the nineteenth century are at all times vivid and dramatic.

## The Story:

In those days, Lavengro and Isopel Berners traveled the English highroads together. Lavengro was a scholar who had become a gipsy tinker, and Isopel, whom he called Belle, was a strapping woman of the roads and dingles. One night they rescued a coachman whose carriage had overturned in a swollen stream, and, while they waited for daylight, he entertained them with the story of his life. In the morning Lavengro forged a new linch-pin for the broken wheel, and the coachman continued on his way. The Man in Black, a Catholic priest whom Lavengro had met before, visited Lavengro again that evening, and the two of them discussed and argued the merits of Catholicism and Protestantism, with an occasional remark from Belle.

The next morning Lavengro informed Belle that Jasper Petulengro and his band of gipsies had camped nearby during the night and that he was going to invite Mr. and Mrs. Petulengro for breakfast. Lavengro's gipsy friend refused his invitation, however, saying that he and his wife would pay a visit later in the day when they were better settled. On the next Sunday they all went to church together. Following the service, Jasper and Lavengro began a lengthy discussion on morals.

Belle had indicated to Lavengro that she thought it about time their paths separated. When she informed him she was going on a journey, he feared she was leaving for good, but she told him she would come back before too long. One evening while she was gone Lavengro had a long talk with Ursula, Mrs. Petulengro's sister, and thus he learned her story. She had been married some years previously. Her husband, escaping from a constable, had met with an unfortunate accident and had drowned. She had been a widow until just two days before, when she had married Sylvester, another member of the gipsy band and a widower with two children. Lavengro and Ursula discussed many subjects, including morals, virtue, marriage customs, and words. It was about the meanings of some of the gipsy words that Lavengro wanted most to talk with Ursula.

Belle returned that night and the next day Lavengro, who had thought the matter over in her absence, asked Belle to marry him and to migrate with him to

America. When she told him that she could not give him her answer immediately, he planned to attend a fair in a nearby village the next day. Belle agreed to consider his proposal during his absence and to give him her reply when he returned. At the fair Lavengro saw a horse which he desired, but he did not have the money to buy the animal and he refused to borrow the money from Jasper, who was willing to lend it to him.

When Lavengro returned to the dingle, Belle had disappeared. At first he thought she had gone only on a short journey, but when two days went by and she did not appear, he began to fear she would not return. A few days later he received a letter from her, telling him that on her previous short journey she had made arrangements to dispose of all her goods and to go to America. When he proposed to her, she had been tempted to accept his offer, but after thinking it over carefully she had decided that her first plan would be the best after all. Lavengro never saw her again.

That night, at a nearby public house, Lavengro again saw the horse he had admired at the fair and learned the animal could be bought for fifty pounds. Jasper insisted on giving Lavengro the money with which to buy the horse, and Lavengro reluctantly agreed. He and Jasper planned to meet about ten weeks later. Lavengro departed the following morning. On his way he met an old man who had just had his mule taken away from him by force. Lavengro rode after the offender and returned the mule.

One afternoon, as Lavengro and his horse were resting at the door of an inn, he met his old friend, the coachman, and through him obtained a job in the hostelry as a keeper of accounts in exchange for room and board for himself and his horse.

After a short while at the inn, Lavengro decided it was time for him to be on his way again. He had decided to go to Horncastle, a town at a distance of about one hundred and twenty-five miles. There he hoped to sell his horse at a good profit. He journeyed at a leisurely pace for several days and was nearing Horncastle late one evening when his horse, frightened by a light on a gig, threw him and knocked him unconscious. When he recovered consciousness, he found himself in the home of the man who owned the gig. The man informed him that his horse was safe and uninjured in the barn. A surgeon came soon after to examine Lavengro and to bandage his injured arm. While recuperating, Lavengro learned his host's story, how at the shattering of all his hopes for happiness with the death of his beloved, he had turned to the study of Chinese as a way to occupy his mind. Through this man, Lavengro learned much of the character of Chinese language and writing.

The surgeon finally declared Lavengro well enough to continue to the fair and gave him a letter to an innkeeper in Horncastle, so that he might find room and board for both himself and his horse. He proceeded to Horncastle, and the next morning, after displaying his horse's abilities to the best advantage, he sold him to Jack Dale, a horse-trader, who was acting as a representative for a Hungarian. Later that evening Lavengro and the Hungarian began a discourse in German, and Lavengro learned much of the history of Hungary. He also heard Jack Dale's life story. Jack, the son of a forger, had experienced a difficult and unhappy childhood. His life had been made even harder because of his physical ugliness. After his father was convicted and sent away to serve a prison sentence, Jack decided to live an upright life, as he had promised his father he would do. After much struggling, he had finally achieved a respectable place in the community.

While walking through the town the next morning, Lavengro saw a thimblerigger chased off by Jack Dale. Lavengro recognized the thimblerigger as a boyhood friend, Murtagh, and followed him. After much recollection of old times he gave Murtagh five pounds to return to Ireland and become a priest, a profession for which Murtagh had studied as a young man, but in which he had never been ordained because of difficulties over card playing.

Lavengro left Horncastle and walked eastward. He continued his journey for two days until he came to a large town. There, on the outskirts, he was accosted by a recruiting sergeant who tried to get him to join the Honorable East India Company and to go to India to fight. Lavengro was struck by the similarity of words the sergeant used and those of the gipsies. But when the sergeant noticed that Lavengro's hair was beginning to turn gray, he withdrew his offer. All of his life Lavengro was to wonder what new adventures he might have encountered if he had gone to India.

# ROME HAUL

*Type of work:* Novel
*Author:* Walter D. Edmonds (1903-    )
*Type of plot:* Regional romance
*Time of plot:* 1850
*Locale:* Erie Canal
*First published:* 1929

Principal characters:
DAN HARROW, a newcomer on the canal
MOLLY LARKINS, his cook
FORTUNE FRIENDLY, a canal character
GENTLEMAN JOE CALASH, a canal highwayman
JOTHAM KLORE, a canal bully

*Critique:*

There is a native tang and sharpness to this novel, which reclaims a segment of the American past in its picture of life along the Erie Canal. The book is vivid in its painstaking detail. The description of a flock of geese becomes more than description for pictorial effect; it becomes a symbol of the passing of a season and a passing of a way of life. There is poignancy and passion in the lives of people like Dan and Molly, Mrs. Gurget and Sol, and even Gentleman Joe Calash, who lived on the big ditch before the railroads destroyed its free, picturesque life. *Rome Haul* is authentic Americana.

*The Story:*

It was early summer. A young man carrying a carpetbag was walking to Boonville, New York, when a peddler named Jacob Turnesa picked him up. The young man said his name was Dan Harrow, lately a farmhand and now looking for work on the Erie Canal. A farm woman stopped them for news and gave them some root beer. She and Turnesa talked about Gentleman Joe Calash, a highwayman on the canal.

While Dan was looking for lodgings in one of the taverns, he saw Gentleman Joe Calash quarreling with Jotham Klore, canal bully. The highwayman struck Klore with his revolver and rode off in the darkness. Dan made no effort to give the alarm, not even for the two

thousand dollars reward. Inwardly he felt sympathy for the robber, who was, like himself, alone and without friends.

Looking for work, Dan went to the *Ella-Romeyn*, the canal boat of Hector Berry. He found Berry playing cards with Sol Tinkle and Mrs. Gurget, Sol's cook. Mrs. Gurget was enormously fat and addicted to rum noggins with lots of lemon in them. Mrs. Berry was away, and so Hector, who could make no decisions without his wife, could only offer Dan a job for the short haul to Rome. Later that day Mrs. Berry came aboard. She was suspicious of Dan because he was a stranger. Dan left the boat on reaching Rome.

At Rome he went to Hennessy's Saloon to see Julius Wilson about a job. While he waited he overheard more talk of Gentleman Joe Calash and of the reward for capturing him. Then Molly Larkins, a pretty canal cook, joined him. Molly cooked for Jotham Klore. When Klore came in, he accused Dan of getting too familiar with Molly. Angry, Dan hit Klore. Gentleman Joe suddenly appeared, knocked out Klore, and held Molly and Dan with his weapon. When they promised not to give the alarm, he made his escape.

A little later Wilson hired Dan for the haul to Albany on his boat, the *Xerxes*. Ben Rae was the captain and William Wampy, the cook and fiddler.

Near Utica they saw a tall thin man running from a crowd that chased him into a haymow. They learned that the man was a traveling preacher who had been paid for six sermons but had tried to sneak out without giving the last one. Cornered, the minister preached a fire-and-brimstone sermon from the mow. After he had finished, Ben Rae took the minister aboard. He explained that though he had been trained for the ministry he was not really a preacher. His name was Fortune Friendly.

At the next stop Dan went ashore and encountered Molly Larkin again. She had given up her job with Klore and was going to Lucy Cashdollar's place to get a new position. Later that night Dan got into another fight with Klore and was knocked out. When he came to, he found that someone had carried him to the boat. He caught a glimpse of Gentleman Joe.

At Albany Samson Weaver, captain of the *Sarsy Sal*, hired him to drive his team. On the first day of their haul they saw a burning canal boat condemned because of cholera. Samson claimed he was not afraid of cholera, but he began to drink hard. Ill, he asked Dan to use his money for a doctor, but before Dan could get a doctor Samson died. While looking for an undertaker, Dan found a funeral director who offered him ten dollars for Samson's corpse. He took the money because he could not afford to pay for Samson's funeral.

Deciding to carry on alone, he headed for Lucy Cashdollar's agency. Lucy supplied girls as cooks for lonely canal men. Whether they married the canal men was no concern of hers, but usually she was glad if they did. By nightfall Molly was installed as the cook aboard the *Sarsy Sal*.

Mr. Butterfield, the agent for whom Samson had worked, offered to keep Dan hauling for him at the rates he had paid Samson. Together they planned to reclaim Samson's body from the surgeon to whom the undertaker had sold it, and

give it decent burial.

On the wharf Dan saw old Fortune Friendly again and hired him as a driver. Molly and Friendly talked about Jotham Klore and agreed that sooner or later there would have to be a show-down fight between Klore and Dan. Molly and Dan found Samson's money hidden aboard the *Sarsy Sal*, over eight hundred dollars. Dan thought it was enough to start a small farm.

When Dan decided to buy a pair of horses at the Utica fair, Molly, Sol Tinkle, Mrs. Gurget, Hector Berry, and Mrs. Berry went with him. While Molly and Dan shopped for a suit for Dan, the clerk treated them as man and wife. Dan almost asked Molly to marry him, but he lost his chance when Hector hurried them along so that his wife could witness the hanging of a woman who had browbeaten her husband and finally killed him. Hector hoped the hanging would be a lesson to his nagging wife. At the fair Dan purchased two well-matched horses.

Autumn was in the air, and soon the canal would be closed for the season. Jotham Klore had not appeared. His fight with Dan would be postponed until spring. Dan and Molly saw Gentleman Joe again, and the highwayman gave them a jeweled pin as a memento. Dan had always linked himself with Gentleman Joe, feeling that neither he nor the highwayman was really part of the canal.

That winter Dan and Molly realized that the initial warmth of their feeling for each other was over. Molly confided to her friends that she intended to stay on the canal and that if Dan decided to go back to the land she would leave him. When spring came, Dan received an offer to work on a farm, but the offer was good only if he were not married. Not knowing what to do and unwilling to desert Molly, Dan headed the *Sarsy Sal* west on the canal. At the Lansing Kill they met Jotham Klore's boat coming toward the lock. Dan and Klore fought on a square of grass that the excited, shouting boaters marked off beside the locks. It was a battle that men talked about on the Erie for years afterward, Dan and Klore pummeling each other under the hot sunshine while Molly Larkin stood by to see what the outcome would be. Dan won, and he and Molly started west once more. But the feeling between them was no longer the same. Dan felt that she was pitying Klore, the beaten bully of the canal.

Then Gentleman Joe was caught and killed, and for the first time Dan saw the highwayman's cruel, mean face. Somehow, he felt that the highwayman's death freed him from life on the canal. One day Molly left him to go back to Klore. Dan took the farm job that had been offered him. He knew that he belonged in the farm country from which he had come.

# ROMEO AND JULIET

*Type of work:* Drama
*Author:* William Shakespeare (1564-1616)
*Type of plot:* Romantic tragedy
*Time of plot:* Fifteenth century
*Locale:* Verona, Italy
*First presented:* c. 1595

*Principal characters:*
ROMEO, son of the house of Montague
JULIET, daughter of the house of Capulet
FRIAR LAWRENCE, a Franciscan
MERCUTIO, Romeo's friend
TYBALT, Lady Capulet's nephew

*Critique:*

This story of two star-crossed lovers is one of Shakespeare's tenderest dramas. Shakespeare was evidently quite sympathetic toward Romeo and Juliet, and in attributing their tragedy to fate, rather than to a flaw in their characters, he raised them to heights near perfection. They are both sincere, kind, brave, loyal, virtuous, and desperately in love, and their tragedy is greater because of their innocence. The feud between the lovers' families represents the fate which Romeo and Juliet are powerless to overcome. The lines capture in poetry the youthful and simple passion which characterizes the play.

*The Story:*

Long ago in Verona, Italy, there lived two famous families, the Montagues and the Capulets. These two houses were deadly enemies, and their enmity did not stop at harsh words, but extended to bloody duels and sometimes death.

Romeo, son of old Montague, thought himself in love with haughty Rosaline, a beautiful girl who did not return his affection. Hearing that Rosaline was to attend a great feast at the house of Capulet, Romeo and his trusted friend, Mercutio, donned masks and entered the great hall as invited guests. But Romeo was no sooner in the ballroom than he noticed the exquisite Juliet, Capulet's daughter, and instantly forgot his disdainful Rosaline. Romeo had never seen Juliet before, and in asking her name he aroused the suspicion of Tybalt, a fiery member of the Capulet clan. Tybalt drew his sword and faced Romeo. But old Capulet, coming upon the two men, parted them, and with the gentility that comes with age requested that they have no bloodshed at the feast. Tybalt, however, was angered that a Montague should take part in Capulet festivities, and afterward nursed a grudge against Romeo.

Romeo spoke in urgent courtliness to Juliet and asked if he might kiss her hand. She gave her permission, much impressed by this unknown gentleman whose affection for her was so evident. Romeo then begged to kiss her lips, and when she had no breath to object, he pressed her to him. They were interrupted by Juliet's nurse, who sent the young girl off to her mother. When she had gone, Romeo learned from the nurse that Juliet was a Capulet. He was stunned, for he was certain that this fact would mean his death. He could never give her up. Juliet, who had fallen instantly in love with Romeo, discovered that he was a Montague, the son of a hated house.

That night Romeo, too much in love to go home to sleep, stole to Juliet's house and stood in the orchard beneath a balcony that led to her room. To his surprise, he saw Juliet leaning over the railing above him. Thinking herself alone, she began to talk of Romeo and wished aloud that he were not a Montague. Hearing her words, Romeo could contain himself no longer, but spoke to her. She was frightened at first, and

3286

when she saw who it was she was confused and ashamed that he had overheard her confession. But it was too late to pretend reluctance, as was the fashion for sweethearts in those days. Juliet freely admitted her passion, and the two exchanged vows of love. Juliet told Romeo that she would marry him and would send him word by nine o'clock the next morning to arrange for their wedding.

Romeo then went off to the monastery cell of Friar Lawrence to enlist his help in the ceremony. The good friar was much impressed with Romeo's devotion. Thinking that the union of a Montague and a Capulet would dissolve the enmity between the two houses, he promised to marry Romeo and Juliet.

Early the next morning, while he was in company with his two friends, Benvolio and Mercutio, Romeo received Juliet's message, brought by her nurse. He told the old woman of his arrangement with Friar Lawrence and bade her carry the word back to Juliet. The nurse kept the secret and gave her mistress the message. When Juliet appeared at the friar's cell at the appointed time, she and Romeo were married. But the time was short and Juliet had to hurry home. Before she left, Romeo promised that he would meet her in the orchard underneath the balcony after dark that night.

That same day, Romeo's friends, Mercutio and Benvolio, were loitering in the streets when Tybalt came by with some other members of the Capulet house. Tybalt, still holding his grudge against Romeo, accused Mercutio of keeping company with the hateful and villainous young Montague. Mercutio, proud of his friendship with Romeo, could not take insult lightly, for he was as hot-tempered when provoked as Tybalt himself. The two were beginning their heated quarrel when Romeo, who had just returned from his wedding, appeared. He was appalled at the situation because he knew that Juliet was fond of Tybalt, and he wished no injury to his wife's people. He tried in vain to settle the argument

peaceably. Mercutio was infuriated by Romeo's soft words, and when Tybalt called Romeo a villain, Mercutio drew his sword and rushed to his friend's defense. But Tybalt, the better swordsman, gave Mercutio a mortal wound. Romeo could ignore the fight no longer. Enraged at the death of his friend, he rushed at Tybalt with drawn sword and killed him quickly. The fight soon brought crowds of people to the spot. For his part in the fray, Romeo was banished from Verona.

Hiding out from the police, he went, grief-stricken, to Friar Lawrence's cell. The friar advised him to go to his wife that night, and then at dawn to flee to Mantua until the friar saw fit to publish the news of the wedding. Romeo consented to follow this good advice. As darkness fell, he went to meet Juliet. When dawn appeared, heartsick Romeo left for Mantua.

Meanwhile, Juliet's father decided that it was time for his daughter to marry. Having not the slightest idea of her love for Romeo, the old man demanded that she accept her handsome and wealthy suitor, Paris. Juliet was horrified at her father's proposal but dared not tell him of her marriage because of Romeo's part in Tybalt's death. She feared that her husband would be instantly sought out and killed if her family learned of the marriage.

At first she tried to put off her father with excuses. Failing to persuade him, she went in dread to Friar Lawrence to ask the good monk what she could do. Telling her to be brave, the friar gave her a small flask of liquid which he told her to swallow the night before her wedding to Paris. This liquid would make her appear to be dead for a certain length of time; her seemingly lifeless body would then be placed in an open tomb for a day or two, and during that time the friar would send for Romeo, who should rescue his bride when she awoke from the powerful effects of the draught. Then, together, the two would be able to flee Verona. Juliet almost lost courage over this desperate venture, but she promised to obey the friar. On the way home she met Paris and modestly promised to be his bride.

The great house of the Capulets had no sooner prepared for a lavish wedding than it became the scene of a mournful funeral. For Juliet swallowed the strong liquid and seemed as lifeless as death itself. Her anguished family sadly placed her body in the tomb.

Meanwhile Friar Lawrence wrote to Romeo in Mantua, telling him of the plan by which the lovers could make their escape together. But these letters failed to reach Romeo before word of Juliet's death arrived. He determined to go to Verona and take his last farewell of her as she lay in her tomb, and there, with the help of poison procured from an apothecary, to die by her side.

Reaching the tomb at night, Romeo was surprised to find a young man there. It was Paris, who had come to weep over his lost bride. Thinking Romeo a grave robber, he drew his sword. Romeo, mistaking Paris for a hated Capulet, warned him that he was desperate and armed. Paris, in loyalty to Juliet, fell upon Romeo, but Romeo with all the fury of his desperation killed him. By the light of a lantern, Romeo recognized Paris and, taking pity on one who had also loved Juliet, drew him into the tomb so that Paris too could be near her. Then Romeo went to the bier of his beautiful bride. Taking leave of her with a kiss, he drank the poison he had brought with him and soon died by her side.

It was near the time for Juliet to awaken from her deathlike sleep. The friar, hearing that Romeo had never received his letters, went himself to deliver Juliet from the tomb. When he arrived, he found Romeo dead. Juliet, waking, asked for her husband. Then, seeing him lying near her with an empty cup in his hands, she guessed what he had done. She tried to kiss some of the poison from his lips that she too might die, but failing in this, she unsheathed his dagger and without hesitation plunged it into her breast.

By this time a guard had come up. Seeing the dead lovers and the body of Paris, he rushed off in horror to spread the news. When the Capulets and Montagues arrived at the tomb, the friar told them of the unhappy fate which had befallen Romeo and Juliet, whose only sin had been to love. His account of their tender and beautiful romance shamed the two families, and over the bodies of their dead children they swore to end the feud of many years.

# ROMOLA

*Type of work:* Novel
*Author:* George Eliot (Mary Ann Evans, 1819-1880)
*Type of plot:* Historical romance
*Time of plot:* 1492-1498
*Locale:* Italy
*First published:* 1863

*Principal characters:*
BARDO, a Florentine scholar
ROMOLA, his daughter
TITO MELEMA, an adventurer
TESSA, a peasant girl
BALDASARRE CALVO, Tito's benefactor

## Critique:

*Romola* is the story of a thoroughly good woman and a thoroughly wicked man. It is not an easy novel to read, for the author has attempted a work involving more than literary craftsmanship. She has dipped into the history of an age of political intrigue and mystical religious personalities, and often the plot of the story becomes lost in the maze of its own environment. But if the plot of this novel fails to stand out clearly from its background, the characters themselves can carry the burden of brilliant development.

## The Story:

Tito Melema arrived in Florence penniless and unknown, but the sale of some rare jewels in his possession soon brought him into the circle of the wealthy, learned men of the city, among them the blind antiquarian, Bardo. Bardo was a great scholar who continued his annotations of Greek and Roman books through the eyes of his beautiful daughter, Romola. Bardo's only interest in life was his library and museum, and he had brought up his daughter in innocence of the outside world. Bardo accepted Tito eagerly, for he was always eager to meet a scholar and a man who had traveled much. He also told Tito of a son whom he had lost.

Tito's fortune had at last come to him with the sale of all his jewels except a single ring. He recalled that the money properly belonged to Baldasarre Calvo, the man who had been almost a father to him, the man who might now be a

slave in the hands of the Turks. If Baldasarre were really alive, Tito told himself, he would spend the money for the old man's ransom. But he was not sure his foster father still lived.

Quickly Tito entrenched himself in the learned society of Florence. At the yearly festival of San Giovanni, patron saint of Florence, Tito, while sitting at a window with a friend, fancied that he saw in the crowd below a monk who gazed upon him with a malicious glance. Also glancing up at Tito from below was the beautiful Tessa, daughter of a milk vendor, whom Tito had met on the day of his arrival in Florence.

Later as he walked through the crowded streets, he rescued Tessa from some jostling revelers. When he had left her, he met the strange monk who had gazed at him from the crowd earlier in the afternoon. The monk, Fra Luca, gave him a note that had been brought from a pilgrim in the Near East. The note was from Baldassare, who pleaded that Tito should rescue him from slavery. Tito wondered what was so familiar about the Fra's face.

Attracted by the lovely, grave Romola, Tito spent many hours reading and writing manuscripts with her blind father. One day, when Tito had the opportunity to be alone with Romola for a brief moment, he declared his love to her, and Romola shyly confessed her love for him. That same day Monna Brigida paid a call on her cousin Bardo. When she accidentally mentioned the name of a

3289

Dominican monk, Dino, Tito discovered that the lost son of Bardo was not dead, but banished from his father's house. Realizing that Fra Luca was Dino, Tito feared exposure of his benefactor's slavery. He felt the time ripe for asking the old man for permission to marry Romola. Bardo readily consented.

Tito learned that Fra Luca was dangerously ill at Fiesole. One evening Romola told him that her dying brother had sent for her. Tito feared that Fra Luca would tell her the story which Tito had hoped would die with him. In despair, he wandered through the city and accidentally met Tessa. In a ribald ceremony which amused the gaping crowd, Tito allowed Tessa to believe that he had really married her. Unwilling to undeceive her, he made her promise to keep the marriage a secret. Meanwhile Dino died without revealing to Romola the story of Baldasarre and the ungrateful Tito. Tito and Romola were married.

Bardo died, leaving Romola to carry on his scholarly work. Meanwhile political events in Florence helped to advance Tito's fortunes; he became an interpreter in negotiations with the French. On the day the French king arrived in the city, the soldiers led through the streets a group of prisoners who begged their ransoms from the Florentines. The mocking mob cut an old man loose from his fetters and allowed him to escape into the crowd. The prisoner ran blindly into Tito, who stood with a group of dignitaries on the steps of San Marco. Tito turned and found himself looking into the face of Baldasarre Calvo, who then disappeared into the crowd.

Fearing Baldasarre's revenge, Tito bought a coat of mail to wear under his clothes as a defense against the thrust of a knife or a spear. Tito begged Romola to sell her father's library and leave Florence with him. When Romola refused, he secretly sold the library and the antiquities it contained.

In his search for a place to stay, Baldasarre came by chance to the house where Tessa and her children by Tito lived

with a deaf old peasant woman. The woman gave the old man permission to sleep in the loft. Tessa eagerly confided in Baldasarre. Tito had not abandoned her after their mock-marriage. At first he had been too flattered by her innocent admiration to tell her they were not man and wife. Instead, he had sent her to live with the old peasant woman, whom he paid well for the care she gave Tessa and his children, and he had sworn the two women to secrecy. While Baldasarre lay in the hayloft, Tito came to see Tessa. Suspecting from her description the identity of the old man, Tito went to his foster father to ask his forgiveness. He had decided that Baldasarre should come to live with him and share his comfort. But the old man did not forgive. He threatened to expose Tito and ruin him.

At a dinner in Florence, Baldasarre appeared to denounce Tito before his political friends. The trembling old man was pronounced mad and sent to prison. During a plague the jails were emptied to make room for the sick, and Baldasarre was released. He spied upon Tito until he learned that the youth had two wives, one noble and brave, the other timid and stupid. He approached Romola to expose Tito. When he told Romola of Tito's betrayal, she was able to piece together all the suspicions she had felt toward her husband, his long absences from home, his strange moods, and his secret fears. One day she found little Lillo, Tessa's son, wandering lost in the streets. She took the child to his home, and there she realized that she had discovered Tito's Tessa.

The final blow came to Romola when her godfather, Bernardo Del Nero, the only person in the world she still loved, was arrested. The Medici had been plotting to return to Florence, and Bernardo was a member of the committee which plotted their return. Romola knew Tito had been a spy for both political factions; he had gained his own safety by betraying others. Romola revealed to Tito her knowledge of Baldasarre's story and the truth of the old man's accusation against him. Then, disillusioned and sorrowful at the execution of Bernardo, she fled from Florence.

Tito also planned to flee from Florence, for his double dealings had been discovered. A mob followed him out of the city. To escape his pursuers, he threw away his money belt, and while the crowd scrambled for it, he jumped into the river. Weakly he pulled himself ashore on the opposite side. There Baldasarre, now a starving beggar, found him. In a final effort the old man threw himself upon his exhausted enemy and strangled him.

After passing many months in another city, Romola returned to Florence to learn of her husband's murder at the hands of an old man who had long been his enemy. Romola understood the justice of Tito's violent end. She found Tessa and the children and brought them to live with her. Hers was the one good deed that resulted from Tito's false and guilty life.

# A ROOM WITH A VIEW

Type of work: Novel
Author: E. M. Forster (1879-     )
Type of plot: Social comedy
Time of plot: Early 1900's
Locale: Florence, Italy, and Surrey, England
First published: 1908

Principal characters:
MISS LUCY HONEYCHURCH, a young Englishwoman
MISS CHARLOTTE BARTLETT, her cousin and chaperon
MR. EMERSON, an Englishman
GEORGE EMERSON, his son
THE REVEREND ARTHUR BEEBE
MRS. HONEYCHURCH, Lucy's mother
FREDDY HONEYCHURCH, Lucy's brother
CECIL VYSE, Lucy's fiancé
MISS CATHERINE ALAN, a guest at the Pension Bertolini
MISS TERESA ALAN, her sister
MISS ELEANOR LAVISH, a novelist

## Critique:

This novel, E. M. Forster's third, was probably conceived in Italy. To Mr. Forster, Italy represents the force of true passion, and the recognition of this passion by his heroine in his theme here. He is singularly aware of the nonexistence of absolutes; his kindest characters have their moments of cruelty and areas of incomprehension. Similarly, those least sympathetic have moments of glory and of true feeling and understanding. Forster is also intensely aware of the structure of society and of the imperfections and merits of each of its spheres. Although smaller in scope than Howard's End and A Passage to India, his two later novels, A Room with a View is equally perceptive and shows a highly developed moral sensibility.

## The Story:

Lucy Honeychurch and Charlotte Bartlett were disappointed by the Pension Bertolini and by the fact that their rooms had no view. They were embarrassed at dinner when Mr. Emerson offered to exchange his and his son's rooms, which had views, with theirs. Their unhappiness decreased when the Reverend Arthur Beebe, whom they had known previously, and who had been appointed rector of Lucy's home parish, joined them at dinner. After dinner he managed to convince Charlotte that the exchange of rooms would not put them under any obligation to the Emersons. The change, although effected, merely confirmed Charlotte's opinion that the Emersons were ill-bred.

At Santa Croce Church Lucy met the Emersons, who guided her to the Giotto frescoes that she had come to see. She found that she was more at ease with Mr. Emerson than she had expected, even though his rejection of artistic and religious cant and his concern about his son confused her.

Late one afternoon Lucy declared that she would go for a walk alone. She bought some photographs of paintings she had seen and then walked through the Piazza Signoria. As she did so, she passed two men arguing over a debt. One stabbed the other and the stricken man, bleeding from the mouth, died at her feet. At the same moment she saw George Emerson watching from across the square. As he reached her side, she fainted. After she had recovered, she sent him to get her photographs. Disturbed because they were covered with blood, he tossed them into the Arno on the way home. When Lucy asked why he had thrown the pictures away, he was forced to tell her. He felt that something very significant had happened to him in the piazza. Lucy stopped with him near the pension and, leaning beside him over the parapet, asked him to tell no one that he had been there. Perturbed by their enforced intimacy, she was puzzled and amazed when George said that the murder would make him want to live.

In a large party the visitors at the pension, together with a resident English chaplain, drove toward Fiesole. Lucy, excluded from Miss Lavish's conversation with Charlotte, asked one of their drivers to direct her to the clergyman. Instead, he led her to George. Lucy found at the end of the path a terrace covered with violets. While she stood there, radiant at the beauty of the place, George stepped forward and kissed her. Charlotte, whom neither had seen at first, called her cousin back.

Charlotte told Lucy that George was a cad and, obviously, was accustomed to stealing kisses. She took advantage of Lucy's need for sympathy to indicate that George's way of life, as she saw it, was merely brutal. In the morning the women took the train for Rome.

Back at her home in Surrey, Lucy became engaged to Cecil Vyse, whom she had visited in Rome. Mr. Beebe, coming to the house for tea, was perturbed by the engagement. Returning from a party with Lucy and Mrs. Honeychurch, Cecil saw a pair of ugly villas that had been put up by a local builder. When the village residents became alarmed as they considered the type of person who might rent them, they were assured that a certain Sir Harry Otway had bought the houses and intended to lease them only to suitable tenants. Lucy suggested the Misses Alan whom she had met in Florence.

After seeing the villas, Cecil and Lucy walked on through the woods. By a pond where Lucy had bathed as a child, Cecil, for the first time, asked if he might kiss her. Their embrace, not successful, only reminded Lucy of the Emersons, whom she then mentioned to Cecil.

Shortly before the Alans' occupancy had been arranged, Cecil met the Emersons in London and suggested that they take one of the villas. Not connecting them with Lucy, he hoped thereby to disrupt the local social order. After the Emersons had moved into their house, Mr. Beebe took Freddy Honeychurch to meet them. The boy immediately asked George to go swimming with him. Together with Mr. Beebe they swam and raced gaily at the pond in the woods. There Lucy came upon George again. Although he greeted her joyously, she bowed stiffly and moved on with her mother and Cecil.

One Sunday, while George was visiting the house, Cecil loftily refused to play tennis. Lucy, George, Freddy, and a friend of his played while Cecil read. After the game Cecil read aloud from his novel. Written by Miss Lavish, it contained a scene describing George and Lucy's kiss. Cecil was ignorant of this fact, but George and Lucy were profoundly moved. On the way into the house, George again kissed her. Charlotte was staying in the house at that time and Lucy was furious that she had thus betrayed her to Miss Lavish. Together they went to George and Lucy asked him to leave. Before he obeyed, he told Lucy that he loved her and that it would be disastrous for her to marry Cecil, who was incapable of intimacy with anyone.

That evening, although she denied to herself that she was attracted to George, Lucy broke her engagement to Cecil. In the meantime Mr. Beebe received a letter from the Misses Alan, who were planning to visit Athens. To escape her confusion, Lucy decided that she must go with them, and Charlotte joined Mr. Beebe in persuading Mrs. Honeychurch to let Lucy go. Lucy, afraid that George would hear of her rejection of Cecil and return to see her, hoped in this manner to avoid another meeting with him.

As Lucy was returning from a day in London with her mother, Charlotte came out of Mr. Beebe's house and asked them to go with her to church. Lucy, declining, went into the house to await their return. There she found Mr. Emerson in the library. George, feeling utterly lost, had gone to London. Lucy finally admitted that she was not to marry Cecil, but when Mr. Emerson revealed his intuitive knowledge that she loved George, she became angry and wept. Although she gradually perceived that all he said was true, she was upset at the prospect of distressing everyone afresh if she acted on her new knowledge. Strengthened by Mr. Emerson's passion, sincerity, and confidence, however, she promised to attempt to live the truth she had learned.

Her family opposing but not defeating her, Lucy married George. They spent their honeymoon in the Pension Bertolini, where they wonderingly realized that subconsciously Charlotte had been on their side. She had known that Mr. Emerson was in Mr. Beebe's house, and she must have realized, too, how he would speak to Lucy when they met there.

# RORY O'MORE

Type of work: Novel
Author: Samuel Lover (1797-1868)
Type of plot: Adventure romance
Time of plot: 1798
Locale: Southern Ireland
First published: 1837

Principal characters:
 RORY O'MORE, an Irish peasant
 MARY O'MORE, his sister
 SHAN REGAN, a villainous neighbor
 KATHLEEN REGAN, his sister
 HORACE DE LACY, an Irish patriot
 DE WELSKEIN, a smuggler
 SCRUBBS, a tax collector

Critique:

Rory O'More never quite succeeds in being a good historical novel, in spite of Lover's patriotic motives in writing the book. The people are the familiar stock characters of Irish fiction, and the plot is clumsy and contrived. But the book lives in its atmosphere of the stirring days of the rebellion of 1798, in its ferocious lampoons of soldiers, magistrates, and collectors, in the terrible and tragic realities of Irish peasant life, and in the pleasant idyl of its love story. Readers of Lover's day felt that in this novel he came close to the heart of his unhappy land.

The Story:

While in Dublin on some business for his widowed mother, Rory O'More made the acquaintance of Horace De Lacy, an Irish patriot who had come from France in order to further the cause of revolution against English oppression. He was a messenger from a French general who was aiding the Irish in order to help Napoleon in his attempted conquest of England. De Lacy was a gentleman, descended from proud blood lines, and Rory and his mother and sister considered it an honor to have him share their home. The O'More women nursed him back to health after an attack of smallpox, and De Lacy felt indebted to the good people for their care. In addition, Rory became a fellow conspirator. De Lacy and Rory did not conspire for personal gain, as did many of the rebels; rather they loved Ireland and wanted her and her people to be free. Although De Lacy was perhaps not aware of it, he was a true democrat.

Rory loved a neighbor lass, Kathleen Regan. Although she returned his affection, she was prevented from marrying him by her brother Shan, a blackguard who had been refused by Mary O'More, Rory's sister. Shan, his pride hurt by Mary's refusal, hated the whole O'More family. Since Shan was the head of the household, Kathleen and her mother feared to disobey him; she and Rory were forced to meet in secret.

Because De Lacy was not well enough to take and receive a message that was expected by his contacts in Ireland, Rory volunteered to act in his place. He was dismayed to learn that Shan was one of his fellow rebels, for he knew that his enemy hoped only for personal gain. Another among the group was De Welskein, a smuggler who cared little which side won since he would profit regardless of the outcome. Shan and De Welskein were made for each other, each one willing to betray their friends for a profit. Rory knew them both to be dangerous.

After he had secured the necessary letter for De Lacy, Rory left the unsavory crowd. Later he was apprehended by the police, but his cleverness and his knowledge of the colonel's affair with a married woman gained his freedom for him. De Lacy was pleased with his success,

3295

and that gentleman's praise was a great reward to Rory. Shan then tried to make trouble for him with Kathleen, and Rory was forced to administer two beatings to the bully before Shan gave him any peace.

It was necessary for De Lacy to return to France to help the cause of the rebellion. He parted sadly from his friends and made his way to a port from which De Welskein was to smuggle him out of Ireland. In the meantime Rory, purely by accident, accompanied Scrubbs, a government tax collector, from a tavern in the village. On their way home they heard people calling for help. Hurrying to the rescue, they found De Welskein, Shan Regan, and other rebels imprisoned in a flooding cave. After saving the lives of the doomed men, the scoundrels repaid Rory by taking him and Scrubbs prisoners and transporting them to the ship which De Welskein had secured for De Lacy's trip to France. Shan, anxious to get rid of Rory in any manner, persuaded the others that Rory was a traitor to their cause. Because Scrubbs was a government official it was not safe to leave him to reveal their names to the authorities.

On board the ship Rory learned that he was on the vessel which carried his friend De Lacy. Knowing that De Welskein would keep the news of his presence from De Lacy, he managed to send a message to his friend. When they were off the coast of France and under the eyes of a battleship commanded by De Lacy's friend, De Welskein was forced to release Rory. Scrubbs, a government official, was of no concern to De Lacy.

In France, De Lacy heard two heartbreaking pieces of news. His unfaithful sweetheart had given her hand to another and Napoleon had decided to withdraw his promised aid to Ireland in his campaign against the English. The first desertion he avenged by inflicting a wound on his rival, but the latter one left a scar on his heart. The approaching death of an uncle kept him and Rory in France, there being no reason for them to hurry back to Ireland. But after the uncle's death Rory and De Lacy embarked once again for Ireland.

Many changes had taken place during the year that they had been gone. Some of the fanatical rebels had attempted to revolt without the help of France, and Ireland had been bathed with blood. The homes of the O'Mores and the Regans had been burned, and the women of the families had banded together and taken a house in the village. Shan was wanted by the authorities as a suspected rebel and because of his attempt on the lives of Mary O'More and an old tinker. The tinker informed the officers of Shan's hideout. Although most of his band escaped by ambushing the police, Shan himself was killed. For his pains, the tinker was hanged as a traitor for leading the officers into an ambush.

Arriving in Ireland, De Lacy stayed in Dublin to transact some business. Rory, meanwhile, went at once to his native village, where he was reunited with his loved ones. On his first night home, however, he was arrested for the murder of Scrubbs, his enemies having testified that Scrubbs was last seen alive in Rory's company. When De Lacy heard the news, he returned to the village and with his lawyer fought for his friend's freedom. The case looked black until Scrubbs, who had escaped from France and returned to Ireland, appeared during the trial. Rory's enemies had tried to keep Scrubbs hidden until after the trial and Rory's hanging, but the collector had eluded his keepers. Although the jury returned a verdict of guilty, so determined were the rogues to be rid of Rory, a humane judge arranged to have the verdict put aside. Rory was set free.

De Lacy, knowing that he and Rory would never be safe in Ireland, persuaded Rory to take his family and Kathleen and her mother and go with De Lacy to America. There De Lacy would buy a farm and make Rory his manager. When Rory and Kathleen were married, De Lacy gave the girl a handsome dowry.

It was with regret that the party left their beloved homeland, but they knew they must do so if they wished to live in peace and safety. Mary O'More had long loved De Lacy but did not dare to show her feeling because she was a peasant and he a gentleman. De Lacy admired the simple lass, but he feared the ridicule he would receive from his friends if he married a peasant. As he thought about the new life in America, however, he began to realize that it would make little difference there if a man and his wife were of different social classes. With Rory and Kathleen already married, De Lacy and Mary seemed likely to join them in that happy state.

# ROSMERSHOLM

*Type of work:* Drama
*Author:* Henrik Ibsen (1828-1906)
*Type of plot:* Social drama
*Time of plot:* Middle nineteenth century
*Locale:* Small coastal town in western Norway
*First presented:* 1887

> *Principal characters.*
> JOHANNES ROSMER, a former clergyman
> REBECCA WEST, his friend
> RECTOR KROLL, the schoolmaster
> ULRIC BRENDEL, a disillusioned liberal
> PETER MORTENSGARD, a publisher
> MADAM HELSETH, housekeeper at Rosmersholm

## Critique:

The last of Ibsen's social dramas, *Rosmersholm* gives us also a first glimpse of the psychological studies he was to write later. The characters are still part of a social class, but toward the end of the play they begin to emerge as individuals, working with their own personal problems and seeking their own values. In this play Ibsen continues the attempt to arouse his readers to raise themselves above the mass, not to be pulled down to the level of the popular majority. This work is written with the dramatist's usual skill and ranks with his other great plays. It was published in 1886, prior to its first presentation.

## The Story:

Since the death of his wife, Beata, Johannes Rosmer had turned more and more to his friend, Rebecca West. Rosmer had had an unhappy marriage with an unsympathetic, neurotic wife who had taken her own life in the millpond that flowed through the estate. Rebecca had been her friend, as well as the husband's. Beata's brother, Rector Kroll, the schoolmaster, was also Rosmer's close friend.

Rector Kroll called on Rosmer to get him to join a political drive against the new liberal party that was gaining power in the village. The party was controlled by Peter Mortensgard, publisher of the *Beacon*, a paper Rector Kroll considered radical and dangerous because it was loud in criticism of the conservative party

which he represented. Kroll was disappointed to learn that Rosmer no longer held his former static views on politics and social structures but, instead, supported the liberals. Rosmer's real concern was not with politics at all, but only with encouraging men to ennoble their souls; he felt the new party was a step toward this goal. Rebecca supported him in his belief.

While they talked, Madam Helseth, the housekeeper, announced Ulric Brendel, a self-styled genius who was going to the village to offer his services to the liberal party. Brendel was in rags and obviously without any means of livelihood, and to Rector Kroll he epitomized the liberals. To Rosmer and Rebecca, however, Brendel was a man living and working as his conscience directed, and they helped him with clothing and money.

This act turned Kroll against them. He now turned on Rosmer savagely and accused him of betraying his class. Because Rosmer had been a clergyman, Kroll attempted to plead with him from a religious point of view, but Rosmer claimed that he had also renounced the Church and become a freethinker. He felt that men were growing so bitter in political struggles that they must be brought back to tolerance and good will. It was his hope that he could aid in this task by renouncing his way of life and working with the new leaders.

Kroll then accused Rosmer of living in sin with Rebecca, even though he had defended Rosmer and Rebecca when town gossips had whispered about them. He accused Rebecca of influencing Rosmer in his new attitude and suggested that she had been responsible for the suicide of Rosmer's wife. He said his sister had believed that Rosmer wished to wed Rebecca and for that reason she had drowned herself. Kroll maintained he had not spoken up before because he did not know that Rebecca was an emancipated woman, and he had not believed her capable of such actions. His worst thoughts about Rosmer and Rebecca were confirmed when Peter Mortensgard appeared at Rosmer's home in answer to a note Rebecca had written him in Brendel's behalf. When Kroll left, he promised to inform the town of Rosmer's treachery.

Mortensgard had come to solicit Rosmer's aid in the liberal cause, but when he learned that Rosmer had left the Church, he did not want the former clergyman's help. He needed Christians, not freethinkers, as he himself was, and so Rosmer was left with no one to support. Mortensgard, too, slyly accused Rosmer and Rebecca of indiscretions and of causing the death of Rosmer's wife.

From that time on Rosmer began to feel guilty about his part in her death and feared that he had not concealed his true feelings for Rebecca from his wife. Determined not to let the past rule his life, he asked Rebecca to marry him. She fled from him sobbing, swearing that she could never marry him, that if he ever asked her again she would die the way his wife had died.

Kroll did his work well. The paper supporting his party accused Rosmer of betraying his class to gain favor with the liberals. The article linked Rebecca and Rosmer in a debasing way. Rosmer wanted to fight back, if only to free men's minds from pettiness and mass thinking, but he felt that he could not accomplish this task because he no longer felt innocent of his wife's death; only the innocent could lead others.

Rebecca decided to give him back his purity of conscience. In Kroll's presence she told Rosmer that she alone was responsible for his wife's suicide. She said that she had come to Rosmersholm for the sole purpose of converting Rosmer to the liberal party. She knew that Brendel had once had great influence over Rosmer, and she hoped to renew that influence and win him to the emancipators. With victory in sight, his wife was a stumbling block. To overcome that obstacle, she made that sick woman believe that she was going to have a child by Rosmer. In desperation the wife threw herself into the millpond. Rebecca's love for Rosmer made her confess so that he could clear his own conscience of all guilt. Kroll and Rosmer left her alone after her confession, and she prepared to leave Rosmersholm forever.

While she packed, Rosmer returned and told her his old friends had persuaded him that the task of ennobling men's minds was not for him, or for anyone. He told her that he knew she had only used him to attain her own goals. Then she made her greatest confession to him. She said that she had first been moved by physical passion. She had plotted to get rid of his wife. Then, after the suicide, Rebecca had come to feel such deep and quiet love for Rosmer that it had taken her free spirit from her. He had ennobled her soul.

Rosmer could not quite believe her story; he feared that she was again using him for her own purposes. As they talked, Brendel appeared and told them that he was leaving town, that his genius was gone, and he was bankrupt. He told them too that Mortensgard was the only one who could win their cause, for he was without ideals. Only those without ideals could gain a victory. He said also that Rosmer could gain victory if the woman who loved him would convince him of her loyalty.

After Brendel left them, Rosmer asked Rebecca to prove that he had ennobled her soul. The price was high. He asked her to throw herself into the millpond as she had caused his wife to do. Because only her self-inflicted death could give him back his faith in himself, she agreed to his plan. Since they no longer believed in a judgment after death, they must punish themselves for their love. At the last minute, Rosmer decided to join Rebecca in death. They stood with their arms entwined, then threw themselves into the pond. The water and Rosmer's dead wife claimed their bodies.

# ROUGHING IT

*Type of work:* Record of travel
*Author:* Mark Twain (Samuel L. Clemens, 1835-1910)
*Type of plot:* Travel sketches and autobiography
*Time of plot:* Mid-nineteenth century
*Locale:* The West
*First published:* 1872

> *Principal characters:*
> MARK TWAIN, a tenderfoot
> BRIGHAM YOUNG, the Mormon leader
> SLADE THE TERRIBLE, a Western desperado
> HANK ERICKSON, a correspondent of Horace Greeley

## Critique:

Mark Twain's recollections are interesting because they present a picture of the still expanding Western frontier. Although the book is badly organized, it is excellent for its eye-witness accounts of Virginia City and the Nevada mining camps, Mormonism, early San Francisco, and the Hawaiian Islands. Always, of course, the book is enlivened by Mark Twain's boisterous, native humor.

## The Story:

When Mark Twain traveled West with his brother, he had no idea that he would stay out there for any long period of time. His brother had been appointed Secretary of the Nevada Territory, and Twain went along as his secretary, with no salary. Instead of the three months he intended to stay, however, he was six years away from home.

The trip itself was exciting. There were many inconveniences, naturally, as well as danger from the Indians and attacks by highwaymen. But Twain saw the country and enjoyed the adventure, nonetheless. On the way he came face to face with Slade the Terrible. Slade was foreman of the stagecoach workers, a man who would kill anyone if crossed, a man whose repute went far and wide. To Twain he seemed very polite, a gentleman, and quite harmless. But Slade's days were numbered. The vigilantes were after him. Although he was warned, he was drunk at the time, and so was unable to avoid capture. Brought to trial by a vigilante court, he was found guilty and ordered hanged. He died

without having seen his wife, probably a fortunate circumstance for the vigilantes. At an earlier time, with blazing six-shooters flaming from under her petticoats, she had rescued Slade from a similar situation.

Twain also met Brigham Young, the Mormon leader, who bemoaned the fact that he had so many wives, wives who were jealous and argumentative. Out of curiosity Twain also read the Mormon Bible.

Twain and some companions set out to prospect for gold in the Nevada mountains. Once they were caught in a snowstorm and seemingly doomed to die. Each of them renounced a particular vice. Twain threw away his pipe, another his cigarettes, and the third his bottle of whiskey. But they did not die. At dawn they discovered that they had been but a few yards away from an inn. Then Twain was sorry he had thrown away his pipe. He found it in the snow and sneaked behind the barn for a smoke. There he came upon one of his comrades drinking from the whiskey bottle and the other rolling a cigarette.

At first they had no luck in their search for gold. True, they found places where there was gold, but the operations needed to extract it were too complicated and expensive. Finally they had real luck. When they found rock that would yield millions of dollars for them, they claimed it and dreamed of spending their lives in luxury. The law specified that some work must be done on each new claim within ten days; otherwise the claimants

3301

lost their right to the claim and anyone else could get control of it. Twain left, having confidence that his partners would work the new claim. But each thought the other would do the work, and so none was done. At the end of ten days the mine was claimed by others. Twain and his partners were relegated to a common, working existence.

He wandered from place to place, working for newspapers, being fired from them, and moving on. Eventually he landed in San Francisco and went from there to the Hawaiian Islands, where he visited the spot on which Captain Cook had been killed by natives. At first the natives had treated the British explorer kindly. Cook, in turn, had made them believe that he was a god, and he had treated them brutally. One day, injured, he showed his pain. Convinced by his hurt that he was not divine, but a man like themselves, the natives killed him — rightly, according to Twain, for he had returned their kindness with cruelty.

Then there was Hank Erickson, the crazy stranger. Erickson had once written a letter to Horace Greeley. A widow had a son who liked turnips. She wanted to find out if turnips sometimes grew into vines. This was the question Erickson asked in the letter he wrote to Greeley.

Greeley replied, but the handwriting was so illegible that nothing could be made of it. In fact, every time Erickson read the letter it seemed different, but always meaningless. Finally he deciphered it and became convinced that Greeley had insulted him. Erickson wrote to Greeley again. The publisher had a clerk copy the letter, which turned out to be informative and not at all insulting. Twain slyly maintained that he never found out why Erickson was crazy.

Twain decided to try his luck at lecturing. At his first appearance he was afraid that nobody would laugh at his jokes. He gave free tickets to various people, and told them to laugh at the right moments. When he got to the auditorium the seats were empty. He sat in the wings and felt sad. However, he soon heard the noise of voices and came out of his dream to find that the hall was crowded. His lecture was a great success; people even laughed when his talk was not funny.

When he returned to San Francisco from Hawaii, Twain planned a trip to Japan. Later he abandoned the idea to go back home. He traveled to New York by way of Panama. So ended his Wild West and Hawaiian adventures.

# ROXANA

*Type of work:* Novel
*Author:* Daniel Defoe (1660-1731)
*Type of plot:* Picaresque romance
*Time of plot:* Eighteenth century
*Locale:* England and Europe
*First published:* 1724

*Principal characters:*
ROXANA, a courtesan
AMY, her maid
MR. ——, her landlord
THE PRINCE DE ——
A MERCHANT

## Critique:

One of the early forerunners of the modern novel, *Roxana, Or, The Fortunate Mistress* holds a special place in English literature. It is a brilliant piece of imaginative writing displaying a talent in the author both original and clever, since he practically invented this form of realism and pretense at fact at a time when his contemporaries were contriving fantastic characters and situations. Roxana herself is a fascinating woman, a matter of perennial interest to lovers of good books. In construction, analyzed in relation to the accepted novel form, the book is rambling, repetitious, and lacking in wit. It is never dull, however, and will always be read. That *Roxana* was written as a didactic study does not detract from its excellence.

## The Story:

Born in France, from which her parents fled because of religious persecution, Roxana grew to adolescence in England. At fifteen she married a handsome but conceited man. After seven years of marriage, during which time her husband went through all their money, Roxana was left penniless with five children.

She appealed for aid to her husband's relatives, all of whom refused her except one old aunt, who was in no position to help her materially. Amy, Roxana's maid, refused to leave her mistress, although she received no wages for her work. Another poor old woman whom Roxana had aided during her former prosperity added her efforts to those of the old aunt and Amy.

These good people managed to extract money from the relatives of the children's father. All five of the little ones were given over to the care of the poor old woman.

Penniless, Roxana was at the point of despair when her landlord, after expressing his admiration for her, praised her fortitude under all her difficulties and offered to set her up in housekeeping. He returned all the furniture he had confiscated, gave her food and money, and generally conducted himself with such kindness and candor that Amy urged Roxana to become the gentleman's mistress should he ask it. Roxana, however, clung to her virtuous independence. Fearing that the gentleman's kindness would go unrewarded, Amy, because she loved her mistress, offered to lie with the landlord in Roxana's place. This offer, however, Roxana refused to consider. The two women talked much about the merits of the landlord, his motive in befriending Roxana, and the moral implications of his attentions.

When he came to take residence as a boarder in Roxana's house, he proposed, since his wife had deserted him, that he and Roxana live as husband and wife. To show his good faith he offered to share his wealth with her, bequeathing her five hundred pounds in his will and promising seven thousand pounds should he leave her. There was a gay celebration that evening and a little joking about Amy's offer to lie with the gentleman. Finally Roxana, her conscience still bothering her, yielded to his protestations of love and bedded with him.

After a year and half had passed and Roxana had not conceived a child, Amy chided her mistress for her barrenness. Feeling that Mr. —— was not her true husband, Roxana sent Amy to him to beget a child. Amy did bear a child, which Roxana took as her own to save the maid embarrassment. Two years later Roxana bore a daughter who died within six months. A year later she pleased her lover by bearing a son.

Mr. —— took Roxana with him to Paris on business. There they lived in great style, until he was robbed and murdered for the jewels he carried on his person. Roxana managed to retain the gentleman's wealth and secured it against the possible claims of his wife, who was still living.

In France the Prince de ——, hoping to make amends to Roxana for the murder of her protector, lavished gifts upon her and flattered her beauty until she consented to be his mistress, this time allowing her virtue to be sullied not because of poverty but through vanity. In order to suppress gossip, Roxana, pretending that she had gone back to England on business, confined herself to her quarters and instructed Amy to admit only Prince de ——.

Roxana's new lover showered her bountifully with gifts. When she bore him a son, he promised to acknowledge the child as his own and never to let it want. After the birth of the child, Roxana thought that she recognized her husband, a member of the gendarmes. Amy visited the man and found him to be the same worthless scoundrel who, years before, had abandoned his wife and five children. When the prince had to go to Italy on an official assignment, he took Roxana with him. There they remained for two years. She bore another son who lived only two months. Then the prince's wife died, and he, repenting his sins, parted from Roxana, who had been his faithful mistress for eight years.

Roxana and her maid, after engaging a merchant to handle Roxana's wealth, sailed for England. Roxana had to go to Holland to receive her money from the merchant. The merchant, arriving in Holland from Paris, took lodgings in the same house, and he and Roxana became well acquainted. The merchant wanted to marry her, but she, too avaricious and calculating to risk her wealth for a mere caprice of love, suspected his motives. She did allow him to seduce her, however, for she felt that she owed him some token of gratitude for his assistance. She was already pregnant when they parted.

Returning to London, Roxana settled her financial affairs and bore her son. Because she established herself in a handsome apartment, she was courted by numerous fortune hunters, but her philosophy, as she chose to call it, would not permit her to marry anyone. As a wife she would have to share her wealth; as a mistress she received riches, and she was determined to amass a fortune.

Roxana gave lavish parties, attended by many fashionable people of London. Soon her name became famous. Her purpose was fulfilled when a rich lord offered her a substantial income if she would be his mistress. Retiring from society, she took a new apartment and saw only the lord. She passed several years in this fashion. By that time she was fifty years old. Tiring at last of her lover, she began to see her friends again.

With Amy's help she began to live a different kind of life so that eventually she could assist her children. She took rooms in another part of the city with a Quaker lady. Amy let people believe that her mistress had gone to Europe.

By chance Roxana met the merchant whom she had known in Holland and whose son she had borne. The merchant renewed his suit. Although Amy sent word from Europe that Prince de —— was trying to find Roxana and wished to marry her, Roxana, having learned that her husband was dead, accepted the merchant's proposal. The pair planned to return to Holland and, taking residence there, declare themselves eleven years married in order to legitimize their son.

One of Roxana's legitimate daughters

had by chance been her maid while Roxana lived in London. At first the mother had tried to help her daughter by giving her, through Amy, money and advantages above her station. When the girl began to suspect that her mistress was her mother, Roxana was distressed, for she would be undone should her past be known now. When Amy, infuriated with the prying girl, threatened to murder her, Roxana, after many years' friendship, dismissed her faithful maid. But at last the persistent daughter's inquiries were silenced and Roxana was able to go to Holland with her husband.

# THE RUBÁIYÁT OF OMAR KHAYYÁM

*Type of work:* Philosophical poem
*Translator:* Edward FitzGerald (1809-1883)
*First published:* 1859

> Awake! for Morning in the Bowl of Night
> Has flung the Stone that puts the Stars to Flight:
> And Lo! the Hunter of the East has caught
> The Sultán's Turret in a Noose of Light.

Thus did Edward FitzGerald, a shy dilettante living in the Victorian Age, open the first edition of what he called his "transmutation" of the quatrains of Omar Khayyám, a Persian mathematician and poet of the eleventh century. So striking are these opening lines, which flash like the rays of the morning sun, it seems almost incredible that anyone could read them and not wish to continue; but FitzGerald's poem, unsigned and privately printed, mouldered in bookshops for years, even though the price dropped to a penny a copy. Not until Dante Gabriel Rossetti stumbled on the poem, realized its worth, and began quoting from it in the proper literary circles did *The Rubáiyát* start its upward climb to great popularity. Fearful that its epicurian flavor would prove too spicy for prudish Victorians, FitzGerald did not allow his name to be associated with the poem during his lifetime. Only the fifth edition, published six years after his death in 1883, gives him credit for taking Omar's random verses and turning them into a poem that has shape, vitality, and a lyrical frivolity. Even after the poem had become famous, a theory was seriously advanced that it was all symbolical, that when Omar mentioned "Wine" he really meant "the Divinity." Such a theory seems as hard to swallow as the one which makes a religious allegory out of the "Song of Solomon." FitzGerald finally won out over the Victorians; by 1900 admirers of *The Rubáiyát* had become a cult. Not so lucky was Omar himself, for he too tried to run counter to a trend: the ancient Persians believed that poetry must have mysticism to be of value; *The Rubáiyát* was so worldly it told them bluntly to eat, drink, and be just as merry as possible. Thus

Omar died unpraised and not until more than seven centuries later, when he was "reincarnated" in FitzGerald, did the world hail his philosophy.

Following the opening quatrain, *The Rubáiyát* quickly establishes that philosophy, for as soon as the cock crows some people standing in front of a tavern demand that the door be opened so that they may drink their wine immediately. Such is the theme of the poem: life is short; therefore, you must put no dependence in Tomorrow or the Hereafter, but must seize on Today with all its sensory pleasures. FitzGerald plays variations on this theme for more than a hundred quatrains and among these are some of the most-quoted stanzas in English literature; for instance, those concerned with "the Bird of Time," with the celebrated "Book of Verses underneath the Bough," with the "batter'd Caravanserai," with "so red the Rose," and with the "Moving Finger." But *The Rubáiyát* is not haphazardly thrown together. It flows smoothly from the praising of wine to the disparagement of logic and wisdom; then from the spoofing of the ordinary conception of Divinity to the finality of death, that simple end to revelry.

One of the most interesting sections, though not the most lyrical, is the group of related stanzas dealing with the Potter and the Pots. Some of the Pots are "loquacious Vessels" and what they say reveals a thought-provoking if somewhat skeptical attitude toward life, the Creator, and death. The first vessel complains that surely the earth will not be molded into a figure and then broken or trampled back to earth again. A second says that since a "peevish Boy" would not break a bowl from which he had drunk with pleasure, the Potter will certainly not in wrath destroy what He created. Then follow these stanzas:

After a momentary silence spake
Some Vessel of a more ungainly Make:
    "They sneer at me for leaning all
        awry:
"What! did the Hand then of the Pot-
    ter shake?"

Whereat some one of the loquacious
    Lot—
I think a Súfi pipkin—waxing hot—
    "All this of Pot and Potter—Tell me,
        then,
"Who is the Potter, pray, and who the
    Pot?"

"Why," said another, "Some there are
    who tell
"Of one who threatens he will toss to
    Hell
    "The luckless Pots he marr'd in mak-
        ing—Pish!
"He's a Good Fellow, and 't will all be
    well."

FitzGerald (or Omar) cannot be taken seriously as a destroyer of faith or as a radical philosopher. He is too light-hearted to be accused of inducing corruption. And when *The Rubáiyát* is looked at closely, one becomes aware that there are really no new ideas here; it has all been said before. Certainly this poem and Gray's "Elegy Written in a Country Churchyard" are highly dissimilar, but in one respect they are alike: both FitzGerald and Gray have taken a series of platitudes, strung them together, and created tremendously effective poems because the words and music blend together so appropriately. Gray's music is slow and stately, a funeral march; FitzGerald sings like a skylark that has become tipsy from eating fermented cherries:

You know, my Friends, with what a
    brave Carouse

I made a Second Marriage in my house;
    Divorced old barren Reason from my
        Bed,
And took the Daughter of the Vine to
    Spouse.

The meter of these lines is plain iambic pentameter, but somehow the unrhymed third line makes each stanza spill into the next, as one might pour wine rapidly from one cup to another. The alliteration and the adroit use of internal part-rhyme (such as "barren Reason") increase the musical effect. And FitzGerald's diction is so fresh, so pert, that *The Rubáiyát* may never become dated, may always sound as if it were written yesterday or (more in the FitzGerald spirit) Today.

In any long poem there are bound to be passages that come as a letdown; *The Rubáiyát* is no exception. A goodly number of its stanzas can be passed over without loss to the reader and even some of the better and best ones are repetitive. In spite of these minor objections *The Rubáiyát* glitters with joy, especially so when one considers it as a product of the Victorian Age, which took itself so seriously. Two fine poets of that era have written poems in which they give their ideas on death. Tennyson's death-poem is, of course, the simple and moving "Crossing the Bar"; in "Prospice" Browning envisions the end of life as a last battle to be won, a fighting-through to heaven. Measured against these two great poems, the final stanza of *The Rubáiyát* may seem flippant, but its very flippancy makes it equally as memorable:

And when like her, oh Sákí, you shall
    pass
Among the Guests Star-scatter'd on the
    Grass,
    And in your joyous errand reach the
        spot
Where I made One—turn down an
    empty Glass!

# RULE A WIFE AND HAVE A WIFE

*Type of work:* Drama
*Author:* John Fletcher (1579-1625)
*Type of plot:* Romantic comedy
*Time of plot:* c. 1600
*Locale:* Spain
*First presented:* 1624

*Principal characters:*
LEON, a young Spanish gentleman
DON JUAN DE CASTRO, a colonel
MICHAEL PEREZ, a captain
CACAFOGO, a fat usurer
THE DUKE OF MEDINA
MARGARITA, a rich and wanton lady
ALTEA, her companion
ESTIFANIA, her maid

## Critique:

From a strictly moral point of view, *Rule a Wife and Have a Wife* leaves a good deal to be desired; Leon wins the beautiful, rich, and wanton Margarita by deceit and transforms her into a dutiful and virtuous wife by bullying her unmercifully. But Fletcher is never much concerned with moral questions. Rather, he is interested in creating comic situations which will give rise to fast-moving action and which will permit the introduction of interesting and humorous characters. These effects he achieves masterfully in *Rule a Wife and Have a Wife*, one of the most tightly knit of his comedies. The main plot, the taming of Margarita by Leon, is carefully balanced against the subplot, the gulling of Michael Perez by Estifania, and the two plots serve to reinforce each other admirably. As a supposedly weak husband asserts and wins superiority over his wife, so a seemingly wealthy and virtuous wife reveals to her husband that she is no better than she should be and makes him like it. The plots are united in their use of dramatic irony, and both are invigorated by a strong and direct language which is saved from vulgarity by its use in broadly comic, sometimes nearly farcical, situations.

## The Story:

As they were discussing the gathering of their companies for the Dutch wars, Michael Perez and Don Juan de Castro were interrupted by two veiled ladies, one of whom desired Don Juan to carry a message to a kinsman serving in Flanders. Perez was much attracted by her companion, and the lady seemed equally drawn to him. In spite of his pleas, however, she would not open her veil, although she did instruct him to have his servant follow her to learn the location of her home and to call there later himself. This was done, and Perez was overjoyed to find that the lady, Estifania, was not only lovely but also the owner of a magnificent town house beautifully adorned with hangings and plate. Perez proposed on the spot and to his delight was accepted. Don Juan, meanwhile, was interviewing Leon, a young man recommended to him as an officer. Although he was strong and handsome and had seen previous service, Leon revealed himself to be the most incredible ass. When he showed himself to be both cowardly and immeasurably stupid, Don Juan dismissed him with little encouragement.

In the country nearby, Margarita, a beautiful young heiress, was making preparations to return to town. She had but one object in view—pleasure—and she declared herself not at all adverse to a bit of wantonness if it should come her way. On the advice of Altea, her gentlewoman, she had decided that her reputation could be best protected if she married a foolish and complaisant man who would wink at her infidelities. In fact, Altea had just the man in mind, a fellow who was presentable enough but who had no more brains than an oyster and no sense of honor whatever. The man was Leon. When Margarita interviewed him she found him perfect for the role he was supposed to play, and she decided to wed him at once. She did not hear Leon whisper to Altea that he was a thousand crowns in her debt.

Margarita's sudden appearance in the city was welcomed by all the gallants, but it interrupted the idyllic honeymoon of Perez and Estifania. The soldier was reveling in the possession of his bride's mansion when Margarita and her entourage arrived at the door. Estifania did not seem altogether surprised; she pacified Perez by telling him that Margarita was a poor cousin trying to make the gentleman who accompanied her believe that she was rich in order to have him propose. The scheme made it necessary for Estifania and Perez to move into temporary quarters for a few days so that the ruse could be carried out. After Perez had left, the relationship between Estifania and Margarita became clear. Far from being a poor cousin, Margarita was the mistress and Estifania only the maid. It was Perez who had been thoroughly gulled.

Again in possession of her house, Margarita wasted no time. New hangings were placed in the rooms, couches were arranged in strategic locations, a magnificent dinner was prepared, and a company of gallants, including Don Juan and the Duke of Medina, in whom Margarita was especially interested, were invited to enjoy the feasting and entertainment.

The party was just beginning when Leon appeared, his air of stupidity and fecklessness entirely gone. Proudly he informed the guests that he was Margarita's husband and master and that he intended to protect his honor to the utmost. Margarita was infuriated, but Leon quickly silenced her. The Duke, too, was sorely displeased that his plans for Margarita had gone so suddenly awry, and he an-

grily drew upon Leon. But the young man was quite ready to fight, and only Don Juan's intercession restored calm and won a grudging apology from the Duke. Don Juan, in fact, was enchanted to see Leon's sudden transformation.

The guests were going fairly amicably in to dinner when Perez burst in. From some women in his new lodging he had heard the truth about Estifania, and he had also learned that he was not the first husband she had cozened. Moreover, she had disappeared with all his possessions.

Having had the women's story confirmed by Margarita, Perez hurried away again, determined to find Estifania and punish her. But when he met her on the street, Estifania was as angry as he; she had attempted to pawn his treasures and had learned that they were all false. In the mutual tongue-lashing that followed, Estifania emerged the winner. Having sent Perez back to Margarita's house again, convinced that it was really his, she began to improve their fortunes by selling Perez's worthless trinkets to Cacafogo for many times their value. She told him that they were Margarita's possessions which her mistress was sacrificing so that she could raise money to escape from Leon.

The Duke had ideas of his own about separating the husband and wife: he had Don Juan deliver to Leon a commission to command a troop of horse and orders to leave for Flanders immediately. When she heard of this plan, Margarita protested, tongue in cheek, that she hardly could bear to be left by her new husband whom she was just coming to love. If only she could accompany him, she sighed, but that, of course, was impossible. At the most ardent point of her discourse she heard the sound of hammers. Leon had checked the Duke's maneuver neatly. He intended to take with him to Flanders not only Margarita but also the complete furnishing of the house so that he could live like a gentleman in the garrison. As a last resort Margarita pleaded that she was pregnant, but Leon calmly reminded her that since they had been married only four days the news was somewhat too sudden to be credible. In spite of the protests of the gallants who were present, Leon remained firm; Margarita would accompany him. In a pique, Margarita gave the house and furnishings to Perez, who had by that time arrived to claim the possessions he believed his own, but Leon was so little troubled by this action that Margarita, almost in spite of herself, was compelled to express her admiration for him. Consequently, the gift was withdrawn, and Perez again was gulled.

Angered beyond measure, he once more sought out Estifania. This time he drew his sword to kill her, but she stopped him by covering him with a pistol. She then took the edge off his wrath by presenting him with the thousand ducats out of which she had gulled Cacafogo. Realizing that there were shortcomings on both sides of the match and that his wife was a great deal cleverer than he, Perez decided that he ought to make the best of his bargain.

Meanwhile, both the Duke and Cacafogo arrived independently to pay suit to Margarita. The usurer was diverted into the wine cellar, where he soon became drunk. The Duke, having gained entry to the house by pretending to be wounded in a duel, soon found a chance to be alone with her, but his passionate speeches were interrupted by Cacafogo's drunken roaring from the cellar, a noise which, at Margarita's suggestion, he took to be a devil haunting him because of his evil purpose. Half afraid and thoroughly ashamed by the lady's virtuous replies, he became utterly discomfited and renounced his suit for good. This development completely satisfied Leon, who had overheard everything that was said. All ended happily as the bride and groom, now completely in love with each other, invited Perez and Estifania to take service with them.

# R. U. R.

*Type of work:* Drama
*Author:* Karel Čapek (1890-1938)
*Type of plot:* Social criticism
*Time of plot:* The future
*Locale:* An unnamed island
*First presented:* 1921; published in 1920

> Principal characters:
> HARRY DOMIN, General Manager of Rossum's Universal Robots
> HELENA GLORY, his wife
> DR. GALL, a scientist
> MR. ALQUIST, head of the works department of R. U. R.
> PRIMUS, a robot
> HELENA, a robotess

## Critique:

R. U. R. is a bitter attack on the trend toward a mechanized civilization which would put millions of men out of work. In this play the crisis of the scientific utopia occurs when the robots are given souls and begin to act like human beings, destroying the men who made them. The characters in the play are deliberately contrived in keeping with Čapek's purpose of protest against the depersonalized march of science and invention. The plot is pure, stark drama. This play has enjoyed continuous success since its first production and has been presented by professionals and amateurs alike.

## The Story:

The Rossum Universal Robot Factory had perfected mechanical men and women. The formula had been developed originally by old Rossum, but it had been left to his son, an engineer, to manufacture the robots. Robots knew no joy, no desire to take a solitary walk, no personal wish of any kind. They were highly developed with mechanisms devised for only one purpose: work.

The robots manufactured by Rossum's Universal Robot Factory were so lifelike, however, that when the president's daughter, Helena Glory, called at the factory and was shown around by Harry Domin, general manager, she could hardly believe they were not human. Helena had been sent by the Humanity League on a mission to gain better living conditions for the robots. Helena knew that when the robots began to act strangely, as they sometimes did, they were destroyed and their parts were used to make new robots. She was dismayed to find that the robots she met and talked with in the factory did not care whether they were killed or starved. They thought of nothing but their work. They talked rationally, answering her questions, but they seemed to have no desires or feelings beyond their given jobs. Domin and the other executives were willing to have her preach to the robots all she wished.

In the warehouses there were hundreds of thousands of robots waiting to be shipped all over the world. Domin tried to convince Helena of the rightness of the new era. Now, man was no longer effective. He was too imperfect, too expensive, too long a child. Although Domin could not agree that robots should be freed and allowed the rights of mankind, he admitted that sometimes they acted queerly. Often one would gnash its teeth, throw things about, and then stand still. The attack was similar to epilepsy, and the robot would have to go to the

R. U. R. by Karel Čapek. Translated by Paul Selver and Nigel Playfair. By permission of the publishers, Samuel French. Copyright, 1923, by Doubleday, Page & Co., 1930, by Thomas H. Dickinson in CHIEF CONTEMPORARY DRAMATISTS, THIRD SERIES. Application for the right to present this play should be made to Samuel French, of 25 West 45th St., New York 36, N. Y., or 7623 Sunset Blvd., Hollywood 46, Calif., or if in Canada to Samuel French (Canada) Ltd., 27 Grenville St., Toronto, Ont.

stamping-mill to be destroyed. Helena believed these were signs of developing a soul. The managers were working on a pain-nerve. They thought that if the robots were to feel pain, these attacks could be foreseen and treated.

The executives tried also to convince Helena of the virtue of robots by pointing out to her that the prices of all manufactured and farm goods had dropped almost to nothing. Where Helena could see only the millions of men out of work, the managers could see a world in which no human being worked. Men could then sit back and enjoy the labors of mechanical workers. Only Mr. Alquist, head of the works department, disagreed with that notion. Alquist could see the joy men found only in working and creating. The others quickly voted him down.

Without prior warning, Domin told Helena that he loved her and could not bear to lose her. Puzzling even herself, she accepted him.

Ten years passed. The managers tried to keep from Helena the news that the robots were causing trouble. All over the world small groups of robots had revolted against their masters. Some governments had turned the robots into soldiers and terrible wars had been fought. Learning of these revolts, she begged Domin and the others to close the factory while there was still time. The men laughed at her fears. They had a gunboat standing by which would protect them from quist agreed with Helena. He even prayed that God would destroy the robots and let mankind return to his rightful work. He knew, as Helena did, that man had stopped reproducing; there had been no births recorded in the past week.

Dr. Gall, the physiologist, began to fear the results when he learned that some of the more intelligent robots, according to their different grades, had begun to feel pain and to have heart flutters. They had also begun to show definite signs of hating and loving. But the R. U. R. shareholders were making too much money and world governments

were growing too powerful with robot soldiers to permit their discontinuance, even if Domin and the others had accepted Helena's and Alquist's views. Feeling that the end was near, Dr. Gall could only warn Helena to look out for herself. The scientist believed they were all doomed.

The only weapon the managers could use against the robots, should they rebel, was the secret of their manufacture, the secret which promised to end a world organization of robots. As soon as the current trouble was over, each country would begin to manufacture its own robots. The differences in language and customs would prevent a world union in the future.

The trouble soon grew into a real danger. A mail boat arrived with leaflets announcing that the world organization ordered all robots to kill every man, woman, and child in the world. The robots claimed that man had become a parasite, that robots were now smarter than man and must rule the world. The orders were to be carried out immediately.

After a gallant fight the humans in the factory were overpowered. Even when he knew death was near, Domin had no regrets. He had wanted to free man from the restrictions of an unfair social system, from poverty, from the slavery of working for another; but something had gone wrong. Somehow the robots had begun to care about the things that man cared about. The mystery was solved when Helena confessed that she had persuaded Dr. Gall to give the robots souls. She had hoped that if the robots were more like human beings both groups could understand each other better. Now the robots were so human that they acted like men.

The only hope was to persuade the robots that they dared not kill the men who knew the secret of their manufacture. Domin prefered death rather than to give up his dream, but the others, hoping to use the formula in their bargaining, outvoted him. Then they learned that Helena, hoping to put an end to the factory and to help children be born again, had burned the formula.

All the humans were killed except Alquist, spared by the robots because he also worked with his hands. Alquist, unable to duplicate the formula, could not save the robots, who were dying by the millions. Before long they would be extinct. The irony was that Alquist needed human beings to study and experiment with in order to rediscover the formula, but there were no humans left.

One day Alquist decided that there was hope. Primus, a robot, and Helena, a robotess made in Helena's image, exhibited all the symptoms of love. At first Alquist planned to dissect them, to see what made them feel human love. When he learned that they were willing to die for each other, but that they would not be parted, he knew that he need search no longer for the secret of robot life. Their love would bring forth new life, and the world would know humanity once more.

# THE SAINT

Type of work: Novel
Author: Antonio Fogazzaro (1842-1911)
Type of plot: Religious romance
Time of plot: Late nineteenth century
Locale: Italy
First published: 1905

Principal characters:
BENEDETTO, the saint
JEANNE DESSALLE, his former mistress
NOEMI D'ARXEL, her friend
GIOVANNI SELVA, a philosopher
DON CLEMENTE, a Benedictine monk

## Critique:

The Saint is the third part of a trilogy dealing with the Maironi family in nineteenth-century Italy. It is, however, complete in itself. The best and most popular novel of the series, it was from its first publication a highly controversial book. In Italy, particularly, its merits are still a matter of debate. Fogazzaro himself was a prominent Catholic layman of the nineteenth century, and the novel has been widely read by those seeking an objective view of the Church of that period.

## The Story:

Three years had passed since Piero Maironi, an artist, had renounced the world, and with it his love for Jeanne Dessalle. Maironi, whose wife was in a lunatic asylum, had fallen in love with Jeanne, who was separated from her husband. Before Maironi's wife died, however, she regained her sanity and called Piero to her side. There he had recovered his sense of honor, and on the night she died he had a prophetic vision concerning his life. He disappeared immediately from the knowledge of his family and friends and none of his old associates had seen him since. Jeanne had received a message from him that told of his sorrow at the sin they had shared. In spite of his message she could not quite accept his decision but still hoped to see him and renew his love for her. Her husband

had died in the meantime, and she thought that if Piero could come to her without guilt he might renounce the holy life he was supposed to have embraced.

With a new friend, Noemi d'Arxel, Jeanne began to travel over Italy in search of Piero. In the hope that he had not yet taken his final vows as a monk, she sought him everywhere. Jeanne herself could not accept God. She knew that this fact would be a hindrance to the relations she hoped to establish with her former lover, but she was too intelligent and too honest to pretend to believe in order to influence him.

At last Jeanne and Noemi found Piero. He was at Jenne, a gardener in the monastery of Santa Scholastica, where he was the pupil and servant of Don Clemente, a Benedictine monk of rare humility and virtue. Piero was now called Benedetto, and no one but Don Clemente knew his real identity. To the people he was known as the Saint of Jenne, and many were cured of afflictions by merely touching his garments. Benedetto claimed no miracles; in fact, he begged people not to glorify him. For Benedetto was a true man of God. He wanted only to pray and to serve others and to rid the Church of her faults. For this last desire he was often reviled, because many dignitaries of the Church could not stand to have their souls bared to the public. Loving the Church with his whole heart, Benedetto sorrowed when he saw corruption and greed weakening it from within. In spite of his sincerity and his humility, he was sometimes hated, sometimes worshipped by those who knew him.

Although Jeanne managed to see Benedetto alone, the interview was not a satisfactory one. He asked her first if she now believed, and honesty made her answer that she did not. Then he asked her if she would promise to live for the poor and to love the afflicted. When she answered that she would, he told her that he would call her to his side at a certain hour in the future. Until then she must never try to see him again. After Benedetto left her, Jeanne was lost in sorrow.

Even though he worked only for the good of others, ruining his health by his frugal habits, Benedetto was forced to leave Jenne because he talked out against the corruption of the Church. Friends helped him, including Giovanni Selva, Noemi's saintly brother-in-law. Selva was a loyal Catholic who loved his Church so much that he wanted to see it rise above the worldly evils which threatened it. He had written some philosophical books on this subject, books which were in danger of being proscribed as unfit for Catholics to read. It was not always safe for Selva to aid Benedetto, but when he could not help the simple man himself he arranged for other friends to do so. Don Clemente, too, had been ordered by his superiors in the Church to abandon Benedetto. Although the monk obeyed, he longed for the time when they would all be vindicated and their teachings accepted.

Benedetto felt an invisible voice telling him to make a pilgrimage to Rome, to the Holy Father himself. Sick and weak, he made the long journey and was ordered to an audience with the pope. As he entered the Vatican, he saw again the vision he had seen on the night of his wife's death. Alone, he found his way to the pope's library, a fact the pope thought singularly strange; however, Benedetto had found the intricate

halls and stairways just as he had seen them in his vision. The pilgrim learned that the pope was also concerned about the Church as it stood at that time, and he told Benedetto that the pope must deal with human beings, not with God alone, and that he had to consider how best to help all people everywhere, not those who believed only as he did. The Holy Father listened earnestly to Benedetto's account of the four sins which he considered the most serious: they were the spirit of falsehood, the domination of the clergy, the spirit of avarice, and the spirit of immobility or the failure to meet the needs of the changing times. The pope agreed with Benedetto on these points but begged him to be patient in waiting for their correction.

Benedetto's last plea to the pope was that Selva's books might not be placed on the Index. The vicar made no promises, but he agreed to consider all the things they had discussed. Then he blessed Benedetto and the pilgrim took his leave.

Not long after the interview friends warned Benedetto that the police were after him. Although she kept her prom ise not to try to see him, Jeanne sent him one message of warning. She did send her carriage for him once, in the hope that the reminder of her might cause him to change his mind, but her ruse was unsuccessful. Though the charges against Benedetto were false, sworn to by his enemies, his friends forced him to heed the dangers and hide himself. By that time he was in poor health because of his life of fasting and praying. Because he often went for days without food or rest, his friends knew that he would soon die.

Benedetto, also realizing that his days were numbered, sent for Jeanne. Before she arrived he saw his true friends once more: Selva, whose books had been kept off the Index because of Benedetto's plea to the pope; Don Clemente, who had come to him in spite of the danger involved; the poor from all over the city. He blessed them all and exhorted them to keep God in their hearts through all obstacles and dangers. Last of all Jeanne went to him. By that time Benedetto was so weak that he could hardly move his head. He did not speak, but stretched out his hand in the direction of the crucifix. When she took it to him, he raised it toward her lips. Taking the crucifix from his weak grasp, Jeanne kissed it passionately. A smile came to the face of the saintly man as he breathed his last.

# SAINT JOAN

*Type of work:* Drama
*Author:* Bernard Shaw (1856-1950)
*Time:* 1428-1456
*Locale:* France
*First presented:* 1923

> *Principal characters:*
> JOAN OF ARC, Maid of Orléans
> CHARLES, Dauphin and later King of France
> PETER CAUCHON, Bishop of Beauvais
> THE EARL OF WARWICK, an English lord
> "JACK" DUNOIS, a French commander
> ROBERT DE BAUDRICOURT, a French squire
> THE ARCHBISHOP OF RHEIMS
> DE STOGUMBER, an English chaplain

In 1920, almost five hundred years after she had been burned at the stake as a heretic, sorceress, and witch, Joan of Arc, Maid of Orléans, was canonized; three and one half years later, with the first performance of *Saint Joan* on December 28, 1923, at the Garrick Theatre in New York City, Joan was Shavianized. That is to say, George Bernard Shaw told the world the truth about Joan in terms of the Shavian dramatic dialectic.

Shaw felt that although Joan had been completely rehabilitated, both by the Church and by secular commentators, the true significance of her life and martyrdom was not yet understood, for in exonerating Joan of the crimes for which it had burned her, the Church had whitewashed Joan and condemned itself. Furthermore, the literary interpretations of Joan, ranging from Voltaire's ribald burlesque to Mark Twain's romantic adulation, were misleading and therefore worthless. Shaw believed that he could rectify all these erroneous interpretations. He proceeded to write *Saint Joan,* basing it on the extraordinary premises, first, that Joan was a harbinger of Protestantism and, secondly, that she was a fomenter of nationalism. Within the framework of the play he concludes that Joan had to die because as a Protestant she threatened the authority of the Church, and as a nationalist she imperiled the power of the feudal lords.

Whether or not these premises and conclusions are valid historically is, of course, conjectural. But such a question is irrelevant since they are valid dramatically. In this play more than in any other, Shaw succeeded in creating characters who lived the theme in addition to preaching it. *Saint Joan* is thus a genuine play, not just a Shavian dialogue.

Joan's Protestantism is rooted in her independence, her insistence on listening to the dictates of her heavenly voices, which she concedes may be figments of her imagination. Convinced that the advice given her by Saint Margaret and Saint Catherine is sensible and practical, she finds the courage to defy bishops, archbishops, and inquisitors. Her nationalism grows out of her almost fanatical zeal to save France from the English and to establish France as an autonomous state dedicated to glorifying God. This zeal, manifested as fervid sincerity and earnestness, enables her to command generals and to crown kings.

Independence, courage, and zeal—these characteristics make Joan a Shavian genius, a superwoman, and the female counterpart of Jack Tanner. Her ability to probe deep into the problems of life and to formulate independent ethical values causes her to be alienated from conventional society. Although Joan is a Shavian genius, she is not a typical one. As a proud, stubborn peasant girl, Joan is profoundly, pathetically human. She can stand as a character without reference to Shaw or his philosophy.

The characterization of Joan is by no means the only original one in the play: the treatment of the minor personages is even less conventional, most notably with the Earl of Warwick, and Cauchon, Bishop of Beauvais. Shaw objected to the traditional interpretation of Warwick and Cauchon as egregious blackguards and set out to rehabilitate them. Within the typically Shavian framework they represent the conservative and reactionary— the established—elements of society who resist and defeat the genius. Within the thematic framework of *Saint Joan,* they represent the power of the Church and of feudalism. Their opposition to Joan is not vindictive; Cauchon, in fact, strives to save her and insures a fair trial for her. Both are forced to resist her because as thinking men they recognize that she threatens their own self-interest within the existing social order. As a feudal lord, Warwick cannot brook Joan's nationalism, which, if unchecked, would diminish his power. As a ruler of the Church, Cauchon cannot tolerate Joan's Protestantism, which, if unchecked, would subvert his authority. Both are reasonable, even virtuous men, and by executing Joan they perform a service to the elements of society which they represent. Far from being villains, they were medieval heroes.

Most of the other characters also represent the conservative elements of society, but they see, for a while at least, the advantage in allying themselves with Joan. To the French, Joan is a new hope for France, a crazy hope, perhaps, but the last hope for driving out the English. Thus Captain Robert de Baudricourt, lord of the province where Joan was born, agrees to furnish her horse and armor as well as an escort to take her to the dauphin. The dauphin, timid and a little silly, a prisoner of his own court, makes Joan his commander-in-chief and succumbs to her efforts to make a man and king of him. The Archbishop of Rheims gives to her enterprise the sanction of the Church. And Dunois, commander of the forces at Orléans, agrees to follow Joan's leadership in a desperate attack across the Loire. Yet all these desert Joan when she has served their purposes. When her plans to complete her mission by driving the English from Paris seem too impractical, too audacious to execute, they withdraw their support, charging her with impudence and pride. By the time Joan has crowned the dauphin at Rheims, they have recovered their conventionality and are embarrassed by their former enthusiasm in accepting a peasant girl's leadership. Therefore they do not move to save Joan when she is captured and sold to Warwick and Cauchon.

This theme of the rejection of the moral genius by the conservative elements of society is recapitulated and generalized in an epilogue. Twenty-five years after her death, on the occasion of her rehabilitation by the Church in 1456, Joan meets again the men who were involved in her career. When a messenger from the Pope appears to announce the canonization of Joan, all, from Cauchon to King Charles, fall to their knees in adoration of the new saint. Yet when Joan acknowledges their praise by asking if she should return from the dead, a living woman, each—except for a common soldier—again rejects her, humbly this time, and disappears. Shaw's message is clear: those who rule society are never ready to accept the moral genius who would change society, even though that genius be a saint.

*Saint Joan* is perhaps the only play in which Shaw succeeded in dramatizing this theme without reference to situations which now seem dated, and without reducing drama to didacticism. Because *Saint Joan* in part transcends Shaw, it must be listed among his masterpieces.

# ST. PETER'S UMBRELLA

*Type of work:* Novel
*Author:* Kálmán Mikszáth (1847-1910)
*Type of plot:* Humorous romance
*Time of plot:* Second half of nineteenth century
*Locale:* Hungary
*First published:* 1895

### Principal characters:

PÁL GREGORICS, a wealthy bachelor
ANNA WIBRA, his housekeeper and cook
GYURY (GYÖRGY) WIBRA, the illegitimate son of Anna Wibra
JÁNOS BÉLYI, a priest in Glogova
VERONICA BÉLYI, his sister
WIDOW ADAMECZ, the priest's housekeeper
JÁNOS SZTOLARIK, a lawyer
JÓNÁS MÜNCZ, a Jewish merchant

## Critique:

Kálmán Mikszáth was a country squire, lawyer, magistrate, journalist, member of parliament, and novelist; but his forte was undoubtedly the ability for superb storytelling, surpassed in Hungary only by Maurus Jókai. He draws his characters with the certainty of a man who knows and understands the people he writes about, mainly the Hungarian peasantry. The ease with which he transforms everyday life into unusual stories reminds one strongly of Maupassant; his sense of humor, as demonstrated in this novel, makes reading a pleasure. The author became a member of the Hungarian Academy and of the Hungarian Parliament, but his parliamentary speeches will be long forgotten when the hilarious episodes of *St. Peter's Umbrella* will be still remembered.

## The Story:

When the new priest, young János Bélyi, arrived in Glogova, prospects for an enjoyable life were extremely dim. The little Hungarian town was a forlorn place where impoverished peasants lived out their lives trying to get as much as possible out of the poor soil. No provisions were made for the priest's subsistence and church property was almost nonexistent. While the priest was contemplating the fact that he would have

to eat less and pray more, the situation became more critical with the arrival of his little baby sister. His parents had died and somebody had decided to send little Veronica to her next relative, the priest. Thus a little baby in a basket was suddenly put at the doorstep of his modest home. In order to find a solution to his problems he took a prayerful walk.

A heavy rain began to fall. Suddenly he remembered the baby, still lying in front of his house, and he was certain the child would be soaking wet before he could arrive. To his surprise he found her completely dry, protected by an old red umbrella. The priest could not imagine who had been so kind to his little sister; however, the townspeople soon found all sorts of explanations. Since the only stranger who had been seen lately was an old Jew, the peasants came to the conclusion that St. Peter had come to show his mercy for the poor child.

At the next funeral on a rainy day the priest used the red umbrella. The men carrying the coffin stumbled and the supposedly dead man, who was merely in a trance, became very much alive. To the villagers this incident was another sign of the supernatural character of the umbrella. On account of the umbrella the priest's conditions improved rapidly, and all kinds of gifts arrived at his house for the baby who had caused St. Peter to come to Glogova. Even Widow Adamecz offered her services as housekeeper free of charge, additional proof of the miraculous power of the umbrella to all who knew the money-conscious widow.

In the beginning the priest tried to resist continuous requests for the presence of the umbrella during church ceremonies, but his parishioners felt so offended when he refused that he finally gave in and used the umbrella on all occasions. Pilgrims came from far away to look at the umbrella and brides insisted on being married under it. Soon the town felt the need for building an inn which carried the name "Miraculous Umbrella." The priest wondered how the umbrella came to Glogova; he was to wait many years for an answer.

In the town of Besztercebánya lived a wealthy bachelor, Pál Gregorics. A spy during the war, he had been seen many times with a red umbrella. Pál Gregorics was in love with his housekeeper, Anna Wibra, who gave birth to an illegitimate son, Gyury Wibra. The townspeople observed how Pál Gregorics devoted all his time to the child. Pál's two brothers and his sister did not like the possibility that they might some day have to share Pál's estate with an illegitimate child. For this reason Pál, afraid that his relatives might try to harm young Gyury, decided to trick them by pretending he did not care for the boy, and he sent Gyury to a distant school. To deceive his brothers and sister, he acted as if he had invested all his money in several estates which required inspection from time to time, but in reality he visited his son.

In spite of great love for his father, Gyury reproached Pál for making himself a laughingstock by always carrying the old red umbrella. Pál disregarded the complaints and promised his son he would one day inherit the umbrella. When Pál felt he was going to die, he asked his lawyer János Sztolarik to prepare his will. Mysteriously, he asked two masons, under strict order of secrecy, to break a wall in order to place a caldron into the wall

and finish the masonry as it had been before. Although he had told his housekeeper to notify Gyury of his illness, she failed to do so, and Pál Gregorics died, without seeing his son, with the red umbrella in his hands.

When Sztolarik read the will, Pál's brothers and sister were horrified to hear nothing about the rich estates which their brother supposedly owned. They spent much time and money to find out what Pál had done with the money. They suspected a secret bequest to Gyury, but investigators reported that the boy was studying and living on a meager income. Finally they discovered the two masons, who revealed for a large sum of money the secret of the caldron in the wall. Certain they had found the answer to their riddle, they bought the house, which had been willed to Gyury, for an extremely high price. When they broke the wall open, they found the caldron filled with rusty nails.

Soon afterward Gyury completed his education and became a lawyer in Besztercebánya. He had heard about the frantic search for his father's estate and he himself began to wonder where it could be. The first clue was given by the dying mayor, who told how Pál Gregorics had carried secret documents in the hollow handle of his umbrella during the war. Gyury's suspicion was confirmed when his mother told him how Pál, even in death, was still clutching the umbrella. The search for the umbrella then began. Gyury's investigations pointed to an old Jew, Jónás Müncz, who had bought for a few coins his father's odds and ends which the relatives did not want. Further inquiries established that the Jew had died, but that his wife owned a small store in Bábaszék. Gyury and his coachman hurried to that town. An interview with Frau Müncz revealed that her husband had been fond of the umbrella and had carried it around at all times. Gyury heard from Frau Müncz's son that the old Jew had been seen putting the umbrella over a little baby in Glogova.

As he was about to leave for Glogova, Gyury found a lost earring for which, according to the town crier, the mayor was searching. Returning the earring to the mayor, he was introduced to its owner, a young and extremely beautiful girl. Furthermore, he learned she was Veronica Bélyi, sister of the village priest in Glogova. She had been on her way home when an accident damaged her vehicle.

Gladly Gyury offered to conduct Veronica and her traveling companion in his carriage, but the two women decided that it was now too late for departure, and Gyury agreed to postpone his trip until morning. During a party in the mayor's house Gyury heard about the miraculous umbrella in Glogova and realized that the umbrella he was seeking was identical with the priest's umbrella. Throughout the night he could hardly sleep from thinking how near and yet how far away the umbrella was. During the night he dreamed that St. Peter advised him to marry the priest's sister; thus he would have a beautiful wife and a legal claim on the umbrella.

On the trip to Glogova, Gyury considered the advantages of the suggestion offered to him in his dream, but he was afraid Veronica might not love him. Not far away from the town the carriage broke down. Searching for some wood needed for repair, he heard faint cries for help; a man had fallen into a deep hole. After several attempts he succeeded in lifting out the unfortunate man, who turned out to be the priest of Glogova; he had fallen into the hole while waiting for Veronica on the previous night. Deeply grateful, the priest wanted to know whether there was anything he could do for his rescuer. Gyury told him he had something in his carriage belonging to the priest. The priest was surprised to find his sister in the vehicle; he informed Veronica of his promise and thus Veronica became engaged to Gyury.

In Glogova the young man had a conversation with the lawyer Sztolarik, who had heard from Gyury about his successful search. The lawyer was concerned because he felt that Gyury could not be sure whether love for Veronica or for the umbrella was the primary motive for his marriage. Veronica, overhearing the conversation, ran away heartbroken.

Gyury was eager to see the umbrella, which the priest gladly showed him. But the old handle had been replaced by a new one of silver. Gyury's last hope for recovering the old handle was crushed when the priest's housekeeper informed him that she had burned it. Meanwhile the priest began to worry about the absence of his sister. Hearing of her disappearance, Gyury was also greatly upset. Suddenly he realized that he could overcome the loss of the umbrella, but not the loss of Veronica. Church bells gave the fire alarm signal and everybody in Glogova appeared for the search. When Gyury found Veronica and told her about the burned handle, she recognized his greater love for her, and she and Gyury were married in the grandest wedding Glogova had ever seen. Although Gyury never knew whether the handle contained the key to his inheritance, the umbrella remained a treasured relic in his family.

# ST. RONAN'S WELL

*Type of work:* Novel
*Author:* Sir Walter Scott (1771-1832)
*Type of plot:* Social criticism
*Time of plot:* Early nineteenth century
*Locale:* Scotland
*First published:* 1824

*Principal characters:*
>FRANCIS TYRREL, a young Englishman posing as an itinerant painter
>THE EARL OF ETHERINGTON, an English nobleman
>CLARA MOWBRAY, daughter of a Scottish laird
>JOHN MOWBRAY, her brother
>MR. TOUCHWOOD, an elderly world traveler
>MEG DODS, mistress of the inn at old St. Ronan's
>LADY PENELOPE PENFEATHER, a society leader at St. Ronan's Well
>CAPTAIN HARRY JEKYL, Etherington's friend

## Critique:

St. *Ronan's Well* is one of the most bitter and scathingly satirical of Scott's novels. Lockhart reports that the original version, in which Clara's forced marriage to Valentine Bulmer was consummated, was so unpleasant that the author's publishers forced him to alter his plot. It is in some ways unfortunate that he followed their advice, because the change weakened the motivation for Clara's later behavior. The members of the idle society at the watering place are easily recognizable individuals, probably modeled after superficial admirers of Scott's work; his own experiences may be reflected in Francis Tyrrel's lack of success in Lady Penelope's circle. The author does not give these characters the sympathy which he reserves for his kindhearted, eccentric figures like Meg Dods, the village parson, or Mr. Touchwood. What is unusual in this novel is the fact that the good intentions of these characters are partly responsible for the final tragedy.

## The Story:

Meg Dods, the proprietress, welcomed Francis Tyrrel, a young Englishman, to her inn at old St. Ronan's, after she had recognized him as a former visitor to the village and not a traveling salesman. She gladly answered his questions about the Mowbray family, telling him that John had inherited his father's title of Laird of St. Ronan's and now spent much of his time gambling at the Well, the fashionable watering place whose growth had caused the old town to fall into ruins. Clara Mowbray, reported to be a little strange, lived with her brother.

Tyrrel saw these old acquaintances a few weeks later when he was invited to tea by Lady Penelope Penfeather, who was delighted to learn that an artist had come into the neighborhood. Her hope that he would be an asset to her social circle was thwarted, for she found him commonplace and was offended that he presumed to sit by her at dinner, far above what she considered his rightful position. Tyrrel was angered to discover that his activities had been the subject of a bet between Sir Bingo Binks and John Mowbray, and only a familiar voice in his ear stopped him from coming to blows with the boorish Sir Bingo.

Leaving the Well, Tyrrel waited in a nearby wood for Clara Mowbray, whose voice he had recognized. When they met they alluded to mysterious and dreadful past events which, the young man immediately realized, had unhinged the girl's mind. Clara, controlling her emotions enough to ask that they meet as friends, invited him to a party she and her brother were to give at Shaws Castle.

Smarting under Tyrrel's supposed insult, Sir Bingo, encouraged by his friend Captain MacTurk, sent a challenge to Tyrrel, who accepted it and agreed to a time for an encounter. However, when Sir Bingo and MacTurk appeared at the appointed place, they waited in vain. Although a public statement was issued at the Well to raise Sir Bingo's status and blacken Tyrrel's name, the young Englishman failed to come forward to defend his reputation.

Meg Dods, upset by her lodger's disappearance, and convinced that Tyrrel had been murdered by his dueling opponents, went to consult the sheriff at a nearby town. Her attention was diverted from Tyrrel by the entrance into the sheriff's office of Mr. Touchwood, who told her that he was thoroughly disgusted with the foolish society at the Well, where he had been staying. When Mrs. Dods promised him better service at her own inn, he agreed to move there.

Once he had given detailed instructions about the angle of his bed and the cooking of his food, Mr. Touchwood set out to make new acquaintances. First he sought out the Rev. Josiah Cargill, the most absent-minded of scholars, but a kind and charitable man. Mr. Cargill, generally vague about the affairs of his parishioners, became unexpectedly agitated when, during a discussion of the Mowbrays' forthcoming fête, he heard the rumor that Clara was to wed a young nobleman. He agreed to join his friend Mr. Touchwood for the party and insisted that he must talk to the girl.

The rumored bridegroom, the Earl of Etherington, had been welcomed at St. Ronan's Well with special cordiality because of the wounds he said he had received at the hands of a highwayman. John Mowbray gambled with Etherington often during his convalescence and would have lost his own fortune and the money he had borrowed from his sister if the earl had not deliberately allowed his opponent to win. He then asked John's permission to marry his sister, explaining that under the will of an eccentric relative a large fortune would be his if he wed a Mowbray. John gave his consent with the provision that Clara must agree to the match.

The mystery of Tyrrel's disappearance was partially explained in a letter which Etherington wrote to a friend, Captain Harry Jekyl. The artist and the earl, bitter enemies who were obviously connected in some way, had met in a wood near St. Ronan's and there fought a duel in which Tyrrel had been injured. Etherington said that he knew nothing of Tyrrel's present whereabouts.

Mr. Touchwood and Mr. Cargill went together to Shaws Castle, where they were entertained with tableaux from *A Midsummer Night's Dream*. Etherington had chosen the part of Bottom, played in an ass's head; it was later made obvious that his object was to prevent Clara from seeing his face. After the play the earl was addressed by the minister as Valentine Bulmer, but the nobleman vigorously denied this name and left abruptly. Mr. Cargill, who had just spoken to Clara and urged her not to sin by considering marriage, was greatly puzzled; however, knowing his own absent-minded nature, he did not pursue the matter further.

Etherington again postponed a meeting with Clara by leaving the banquet before she arrived, but he sent word to John the next morning that he wished to meet her that day. When Clara told her brother that she would not see him or any other man who came proposing marriage, John left her alone to look for the bearer of an anonymous note which declared that Etherington had usurped his title. Just then the earl entered Clara's room; she screamed as she recognized him and asked why he had broken his promise never to see her again. He answered that the fact that she had spoken to Tyrrel absolved him of his promise.

Etherington's ensuing conversation with John and his second letter to Captain Jekyl explained the complicated relationship between himself, Clara, and Tyrrel. The two young men were half-brothers, both claiming to be their father's legitimate son. At one time they had been sent to Scotland, where the future earl took the name of Valentine Bulmer. When Tyrrel fell in love with Clara, the two planned a clandestine marriage with Bulmer's help. Meanwhile, Bulmer had learned of the strange bequest hinging upon his marriage with a Mowbray, and he treacherously substituted himself for the bridegroom in the ceremony performed by Mr. Cargill. When Tyrrel stopped the newly wedded couple a short distance from the church and fought with his half-brother, Bulmer fell under the wheels of his carriage and was seriously injured. Clara had returned home, horrified, and the two young men, both still in their teens, vowed never to see her again. The old earl died soon afterward and, having made no effort to acknowledge Francis Tyrrel's legitimacy, named Etherington as his heir.

Soon after Etherington's interview with Clara, Tyrrel returned to the inn, where he was befriended by Mr. Touchwood. When Captain Jekyl came there to try to persuade him to soften his hatred for his brother, Tyrrel showed his visitor a list of documents which proved his legal title to the earldom; he offered to withhold this evidence, however, if Etherington would agree to leave Clara alone for the rest of her life. Captain Jekyl reported this interview to the earl, who denied that such proofs existed. As soon as his friend had gone, however, he plotted with his valet to steal the documents from the post-office, thus substantiating Tyrrel's claim that his brother already knew about the papers.

By coincidence Lady Penelope led the earl to the deathbed of the one person who could prove his treachery conclusively. She was Hannah Irwin, Clara's former maid, who had helped him carry out his plot. Etherington kept Lady Penelope from hearing much of the dying woman's confession, but he was disturbed by the knowledge that his trickery could so easily be disclosed. His consternation increased when the stolen packet was found to contain only copies of the vital documents. In danger of losing his earldom, he was more anxious than ever to acquire the estate which would come with Clara. He gambled again with John Mowbray and won heavily enough to make the young man agree to persuade Clara to accept marriage to a husband she detested.

John first confronted Clara with the ugly rumors about her character, reports spread by Lady Penelope, who based her gossip on Hannah's half-heard confession. Then he literally forced the poor girl to swear to submit to marriage with the earl. He left her, trembling, in her room and went to greet an unexpected visitor, Mr. Touchwood, who identified himself as the son of the man who had left the estate coveted by Etherington and the senior partner in the law firm which held the documents proving Francis Tyrrel's legitimacy. Mr. Touchwood, having pieced together the complicated affair between Clara and the two young men, told John the whole story, partly extracted from the earl's servant, Solmes.

Ironically, this revelation came too late. When John went to rouse his sister and tell her that he at last knew the truth, he found that she had fled. Her nightly wandering had led her first to Mr. Cargill's house, where Hannah Irwin had been moved by Mr. Touchwood. There she heard Hannah ask for forgiveness before she went on, distractedly, to Tyrrel's room at the inn. She collapsed after begging him to flee with her and died the next morning under the care of Meg Dods. Tyrrel rushed out to take vengeance on the man responsible for the tragedy, only to learn from Mr. Touchwood that John Mowbray had preceded him and had already killed the earl.

John, in flight to England, sent back word that the whole town of St. Ronan's Well should be pulled down. He gradually developed habits of economy, and it was generally believed that he would eventually inherit Mr. Touchwood's estate. That gentleman had tried to make a protégé of Francis Tyrrel, but the latter said that he had lived too much of his life too young and wanted only a quiet future. Refusing to claim his title, he went to the Continent, where he was reported to have joined a Moravian mission. Mr. Touchwood, who might have forestalled the final tragedy if he had not been so anxious to work everything out himself, lived on, alone, making empty plans and increasing his fortune.

# SAKUNTALA

*Type of work:* Drama
*Author:* Kalidasa (c. sixth century)
*Type of plot:* Exotic romance
*Time of plot:* Golden Age of India
*Locale:* India
*First presented:* c. sixth century

### Principal characters:

SAKUNTALA, beautiful daughter of a Brahman and a nymph
KANWA, Sakuntala's foster father and a wise hermit
DUSHYANTA, King of India, in love with Sakuntala.
MATHAVYA, the court jester

## Critique:

Kalidasa has been termed the Shakespeare of India, and this particular drama is usually considered his best work. There is little of the realism found in this play that may be found in earlier Hindu drama, such as *The Clay Cart,* done by an unknown author a century or two before *Sakuntala.* The greatness of Kalidasa's drama lies in its tremendous lyric power. The play was originally written in a combination of verse and prose, a form which most modern translators from the original Sanskrit have striven to emulate, though not always successfully. While almost nothing is known of Kalidasa, legend has it that he was the son of a good family of high caste, but that he was abandoned as a baby and reared as a common laborer. In spite of that handicap, says the legend, he became a great poet and dramatist, as well as the favorite of an Indian princess.

## The Story:

Dushyanta, King of India, was hunting one day when his chariot took him into the sacred grounds of a religious establishment. A hermit stopped the king and reminded him that he had sworn to protect the religious people who lived there. The king left his chariot and wandered through the hallowed groves. As he walked, he heard voices and saw three young women passing through the grove to water the plants growing there. When a bee, angered by their presence, flew at her, Sakuntala, not knowing that the king was anywhere near, playfully called on Dushyanta to rescue her.

Dushyanta, stepping from his hiding place, announced himself, not as the king, but as the king's representative appointed to oversee the safety of the grove and its inhabitants. While they talked, Dushyanta learned that Sakuntala was no ordinary maid, but the child of a Brahman and a water nymph. Dushyanta fell in love with her. Sakuntala also felt the first pangs of love for the king and believed that the Hindu cupid had struck her with his five flower-tipped arrows.

Mathavya, the king's jester, complained to his master that too much time was being spent in hunting and that the life was too hard on him. Ostensibly to humor the jester, but actually to have more time to seek out Sakuntala, the king called off any further hunting and ordered his retinue to camp near the sacred grove in which Sakuntala lived with her foster father, a hermit-wiseman named Kanwa. A short time later word came to the camp that the king's mother wished him to return to the capital to take part in certain ceremonies, but Dushyanta was so smitten with love for Sakuntala that he sent his retinue back while he himself, in hopes of seeing Sakuntala again, remained at the sacred grove.

After their first meeting, both the king and Sakuntala had languished with love. At last Dushyanta found excuse and opportunity to revisit the grove, and there he met the girl again. Both were obviously in love, but neither one knew how to tell the other. One of Sakuntala's attendants finally conceived the idea of having her send a love note to the king. As Sakuntala wrote the note, Dushyanta heard her speaking the words aloud. He stepped from his place of concealment and told her of his determination to make her his consort and the head of his household, above all his other wives. Sakuntala left, telling him that she would have to talk over the subject of marriage with her attendants, for her foster father, Kanwa, was absent and so could not give his consent.

Sometime later a scurrilous and eccentric sage came to the sacred grove. He felt himself slighted by Sakuntala, who had not heard of his arrival and so did not accomplish the rites of hospitality to suit him. In his anger he called down a curse upon the girl, though she did not know of it. The curse was that her lover should not remember her until he saw once again the ring of recognition that he would give her. The attendants who heard the curse were afraid to tell Sakuntala for fear she would become ill with worry.

Before Dushyanta left the sacred grove to return to his palace, Sakuntala agreed to a secret marriage and became his wife, but she decided to remain at the grove until the return of her foster father. Before he left, the king gave her a ring, as a sign of her new status. Not long after the king's departure, Kanwa returned. Having the gift of omniscience, he knew all that had taken place, and, as Kanwa reëntered the sacred grove, a supernatural voice told him that Sakuntala should give birth to a son destined to rule the world. Kanwa, thus assured of the future, gave his blessing to the union of Sakuntala and the king. He had his people make the necessary preparations for sending the bride to her husband, to appear as the royal consort.

When the time came for her departure, Sakuntala was filled with regret, for she loved the sacred grove where she had been reared. In addition, she had premonitions that her future was not to be a happy one. Kanwa insisted, however, that she make ready to leave, so that her son could be born in his father's palace.

But when the hermits of the sacred wood appeared in Dushyanta's presence with the girl, the curse proved true, for King Dushyanta failed to remember Sakuntala and his marriage to her. The hermits, feeling that they had done their duty in escorting Sakuntala to her husband, left her in the king's household. Sakuntala, heartbroken at her husband's failure to remember her, looked for the ring of recognition he had given her. But the ring had been lost during the journey from the sacred wood to the palace.

Not long after Dushyanta had sent Sakuntala from his presence, his courtiers came to tell him that a strange, winged being had flown into the palace gardens, picked up Sakuntala, and carried her away into the heavens. The king was much disturbed over the event, but resolved to put it from his mind. Later the ring of recognition, bearing the king's crest, was discovered in the hands of a poor fisherman; he had found it in the belly of a carp. The ring was carried to Dushyanta; no sooner had he set eyes upon it than he remembered Sakuntala and their secret marriage, for the sight of the ring removed the curse.

Remembrance of Sakuntala did him no good; when she had been snatched from the palace garden, she had been lost to mortal eyes. Dushyanta grew sad and refused to be comforted. Meanwhile the nymph who had stolen Sakuntala from the palace garden kept watch and took note of the king's unhappiness. Finally she took pity on him and had the chariot of the god Indra sent down to earth to convey King Dushyanta to heaven for a reunion with Sakuntala.

In heaven the king found a young boy playing with a lion. He was amazed to see what the child was doing and felt a strong attraction for him. While he watched, an amulet fell from the child's neck. The king picked it up and replaced it on the boy's shoulders, much to the surprise of the boy's heavenly attendants, for the amulet was deadly to all but the child's parents. Dushyanta, recognized as the true father, was taken to Sakuntala, who readily forgave her husband, for she had heard the story of the curse. The gods, happy to see the pair reunited, sent them back to earth, along with their little son Bharata, to live many years in happiness together.

# SALAMMBÔ

*Type of work:* Novel
*Author:* Gustave Flaubert (1821-1880)
*Type of plot:* Historical romance
*Time of plot:* Third century B.C.
*Locale:* Carthage
*First published:* 1862

*Principal characters:*
HAMILCAR, Suffete of Carthage
SALAMMBÔ, his daughter
MATHÔ, a Libyan chief
SPENDIUS, a Greek slave
NARR' HAVAS, a Numidian chief

## Critique:

Salammbô is a monumental description of Carthage while that city-republic was still a great power. Into this novel Flaubert put five years of reading, years when he read every scrap of information he could find about Carthage during the Punic Wars. The result is a vast, erudite reconstruction for which there are few parallels. Flaubert was a careful, slow worker, and this novel demonstrates his exact style. Character analysis is scant and the plot little more than animated history, but critical opinion accords it a distinguished place because of its faithful picture of the people and the times.

## The Story:

Inside the walls of Carthage a vast army of mercenaries gathered in the gardens of Hamilcar. There were Ligurians, Lusitanians, nomadic barbarians from North Africa, Romans, Greeks, Gauls, and Egyptians. A feast for these thousands of hired warriors was in preparation. Odors of cooking food came from Hamilcar's kitchens, and the Council of Elders had provided many oxen to roast over the open fires in the gardens. The men, tired from their defeat at the hands of the Romans and weary from the sea journey over the Mediterranean, waited with ill-concealed impatience for the feasting to begin.

More than that, they were in an ugly mood because they had not been paid. Hamilcar, their beloved leader even in defeat, had promised them their pay

many times. The elders, however, parsimonious and afraid of this huge assembly of fierce foreigners, withheld their pay. Offers of token payment had been angrily refused.

While the revelry was at its height, many men were emboldened by drink and began to pillage the palace of Hamilcar. In a private lake, surrounded by a heavy hedge, they found fish with jewels in their gill flaps. With joy they ruthlessly tore off the gems and boiled the sacred fish for their feast. The slaves brought new foods and fresh casks of wine for the drunken revelers. Then above them on a high balcony appeared Salammbô, the priestess of the moon goddess and daughter of Hamilcar. Her great beauty stilled the wild barbarians. She called down a malediction on their heads and in a wailing refrain lamented the sad state of Carthage.

Among those who watched the young girl, none was more attracted than Narr' Havas, a Numidian chief who had been sent by his father to Carthage to serve with Hamilcar. Although he had been in Carthage six months, this was his first sight of Salammbô. Also watching her keenly was Mathô, a gigantic Libyan. He had heard of Salammbô, and already loved her. With Mathô was Spendius, a former Greek slave who, tricky and shrewd, played the jackal to brave Mathô. Spendius had been long in service to Carthage, and he whispered the delights of Salammbô to his master.

The elders gave each soldier a piece of gold if he promised to go to Sicca and wait for the rest of his money to be sent to him. The gold and the solemn promises enticed many, and finally all the mercenaries and barbarians joined the march to Sicca. Many of their leaders distrusted the words of the elders, but they were sure of better treatment when Hamilcar returned to Carthage.

Mathô lay in his tent all day long at Sicca. He was in love, and since he had no prospect of ever seeing Salammbô again, he despaired. Finally the wily Spendius profited greatly by Mathô's inaction and ingratiated himself with the Libyan.

At Sicca the enormous Hanno appeared in his costly litter. Hanno, one of the Council of Elders, was tremendously fat; the fat on his legs even covered his toenails and his body was covered with weeping sores. Pompously he addressed the crowd, telling them of Carthage's intent to pay later and urging them all to return to their homes. But the Gauls and the Campanians and the rest understood not a word of Punic. Spendius leaped up beside Hanno and offered to translate. Falsely he told the soldiers that Hanno was exalting his own gods and reviling theirs. The mob became unruly and Hanno barely escaped with his life.

Soon the inflamed barbarians were on the march again, this time to besiege Carthage. At their head rode Mathô, Narr' Havas, and Spendius, now a leader.

The mob camped at the gates of Carthage. The city sent Gisco, a famous warrior, to treat with them. In fear the Carthaginians raised a little money and began to pay the soldiers. They felt powerless without Hamilcar. But the payment was slow. Gisco had insufficient funds, and many barbarians claimed more pay than they merited.

As the unrest grew, Spendius went to Mathô with a project of his own. He was sure he had found a way into the city, and if Mathô would follow his lead and help him in his own private errand, he would take Mathô to Salammbô.

Outside the walls Spendius had found a loose stone in the pavement over the aqueduct that supplied the city with water. Mathô with his giant strength lifted the stone, and the two swam with the current in the darkness until they came to a reservoir inside the city itself. Then Spendius revealed his project. He and Mathô were to steal the zaïmph, the mysterious veil of Tanit, goddess of the moon. Since the Carthaginians put their trust in Tanit, and Tanit's strength lay in the veil, Spendius hoped to cripple the morale of the city. Mathô was fearful of committing sacrilege, but he was forced to consent in order to see Salammbô.

While the female guards slept, the two stole into Tanit's sanctuary and Mathô seized the veil. Then quietly Spendius led the trembling Mathô, who wore the sacred robe, into Salammbô's sleeping chamber.

As Mathô advanced with words of love to Salammbô's bed, the terrified girl awoke and shouted an alarm. Instantly servants came running. Mathô had to flee, but while he wore the sacred veil no one dared to lay a hand on him. So Mathô left the city and returned to the barbarians with his prize.

Hamilcar returned to Carthage in time to organize the defense of the city, and the siege melted away. Because the barbarians were short of food, they marched to Utica to demand supplies. Only loosely bound to Carthage, Utica was glad to harass Carthage by aiding its enemies.

Newly supplied with arms and food, the barbarians were a more formidable host. Hamilcar, however, had brought his army out of Carthage and joined the battle on the plain. Although the Carthaginians were few in number, they were disciplined and well led. They engaged the barbarians several times, always indecisively. Finally, by a stroke of luck, the army of Hamilcar was trapped, and the barbarian's surrounded the city's defenders.

Meanwhile Salammbô was goaded by the high priest into retrieving the sacred veil. Disguised and with a guide, she made her way into the barbarian camp, under priestly injunction to do whatever might be necessary to reclaim the robe. Finding Mathô's tent, she went in and asked for the veil which hung among his trophies of war. Mathô was thunderstruck and stammered eager protestations of love. Remembering the commands of the priest, Salammbô submitted to Mathô. While the Libyan slept, she took the veil and went unmolested into her father's camp.

Hamilcar noticed immediately that the thin golden chain linking her ankles was broken, and in his shame he promised her to Narr' Havas, who had long since deserted the barbarians and returned to help Hamilcar. But the marriage was delayed until after the final defeat of Hamilcar's enemies.   ·  ·

Hamilcar, wary of the stalemate in the battle, led his followers back to Carthage and the barbarians again laid siege to the city. Spendius sought to end the siege by breaking the aqueduct. Thirst and famine threatened the city from with-in. When pestilence broke out, the children of Carthage were burned in sacrifice to Moloch. Moloch was appeased, and torrential rains saved the city.

With help from his allies, Hamilcar began to reduce the forces of the enemy. A large part of the army was trapped in a defile in the mountains and left to starve. Mathô was taken prisoner.

On the wedding day of Narr' Havas and Salammbô, Mathô was led through the city and tortured by the mob. Still alive but with most of his flesh torn away, he staggered up to the nuptial dais of Salammbô. There he fell dead. Salammbô recalled how he had knelt before her, speaking gentle words. When the drunken Narr' Havas embraced her in token of possession and drank to the greatness of Carthage, she lifted a cup and drank also. A moment later she fell back on the wedding dais, dead. So died the warrior and the priestess who by their touch had profaned the sacred robe of Tanit.

# SAMSON AGONISTES

*Type of work:* Drama
*Author:* John Milton (1608-1674)
*Type of plot:* Heroic tragedy
*Time of plot:* c. 1100 B.C.
*Locale:* Palestine
*First published:* 1671

Principal characters:
SAMSON, Hebrew champion, one of the Judges
MANOA, his father
DALILA, a Philistine woman, Samson's wife
HARAPHA, Philistine giant
CHORUS OF HEBREW ELDERS

*Critique:*

Samson Agonistes is Milton's profound treatment of the Biblical story in the form of the classical Greek tragedy. Although the play, published with *Paradise Regained* in 1671, was not designed for the stage, the author modeled his work on Greek tragedy because he found it "the gravest, moralest, and most profitable of all other poems." The story of Samson is one of the most dramatic episodes in the Old Testament; the parallels between the life of the blind Hebrew hero and his own must have encouraged Milton to base his last work on the story, told in *Judges,* of the man singled out before his birth as a servant of God. Milton opens his play during Samson's imprisonment. He refers frequently to the Biblical accounts of the events of Samson's youth, but the episodes which make up most of the play are his own creation. Each affects Samson's character, renewing his faith in God and influencing his decision to go to the Philistine temple where he dies, according to the Biblical tradition, when he pulls down the roof upon himself and his enemies. *Samson Agonistes* is a powerful and moving drama. The poetry is both majestic and simple, different from the rich verse of *Paradise Lost* and *Paradise Regained,* but perfectly suited to the subject. The play is the masterpiece of an old man, one who has suffered like Samson and who has, in his own way, triumphed over suffering.

*The Story:*

Samson, eyeless in Gaza, had been given a holiday from his labors during the season of a Philistine religious festival. He sat alone before the prison, lamenting his fallen state. His hair had grown long again and his physical strength had returned; but to him life seemed hopeless. Although he wondered why God had chosen him, who seemed destined to live out his days as a miserable, blinded wretch, he nevertheless blamed his misfortunes on himself. He should not have trusted in his strength without the wisdom to protect him from the wiles of Philistine women. He mourned also the blindness which made him live a life that was only half alive.

A chorus of Hebrew elders joined him. They recalled his past great deeds and spoke of the present state of Israel, subject to Philistine rule. Samson accused his people of loving bondage more than liberty because they had refused to take advantage of the victories he won for them in the days of his strength.

Manoa, Samson's aged father, also came to see his son, whose fate had given him great distress. He brought news which plunged Samson still deeper into his mood of depression; the Philistine feast was being given to thank the idol Dagon for delivering the mighty Hebrew into the hands of his enemies. Samson realized then the dishonor he had brought to God, yet he was able to find hope in the thought that the contest now was be-

3332

tween Jehovah and Dagon. He foresaw no good for himself, cast off by God, and he prayed only for speedy death.

As the chorus mused over God's treatment of his chosen ones, Dalila approached. When she offered Samson help as recompense for her betrayal of him, he scorned her. She tried to excuse herself, pleading weakness and patriotism, but Samson refused to compound his sins by yielding to her again; he was regaining spiritual as well as physical might. He again accepted his position as God's champion when Harapha, a Philistine giant, came to gloat over his misfortune. It was too bad that Samson was now so weak, said Harapha; had he met him sooner he would have won great honor by defeating him. But he could not defile himself by combat with a slave. Samson, enraged, invited Harapha to come within his reach. The giant refused to accept the challenge, however, and left.

When a public officer came to summon Samson to the feast, the blind man refused to go. His presence there would violate Hebrew law, and he had no desire to have the Philistine mob make sport of his blindness. But as Samson told the chorus why he would not go, he felt a sudden inner compulsion to follow the messenger. He sensed that the day would mark some remarkable deed in his life. When the officer brought a second summons, and more imperative, Samson accompanied him.

Manoa, returning with the news that he had been able to persuade the Philistine lords to ransom his son, gladly planned to sacrifice his patrimony and spend his old age caring for Samson. Just as he was speaking of his hopes that Samson would recover his sight, horrible shouting broke out in the temple. A Hebrew messenger, fleeing the awful spectacle, told Manoa and the chorus that he had just seen Samson pull the temple down upon himself and thousands of Philistines. Manoa decided that Samson had conducted himself like Samson, and heroically ended a heroic life.

# SANCTUARY

*Type of work:* Novel
*Author:* William Faulkner (1897-1962)
*Type of plot:* Psychological melodrama
*Time of plot:* 1929
*Locale:* Mississippi and Memphis, Tennessee
*First published:* 1931

#### Principal characters:

POPEYE, a racketeer
HORACE BENBOW, a lawyer
TEMPLE DRAKE, a girl attacked and held by Popeye
TOMMY, a moonshiner killed by Popeye
LEE GOODWIN, a moonshiner accused of Tommy's murder
RUBY LAMAR, Goodwin's woman
REBA RIVERS, madam of a Memphis bawdy house
GOWAN STEVENS, a college student

## Critique:

Sanctuary is a harsh and brutal book which on one level reads like a sensational and motiveless recital of horrors enacted by a sinister cast of grotesques and perverts. Beneath its surface violence, however, the novel has a deeper meaning for which an interesting allegorical interpretation has been suggested: The social order of the old South has been corrupted and defiled by progressive modernism and materialistic exploitation, represented by Popeye and his bootlegging activities, so that historic tradition, symbolized by Horace Benbow, is powerless to act because it is opposed by middle-class apathy and inbred violence which victimizes both the Negro and poor white trash. Viewed in this light, Sanctuary is a social document which has its proper place in William Faulkner's tragic legend of the South.

## The Story:

Horace Benbow, on his way to Jefferson one afternoon, stopped to drink from a spring on the Old Frenchman place. When he rose he saw an undersized man in a black suit watching him, the man's hand in a pocket which held his gun. Satisfied at last that the lawyer was not a revenue officer, Popeye led Benbow to the gaunt, gutted ruins of a plantation house. That night the law-

yer ate with Popeye, several moonshiners, and a blind and deaf old man, the father of Lee Goodwin, one of the moonshiners. They were fed by Ruby, Goodwin's woman. Later Benbow was given a lift into Jefferson on a truck loaded with whiskey on its way to Memphis.

The next afternoon, at his widowed sister's home, Benbow watched her walking in the garden with young Gowan Stevens. Stevens left that evening after supper because he had a date with a girl at the State University the following night. The girl was Temple Drake.

After a dance Stevens got drunk. He awoke the next morning in front of the railroad station. A special train taking university students to a baseball game had already left. Driving rapidly, Stevens caught up with the train in the next town. Temple jumped from the train and climbed into his car. Disgusted with his disheveled appearance, she ordered him to drive her back to the university. Stevens insisted that he had promised to drive her to the game. On the way he decided to stop at Goodwin's place to buy more whiskey.

Stevens wrecked his car when he struck a barrier across the lane leading to the house. Popeye took Temple and Stevens to the house. Temple went into the kitchen, where Ruby sat smoking and watching the door.

When she saw Stevens again, he was drunk. Then Popeye refused to drive them back to town. Temple was frightened. Ruby told Temple to go into the dining-room to eat with the men.

One of the men tried to seize her and Temple ran from the room. Tommy, one of the moonshiners, followed her with a plate of food. The men began to quarrel and Stevens was knocked unconscious and carried into the house. Goodwin and a moonshiner named Van tussled until Popeye stopped them. When Van found Temple in one of the bedrooms, Goodwin knocked him down.

Then began a series of comings and goings in the bedroom. Ruby came to stand quietly in the darkness. Later Popeye appeared and stood silently over the girl. After he had gone, Goodwin entered to claim a raincoat in which Temple had wrapped herself. Popeye returned once more, followed noiselessly by Tommy, who squatted in the dark beside Ruby. When the men finally left the house to load the truck for its run to Memphis, Ruby took Temple out to the barn and stayed with her until daylight.

Stevens awoke early and started out for the nearest house to hire a car. Feeling that he could not face Temple again after his drunken night, he paid a farmer to drive to the house for Temple, while he thumbed a ride into town.

Learning that Stevens had already gone, Temple went into the kitchen with Ruby. When she left the house again, she saw the shadowy outline of a man who was squatting in the bushes and watching her. She returned to the house. Seeing Goodwin coming toward the house, she ran to the barn and hid in the corncrib.

Watching, Popeye saw Goodwin looking from the house toward the barn. In the barn Popeye found Tommy at the door of the corncrib. While Tommy stood watching Goodwin, Popeye shot him. A short time later Goodwin told Ruby that Tommy had been shot. He

sent her to the nearest house to phone for the sheriff.

Benbow stayed with his sister for two days. When Goodwin was brought in, charged with Tommy's murder, Benbow agreed to defend the prisoner. Goodwin, afraid of Popeye, claimed only that he had not shot Tommy. It was Ruby who told Benbow that Popeye had taken Temple away in his car.

Benbow attempted to trace the girl's whereabouts. State Senator Snopes told him that Judge Drake's daughter was supposed to be visiting an aunt in Michigan after an attempted runaway marriage.

A week before the opening of the court session Benbow met Senator Snopes again. For a price the politician was willing to reveal that Temple was in Reba Rivers' bawdy house in Memphis. Benbow went at once to see the girl. Temple, although reluctant to talk, confirmed many details of Ruby's story. The lawyer realized that without the girl's testimony he could not prove that Goodwin was innocent of Popeye's crime.

One morning Temple bribed Reba's colored servant to let her out of the house to make a phone call. That evening she managed to sneak out again, just as a car with Popeye in it pulled up at the curb. When she refused to go back to her room, he took her to the Grotto, where Temple had arranged to meet a young man called Red, whom Popeye had taken to her room.

At the Grotto she danced with Red while Popeye played at the crap table. She begged Red to take her away with him. Later in the evening two of Popeye's henchmen forced Temple into a car waiting outside. As they drove away, Temple saw Popeye sitting in a parked car.

Red's funeral was held in the Grotto. For the occasion the tables had been draped in black and a downtown orchestra had been hired to play hymns. Drinks were on the house.

The night before the trial Benbow learned from Reba Rivers that Popeye and Temple had left her house. Ruby took the witness stand the next day and she told the story of Tommy's murder. She and Benbow spent that night in the jail cell with Goodwin, who was afraid that Popeye might shoot him from one of the buildings across the street.

Temple, located through the efforts of Senator Snopes, was called to testify the next morning. She indicated that Goodwin was the man who had first attacked her on the day of Tommy's murder. Goodwin was convicted. That night a mob dragged the prisoner from the jail and burned him.

Popeye, on his way to Pensacola, was arrested for the murder of a policeman in Birmingham. The murder had occurred the same night Red was shot outside the Grotto. Popeye made no defense, and his only claim was that he knew nothing about the Birmingham shooting. Convicted, he was executed for a crime he had not committed.

Judge Drake took his daughter to Europe. In the Luxembourg Gardens with her father, listening in boredom to the band, Temple sat in quiet, sullen discontent.

# SANDFORD AND MERTON

*Type of work*: Novel
*Author*: Thomas Day (1748-1789)
*Type of plot*: Didactic romance
*Time of plot*: Late eighteenth century
*Locale*: England
*First published*: 1783-1789

> *Principal characters*:
> HARRY SANDFORD, a farmer's son
> TOMMY MERTON, a gentleman's son
> MR. BARLOW, a clergyman, teacher of Sandford and Merton
> MR. MERTON, a very sensible gentleman, Tommy's father

*Critique*:

This novel is one of those which during the eighteenth century appeared in England to popularize certain social theories which were originating in France. The theory which *Sandford and Merton* attempted to promulgate was that of education by example rather than coercion: the same theme had been presented in Rousseau's *Émile,* which had been published in France twenty-one years earlier. In Thomas Day's novel the reader finds also the belief that a proximity to nature is one of the ingredients of a healthy personality. Little Harry Sandford, a farmer's son, having been in contact with nature in his most formative years, is healthy, kindly, and sensible; young Tommy Merton, on the other hand, enters the novel with a background of artificiality and is a headstrong weakling. Like most novels of doctrine, this one depends for its force upon its didactic elements.

*The Story*:

Little Tommy Merton was a headstrong, ill-tempered, and weak lad when he returned with his family to England from Jamaica. His first years had been spent in the company of slaves who pampered his whims, and his mother, who could see no wrong in her child, condoned everything he said or did. The child had no inclination to study, and so he could not read, write, or do arithmetic when he arrived in England. Mr. Merton, who was very wealthy, wished to improve his son, but he was at a loss to know where to begin.

Thanks to a lucky chance, Mr. Merton's problem solved itself. One day, when Tommy Merton was walking through the fields, a snake coiled itself about his leg. Only the timely appearance of a farmer boy, who tore the snake from Tommy's leg, prevented serious injury. As a reward for his brave action, the farm boy, Harry Sandford, was invited to the Merton mansion for dinner. During the meal he greatly displeased Mrs. Merton, for he refused to believe that the artificialities of the Merton home and all the paraphernalia of the rich were really worth-while. But his philosophic attitude interested Mr. Merton, who, upon inquiry, learned that Harry Sandford was under the tutelage of the local clergyman, Mr. Barlow. Thinking that his son needed some training to make him a better social being, Mr. Merton made arrangements for Tommy to be boarded at Mr. Barlow's vicarage and educated with little Harry.

The first few days at the vicarage were trying ones for Tommy. When he refused to help with the gardening, Mr. Barlow refused to let him eat. Then, when he went into tantrums, no one paid the least bit of attention to him. Gradually he learned that getting on in the world took greater abilities than simply demanding whatever one wanted. Under the tutelage of Mr. Barlow, and with the example of Harry, he began to take an interest in what was going on about him. He became ashamed that he did not know how to read, and with great effort he taught himself to do so. His desire was to read stories aloud, as Harry did. By means of these stories Mr. Barlow imparted a great deal of information to the children.

From their reading the boys also got ideas for various projects. They embarked for example, on the building of a hut, to see if they could build one that would protect them from the weather, after they had read of sailors being cast away on islands which were uninhabited. Tommy also became interested in gardening after he learned that bread did not simply happen on the table at mealtimes. From the gardening he went on to visit, along with Mr. Barlow and Harry, a mill where the grain was ground to make flour. These processes he had never even heard of in his earlier years when he was pampered as a rich man's son.

The first sign of generosity on the part of Tommy came when he and Harry were befriended by a poor woman who gave them some lunch one day after they had strayed from home. While the boys were in the cottage, bailiffs came to take away the family's belongings to settle a bill that the father of the family had signed for a relative. Little Tommy went to his father and got the money, a relatively large sum, and gave it to the man and his wife. Keeping his generosity a secret from his family, he said that he would save the money out of his allowance, a sizeable one, and pay it back to his father. When the secret was finally made known by the poor people, Mr. Merton was very pleased, not only with his son but also with the instruction he was getting from Mr. Barlow and Harry.

After some months had passed, Tommy went home for a vacation and took Harry with him. The guests at the Merton house, astonished and displeased that a gentleman's son should be permitted the companionship of a farmer's son, showed their disapproval. Other children at the house, imitating the grownups, made life miserable for Harry, who took their malice with the best possible grace, even when Tommy, whom he thought his best friend, turned against him. One day a group of youngsters disobeyed their parents and went to a bull-baiting. Harry tried to dissuade them from going, but he received only blows and ill will for his efforts. At the bull-baiting the infuriated animal broke its tether and ran amuck. Only quick thinking on the part of Harry and a colored beggar saved Tommy's life.

After saving Tommy's life, Harry and the Negro went to Harry's father's farm. The other children tried to blame Harry for their having gone to the bull-baiting, but the truth came out and little Harry was the hero of the day. As much as he had been the underdog before, he became the hero of the adults and the children. Tommy asked Harry's forgiveness and apologized for his selfish and proud behavior. Harry, of course, forgave him.

One day Tommy, while on a walk by himself, saw a lamb attacked by a dog. Tommy rescued the lamb, although he himself had to be rescued by a Highlander who happened along the road. Filled with gratitude, Tommy took the Highlander and his motherless children home, where the Scots were given a hearty meal. After dinner the Highlander told of his adventures while serving as a soldier in America. As he told his story, it came out that he was a friend of an officer in America who was related to one of the Mertons' guests. Because of his help in rescuing Tommy and the lamb, as well as his connection with the guest's relative, the Highlander was given employment on one of Mr. Merton's farms.

By that time Mr. Merton was convinced that Harry Sanford and Mr. Barlow had changed his son into a healthy, generous, straight-thinking young lad. It was time, however, for Tommy to begin a more formal education. Mr. Merton went to the Sandford farm to make a present of a large sum of money to Mr. Sandford for what Harry had done. Mr. Sandford, a virtuous, self-sufficient man, refused to accept payment, saying that he had got along well without it and that he was afraid it would only cause trouble in his household, where heretofore everyone had been content. He did, however, agree to accept a fine team of workhorses. When Tommy left with Mr. Merton, he told Harry that he would look forward to seeing him as often as possible, for he realized that Harry had taught him how to be sincere and useful, not merely a gentleman's son.

# SANINE

*Type of work:* Novel
*Author:* Mikhail Artsybashev (1878-1927)
*Type of plot:* Philosophical romance
*Time of plot:* 1906
*Locale:* Russia
*First published:* 1907

Principal characters:
> VLADIMIR PETROVITCH SANINE, an individualistic young Russian
> LIDIA (LIDA) PETROVNA, his sister
> MARIA IVANOVNA, his mother
> CAPTAIN SARUDINE, in love with Lida
> DR. NOVIKOFF, also in love with Lida
> SINA KARSAVINA, briefly the mistress of Sanine
> YOURII NICOLAIJEVITSCH SVAROGITSCH, in love with Sina Karsavina

## Critique:

Following the abortive revolution of 1905, many of the Russian intelligentsia made hedonism a popular cult, with pleasure and freedom from sexual morality the hallmarks of their changed attitudes. Artsybashev, in *Sanine* (the English variant of the Russian *Sanin*), took advantage of the prevalent climate of opinion and with this novel achieved great popularity—even notoriety—both in Russia and abroad. While critics of Russian literature have refused to grant greatness to the book or its author, students of Russian history have felt that *Sanine* not only mirrored the lapse in morality in Russia at the time of its publication but that it actually contributed to that lapse. The novel can best be described by saying that it preaches a kind of nihilism as the only satisfactory answer to human life. It has been termed a sermon based on the text of being one's self and following one's inclinations. *Sanine,* the first novel written by Artsybashev, is typical of his plays, short stories, and novels in its treatment of brutality, death (especially suicide), and sexual irregularity.

## The Story:

During the formative years of his life Vladimir Petrovitch Sanine was away from the influence of his family and their home. When he returned, a young man, to his mother's house in a provincial garrison town, he came as a person believing only in himself, his strength, and the desirability of following his inclinations wherever they might lead him. His mother, Maria Ivanovna, could not understand her son. His sister Lida, however, found him strangely attractive, even though she distrusted and feared his thinking and its influence.

Lida, having many admirers among young civilians and the junior army officers, was the belle of the little garrison town. Her two most serious admirers were Dr. Novikoff, who wished sincerely to marry her but was awkward as a suitor, and Captain Sarudine, a brutal and lascivious army officer who wished only to make a sexual conquest and was well on his way to success with the young woman. Sanine, giving the same freedoms to others as he believed in for himself, made no serious attempt to interfere in his sister's affairs.

Before long Sanine was caught up in the social life among the young intelligentsia of the town. Among those in the group were Sina Karsavina and Yourii Svarogitsch. The former was a pretty young schoolteacher of strong emotions who found herself drawn strangely to Sanine, although she was very much in love with Yourii, a young student who had been exiled to the provinces for his part in revolutionary activities. Although

SANINE by Mikhail Artsybashev. Translated by Percy Pinkerton. By permission of the publishers, The Viking Press, Inc. Copyright, 1926, by The Viking Press, Inc. Renewed. All rights reserved.

attracted to Sina, Yourii felt that his political duties and ambitions would be hampered if he were married. Because of his beliefs in political duty, and because of bashfulness as well, he tried to avoid becoming emotionally involved with the young schoolteacher.

As the weeks passed, Lida was drawn closer to Captain Sarudine. So strong was his physical attraction that she refused a proposal of marriage from Dr. Novikoff, whose jealousy almost became hate. Soon afterward Lida became Captain Sarudine's mistress. Discovering that she was pregnant, she turned for help to her lover, only to learn that he was now finished with her, having made his conquest. Lida, distraught, thought of drowning herself, but she was found by her brother in time. He convinced her that she needed to live and that she should become Dr. Novikoff's wife. Having his sister's agreement, Sanine went to Dr. Novikoff, who was about to leave the town. Little persuasion was needed, even with a knowledge of the facts, to get the doctor's agreement to marry Lida.

About this time Captain Sarudine had a visitor from St. Petersburg. When Captain Sarudine and his friend paid a visit to the Sanine home so that the officer might show off the beautiful woman he had seduced, Sanine ordered the captain to leave the house and suggested further that he leave town. Captain Sarudine, true to the code of his corps, challenged Sanine to a duel. Because he believed that dueling proved nothing, the young man refused the challenge. He learned that his sister, on the other hand, expected him to fight the duel. Realizing that his sister, like his mother, was a conformist to opinion and tradition, Sanine felt alienated from them because of their attitudes and their failure to understand his ideas.

Even more angered by the refusal of his challenge, Captain Sarudine feared that his failure to avenge his honor might put him in a disgraceful position with his brother officers. That he had disgraced himself in some people's eyes by his treatment of Lida did not enter his mind.

One evening, as Sanine and some friends were strolling along the boulevard, they unexpectedly met Captain Sarudine and several of his brother officers. Captain Sarudine spoke harshly to Sanine and threatened him with a riding crop. Sanine, in self defense, knocked down the officer with his fist. Captain Sarudine, not much hurt physically but humiliated by the indignity of the blow, almost went out of his mind. Taken back to his quarters, he refused to see even his friends or his orderly.

After the brief but violent encounter Sanine walked home with a Jewish friend, Soloveitchik. The two sat for a long time discussing human life and its meaning. Sanine refused to accept any blame for his behavior, even though he might have ruined Captain Sarudine's career and life. The Jew asked Sanine if a man who worried and thought too much might not be better off dead. Sanine replied that a man or woman who could not enjoy life was already dead. Shortly afterward he left. On his way home he met Captain Sarudine's orderly, who informed him that the officer had committed suicide by shooting himself. The next morning word came, too, that Soloveitchik had hanged himself. The two sudden deaths caused a great furor in the little town, but Sanine steadfastly refused to admit that he was in any way responsible.

One morning Yourii received a letter from Sina asking him to meet her at a monastery near the town. He met her as requested, and a tender but awkward love scene ensued. Because Yourii hated to admit he needed the girl, his conscience bothered him in strange ways. When Sina was suddenly called back to town that evening, Sanine, who was also visiting at the monastery, offered to escort her. On the way both Sanine and the girl were overcome by their emotions, and she surrendered to him. Though she was much upset afterward, she decided that the best thing for her to do was forget what had happened. In the meantime Yourii's sister tried to persuade her brother to marry.

3341

The problems that marriage raised for him were so great that the young man could not face them, and he shot himself. At the funeral Sanine, asked to say a few words, declared that there was one fool less in the world. His response horrified everyone. Soon afterward Sanine left the town again by train. Early one morning, as the train was crossing the plains, he jumped off to glory in the beauty of an autumn sunrise.

# SAPPHO

*Type of work:* Novel
*Author:* Alphonse Daudet (1840-1897)
*Type of plot:* Naturalism
*Time of plot:* Nineteenth century
*Locale:* Paris
*First published:* 1884

> *Principal characters:*
> JEAN GAUSSIN, a student
> FANNY LEGRAND, his mistress
> IRÈNE, his fiancée
> BOUCHEREAU, a famous physiologist
> DÉCHELETTE, a wealthy engineer
> LaGOURNERIE, a poet
> DE POTTER, a composer
> ROSA, de Potter's mistress
> FLAMANT, convict engraver
> CÉSAIRE, Jean's uncle

*Critique:*

To many people Daudet's name is a synonym for naturalism, and in some respects Daudet is the outstanding representative of his school. His writing is carefully documented; his style releases a sustained emotion. Above all Daudet is an intuitive psychologist. *Sappho,* concerned with the half-world of prostitutes and crime, is generally considered a surprisingly delicate and sure study of a distasteful milieu.

*The Story:*

Déchelette, a vigorous though aging engineer, spent all but two months of the year on construction projects far from Paris. Each summer, however, he returned to the gay city to compress into two months enough pleasure to make up for his enforced absences. To one of his masquerade parties came Jean Gaussin, a young student from the south of France. Jean was bewildered at the extravagant ball. Unhappy and lost, he wandered into a gallery and found there a woman dressed as an Egyptian.

When he was ready to leave, the woman stopped him and asked him to take her to his room. In this way he became her lover. Her name, she told him, was Fanny Legrand.

She continued to come to his room frequently. When he finally visited her apartment, he was astonished at the luxury of the place. In the morning before he was up, the servant announced a visitor. Fanny went into another room to see the early caller, and Jean was horrified to overhear a violent quarrel. Fanny was shouting insults and curses at the man in the language of the gutter. Finally the man began to sob and pressed money on Fanny. He begged her not to dismiss him, whatever else she did. Jean went back to his classes much disturbed.

Unable to end the affair, he rented an apartment and set up housekeeping with Fanny. She proved to be a capable housewife and a demanding mistress. Jean felt settled and at ease. He made good progress in his consular studies.

The following summer he met Déchelette and Caoudal, a sculptor, at a café and learned the past history of his mistress. Thirty years before, she had lived with Caoudal and had been the model for his well-known figure of Sappho. She had lived with Déchelette at various times and LaGournerie, the poet, had kept her for some years. Jean felt nauseated when he came to understand that she owed her imaginative diction to LaGournerie, her graceful gestures to Caoudal, her ample spending money to Déchelette. One of her latest lovers had been Flamant. The poor man, an engraver, had counterfeited some bank notes and had been sentenced to prison. Jean learned that Fanny was nearly fifty, almost thirty years older than he.

When he taxed Fanny with his knowledge, she readily admitted her past. When she protested her love for him alone, Jean asked for her box of keepsakes. In her letters he traced her history of loose love for nearly thirty years. The farewell letter from Flamant asked Fanny to look after his young son. Jean suspected that the child was Fanny's also. But in spite of this knowledge, Jean could not leave his mistress after Fanny meekly submitted to his reproaches. They continued to live together.

Césaire, Jean's uncle, came to Paris with news that Jean's family had been ruined by failure of the grape crop and that he had been sent to Paris to collect an old debt of eight thousand francs. With Fanny's help, Césaire collected the money but soon lost it gambling. Fanny volunteered to get more money from Déchelette. Jean and Césaire awaited her return anxiously. Jean tortured himself by imagining how she would get it. After some hours Fanny returned with the money. Césaire left for home, loudly asserting the goodness of Fanny and promising to keep silent about Jean's loose life.

With the decline in the Gaussin fortunes, Jean and Fanny decided to separate. Fanny went to work managing an apartment for Rosa, mistress of the wealthy composer, de Potter. She and Jean were together each Sunday on her day off. After reckoning his decreased allowance, Jean found that they could take a small hut in the country. He was sure they could exist there for another year, and then he would be through with his course of study. But Jean hated their life in the country. The grumbling old servant Fanny hired had been revealed as Fanny's mother. Her father, a dissolute cab driver, came to visit them. Flamant's child, a savage boy of six, lived with them. Jean counted on an appointment to a consular office to break away from Fanny.

On his trips into town, he became acquainted with Bouchereau, the eminent physiologist. Then he met and fell in love with Bouchereau's niece, Irène. Jean hoped that he would receive an appointment in South America and that Irène would go with him as his wife.

As he was gradually permitted to see Irène more often, Jean became troubled. Her innocent enjoyment of simple things was disturbing, for he had become so satiated with his experienced courtesan that other women had little attraction for him. When he told Fanny of his approaching marriage, a furious quarrel broke out.

Shortly afterward Jean met de Potter, who congratulated him on his approaching marriage. De Potter's story was a horrible warning to Jean; the composer had never been able to get away from his mistress, and the attraction of her flesh had held him fast for many years. De Potter's wife rarely saw him; his children were almost strangers. De Potter was bitter about his wasted life, but he could not leave the aging Rosa, whom he supported in luxury.

Despite de Potter's example, despite his engagement to Irène, Jean resolved to keep Fanny. On the eve of his departure for his post in South America, he broke his engagement to Irène and wrote to Fanny to join him in Marseilles. Waiting with tense expectancy in a hotel room in the Mediterranean port, Jean received a letter from Fanny. She had gone back with Flamant on his release from prison. Fanny was too old to go traveling about. She could not leave her beloved Paris.

# SAPPHO

*Type of work:* Drama
*Author:* Franz Grillparzer (1791-1872)
*Type of plot:* Romantic tragedy
*Time of plot:* Sixth century B.C.
*Locale:* The island of Lesbos
*First presented:* 1818

Principal characters:
SAPPHO, the renowned Greek poetess
PHAON, a young man loved by Sappho
MELITTA, Sappho's young and beautiful slave
RHAMNES, an elderly male slave owned by Sappho

*Critique:*

The legend that Sappho hurled herself to her death from the Leucadian rock when her love was spurned by a young man named Phaon has persisted through the centuries, although there seems to be no historical foundation for the legend. Using this tale as his starting point, Franz Grillparzer wrote a play that goes beyond a mere love story in several ways. Sappho is portrayed in the drama as the victim of love for a man, many years her junior, who turns to love a woman his own age. Sappho is also presented as a poetic genius who cannot meet the demands of ordinary mortal love and domestic relations. Finally, realizing that she cannot meet those demands, she foregoes love to hurl herself to her death, seeking not vengeance or escape, but rather trying to find her place among the immortals. The conflict within Sappho between the demands of love and genius probably reflects the fact that Grillparzer himself believed, as a result of personal experience, that the two conflicting forces were incompatible. The central aspect of the play is really to be found in Phaon's error in mistaking his love of her poetic genius for love of Sappho the woman.

*The Story:*

Sappho, beloved by all and treated as the queen of her native island of Lesbos, went to Olympia to compete for the prize to be awarded for poetry and song. Because of her genius she won the laurel wreath accorded the victor and returned in triumph to her island home. To her countrymen's surprise she brought with her on her return a handsome, pleasant, but very young man named Phaon, with whom she had fallen deeply in love. Phaon, having heard the poems of Sappho read in his father's home, had great admiration for the poetess before he journeyed to Olympia to compete in the games as a charioteer. There he and Sappho had met and fallen in love.

Phaon, a young man simple in his tastes, was almost overwhelmed by Sappho's home, her way of life, and her place of importance on the island. Sappho, deeply in love with Phaon, tried to make him comfortable and at ease in his new environment by constantly expressing her love for him and telling him how much he meant to her happiness.

In Sappho's household was a very beautiful young female slave named Melitta, taken into Sappho's home when the slave was a small child. For some years the girl had been very close to her mistress. On Sappho's return from Olympia she suddenly realized that the child had become a woman. Realization of the change caused Sappho some pangs, for it brought home the fact that Sappho herself was no longer young. For the first time the poetess wished she were younger again, for the sake of Phaon.

One day Phaon, who still was uncomfortable in the luxurious household of his mistress, found refuge in a grotto from the noisy merrymaking of Sappho's guests. While he was enjoying the silence of the place, Melitta wandered nearby, having been sent to the gardens to pick some flowers. As she walked along she voiced her grief at being a slave in a foreign land, lonely for a home and family. Phaon, hearing the girl's lamentations, was greatly moved, for he too was lonesome in a strange land. He went to the slave girl and tried to cheer her. The climax of their interview was a kiss, observed by Sappho as she came looking for Phaon. Upset, she left Phaon to himself for a time. Later she found him asleep in the grotto and awakened him with a kiss. As he awoke, Phaon murmured Melitta's name. Fully awake, he told Sappho of a dream in which he saw himself in love with Melitta, who had usurped the place of Sappho. Sappho told him not to believe in lying dreams.

Although she concealed the fact from him, Sappho's pride was badly hurt by his account of the dream and by the kiss she had seen him bestow upon Melitta. Coming upon Melitta, Sappho accused the girl of maliciously trying to steal Phaon's love. After heated words had passed between the mistress and her slave, Sappho drew a dagger and threatened Melitta's life. Phaon's appearance probably saved the girl from injury at Sappho's hands. Phaon then announced his love for the slave girl and accused Sappho of trying to weave magic spells with her poetry to make him believe he loved her.

Later that same day Sappho called her most trusted slave, Rhamnes, to her and commanded him to take Melitta away from Lesbos to Chios, across the sea, to be placed in the household of one of Sappho's friends. That night Rhamnes tried to lure the girl from her quarters to a boat on the beach. Melitta, suspecting a trap, protested.

Phaon, fearful for Melitta's safety, had remained awake and had heard Rhamnes enter Melitta's quarters. When he discovered Rhamnes' trickery, he made him relinquish the girl.

Alarmed by what had happened, Phaon decided to flee Lesbos and Sappho's household. Taking Melitta with him, he embarked in the boat Rhamnes had planned to use in spiriting the girl away.

As soon as he was free of the threat of Phaon's dagger, Rhamnes sounded the alarm and told of Phaon's flight with Melitta. Planning revenge, Sappho called the people of the island to her and promised a handsome reward of gold for the return of the fugitives. Spurred by the reward and their love for Sappho, the islanders hurried after Phaon and Melitta. When they came up with the fugitives upon the sea, Melitta was struck on the head by an oar during the struggle. Phaon then yielded to their captors.

Back in the house of Sappho, Phaon demanded to know why she should be given the privilege of judging him, as if she were a queen. The islanders told him that they regarded her as their queen. Sappho demanded the return of Melitta, but Phaon said that in threatening the slave girl's life Sappho had relinquished all her rights to the girl. Sappho then accused Phaon of being a deceiver in love. Phaon defended himself by saying that he had been mistaken in his love, that the love he had felt for Sappho was love of her genius. He added that he had really loved her as a goddess, not as a woman, not knowing the difference, he claimed, until after he had met and fallen in love with Melitta.

Sappho was disturbed by what had happened and by what Phaon had said. At first, thinking that she was being asked too great a price for having poetic gifts, she wished to disown her genius in order to live and love as an ordinary mortal woman. She left the company to think in solitude. As she looked out across the sea, her lyre suddenly clanged loudly, as if warning her, and she decided not to try to escape the genius given her by the gods. She asked the gods only to keep her from being an object of men's derision. Returning, she forgave the young lovers with a kiss and then walked to an altar of Aphrodite which stood on a cliff overlooking the sea. Calling upon the gods to take her to them, Sappho hurled herself over the brink into the water below. Phaon and Sappho's people ran to rescue her, but they were too late. The ocean currents had dashed her to her death against the rocks.

# SARAGOSSA

*Type of work:* Novel
*Author:* Benito Pérez Galdós (1845-1920)
*Type of plot:* Historical romance
*Time of plot:* 1808-1809
*Locale:* Spain
*First published:* 1874

> *Principal characters:*
> Don José de Montoria, a Spanish patriot
> Augustine de Montoria, his son
> Araceli, Augustine's friend
> Candiola, a miser
> Mariquilla, his daughter

## Critique:

*Saragossa* is one of a series of novels by Galdós which cover the period of Spain's wars with Napoleon. Here the story of the second siege of Saragossa is presented as a historic example of Spanish patriotism. Because of its dramatic scenes and accurate descriptions of the siege, the novel has been ranked by some critics with the better-known work of Zola and Tolstoy.

## The Story:·

The French armies of Napoleon had laid siege to Saragossa from mid-June to mid-August in the year 1808. Although the city had defended itself so bravely that the French finally withdrew, the people of Saragossa knew that Napoleon would never leave them in peace until he had conquered them. When warnings of a second siege came early in December of the same year, citizens of the town were not surprised. The fame of the first defense of Saragossa had spread over all Spain, and many men went to aid the city in the coming struggle. Among these was Araceli, a young man well-known to a brave Saragossan, Don José de Montoria.

Don José, delighted to have Araceli in Saragossa, enrolled him in the battalion of the Peñas of San Pedro. Don José himself had two sons, Manuel and Augustine. Manuel, the older, was to carry on the family line. Augustine was to enter the Church. Araceli quickly made friends with Augustine and discovered that the boy was a better soldier than he was a theological student.

When French troops began their attack on the city, Augustine and Araceli fought side by side in the front lines. During the first days of the siege everything seemed to be going well for the defenders. One night, when the two were off duty, Augustine told Araceli about his love for Mariquilla, daughter of the old miser, Candiola. Augustine knew that he was destined for the Church, but he also knew that he and Mariquilla loved each other. During the first siege Candiola had won the enmity of everyone because he had done nothing to help the town, and Augustine did not dare tell his family that he loved the miser's daughter. The two tried to see the girl secretly that night but, as they were about to be let into the garden of her house by a maid, Candiola appeared and they had to leave.

The fighting continued, neither side making much headway until the French attacked the Redoubt del Pilar and finally breached the walls. As the Spanish defenders prepared to retire, they saw that someone had mounted the walls and was trying to hold back the French alone. When the soldiers saw that this brave person was a girl, Manuela Sancho, they were inspired to hold their positions. The fortification did not fall that day.

As the battle for the city went on, food and materials of war became scarce. Don José was authorized to seize any wheat that he could find and pay a stipulated sum for it. Because Candiola was known to have a large supply of grain in his house, Don José went there to get it. But Candiola refused to sell the wheat at the price offered. Angry, Don José knocked the old man down and ordered the soldiers to take the wheat. Mariquilla, rushing from the house, tried to protect her father, who lay shaking in the dust. When Don José offered her the money he had been ordered to pay for the wheat, she took it and threw it in his face.

A few days later Augustine and Araceli visited Mariquilla at night. The girl's first words to Augustine were about the man who had struck her father, for she did not know that Augustine was Don José's son. Augustine was at a loss for something to say. Mariquilla loved her father despite his faults, and Augustine could not let her know that it had been his father who had struck the old miser. A few days later, after Candiola's house had been hit by a bomb, Augustine and Araceli rushed to the spot to see if any harm had come to Mariquilla. They found the family safe, but the house was in ruins. Candiola was disgusting in his concern over his lost treasures in the very face of the dead about him, and he refused to leave his house for fear looters would steal something from the rubble. Augustine arranged to have Mariquilla stay with the brave Manuela Sancho.

Meanwhile the French had broken into the city, and the defenders fought from street to street, from house to house. During the fighting Manuel de Montoria was killed. The tragedy worked a great change in Don José. When he met Candiola in the street, he asked to be forgiven for striking him, but Candiola would not forgive the insult. During their conversation Candiola charged that Don José's son had led his daughter astray by taking her to nurse the wounded and care for the sick.

The next day Augustine and Mariquilla were sitting together on a sidewalk talking over the plans for their marriage

after the war was over. Araceli joined them. All thought they could hear sounds of digging under them. For the past several weeks the French had been trying to dig tunnels under the city to aid them in blowing up strategic buildings, but the defenders had dug as many tunnels in defense and felt sure that all was protected from surprise. The three investigated as well as they could, but decided that a tunnel at that spot would be of no danger to the city.

The next day the convent of San Francisco in the center of the city was destroyed. The Saragossans soon discovered that the French had penetrated to the convent through a tunnel from Candiola's house, to which the miser had guided the enemy. The town demanded death for the traitor.

As soon as she heard that her father was to be killed, Mariquilla left the hospital where she had been working and went to look for Augustine. Sure that her father was innocent, she begged Augustine to save Candiola. At that moment Don José appeared and Mariquilla learned that Augustine was his son. When she learned further that Augustine was in charge of the firing squad for Candiola's execution, she threw herself at his feet and again begged him to spare her father's life. Don José told his son to remember the cause for which he fought. Torn between love and honor, Augustine broke his sword and walked away. Mariquilla, overcome with grief, was befriended by sympathetic spectators.

Still Saragossa held out. Weeks dragged by. Finally, on the twenty-first of February, 1809, the city was forced to surrender. Hardly a wall stood to shelter the defenders.

A few days later Araceli was accosted by a man he scarcely recognized. It was Augustine, come to entreat his friend to help dig a grave for Mariquilla, who had died neither of war nor of the plague, but of grief. Don José came up to them and begged his son to forget the girl now that she was dead, and to come back to his family and carry on the Montoria name. But Augustine told his father that he intended to enter a monastery as soon as he had finished with Mariquilla's grave. Thus ended Don José's hopes for his family. Araceli left the destroyed city of Saragossa, the lesson of its bravery still deep in his heart when in other cities, in later days, he continued the fight for Spanish freedom.

# SARTOR RESARTUS

*Type of work:* Philosophical satire
*Author:* Thomas Carlyle (1795-1881)
*First published:* 1835

This ecstatic, involved work—"The Life and Opinions of Herr Teufelsdröckh," to quote its subtitle—is in many ways one of the most characteristic works of Thomas Carlyle, the "sage of Chelsea" and a crusty censor of the optimistic Victorian era.

Carlyle, a familiar gibe has it, preached the virtues of silence in a long series of volumes. *Sartor Resartus* ("the tailor reclothed") is an early preachment on silence, work, duty, and the world as spirit. These were topics that Carlyle was never able to abstain from, whether he was writing about a medieval abbot (*Past and Present*), about heroes (*On Heroes, Hero-Worship, and the Heroic in History*), or about fairly recent historical events (*The French Revolution*). Of Carlyle it is fair to paraphrase and say: Scratch the historian, and you will find the prophet. In *Sartor Resartus*, at any rate, Carlyle is nearly all prophet.

In a style that is crabbed, Germanic, allusive, ironic, hectoring, and paradoxical, Carlyle gave to the age of the Reform Bill (1832), John Stuart Mill, utilitarianism, and the Industrial Revolution the "gospel" he thought it needed. It was a message that, in Carlyle's opinion, the age was likely to overlook. Historically, this is one reason why *Sartor Resartus* and other of his works are worthy of attention today.

*Sartor Resartus* is a title pointing to the "clothes-philosophy" at the center of the book. But no reader reaches the center of the book without penetrating the formidable framework and bastion of mystification both playful and perverse that Carlyle sets up in early chapters. Carlyle, already an admirer, translator, and popularizer of German literature when he began this work, writes much of the time as if in his own person. That is, he is supposedly the English editor

who has been faced with the task of rearranging and commenting upon the mss. contents of six paper sacks which have come to him from Germany. These sacks contain the disorderly, fervid lucubrations of a learned German philosopher named Teufelsdröckh (literally, "Devil's-dung"). Out of these scrambled materials, the English "editor" and interpreter wishes to write a "life" of the German savant and also to effect a presentation of the key ideas of the great foreign thinker.

The "life," which does not come to much, is obviously a reflection of Carlyle's admiration for Goethe's *The Sorrows of Young Werther* and other *Bildungsromane* or tales of youthful growth. Teufelsdröckh has a mysterious birth and grows up lovingly cared for by foster parents. His mind soon shows its powers and feeds omnivorously on books. The future sage falls in love with a young woman named Blumine, is jilted by her, and goes on typical early nineteenth-century wanderings. Driven by *Weltschmerz*, he goes to the Alps and finally to Paris; for sufficient reason, he utters his Everlasting No, his sweeping and bitter rejection of the structure of society and its conventions. Shortly thereafter, Carlyle's hero goes to Northern Scandinavia, outfaces a murderous Russian, and utters his Everlasting Yea. This is his acceptance, in a deeper sense, of the same texture of life and convention that he had rejected in Paris. After this climactic experience, Teufelsdröckh returns to his native city of Weissnichtwo (Don't-Know-Where), puffs his pipe, drinks his beer, and now and then sits at his desk in a top-floor room and meditates upon his little town and the world beyond it.

This "life," however, takes second place to the long quotations of his opinions, also deposited in the paper bags for

3351

the benefit of his English editor and, of course, England. On many pages Teufelsdröckh is allowed to speak for himself. But in almost as many pages the editor speaks for him, extending the application of the supposedly Germanic ideas to the turmoils of contemporary England. By this transparent subterfuge, the life and opinions of the imaginary German philosopher become a tract for the time, in which Carlyle is able to utter his own Everlasting No to the anti-idealist movements of the Victorian Age: the growth of democracy, the trust in utilitarian philosophy and its cold and (to Carlyle) petty calculation of pleasure and pain, profit and loss.

Carlyle is also able to utter his Everlasting Yea, which amounts to this: clothes and human institutions and religions of the past and their empty rites must be regarded, when they are properly viewed, as the obscure and yet wonderful expression of the ongoing life of the soul. And the life of the soul must be regarded in two supplementary but noncontradicting ways: It is the destiny of each man to create or re-create the "clothes" that he himself wears. It is a gift of world destiny that man over outnumbered genera-

tions may trace the biography of the human race itself by study of the institutions it sets up, the buildings it erects, and, most important of all, the thoughts that it thinks and, by religion and in books, transmits to future generations.

To do all this is to be a good Teufelsdröckh, but to practice an imitation of Richter and Goethe, if not Christ, each man must trace the arc of denial and affirmation in his own life. As Carlyle points out in *Sartor Resartus*, each man must deny "the dandiacal body"—life smart, modish, and empty—and he must sink into a condition of receptive silence. Out of this silence will come the true words, the words that emancipate man from illusions and which clear the way to *work*. This work can be humble and anonymous like the digging of a gardener, or it can be noble and widely known, like the notations of Teufelsdröckh at his desk.

Such are the main outlines of the "good news" of Carlyle's early book. Readers who are just will concede that Carlyle was a kind of pre-Existentialist like his contemporary Kierkegaard, though it is Kierkegaard who is accepted as a master by modern Existentialist thought.

# SATANSTOE

*Type of work:* Novel
*Author:* James Fenimore Cooper (1789-1851)
*Type of plot:* Historical romance
*Time of plot:* 1751-1758
*Locale:* New York State
*First published:* 1845

*Principal characters:*
CORNELIUS LITTLEPAGE, called Corny, the narrator
HUGH ROGER LITTLEPAGE, Corny's grandfather
DIRCK VAN VALKENBURGH, called Dirck Follock, Corny's friend
ABRAHAM VAN VALKENBURGH, called 'Brom Follock, his father
HERMAN MORDAUNT, a wealthy landowner
ANNEKE MORDAUNT, his daughter
MARY WALLACE, her friend
GUERT TEN EYCK, Corny's friend, in love with Mary
THE REVEREND THOMAS WORDEN, a clergyman
JASON NEWCOME, a schoolmaster from Connecticut
MOTHER DOORTJE, a fortune-teller
MAJOR BULSTRODE, a British officer, in love with Anneke
JAAP, Corny's Negro slave
MR. TRAVERSE, a surveyor
SUSQUESUS, and
JUMPER, Indian guides and runners

## Critique:

*Satanstoe, or, The Littlepage Manuscripts,* combines the social criticism of Cooper's later life with his talents as a romanticist. Unlike his best work, however, this novel lacks the action and melodrama that brought him fame. The story, narrated by Corny Littlepage, son of a landed proprietor, takes place mainly in Albany, New York, with an adventurous climax in the forests of New York State. The value of the book as social criticism rests in its descriptions of life in Albany and New York City and in the author's comments on the Dutch characters of these cities. Cooper's intense romanticism led him to create idealized heroes who are unreal and often boring. Much of the book dwells on a poorly developed love affair between Corny and Anneke who, in the end, marry and live happily ever after. The novel seems to lack direction and the action barely gets off the ground before the novel ends.

## The Story:

As a lad, Cornelius Littlepage, usually called Corny, studied classics under the Rev. Thomas Worden at Satanstoe as a preparation for going to an American university. Satanstoe was owned by Corny's father and was so named because it was a peninsula shaped like an inverted toe. When Corny's father felt that he was prepared to attend a university, a discussion was held with Abraham Van Valkenburgh, or 'Brom Follock, as he was called, to decide on which university Corny was to attend. Follock also had a son, Dirck, the same age as Corny. After comparing the New England manners at Yale with the manners of Newark, later Princeton, it was decided to send Corny to Princeton.

Before settling at Newark, Corny went with his father to visit New York City. They arrived there during a holiday and toured the streets. Because the Patroon of Albany was visiting the city, a crowd had gathered. Corny noticed a beautiful girl named Anneke who had been insulted when a butcher's boy knocked an apple from her hand. Corny gave the boy a dig in the ribs and then exchanged blows with him. Turning to see the girl again,

Corny found that she had disappeared.

In 1755, after completing the four-year course at college, Corny returned to Satanstoe. There he renewed his boyhood friendship with Dirck Follock and met Jason Newcome, the new schoolmaster from Danbury. Newcome took strong exception to New York habits and manners, as exampled by the Rev. Mr. Worden, who played whist with Corny's mother. Newcome, because of his Connecticut upbringing, was not as well educated as were the Littlepages, and he could not understand their leisure. He felt that Corny should work for a living.

When Corny was twenty, he and Dirck traveled to New York City. On the journey Corny learned that their fathers had jointly purchased some land from the Indians and that probably, next year, they were to be sent to look over the land, which was not far from Albany. While on the road, Dirck pointed out Lilacsbush, the summer home of Herman Mordaunt, his mother's cousin. Corny suggested that they stop there, but Dirck explained that Mordaunt and his motherless daughter Anneke remained in their winter home in New York City until after the Pinkster holidays, around Easter time. Dirck declared that Anneke was one of the prettiest girls in the colony. The pair stopped at Mrs. Light's inn where they heard some gossip about Anneke's many admirers.

In New York City, Corny visited his aunt, Mrs. Legge, while Dirck stayed with relatives in the town. Jason Newcome, being on a holiday, also made his appearance. Soon after their arrival the three young men went to the town common to watch the Pinkster frolics, a Negro holiday. There they met Anneke Mordaunt, Dirck's cousin, who remembered that Corny had fought the butcher's boy for her sake. The group visited a lion's cage and Corny was able to save Anneke's life when the crowd pressed her close to the bars and the animal seized her with one paw. In addition to Anneke's gratitude Corny also earned that of her father, who invited Corny and Dirck to dine with him. At the Mordaunt house Corny met several British officers who were numbered among Anneke's admirers. One, Major Bulstrode, asked Corny why he had not enlisted to fight in the war against the French. Corny replied that his grandfather would not have allowed him to join the colors. Later he expressed his opinion that the war was not really the concern of the settlers but a quarrel between the English and the French.

During the stay in New York, Corny and Dirck frequently visited the Mordaunts. When the officers gave a dramatic performance to which the Mordaunts and their friends were invited, Bulstrode, the starring performer, was offensive to Anneke's sensitivities, theatrical performances not being highly considered in the colonies. Corny and Dirck -then rode with the Mordaunts and Mary Wallace to Lilacsbush. In spite of Corny's efforts to prevent him, Jason Newcome managed to travel with them on the journey back to Satanstoe. On their return home, Corny related the events of his trip, including his meetings with Anneke, to his mother, who was greatly pleased.

In the following March, Dirck and Corny traveled to Albany in order to inspect the land their fathers had bought. With them they carried a quantity of merchandise to sell to the army, which was stationed in Albany. At the inn where they stopped they learned that the Mordaunts were also there as well as Bulstrode's regiment and that Herman Mordaunt wanted Anneke to marry Bulstrode. Corny and Dirck had Mr. Worden and Jason as their companions, as well as Jaap, a faithful colored servant. In order to reach Albany they were forced to cross the Hudson on ice. Although many other wagons had made the crossing, Mr. Worden refused to ride in the sleigh and ran alongside, thus acquiring in Albany the title of the "loping Dominie." In Albany, Corny met Guert Ten Eyck, an irresponsible young man who took Corny sledding in the center of the town and humiliated him by guiding the sled to the feet of Anneke and her friend, Mary Wallace; sledding was considered a child's sport. Guert was in love with Mary, who admonished his action severely.

Guert, who helped Corny dispose of the goods he had brought from Satanstoe, invited his friends to dinner. Discovering that the army had stolen his dinner, he tricked Corny and Mr. Worden into helping to steal their dinner from the mayor. That official, learning of Guert's trick, invited them to a second dinner that night. Present at the mayor's house were the Mordaunts and Mary Wallace. That same night Corny told Anneke that Guert loved Mary and then admitted that he loved her. Anneke, hearing his declaration, turned pale.

When Corny met Bulstrode in Albany, the British officer spoke of his love for Anneke and of his hopes of obtaining his father's permission for their marriage. They discussed the war and the relationship between England and the colonies. Guert Ten Eyck, wishing to go riding with Mary, asked Corny to try to obtain Mr. Mordaunt's approval of a sleigh ride he was planning.

Mr. Mordaunt agreed to accompany Anneke and Mary on the sleigh ride with Guert, Corny, and Dirck on the following Monday. Then, over the weekend, the ice melted on all the roads because spring had arrived suddenly; Guert and Corny feared their trip would have to be postponed until the following year. The Hudson River was still frozen over, however, and Guert's suggestion that they go for a ride on the river itself proved a plan agreeable to the whole party.

The sleighs rode on the ice to Kinderhook without mishap. On the return trip people frequently called out from the land, but the sleighs were going too fast for the occupants to understand what was being told them. Suddenly, to their dismay, they realized that the warm weather had caused the river to flood, breaking the ice apart and separating the sleighs from dry land. Fearing for the safety of the women, Corny promised to care for Anneke's life and Guert promised to look

after Mary. In their efforts to reach shore safely, the groups were separated, each attempting to save themselves by another route. Through courage and effort, everybody reached shore safely.

Because of their heroism on the ice, Guert and Corny became well known in Albany. Bulstrode, congratulating Corny, learned for the first time that the young man was in love with Anneke. Although he received this news coolly, Bulstrode said that he saw no reason why he and Corny could not remain friends.

Disappointed in his courtship of Mary, Guert proposed that Corny accompany him on a visit to Mother Doortje, a fortune-teller. Mr. Worden, not a strictly moralistic man, went with them, as did Dirck Follock. Although they disguised themselves, the seer recognized them and advised Guert to follow Corny into the woods during the summer. She also identified Mr. Worden as the loping Dominie and advised Jason Newcome to buy land for making a mill-seat. When Guert was told he might never marry, the fortune-teller's words caused him to give up almost all hope of winning Mary.

After the arrival of Lord Howe, the British troops moved northward. A short time later Mr. Mordaunt announced that he was going to visit land of his own, a tract known as Ravensnest, which was very near the Littlepage and Follock property of Mooseridge. The group traveled together to Ravensnest. From there Corny, Dirck, Guert, the surveyor Mr. Traverse, two axmen, two chainbearers, Jaap, and Guert's colored servant Pete set out to find Mooseridge. On the way they met Jumper, an Indian whom they hired as a guide. Later a second Indian, Susquesus, or Trackless, was added to the party. Because of Susquesus' skill in woodcraft, they soon located the boundary marker and immediately began the work of surveying the tract. For shelter they built a rude but comfortable log cabin.

Learning from the woods runner that the English were about to begin operations against Ticonderoga, Corny, Dirck,

Guert, and Jaap, guided by Susquesus, set out to join the expedition. The British were badly defeated at the battle by a smaller force of French and Indians and Lord Howe was killed. Under Guert's leadership the volunteers escaped after learning that Bulstrode had been seriously wounded and sent to Ravensnest. Jaap had taken a Canadian Indian, Musquerusque, but he was forced to release his prisoner so that the group could make an escape. Jaap thrashed the Indian before freeing him; Susquesus warned that Jaap had done a very foolish deed. Guided by Susquesus, the party returned to Mooseridge, where they found the surveying party gone.

Susquesus, going to warn the surveyors of the danger of Indian raids, found strange Indian tracks and followed them. That night the men returned from Ticonderoga and all slept in the locked hut. In the middle of the night Corny was awakened by Susquesus, who led him in the direction of cries for help. They found Guert's colored servant, who had been with the surveyors, tortured and scalped. Later they found the body of one of the hunters and axmen and, a little farther on, the surveyor, his two chainbearers, and the second axman, also scalped and dead. Susquesus said that Musquerusque had taken his revenge for the beating.

Returning to Mooseridge, they found Jumper, the Indian scout, with a letter from Mr. Mordaunt inviting them to join him at Ravensnest. On the way they came upon a party of Indians and dispersed them in a surprise attack.

At Ravensnest, Corny took the opportunity to press his suit. Anneke, in turn, confessed her love for him, adding that she had never loved Bulstrode. Mary Wallace, however, refused to marry Guert. During an Indian raid on the house Guert fought with reckless courage. After he and Jaap had been captured, Mary realized that she loved him after all. Guert was mortally wounded, however, while escaping with Jaap from the Indians, and he died in Mary's arms. Bulstrode, confined to his bed because of his wound, did not learn until much later Anneke's decision to marry Corny. When the two men met again at Lilacsbush, Bulstrode offered his rival his hand and best wishes.

Corny's mother was overjoyed to hear of her son's approaching marriage, and Mr. Mordaunt, who had originally favored Bulstrode for his daughter's hand, decided to settle his property on Corny and his bride. After their marriage Anneke and Corny settled at Lilacsbush. On the death of his grandfather Corny acquired still more land. He and Anneke lived for many years in peace, and became the happy parents of a son whom they named Mordaunt.

Jason Newcome acquired a mill-seat from Mr. Mordaunt on a cheap lease. Mr. Worden returned to Satanstoe. He had decided that missionary life was too difficult and that the only people who should be Christians were people who were already civilized.

# SATIRES

*Type of work:* Poetry
*Author:* Juvenal (Decimus Junius Juvenalis, c. 55-c. 135)
*First transcribed:* 112-128

Greatest of the Latin satirists, Juvenal was born in Aquinum, southeast of Rome, also the birthplace of St. Thomas Aquinas. Few facts about him have come down outside his own writing, though a biography written in the fourth century said that he was the son of a freedman and practiced rhetoric until middle age for his own amusement — perhaps until he took up poetry. As a satirist, the vices of his age gave him material.

Born during the reign of Nero, he lived under nine other emperors, including Otho, of whom he was especially critical, and tyrannical Domitian. Juvenal's pictures of life in Rome are gloomy and bitter. He feared the growing power of the moneyed classes, the traders, and the freedman. He disapproved of the softening influences of Greek and Eastern cultures and the vices they introduced. Some scholars have accused him of dwelling on vice for the pleasures he took in writing about immorality; his own claim was that he wrote to exalt virtue and encourage men to seek it.

He explained his choice of medium in his first satire. Having no desire to rewrite old plays or endless epics, and having seen a barber become wealthier than a patrician and an idiotic Egyptian advance himself at the expense of the Romans, he declared that "it is difficult not to write satires." His writing was little appreciated during his lifetime. Indeed, his satires disappeared for several centuries. Rediscovered, Juvenal was esteemed as an epigrammatist and social historian because of his vivid pictures of Latin life.

Sixteen satires, totaling 3,775 lines, made up the total preserved work of Juvenal. The poems vary in length from the little more than sixty lines of the unfinished XVI, which deals with the prerogatives of a soldier, to the 661 lines of VI, directed against women, which is long enough to fill a papyrus roll by itself. His first book, containing 690 lines in all, includes his first five satires of which Satire I, appropriately, explains why he turned to this form of literary activity. He declared that he began writing to pay back the many poets who had been boring him, from crude Cordus with his lengthy epics to the writers of comedies and elegies. Since depravities on every side "rate the midnight oil of Horace," he bade the writer of satires to "set sail." Pondering, however, the advice of those who had warned him against the wrath of rulers, he declared his intention to dedicate his attention to the dead, those whose ashes lie along the roads outside Rome.

Satire II, directed against effeminate men, put into circulation the familiar proverb that "one rotten apple spoils a whole barrel." This work describes the pretty boys with their long hair and their togas of pastel colors.

The whole of Rome was his target in Satire III. Hearing that his friend Umbritius was moving to Cumae to escape the vices of the capital, Juvenal commended his decision:

After all, it is something even in a
lonely corner
To make yourself the landlord of a
single lizard.

In Satire IV he considered those able to escape the consequences of any crime because they were wealthy or highborn. In Number V, he inveighed against stingy patrons and clients who had no sense of shame. He described the tasteless food provided for clients who came to the rich man's table, contrasting this fare with the delicious banquets served when only a few friends were invited in to dine.

3357

The approaching marriage of Postumus gave the poet a motive for a coarse diatribe against the women of Rome in Satire VI. Back in primitive times, he asserted, chastity existed on earth, but not among the Roman matrons of his time. He described their beauty aids, their aimless lives, their extravagances, and their pretense to culture. Some even went as far as to forget their sex in their desire to be gladiators. And the remedy? End the evils of an extended peace and the luxury that had taken the place of frugality and self-sacrifice.

Satire VII laments the evil plight of men of culture when poets and historians cannot make a living and teachers, after years of preparation, get less money in a year than a successful jockey after one race.

Blood is no reason for expecting respect, said Juvenal in Satire VIII. Retraced a few generations, even the noblest blood is mixed with the common. Deeds are more important. The brief Satire IX is a poem on pimps and informers. It is followed by the famous Number X, adapted by Johnson to the English scene under the title "On the Vanity of Human Wishes." This poem states that few human beings know what is good or bad for them. Most people wish for health or honor. Students of rhetoric crave eloquence, the ruin of Demosthenes and Cicero. The ambitions of Alexander and Xerxes were their undoing. People desire long life, which brings ills, or beauty which causes unhappiness. If we were wise, we would let the gods make the decision for us. As Johnson translated it:

So raise for good the supplicating voice,
But leave to Heaven the measure and
    the choice.

If we must pray, ask for a healthy mind in a healthy body and a spirit reconciled to trouble or death.

Extravagance is the theme of Satire XI, sent to Persicus along with an invitation to dinner. Many in Rome beggar themselves for pleasure, said Juvenal; but at my table, friend, you will eat what I can afford, simply served, and without lavish entertainment.

In a more mellow vein, Juvenal devoted Number XII to his joy that his friend Catullus had been rescued after a shipwreck. His ceremonies of thanksgiving, however, were to be simple. He would not offer rich treasures to the gods as some legacy hunters had done. Then, not able to remain benevolent long, he ended with a jibe at Pacuvius, who profited from the misfortunes of others.

Calvinus, who complained loudly at being defrauded, was satirized in Number XIII, and the avaricious Fuscinus in Number XIV was urged to provide a better example to his children. Satire XV differs from the preceding, being in effect a parable about the rivalry of neighboring towns: Once man was kind to man; now vipers are less cruel to their fellows. Pythagoras, should he return, would be certain the beasts of the fields are superior to humans.

The final, unfinished Satire XVI represents a new departure for the poet. Here he lists the special advantages that soldiers have over everyone else. The work breaks off with an unfinished sentence, in the middle of a line, without leaving the reader sure whether Juvenal really intended to praise the soldiers, or whether he was preparing to deflate the military caste. There is no explanation of why Juvenal failed to finish the poem. Perhaps there is some truth in the tradition that he was either summarily banished or sent on a mission from which he never returned.

# SATIROMASTIX

*Type of work:* Drama
*Author:* Thomas Dekker (c. 1572-1632?)
*Type of plot:* Satirical romance
*Time of plot:* c. 1100
*Locale:* England
*First presented:* 1601

*Principal characters:*
WILLIAM RUFUS, King of England
SIR WALTER TERRILL, his noble follower
CAELESTINE, Sir Walter's bride
SIR QUINTILIAN SHORTHOSE, the bride's father
MISTRESS MINIVER, a wealthy widow
SIR VAUGHAN AP REES, a Welshman, suitor of the widow
SIR ADAM PRICKSHAFT, another suitor of the widow
CRISPINUS, a poet
DEMETRIUS, another poet
HORACE, the humorous poet
ASINIUS BUBO, Horace's admiring follower
CAPTAIN TUCCA, a roaring roisterer

## Critique:

Thomas Dekker's *Satiromastix* owes its present interest almost solely to the plot dealing with "The Untrusting of the Humourous Poet," the poet being Ben Jonson under the thin disguise of the name Horace. Apparently the play was patched up in some haste after the production of Jonson's *Poetaster,* which caricatured Dekker and John Marston. The three plots are not well joined. Perhaps the triangle containing Sir Walter Terrill, his beautiful bride Caelestine, and King William Rufus, was the plot of an original play on which Dekker was working when the controversy between Jonson and the "poetasters" broke out. It remains the central plot. The second, which has little bearing on the first, is concerned with the wooing of Mistress Miniver by Sir Quintilian, Sir Vaughan, and Sir Adam. Filled with a veritable glut of puns ranging from the risqué to the obscene, this farcical plot would doubtless have been a success on the Elizabethan stage as an independent work. The third plot depends on its relation to Jonson's *Poetaster,* performed earlier in the year (1601). *Poetaster* contains two plots, somewhat loosely connected: the love story of Ovid and Julia, the daughter of Augustus Caesar, and the discomfiture of Horace's enemies, par-ticularly Crispinus the poetaster and Demetrius the playdresser. For a long time scholars of Jonson devoted themselves to identifying the characters of *Poetaster* with actual Elizabethans. There is, however, no reason to doubt that *Poetaster* contains attacks on Marston and Dekker, and possibly other contemporaries. And there is no ambiguity about Dekker's Horace: he is England's Ben Jonson, brilliantly caricatured.

## The Story:

While Sir Quintilian Shorthose supervised the preparations for the marriage of his daughter Caelestine, Sir Adam Prickshaft, Sir Vaughan ap Rees, and Mistress Miniver came to share in the festivities. All three knights were enamored of the widow. When the bridal party entered, Sir Walter Terrill, the groom-to-be, announced that King William Rufus would grace the wedding with his presence. The groom had sent to the poet Horace for a wedding song.

Horace was laboring by candlelight, surrounded by books, when his admiring friend Asinius Bubo visited him. Bubo warned that Crispinus and Demetrius planned to put Horace in a play as a bricklayer. To the great embarrassment

3359

of Horace, Crispinus and Demetrius entered and accused him of unfair attacks on them.

Soon Blunt, accompanied by Captain Tucca, came to get the wedding verses; but Horace confessed he had not been able to finish them in the three days allotted him. Captain Tucca blasted Horace with a stream of Rabelaisian abuse for writing satires about him. Quivering with fear, Horace apologized and promised future good behavior. The captain tipped him generously, and the visitors left.

The three knights urged Mistress Miniver to choose one of them for her second husband, but their talk was interrupted by the arrival of King William Rufus and his train. The king greeted the bride with a kiss, obviously taken with her beauty and charm. During the dance he managed to single her out frequently, engaging in risqué banter. When the ladies withdrew, the king dared Sir Walter to postpone the wedding night and to trust his bride at court alone with the king. Goaded with lack of faith in her, Sir Walter unwisely promised to send her.

In spite of Horace's love letters purchased by Sir Vaughan, the widow refused him, favoring Sir Adam. Enraged, Sir Vaughan asked Horace to write a satire on baldness, since Sir Adam was bald. Sir Quintilian, needing a messenger to speak for him, turned to raucous, foulmouthed Captain Tucca. The captain also agreed to carry rich gifts to the widow from Sir Adam. However, Captain Tucca wooed for himself. Later, the captain was shown a new series of satirical epigrams by Horace on him.

Sir Vaughan entertained the widow at a banquet, at which Horace read his satire on baldness. Mistress Miniver announced she could never be "enameled" of a baldheaded man again. Captain Tucca burst in and threatened Horace; Sir Vaughan drove him out, but Mistress Miniver called after the captain demanding that he return the money she had lent him. Sir Vaughan rushed after the

captain to punish him. Bubo showed Horace a challenge left by the fire-eating Captain Tucca.

Captain Tucca promised Sir Adam he would have Crispinus and Demetrius praise baldness in verse. Bubo and Horace came to the captain for a parley, and the three made peace again. Captain Tucca convinced Sir Vaughan that borrowing the money had been part of his plan to help the knight win the widow. At the next gathering of the widow's friends, Crispinus read his praise of baldness; then Captain Tucca aroused the whole group to take Horace to court and punish him for his sharp satires.

Sir Walter, Sir Quintilian, and Caelestine lamented her danger; and Sir Quintilian proposed that she drink poison. Grief-stricken, Sir Walter consented to the loss of his wife in order to save her honor. When revelers came to escort the couple to court, Sir Walter announced his wife's death and requested that they go with him in procession to the king.

King William Rufus, laughing at the gullibility of Sir Walter, waited eagerly for the coming of the bride. Sir Walter, dressed in black, escorted the body into the king's presence. Seeing Caelestine lifeless, the king cried out in horror. Sir Walter accused the king of tyranny and explained that Caelestine had chosen to die rather than to lose her honor; Sir Walter's oath was kept by his bringing her body to the king. Shame overcame the repentant monarch. Caelestine revived, and Sir Quintilian told how he had given her a potion which gave the appearance of death, though both Sir Walter and she had believed it poison. The king restored the wife unharmed to her husband.

Crispinus offered an interlude for comic relief after the seriousness of the situation. Captain Tucca led Horace and Bubo, both wearing horns, into the royal presence. Bubo was made to swear he would abandon Horace and his poetry; upon swearing this, he was released. Horace, crowned with nettles instead of laurels, promised at great length to amend as a writer and to give up sour criticisms and complaints. Captain Tucca announced that he and Mistress Miniver were to be married. The disgruntled knights accepted defeat, and Captain Tucca promised to repay them what they had given him for their wooing of the widow. A dance followed, and all ended happily.

Captain Tucca delivered an epilogue promising future theatrical battles between Horace and the poetasters.

# THE SATYRICON

*Type of work:* Fictional miscellany
*Author:* Gaius Petronius Arbiter (?—A.D. c. 66)
*Type of plot:* Social criticism
*Time of plot:* First century
*Locale:* Italy
*Earliest extant printed version:* 1664

Principal characters:
ENCOLPIUS, the narrator
ASCYLTUS, his friend
GITO, their attendant
EUMOLPUS, a poet
TRIMALCHIO, a wealthy vulgarian

## Critique:

This vast work of Petronius is extant only in a fragment of 146 chapters of books 15 and 16. The chapters consist of a miscellany of anecdotes without much unity. It is generally thought that Petronius wrote the tales as a sort of parody or protest of the orgies and debauches of Nero's reign. The pictures of Roman life presented are a vast canvas of licentiousness. By their worship of Priapus the Romans signaled their decadence and fall. Modern readers, even though hardened by the present-day cult of frankness, tend to turn in disgust from the excesses here depicted.

## The Story:

Encolpius railed at the growth of artificiality in modern rhetoric and the ill-prepared students who came to the school. Agamemnon, the professor, agreed with him, but placed the blame entirely on parents who refused to make their children study. Weary of the dispute and far gone in drink, Encolpius fled the school. An old woman, who made indecent proposals to him, showed him the way back to his inn.

Gito, his sixteen-year-old slave, had prepared supper, but the comely boy was crying: Ascyltus had made violent love to him. Encolpius was soothing the boy with caresses and tender words when Ascyltus broke in on them. A quarrel en-

sued between the two friends as to who should enjoy Gito's favors. The dispute was settled only when all three agreed to pay a visit to Lycurgus, a rich friend of Ascyltus.

Lycurgus received them most cordially and introduced them to Lichas, his friend. Lichas, completely taken with Encolpius, insisted that Encolpius and Gito come home with him. On the way, Tryphaena, a beautiful woman attached to Lichas' entourage, made surreptitious love to Encolpius, who resolved to have little to do with Lichas. But, when the party arrived at Lichas' villa, Tryphaena deserted Encolpius for the bewitching Gito. Smarting under her desertion, Encolpius made love to Doris, Lichas' attractive wife. All went fairly well until Gito tired of Tryphaena. Then she accused both Gito and Encolpius of making improper advances, and the two returned in haste to Lycurgus' house.

Lycurgus at first supported the two adventurers, but as the jealous Lichas increased his complaints, Lycurgus turned against the pair. At the suggestion of Ascyltus, the three set out again to seek what love affairs and plunder they could find. They were well supplied with gold, for Encolpius had thoughtfully plundered one of Lichas' ships before leaving.

At a nearby small town a fair was in progress. There they came upon a groom who was saddling a rich man's horse. When the groom left for a moment, Encolpius stole the rich man's riding cloak. Soon afterward Ascyltus found a bag of coins on the ground. The two friends hid the gold by sewing it under the lining of Encolpius' threadbare tunic. Just as they finished, the rich man's retainers gave chase to recover the riding cloak. Dashing through a wood, Encolpius was separated from his friend and lost the tunic.

They met again at a market. There they saw the tunic up for sale with the gold pieces still hidden in the lining. When they offered to trade the riding cloak for the tunic, the bystanders became suspicious and tried to make the two friends appear before a judge. Dropping the riding cloak and seizing the tunic, they fled.

After telling Gito to follow later on, they set out for the next town. Seeing the dim forms of two comely women hurrying through the dusk, they followed them unobserved into an underground temple. There the two men saw a company of women in Bacchanalian garb, each with a phallic emblem in her hand, preparing to worship Priapus. They were discovered by the horrified women and chased back to their inn.

As they were dining with Gito in their rooms, the maid of one of the women whom they had followed to the sacred rites came in and begged them to listen to her mistress, who was a respectable matron. Even though Encolpius swore never to tell of the forbidden rites, the matron had the three seized and taken to her villa. The men were bound and given powerful love potions, and then all the women of the household made love to them. After escaping from the love-maddened ladies, Encolpius had to rest for three days; Gito seemed little affected.

Next the three attended a huge banquet given by Trimalchio, a rich and vulgar freedman. Every dish served was disguised as something else. After hours of eating and drinking, they were glad even for the respite of story telling. Trimalchio started off with a boring elucidation of the signs of the zodiac, and many of the guests told pointless anecdotes. From Niceros, however, they heard an absorbing tale.

Niceros was staying, while he was still a slave, at an inn where he was in love with the landlord's complaisant wife, Melissa. One day he induced a soldier to go for a walk with him. When they came to a graveyard, the soldier took off his clothes and threw them beside the path. Making a magic circle around the clothes, he straightway turned into a wolf and went howling away. When Niceros saw to his horror that the clothes had turned to stone, he hurried home to Melissa. She told him that a wolf had just come into the yard and killed some sheep. A servant drove a spear through the animal's neck but the wolf got away.

Niceros ran back to the cemetery where he found that the stone clothes had dissolved in blood. In the morning he went to the soldier's room. There a physician was stanching the blood from a wound in the soldier's neck.

Encolpius, Ascyltus, and Gito were finally so stuffed and bored they could stand no more. To their relief, the company moved outdoors to exercise. From the conversation they learned that another banquet was to follow, this one given by Trimalchio's wife. They left hurriedly.

Following another quarrel over Gito, Encolpius and Ascyltus parted company. To the distress of Encolpius, Gito elected to go with Ascyltus.

After sorrowing uselessly for days, Encolpius fell in with an old man, the poet Eumolpus. When the two went to the baths to cement their friendship, Encolpius was overjoyed to find Gito acting as attendant for Ascyltus, who was in another room. Gito confessed that he really liked Encolpius better, and the latter, in a happy mood, took the boy back to his apartment.

Matters would have been smoother for Encolpius if he had not tried to make love to Circe. Because of his past tribulations and hardships, he had no strength for her ardors. Suspecting him of trifling with her, she raised such an outcry that Encolpius judged it wise to leave town.

On Eumolpus' advice, the comrades embarked secretly at night on a ship lying in the harbor. In the morning Encolpius discovered to his chagrin that they were aboard Lichas' ship. The owner and Tryphaena were aboard. Eumolpus tried to disguise Encolpius and Gito with burnt cork. Their subterfuge was discovered, however, and for a while it looked as though they would be flogged. But Lichas remembered his old attraction to Encolpius and Tryphaena was smitten anew with Gito; so they were spared.

When Lichas' ship was wrecked in a storm, the three comrades got ashore at Croton. Eumolpus posed as a rich landowner and Encolpius and Gito passed as his slaves. By cleverly deluding the inhabitants, they lived luxuriously as guests of the town. After a year suspicion grew as to Eumolpus' supposed wealth. Seeing an end to their pleasant stay, Encolpius and Gito escaped just in time. The aroused townspeople used Eumolpus as a scapegoat. They decked him out with boughs and sacred vestments, led him through the city, and finally hurled him down a cliff.

# THE SCARLET LETTER

*Type of work:* Novel
*Author:* Nathaniel Hawthorne (1804-1864)
*Type of plot:* Psychological romance
*Time of plot:* Early days of the Massachusetts Colony
*Locale:* Boston
*First published:* 1850

*Principal characters:*
HESTER PRYNNE, a woman convicted of adultery
ARTHUR DIMMESDALE, a minister of the community
ROGER CHILLINGWORTH, a physician, and Hester's husband
PEARL, Hester's daughter

## Critique:

Critics have called *The Scarlet Letter* the greatest book ever written in the Western Hemisphere. The theme of the novel is the universal subject of sin. Specifically, Hawthorne traces the effect of one particular sin on the lives of four people. In the pages of *The Scarlet Letter* we watch the almost beneficial effect of her sin upon Hester Prynne, who wears her shame openly for all the world to see; upon the Reverend Arthur Dimmesdale, who is killed by the distressing secret which he keeps hidden in his own breast; upon Roger Chillingworth, who becomes a devil incarnate; and upon little Pearl, who develops into a capricious, wayward child, but still sympathetic and lovable.

## The Story:

On a summer morning in Boston, in the early days of the Massachusetts Colony, a throng of curious people had gathered outside the jail in Prison Lane. They were there to watch for Hester Prynne, who had been found guilty of adultery by a court of stern Puritan judges. Condemned to wear on the breast of her gown the scarlet letter, the A which stood for adulteress, she was to stand on the stocks before the meeting house, so that her shame might be a warning and a reproach to all who saw her. The crowd waited to see her ascend the scaffold with her child in her arms, and there for three hours bear her shame alone.

At last, escorted by the town beadle,

the woman appeared. She moved serenely to the steps of the scaffold and stood quietly under the staring eyes that watched her public disgrace. It was whispered in the gathering that she had been spared the penalty of death or branding only through the intercession of the Reverend Arthur Dimmesdale, into whose church she had brought her scandalous sin.

While Hester stood on the scaffold, an elderly, almost deformed man appeared from the edge of the forest. When her agitation made it plain that she had recognized him, he put his finger to his lips as a sign of silence.

Hester's story was well-known in the community. She was the daughter of an ancient house of decayed fortune, and when she was young her family had married her to a husband who had great repute as a scholar. For some years they had lived in Antwerp. Two years before, the husband had sent his wife alone across the ocean to the Massachusetts Colony, intending to follow her as soon as he could put his affairs in order. There had been news of his departure, but his ship had never been heard of again. Hester, a young, attractive widow, had lived quietly in Boston until the time of her disgrace.

The scaffold of the pillory on which Hester stood was situated next to the balcony of the church where all the dignitaries of the colony sat to watch her hu-

THE SCARLET LETTER by Nathaniel Hawthorne. Published by Houghton Mifflin

miliation. The ministers of the town called on her to name the man who with herself was equally guilty, and the most eloquent of those who exhorted her was the Reverend Arthur Dimmesdale, her pastor. Still Hester refused to name the father of her child, and she was led back to the prison after her period of public shame had ended.

On her return to prison Hester was found to be in a state of great nervous excitement. When at last medical aid was called, a man was found who professed knowledge of medicine. His name was Roger Chillingworth, he told the jailer, recently arrived in town after a year of residence among the Indians. Chillingworth was the stranger who had appeared so suddenly from the forest while Hester stood on the scaffold that afternoon, and she knew him as her husband, the scholar Prynne. His ship had been wrecked on the coast and he had been captive among the Indians for many months.

He also asked Hester to name the father of her child. When she refused, he stated that he would remain in Boston to practice medicine, swearing at the same time that he would devote the rest of his life to discovering the identity of the man who had dishonored him. He commanded Hester not to betray the relationship between them, and she swore she would keep his secret.

When Hester's term of imprisonment was over, she found a small house on the outskirts of town, far removed from other habitation. There with her child, whom she had named Pearl, she settled down to earn a living from needlework, an outcast from society and still wearing the scarlet emblem on her breast.

Hester Prynne dressed her child in bright highly-ornamented costumes, in contrast to her own sober dress. As she grew up, Pearl proved to be a capricious, wayward child, hard to discipline. One day Hester called on Governor Bellingham to deliver a pair of embroidered gloves. She also wanted to see him about the custody of Pearl, for there was a movement afoot among the strict church members to take the child away from her. In the garden of the governor's mansion, Hester found the governor, Dimmesdale, and old Roger Chillingworth. Because the perverse Pearl would not repeat the catechism, the governor was about to separate the child from her mother. Dimmesdale saved the situation, however, by a persuasive speech which resulted in the decision to let Hester keep Pearl, who seemed to be strangely attracted to the minister.

Roger Chillingworth had become intimately acquainted with Arthur Dimmesdale both as his parishioner and his doctor, for the minister had been in ill health ever since the physician had come to town. As the two men lodged in the same house, the physician came to know Dimmesdale's inmost thoughts and feelings. The minister was much perturbed by thoughts of conscience and guilt, but when he expressed these ideas in generalities to his congregation, the people thought him only the more righteous. Slowly in Chillingworth the conviction grew that Dimmesdale was Pearl's father, and he conjured up for the sick man visions of agony, terror, and remorse.

One night, unable to sleep, Dimmesdale walked to the pillory where Hester Pyrnne had stood in ignominy. He went up the steps and stood for a long time in the same place. A little later Hester, who had been watching at a deathbed, came by with little Pearl. The minister called them to the scaffold, saying that they had been there before when he lacked courage to stand beside them. Thus the three stood together, Dimmesdale acknowledging himself as Pearl's father and Hester's partner in sin. This striking tableau was not unobserved. Roger Chillingworth watched them from the shadows.

Hester Prynne was so shocked by Dimmesdale's feeble and unhealthy condition that she determined to see her former husband and plead with him to free the sick minister from his evil influence.

One day she met the old physician gathering herbs in the forest and begged him to be merciful to his victim. But Chillingworth was inexorable; he would not forego his revenge on the man who had wronged him. Hester then advised him that she would tell Arthur Dimmesdale their secret and warn him against his physician. A short time later, Hester and Pearl intercepted Dimmesdale in the forest as he was returning from a missionary journey to the Indians. Hester confessed her true relation with Chillingworth and warned the minister against the physician's evil influence. She and the clergyman decided to leave the colony together in secret, to take passage in a ship then in the harbor and return to the Old World. They were to leave four days later, after Dimmesdale had preached the Election Sermon.

Election Day, on which the new governor was to be installed, was a holiday in Boston, and the port was lively with the unaccustomed presence of sailors from the ship in the harbor. In the crowd was the captain of the vessel, with whom Hester had made arrangements for her own and Dimmesdale's passage. During the morning the captain informed Hester that Roger Chillingworth had also arranged for passage on the ship. Filled with despair, Hester turned away and went with Pearl to listen to Dimmesdale's sermon.

Unable to find room within the church, she stood at the foot of the scaffold where at least she could hear the sound of his voice. As the procession left the church, everyone had only words of praise for the minister's inspired address. Dimmesdale walked like a man in a dream and once he tottered and almost fell. When he saw Hester and Pearl at the foot of the scaffold, he stepped out of the procession and called them to him. Then, taking them by the hand, he climbed the steps of the pillory. Almost fainting, but with a voice terrible and majestic, the minister admitted his guilt to the watching people. With a sudden motion he tore the ministerial band from across his breast and sank dying to the platform. When he thus exposed his breast, witnesses said that the stigma of the scarlet letter A was seen imprinted on the flesh above his heart.

Chillingworth, no longer able to wreak his vengeance on Dimmesdale, died within the year, bequeathing his considerable property to Pearl. For a time Hester disappeared from the colony, but years later she returned alone to live in her humble thatched cottage and to wear as before the scarlet emblem on her breast. But the scarlet letter, once her badge of shame, became an emblem of her tender mercy and kindness — an object of veneration and reverence to those whose sorrows she alleviated by her deeds of kindness and mercy. At her death she directed that the only inscription on her tombstone should be the letter A.

# SCEPTICISM AND ANIMAL FAITH

*Type of work:* Philosophy
*Author:* George Santayana (1863-1952)
*First published:* 1923

*Scepticism and Animal Faith* was written as an introduction to a system of philosophy, a system later made explicit in Santayana's four-volume *The Realms of Being: The Realm of Essence* (1927), *The Realm of Matter* (1930), *The Realm of Truth* (1938),*The Realm of Spirit* (1940). Despite the fact that the author believed that his ideas needed the extended treatment he gave them in these volumes, the introductory work remains the clearest, most concise, and most representative of Santayana's works. Almost every important contribution which the author made to philosophy can be found here; and the advantage of this single work is that the reader can gain a synoptic vision of the relations of the ideas to each other, something he might fail to achieve if he centered his attention initially upon one of the volumes of *The Realms of Being* or *The Life of Reason* (1905-1906).

Santayana's principal thesis is that knowledge is faith "mediated by symbols." The symbols of human discourse, when man is talking to himself about the world of facts, are the elements in his experience: sensations, images, feelings, and the like. "The images in sense are parts of discourse, not parts of nature: they are the babble of our innocent organs under the stimulus of things," writes Santayana. Since we cannot be certain that the given elements, the essences, are signs of physical objects affecting us as physical organisms, there is a sense in which we cannot be said to be free of the possibility of error. Nevertheless, as animals, as active beings, we find ourselves compelled to take our experiences as the experiences of a living organism in the process of being shocked and stimulated by the world. Our belief in a nature of change is made possible by our interpretation of the given—the data, the essences—but it cannot be justified by the

given; hence, it is animal faith.

To prepare himself for the statement that all knowledge is the faith that certain given elements are signs of things and events, Santayana develops a thorough skepticism which ends with the cryptic statement that "Nothing given exists." To understand the meaning and ground of this claim it is necessary to understand Santayana's conception of the given—his theory of essences.

It is difficult to make all the proper qualifications in a brief description, but if one begins by supposing that essences are characteristics of actual and possible things, whether physical, psychical, mathematical, or whatever, a beginning has been made. If a person were to have two or three sense experiences of precisely the same sort—three sense images of a certain shade of yellow, for example —that shade of yellow would be an essence that had been given to him in sense experience. Even if he had not had the experience, he could have had it; the essence is a character his experience might come to have. Essences, then, are universals, not particulars; they are characteristics which may or may not be the characteristics of existing things.

It makes sense to say of a particular thing that it is, or was, or shall be; but we cannot sensibly talk that way about the characteristics of things. Considered in themselves, as they must be, essences are immutable, eternal, never vague, and neither good nor bad. In Santayana's terms, the realm of essence "is simply the unwritten catalogue, prosaic and infinite, of all the characters possessed by such things as happen to exist, together with the characters which all different things would possess if they existed."

If this definition of essence is kept clearly in mind, if an essence is simply a character but not necessarily the character of anything, then it becomes clear that if essences are given—and they are —then nothing given exists. If we are correct in our suppositions, then, whenever an essence is given, it is given to a self; i.e., someone has an experience, and the experience has a certain character, an essence. The self that has experiences exists; the "intuition," i.e., the apprehension of the character of the experience, exists; and, if the self is not mistaken in its interpretation of the given, of the "datum," a physical event or object exists as signified by the datum. In conventional language, there are persons, sense experiences, and the objects which give rise to the experiences. But it is improper now, and false, to say that the essence of the experience exists. To say this would violate Santayana's definition of essence and, accordingly, lead to a paradox. For example, if an essence is a character, and if on three occasions the same character were given, then the consequence of saying that on each occasion the essence existed is that the essence will have gone in and out of existence three times. If two persons have the same kind of experience—i.e., intuit the same essence—then we would have to say that the essence is in two places at the same time. As long as one remembers that, by definition, an essence is a character considered as a character, it is clearly nonsense to think of essences as existing.

The discovery of essence is the reward of a relentless skepticism. In Santayana's view, we have no final justification for our claims about the existence of external objects, and all of our beliefs about selves and change and memory are open to critical challenge. "Scepticism may . . . be carried to the point of denying change and memory, and the reality of all facts," he writes.

But Santayana had no great affection for this ultimate skepticism. In his terms he was a "wayward sceptic," entertaining the notion of an ultimate skepticism only to show that critical challenge of our customary beliefs is possible. It is customary and unavoidable for a human being to suppose that he himself lives and thinks, and Santayana's rejoinder is, "That he does so is true; but to establish that truth he must appeal to animal faith."

In order to discuss the human being in his response to the data of experience Santayana introduces his special senses of the terms "spirit," "psyche," and "intuition." Intuition is the apprehension of essence; the spirit is the cool contemplator, that which intuits; and psyche is the self that acts, has preferences, takes data as signs. Of course, when we begin to use these terms as descriptive of facts, we are expressing our own animal faith; when we say that the spirit confronts essences and that the psyche acts accordingly, taking the essences as signs of a physical world, we are saying what the ultimate skeptic cannot allow—but we are animals, and the psyche has other business than philosophy.

There is something appealing and liberating in Santayana's conception of animal faith. No one could be more careful than he in examining and challenging the pretensions of the pretenders to knowledge and wisdom: the paradox that knowledge is animal faith reveals that what we call "knowledge" is merely unwarranted, but stubborn, animal conviction. That same paradox brings out the positive side of Santayana's philosophy: as animals taking data as signs we make sense out of what would otherwise be a static complex of essences and give order both to our world and ourselves.

In the description of the consequences of animal faith in action, Santayana considered first the belief in discourse which arises once one has given up "passive intuition." From the belief in discourse one passes to belief "in experience, in substance, in truth, and in spirit." This progression of beliefs is a natural one, and the description of the life of reason in various areas was undertaken by Santayana in his earlier five-volume work *The Life of Reason. The Realms of Being* naturally followed *Scepticism and Animal Faith* as a careful elaboration of the terms "essence," "matter," "truth," and "spirit."

Unlike many philosophers, Santayana had self-confidence enough to know the limits of his inquiry. He did not pretend to be able to discover what the physicist, for example, can discover by acting on his scientific animal faith. Once we pass from the intuitive contemplation of essences to the recognition of the human use of data as signs, we soon come to the discovery of our assumptions of an experiencing self coming up against substance —the presumed cause of the data. The philosopher can clarify the idea of substance, explaining that it is extended, in space and time, with a structure, and so forth; and he can go on to identify substance with such homely examples as "the wood of this tree . . . the wind . . . the flesh and the bones of the man. . . ." But he need not, and Santayana does not, try to do what the physicist and the chemist do in their specialized ways.

By this practice, then, Santayana fulfilled the promise of his introduction to *Scepticism and Animal Faith* in which he said: "Here is one more system of philosophy. If the reader is tempted to smile, I can assure him that I smile with him. . . . I am merely trying to express for the reader the principles to which he appeals when he smiles."

In this book, as in all his others, Santayana presents his ideas by means of a beautifully articulated, poetic style. Even if his vision of knowledge as animal faith had no value, this work would endure as the most fascinating portrayal of the realm of essence which has yet appeared in literature. That this moving survey of the timeless, changeless realm of essence should have come from a naturalistic philosopher is one of those pleasant paradoxes to which we turn with classic delight after coming from *Scepticism and Animal Faith.*

# THE SCHOOL FOR HUSBANDS

*Type of work:* Drama
*Author:* Molière (Jean Baptiste Poquelin, 1622-1673)
*Type of plot:* Social satire
*Time of plot:* Seventeenth century
*Locale:* Paris
*First presented:* 1661

Principal characters:
SGANARELLE, a gentleman of means
ARISTE, his brother
ISABELLE, Sganarelle's ward
LÉONOR, her sister and Ariste's ward
VALÈRE, Isabelle's lover

## Critique:

Molière has been called the first great modern in the sense that he portrayed the actual in life, the true manners of his times. In *The School for Husbands* he lives up to his reputation as a satirical critic and comic dramatist. The outspoken frankness and amusing anecdote of the play delighted the theatergoers of Paris, and it met with striking popularity which it has retained to this day.

## The Story:

Léonor and Isabelle, orphaned on the death of their father, were committed by his deathbed wish to the guardianship of his friends, Sganarelle and Ariste, with the additional charge that if they themselves did not marry the young women they were to provide suitable husbands for their wards. The two brothers had different ideas about the upbringing of the orphans. The elder, Ariste, chose to conform to the fashions of the day but without going to extremes. He gave his ward Léonor the opportunity to attend balls and dances and meet the gallants of the city. Although he himself wished to marry her, he loved Léonor sufficiently to leave the choice to her. Sganarelle, however, thought all this was foolish. Where Ariste hoped to govern only by affection, Sganarelle believed in the effectiveness of severity. He confined Isabelle strictly to her quarters and to household duties, thus keeping her from meeting any eligible young men. Determined to marry her

himself, he hoped to discipline her to that end. When Sganarelle scoffed at his brother's leniency and predicted that he would in the end be tricked by so young a wife, Léonor declared that if she married her guardian she would be faithful to him, but that if she were to be Sganarelle's wife she would not be answerable for any of her actions.

Meanwhile, Valère, Sganarelle's new neighbor, had fallen in love with Isabelle, whom he had seen at a distance, and Isabelle reciprocated his love; but with no means of communication neither knew the true feelings of the other. Isabelle finally worked out a plan to test Valère. She told Sganarelle about Valère's attentions and, knowing her guardian would then angrily accost Valère, declared that they were distasteful to her. Sganarelle asked Valère to cease molesting his ward and told him that, even though Isabelle knew of Valère's hopes, his was an unrequited passion, that her only wish was to find happiness in marrying her guardian. Valère sensed in this message something more that Isabelle hoped to convey to him.

Sganarelle told Isabelle that Valère had been crushed by her harsh message. Isabelle, under the pretense of returning a letter which, according to her story, an accomplice of Valère's had thrown into her chamber, persuaded her guardian to deliver the note. Actually, it was a love letter that she had written to Valère.

3371

Sganarelle, taking her request as a touching example of model womanly behavior, delivered the letter, which told of Isabelle's resolve to get free of her prison at any cost during the six days remaining before her enforced marriage to her guardian. Valère, making use of Sganarelle to take back to Isabelle words showing the sincerity of his attachment, declared that his only hope had been to make her his wife and that, although he now realized the hopelessness of his suit, he would always love her. First he flattered Sganarelle as an opponent no one could possibly displace, and showed himself so completely crestfallen and hopeless in surrendering all thought of winning his fair prize that Sganarelle even came to feel a little sorry for his rival.

Isabelle, trying to trick her guardian into appearing despicable in the eyes of her lover, pretended to fear an attempt by Valère to force her from her chamber and carry her off before her marriage to Sganarelle. Bursting with pride at what he considered the womanly discretion of his ward, discretion obviously reflecting his own wisdom in her upbringing, Sganarelle offered to return to Valère and berate him for his bold and mischievous scheme. All turned out as Isabelle hoped. In reply, Valère declared that if what Sganarelle reported were possibly true, then his passion was indeed hopeless. Sganarelle, to make matters perfectly clear, took Valère directly to Isabelle to hear the cruel decision from her own lips. By words that could be understood two ways, Isabelle and Valère declared their love for each other under the nose of their dupe. Then on Isabelle's order Valère departed, promising that in three days he would find a way to free her from her jailer. But Sganarelle could not wait three days. Overjoyed at the exhibitions of what he took to be his ward's fond regard for him, he was eager to consummate the marriage. He told Isabelle the ceremony would be performed the next day.

Isabelle realized that her last resource was to commit herself unreservedly to her lover at once, but as she prepared for flight Sganarelle saw her and informed her that all preparations had been made for their union. Isabelle trumped up a story that she was about to leave the house to spend the night with a worthy friend, Lucrèce, because Léonor, in desperation, had asked for the use of Isabelle's room that night. Against her better judgment, she declared, she had consented and had just locked her sister in. Isabelle pretended that Valère had really been Léonor's lover for more than a year, but had abandoned her when he became infatuated with Isabelle. She said that Léonor, hoping to win back his love, planned to meet him in the lane near the house. Sganarelle, declaring this plan immodest, wanted to drive Léonor out of the house at once. Isabelle restrained him, however, and persuaded him to let her take the message to Léonor, after insisting that Sganarelle must hide himself and promise to let her sister leave without his speaking to her. Sganarelle agreed, secretly pleased at the thought of his brother's discomfiture over the wanton doings of his ward.

Isabelle, pretending to be Léonor, left the house. Curious, Sganarelle followed. He saw Valère and Isabelle meet and, after declaring their love, enter Valère's house. Thinking that Léonor was with Valère and wishing to keep scandal from touching Isabelle through her sister, he hurriedly called a magistrate and urged him to marry the pair. The magistrate was to wait, however, until Sganarelle could return with the bride's guardian to witness the ceremony.

Ariste, although he could not believe his ears when Sganarelle gloatingly insisted that Léonor was with Valère, was induced nevertheless to accompany his brother. Valère, who had hidden Isabelle in a separate room, had the magistrate prepare a formal contract, to be signed by all parties present, indicating their consent to the marriage. Still under the delusion that the bride to be was his brother's ward Léonor, Sganarelle agreed to the wedding; and Ariste, placing the desires of his supposed ward above his own dreams, assented also.

Meanwhile, Léonor returned early from the ball she had attended. Ariste gently chided her for not confiding in him her love for Valère; but Léonor, amazed, protested that she loved only Ariste, her beloved guardian, whom she was ready to marry immediately. Angered, Sganarelle realized too late the trick played on him by Isabelle. All women, he declared, were to be disbelieved and shunned. In the schooling of husbands it was he and not his brother Ariste who had failed.

# THE SCHOOL FOR SCANDAL

*Type of work:* Drama
*Author:* Richard Brinsley Sheridan (1751-1816)
*Type of plot:* Comedy of manners
*Time of plot:* Eighteenth century
*Locale:* London
*First presented:* 1777

### Principal characters:

SIR PETER TEAZLE, an elderly nobleman
LADY TEAZLE, his young wife
MARIA, Sir Peter's ward
SIR OLIVER SURFACE, Sir Peter's friend
JOSEPH SURFACE, and
CHARLES SURFACE, Sir Oliver's nephews
LADY SNEERWELL, Lady Teazle's friend
ROWLEY, Sir Peter's servant

## Critique:

The School for Scandal contains elements of Restoration comedy as well as the usual sentimentalism of the comedy of sensibility. There are two plots: Lady Sneerwell's love for Charles and her scandalous tales about Lady Teazle and the latter's relations with Joseph, and Sir Oliver Surface's tests to discover the worthier of his two nephews. Sheridan brilliantly brings the two plots together in the famous screen scene, which demonstrates his adeptness as a writer of comedy. The School for Scandal, revived from time to time as a costume play, continues to hold the interest of audiences everywhere.

## The Story:

Lady Sneerwell, who in her youth was the target of slander, had set her life upon a course to reduce the reputations of other women to the level of her own. Aided by her intimate, Snake, she was intriguing to involve the Teazles in scandal, to bring Joseph Surface's true character to light, to wreck the love of Charles and Maria, and to gain Charles for herself along with Sir Oliver's fortune. To her the world was nothing but scandal and scandalous intrigues, and she did her best to make her vision a reality. But when she abused Charles Surface, Maria, Sir Peter Teazle's ward, refused to listen to her. Instead, Maria trustingly confided in Lady Candour, whose defense of a reputation insured its complete annihilation.

Sometimes Sir Peter Teazle pondered the wisdom of his marriage to Lady Teazle, doubting the judgment of an old bachelor in marrying a young wife. Lady Teazle was a country-bred girl who was extravagantly enjoying London life to the full. Sir Oliver Surface was concerned about his two nephews, his problem being the disposal of his great fortune. Sir Oliver, having been abroad for the past fifteen years, felt that he did not know their real natures, and he hoped by some stratagem to catch them unawares and test their characters.

One day Sir Peter and Lady Teazle quarreled because Sir Peter objected violently to her attendance at the home of Lady Sneerwell. Lady Teazle accused Sir Peter of wishing to deprive her of all freedom and reminded him that he had promised to go to Lady Sneerwell's with her. He retorted that he would do so for only one reason, to look after his own character. When he arrived, Lady Sneerwell's rooms were full of people uttering libelous remarks about their enemies and saying even worse things about their friends. Sir Peter escaped as soon as possible.

THE SCHOOL FOR SCANDAL by Richard Brinsley Sheridan. Published by The Macmillan Co.

When the rest of Lady Sneerwell's guests retired to the card room, leaving Maria and Joseph alone, Joseph once more pressed his suit for Maria's hand. He insinuated that she was in love with Charles and was thus running counter to Sir Peter's wishes. Lady Teazle interrupted as Joseph was on his knees avowing his honest love. Surprised, Lady Teazle told Maria she was wanted in the next room. She then asked Joseph for an explanation. Joseph informed her that he was pleading with Maria not to tell Sir Peter of his tender concern for Lady Teazle.

Sir Oliver consulted Rowley, Sir Peter's shrewd and observing servant, in an attempt to learn more of his nephews' characters. Rowley himself believed that Joseph had less good character than his reputation seemed to indicate and that Charles had more. Sir Peter was also consulted. He declared that he was ready to stake his life on Joseph's honor. He was much put out, therefore, when Maria once more refused to marry Joseph.

Sir Peter, Sir Oliver, and Rowley planned to test the worthiness of the nephews. Charles, as usual, was in dire need of money. Since Moses, a Jew, was going to see Charles, Sir Oliver was to accompany him as Mr. Premium, a man who could supply the money Charles needed.

When they arrived at Charles' lodging, a drinking party was in progress. Some of the guests were at games of dice. Sir Oliver was not at all impressed with Trip, Charles' footman, who gave himself the airs of a fashionable man about town. Upon investigation, Sir Oliver discovered that Charles had turned his inherited possessions into cash with the exception of the portraits of his ancestors. Convinced that Charles was a scamp, Sir Oliver, still calling himself Premium, agreed to buy the paintings, and he purchased each picture as presented except his own, which Charles would not sell for any amount of money. Sir Oliver was pleased by this fact and discounted Charles' reputation for extravagance. Charles received a draft for eight hundred pounds for the portraits and immediately sent one hundred pounds to Mr. Stanley, a poor relation in even more straitened circumstances.

During an assignation between Joseph Surface and Lady Teazle in Joseph's library, he advised her to give her husband grounds for jealousy rather than suffer his jealousy without cause. He argued that to save her reputation she must ruin it and that he was the man best able to help her. Lady Teazle said that such a doctrine was very odd.

While they were talking, Sir Peter arrived unexpectedly, and Lady Teazle hid behind the screen which Joseph ordered placed against the window. Joseph pretended to be reading when Sir Peter walked in. The purpose of Sir Peter's call was to inform Joseph of his suspicions that Lady Teazle was having an affair with Charles, and he showed Joseph two deeds he had brought with him. One deed settled eight hundred pounds a year upon Lady Teazle for her independent use, the other gave her the bulk of his fortune at his death. Joseph's dissimulation before Sir Peter and Sir Peter's generosity to her were not lost on Lady Teazle. Then Sir Peter began to discuss Joseph's desire to wed Maria. Hidden, Lady Teazle realized that Joseph had been deceiving her.

Below stairs, Charles inopportunely demanded entrance to the house to see his brother. Not wishing to see Charles Sir Peter asked where he could hide. Sir Peter caught a glimpse of a petticoat behind the screen, but Joseph assured him that the woman was only a French milliner who plagued him. Sir Peter hid in a closet; Lady Teazle remained behind the screen.

When Charles came in, he and Joseph discussed Lady Teazle and Sir Peter's suspicion that Charles was her lover. Charles mentioned that he believed Joseph to be her favorite and recounted all the little incidents which led him to think so. Embarrassed by this turn in the conversation, Joseph interrupted to say that Sir Peter was within hearing. Placed in a difficult position, Charles explained to Sir Peter that he was merely playing a joke on Joseph. Sir Peter knew a good joke on Joseph, too, he said; Joseph was having an affair with a milliner. Charles decided that he would have a look at the milliner and threw down the screen. Joseph was undone because Lady Teazle refused to agree with any excuses he made. She angrily informed her husband of the whole nature of Joseph's intentions and departed. Sir Peter followed her, leaving Joseph to his own conscience.

Sir Oliver, masquerading as Mr. Stanley and badly in need of assistance, gained admittance to Joseph's apartment. Joseph refused to help Mr. Stanley, saying that he received very little money from Sir Oliver and claiming that he had advanced all his funds to Charles. After Sir Oliver left, Rowley, who was a party to the whole scheme, came to tell Joseph that Sir Oliver had arrived in town.

Sir Oliver went again to see Joseph. Still believing that his uncle was Mr. Stanley, Joseph was showing him out just as Charles entered. Charles, surprised to see Mr. Premium in his brother's apartment, also insisted that he leave. But at that moment Sir Peter Teazle arrived and addressed Sir Oliver by his right name. Both Sir Oliver and Sir Peter were now aware of Joseph's real character. Charles, promising to try to reform, got Maria and his uncle's inheritance as well. Then Lady Sneerwell was exposed by Snake, who was paid double to speak the truth, and Lady Teazle returned her diploma to the School for Scandal of which Lady Sneerwell was president. Everyone was happy except Lady Sneerwell and Joseph Surface.